FDR's Long New Deal

Robert E. Wright

FDR's Long New Deal

A Public Choice Perspective

palgrave
macmillan

Robert E. Wright
Department of Economics
Central Michigan University
Mount Pleasant, MI, USA

ISBN 978-3-031-74140-1 ISBN 978-3-031-74141-8 (eBook)
https://doi.org/10.1007/978-3-031-74141-8

This Palgrave Macmillan imprint is published by the registered company Springer Nature Switzerland AG
The registered company address is: Gewerbestrasse 11, 6330 Cham, Switzerland

Preface

Though often revered, America's thirty-second President, Franklin Delano Roosevelt (1882–1945, hereafter FDR), pushed a series of policies, collectively known as the New Deal, that caused Americans much misery because they denigrated the nation's tradition of individualism and extolled collectivism. In the process, FDR's policies helped some, while hurting others, often society's most vulnerable. His policies also prevented the economy from recovering from the depths of depression. If such sentiments are new to you, read on for a full explanation and all the "receipts" because understanding the New Deal's many problems may help policymakers and voters to avoid similar costly mistakes in the future.

A few other scholars have also critiqued the New Deal from the standpoint of Public Choice Theory, an economic theory of governance that posits that policymakers may implement policies that aid themselves, or their political parties, rather than some sense of the common good or public interest. The bulk of the work on the New Deal, however, remains almost hagiographic, even though the New Deal largely consisted of one costly mistake[1] after another. FDR often ranks second only to Abraham Lincoln in assessments of presidential crisis leadership, largely due to the economic policy naivety of the scholars who make such assessments.[2] Historian John Steele Gordon, for example, somehow concluded that although "many of the New Deal programs were unsuccessful and many of its economic principles shortsighted, in its totality it was an enormous success."[3] Its main "success" was that it continued an economic crisis for partisan gain by making the masses feel beholden to the Democrats as their saviors in troubled times. Like dogs, people rarely bite the hands that feed them, even when those hands prove cruel or incompetent.[4]

FDR's reforms caused so many problems, in fact, that they may appear to have been deliberately destructive. After all, as financial journalist Garet Garrett (pronounced, according to the daughter of one of his employees I met by happenstance in May 2023, "Guh – rett") put it, "depression is the New Deal's meat and drink."[5] U.S. Army officer and political economist E.C. Harwood called New Dealers "God Sakers" clamoring "for a Dictator, or for almost any sudden and arbitrary action which came into their minds." "Genuine repairs to the machine," he predicted in 1932, will "baffle their ingenuity."[6] Subsequent events proved him correct, though it remains to a large extent verboten to claim it publicly.

FDR was not America's savior. As Walter Lippmann said, the country's only 4-term president was more of a "kind of amiable boy scout ... a pleasant man who, without any important qualifications for the office, would very much like to be President."[7] "Is it reasonable," New Deal doyen William Leuchtenburg once asked, "to criticize the New Dealers for not grasping the nuances of the environmentalist theories that did not emerge until a generation later?" Of course not, but it is incumbent upon scholars to criticize them for brashly implementing policies, the effects of which they knew not. It also behooves scholars to criticize attempts to whitewash the truth.

FDR and other New Dealers—shorthand for the top advisers, cabinet members, and strategists most closely aligned with FDR—wielded power far beyond their understanding of societal and economic dynamics.[8] It's not that they were boy scouts intellectually, simply that they were naïve enough to believe that they could micromanage the economy sufficiently to improve matters. They fancied themselves technocrats or social engineers with the knowledge and technical skills to reorder society as they saw fit.[9] A similar conceit infected the leaders of other nations on both sides of the political spectrum, leading to the creation of totalitarian and collectivist communist and fascist states throughout much of the northern[10] hemisphere. Thankfully, FDR remained somewhat checked by the Constitution. Where governments gained total power, as in Italy, Germany, China, and the Soviet Union, the result was intense human misery, death, and destruction.[11] In America, as one contemporary put it, the New Deal was only "tinged with the color of socialism and with the idea of a managed economy."[12]

In fact, collectivist countries eventually became so discredited that for a time the world's people successfully used the power of "democracy" to keep the keys away from new generations of naïve policymakers eager to remake the economy. As FDR once noted, however, "history does in fact repeat."[13] In 2020, policymakers across the world leveraged a global health crisis, the origins of which remain murky, to seize more power, attack private property, and question other civil rights like privacy and speech.[14] Those who truly seek prosperity for all must first understand the problems caused by the New Deal and other forms of collectivist thought so that they may resist the temptation of thinking that the right laws and leaders can fix our problems when only reason can.

Ocean View, New Jersey
August 2024

Robert E. Wright

Notes

1. William F. Shughart, "Bending Before the Storm: The U.S. Supreme Court in Economic Crisis, 1935–1937," *The Independent Review* 9, 1 (Summer 2004), 55; Paul Moreno, "An Ambivalent Legacy: Black Americans and the Political Economy of the New Deal," *Independent Review* 6, 4 (Spring 2002), 513; Betty Houchin Winfield, *FDR and the News Media* (New York: Columbia University Press, 1994), xii–xiv.
2. David T. Beito, *The New Deal's War on the Bill of Rights: The Untold Story of FDR's Concentration Camps, Censorship, and Mass Surveillance* (Oakland: Independent Institute, 2023), 1; Winfield, *FDR and the News Media*, 1; Robert S. McElvaine, *The Great Depression: America, 1929–1941* (New York: Random House, 1984).
3. John Steele Gordon, *An Empire of Wealth: The Epic History of American Economic Power* (New York: HarperCollins, 2004), 343.
4. Winfield, *FDR and the News Media*, ix.
5. Garet Garrett, "For Five Years, There Has Been No American System," in Amity Shlaes, ed. *New Deal Rebels* (Great Barrington, Mass.: American Institute for Economic Research, 2023), 238.
6. E.C. Harwood, "What To Do About It?" (Nov. 1932) Box 1, E.C. Harwood Archives, AIER, Great Barrington, Mass.
7. John Morton Blum, ed., *Public Philosopher: Selected Letters of Walter Lippmann* (New York: Ticknor & Fields, 1985). John T. Flynn at least had FDR pegged as an adult in his 1940 *Country Squire in the White House* (New York: Doubleday).

8. New Dealers included, but are by no means limited to, Paul Appleby, Thurman Arnold, Louis Bean, Beany Baldwin, Adolf Berle, Tom Blaisdell, Louis Brandeis, Ben Cohen, Thomas Corcoran, Fred Delano (FDR's uncle), Harry Dennison, William Douglass, Mordecai Ezekiel, Jerome Frank, Felix Frankfurter, John Nance Garner, Herb Gaston, Richard Gilbert, Harry Hopkins, Harold Ickes, Robert Jackson, Hugh S. Johnson, Isador Lubin, Gardiner Means, Sherman Minton, Raymond Moley, Henry Morgenthau, Bob Nathan, Basil O'Conner, Herman Oliphant, Frances Perkins, Lee Pressman, Beardsley Ruml, Charles Taussig, Henry Tolley, Rexford Tugwell, Henry Wallace, James Warburg, George F. Warren, Harry White, Aubrey Williams, and Milburn L. Wilson. Some New Dealers, like Douglass, Garner, Johnson, Moley, and Warburg, eventually split with the administration. A few, like Morgenthau, exhibited some independent policy views at times. Gary Dean Best, *Pride, Prejudice, and Politics: Roosevelt Versus Recovery, 1933–1938* (New York: Praeger, 1991), 207–211.
9. John M. Jordan, *Machine-Age Ideology: Social Engineering and American Liberalism, 1911–1939* (Chapel Hill: University of North Carolina, 1994), 232–254.
10. Kiran Klaus Patel, *The New Deal: A Global History* (Princeton: Princeton University Press, 2016), 1–9.
11. Jean-Louis Panne et al, *The Black Book of Communism: Crimes, Terror, Repression* (Cambridge: Harvard University Press, 1999). The Fascists were of course no better.
12. James Ledbetter and Daniel B. Roth, eds., *The Great Depression: A Diary by Benjamin Roth* (New York: Public Affairs, 2009), 160.
13. As quoted in William Shughart, "The New Deal and Modern Memory," *Southern Economic Journal* 77, 3 (2011), 515.
14. Richard Florida, *The Great Reset: How the Post-Crash Economy Will Change the Way We Live and Work* (New York: HarperCollins, 2010); World Economic Forum, "The Great Reset," https://web.archive.org/web/20230619080247/https://www.weforum.org/great-reset/; Klaus Schwab and Thierry Malleret, *Covid-19: The Great Rese*t (Geneva, Switzerland: World Economic Forum, 2020); Anthony P. Charles, *The Great Reset Explained: Corporate Plot, Economic Pipe Dream, or Global Panacea?* (New York: Kindle, 2022).

Acknowledgments

The American Institute for Economic Research (AIER) allowed me to work fulltime on the manuscript when I was employed there during the Covid pandemic and funded a manuscript workshop in Alabama in February 2023. The participants in that two-day workshop all read an earlier version of the manuscript and made numerous substantive comments that improved this book. The conferees were David Black, Art Carden, Leslie Corbly, Ranjit Dighe, Lenore Ealy, James Harrigan, Jason Jewell, Phil Magness, Keith Malone, Steve Miller, Patrick Newman, Ray Niles, Paul Schwennesen, Nathaniel Smith, and Jason Taylor. Moreover, one AIER intern, Warren Barge, identified, acquired, and evaluated several key sources for me while another, James Peterson, offered important suggestions on a late draft. Lee Ohanian and David Beito kindly read and commented on the improved draft, offering many suggestions that further improved the book. Unfortunately, many pro-New Deal/pro-FDR scholars declined the offer to attend the Alabama workshop and did not offer to critique the manuscript. I am sure that their input would have helped me to write a better book by offering a different perspective. Nevertheless, the book's shortcomings remain my sole responsibility.

Contents

About the Author

Robert E. Wright (Ph.D., History, SUNY Buffalo, 1997) currently teaches economics at Central Michigan University. Previously, he taught courses in business, economics, and policy at Temple, New York, and Augustana universities, and the University of Virginia. In 2020, he served Georgia State College and University as its Paul Coverdell Visiting Distinguished Faculty of Policy Studies and PERC as a Julian Simon Fellow. He then served AIER for three years as a policy analyst, writing extensively about Covid, DEI, and ESG policies. Wright has (co)authored two dozen books and scores of peer-reviewed journal articles and book chapters on topics ranging from bailouts and corporate governance to UBI and wildlife policy. He has also (co)edited half a dozen other books, including *The C.Q. Guide to U.S. Economic Policy.*

Abbreviations

AAA	Agricultural Adjustment Administration
ACA	Affordable Care Act
AFDC	Aid to Families with Dependent Children
AIER	American Institute for Economic Research
AMA	American Medical Association
BIA	Bureau of Indian Affairs
BLM	Bureau of Land Management
Blue Eagle	National Industrial Recovery Act (NIRA)
BSC	British Security Coordination
CCC	Civilian Conservation Corps
CPUSA	Communist Party of the United States of America
CWA	Civil Works Administration
EHFA	Electric Home and Farm Authority, Inc.
EPA	Environmental Protection Agency
ER	Eleanor Roosevelt
FBI	Federal Bureau of Investigation
FCA	Farm Credit Administration
FCC	Federal Communications Commission
FCIC	Federal Crop Insurance Corporation
FDIC	Federal Deposit Insurance Corporation
FDR	Franklin Delano Roosevelt
Fed	Federal Reserve System
FEPC	Fair Employment Practice Committee
FERA	Federal Emergency Relief Administration
FFMC	Federal Farm Mortgage Corporation
FHA	Federal Housing Administration

FHLB	Federal Home Loan Banks
FRBNY	Federal Reserve Bank of New York
FRC	Federal Radio Commission
FRN	Federal Reserve Notes
FSA	Farm Security Administration
FSLA	Federal Savings and Loan Associations
FSLIC	Federal Savings and Loan Corporation
FTC	Federal Trade Commission
FTP	Federal Theater Project
HOLC	Home Owners' Loan Corporation
ICC	Interstate Commerce Commission
IRS	Internal Revenue Service
JNG	John Nance Garner
KKK	Ku Klux Klan
LBJ	Lyndon B. Johnson
LEC	London Economic Conference
LLR	Lender of Last Resort
NAM	National Association of Manufacturers
NCUCG	National Committee to Uphold Constitutional Government
NIRA	National Industrial Recovery Act
NLRA	National Labor Relations Act
NLRB	National Labor Relations Board
NRA	National Recovery Administration
NYA	National Youth Administration
OPA	Office of Price Administration
PBA	Public Buildings Administration
PRA	Public Roads Administration
PUD	Public Utility District
PWA	Public Works Administration
REA	Rural Electrification Administration
RFC	Reconstruction Finance Corporation
RRA	Railroad Retirement Act
SCOTUS	U.S. Supreme Court
SEC	Securities and Exchange Commission
SSDI	Social Security Disability Insurance
TNEC	Temporary National Economic Committee
TVA	Tennessee Valley Authority
USFS	U.S. Forest Service
USFW	U.S. Fish and Wildlife
USHA	U.S. Housing Authority
WPA	Works Progress Administration

CHAPTER 1

The Great Depression, New Deal, and War

Franklin Delano Roosevelt (FDR) used the crises engendered by the global Great Depression and Second World War to engineer the "radical" (FDR's word)[1] reordering of American constitutional and economic traditions in the name of collectivist notions of "safety" and "social justice."[2] FDR, his Marxist economic advisor Lauchlin Currie later admitted, "was glad to use economic arguments for something he wanted to do on other grounds." "He was the first President," Currie continued, to favor "the active intervention of the State to protect the economically weak and to check the abuses of the economically strong," or at least the first since Andrew Jackson to claim to do so.[3] To further his agenda of transformation, FDR crushed the very states' rights he had championed as the Democratic governor of New York from 1929 through 1932.[4] And as historian David Beito shows, FDR virtually waged war on the Bill of Rights, from freedom of speech to due process.[5] Within 2 weeks of his inauguration, an astute journalist noticed that Americans "instinctively" spoke of a *new government*, rather than a *change in administration,* because they knew that the more rapid and vapid "tempo and temper in government" would lead to increased presidential authority.[6]

FDR indeed greatly strengthened the office of the presidency through his use of executive orders and strong man techniques. A Gallup poll taken in August 1936 revealed that 45% of Americans, including eight in ten Republicans, believed that "the acts and policies of the Roosevelt

R. E. Wright, *FDR's Long New Deal*,
https://doi.org/10.1007/978-3-031-74141-8_1

administration may lead to dictatorship."[7] Fear of presidential dictatorship led to the defeat of the Executive Reorganization Bill of 1938.[8] Even FDR's friends in the administration and the press corps began to fear the worst.[9] Such fears might have been overblown but they were not unfounded. FDR ushered in the supremacy of the national administrative state, the ability of the executive branch to implement administrative rules with the force of law largely unreviewable by Congress or the courts. The New Deal, in other words, undermined the Constitution's core doctrine, the separation of powers between the three branches of government.[10]

In the late nineteenth century, serving in Congress in peacetime was a leisurely affair.[11] Not so during the New Deal, during which numerous transformative bills were passed, some without being read, at the mere behest of the executive. Little wonder that many Americans sensed that the nation and its economy stood at a great crossroads and that FDR's policies would influence America's path for the next century. His policies in fact largely did so.[12]

Those are strong words, but the author holds no personal animus against FDR. Had Giuseppe Zangara's bullet found its mark, this book might well be about the ill effects of the economic policies of JNG, John Nance Garner of Uvalde, Texas, FDR's vice president during his first two terms.[13] For a vice president, "Cactus Jack" played an unusually active role in the cabinet during FDR's first term, breaking with the New Deal agenda only in 1937. He unsuccessfully challenged FDR for the nomination in 1940 only because his opponent was by then unbeatable due to his control of federal relief programs and bureaucrats like SEC chairman Jerome N. Frank, who relayed information about the Willkie campaign to the incumbent.[14] Garner lived until age 99, so had Zangara's assassination attempt been successful, and had JNG built the same election apparatus that FDR did, he could have kept getting re-elected through the 1964 presidential cycle. But Zangara missed, hitting Chicago mayor Anton Cermak instead, so FDR must bear the primary responsibility for the collectivist policies that the New Deal inflicted, and continues to inflict, on Americans.

The *Cleveland Plain Dealer* clearly articulated the collectivist nature of the New Deal, noting that FDR had "gone further along the path of social justice than anyone else who ever held the office."[15] Yes, the term *social justice* was widely used already in the 1930s.[16] Depression-era Americans also employed the concept of equity, usually in a phrase like "in an equitable manner," in today's sense, too.[17] That is far from the only parallel between the 1930s and the 2020s.

The Great Delusion

The Great Depression and New Deal remain among the most widely studied events in American history, and FDR among the most chronicled presidents.[18] Nevertheless, most of the books and articles on FDR and the New Deal, whether intentionally or not, distort the historical record so severely that the literature on those subjects could be considered hagiographic or "court" history at best and disinformation at worst.[19] The winners, they say, get to write history and the New Dealers certainly won. For example, Rexford Tugwell, an economist who purported to know more about farming than farmers did, lived until 1979. After inspiring a dystopian novel and serving as the central planning governor of Puerto Rico, he devoted his life to creating propaganda designed to cover up what FDR (1957, 1967, and 1972 bios), his "*Brains Trust*" (Viking 1968), and Tugwell himself (autobiographies in 1947, 1955, 1962, 1971, 1977) had done. All those books became primary sources eagerly devoured by the New Deal's many court historians, who threatened even luminaries like Charles Beard with cancellation for the slightest deviation from the accepted narrative of adulation.[20]

To this day, much of the scholarship on FDR and the New Deal relies upon high-level generalizations and under-specified concepts like "capitalism."[21] Harvard Business School's longtime dean, Wallace Brett Donham, or Syracuse University Chancellor Charles W. Flint, may have started the tradition when they independently claimed early in the Depression that "capitalism is on trial," without defining capitalism or explaining why *an idea* should be on trial given that agents of the federal government exacerbated a routine economic contraction and created a period of unemployment unprecedented in its length and severity by stymieing private recovery efforts at every turn.[22]

Too few general histories of the period contend seriously with the economics of the Great Depression and New Deal. That's a shame because "economics may be dull, and it may be imperfect," as Currie put it, "but in the light of the record, nobody can say that it is not vitally important."[23] This book aims to bring some of the economics back in, not to bore readers but to allow them to see the New Deal's many often unspoken or underappreciated costs. It owes much to Amity Shlaes's *The*

Forgotten Man but is more analytical, like Burton Folsom's *New Deal or Raw Deal?* and Jim Couch and Bill Shughart's *The Political Economy of the New Deal*, yet even more focused on the failed monetary management of the era.[24] The closest rivals are Gary Dean Best's *Pride, Prejudice, and Politics* published in 1991 and Jim Powell's 2003 book, *FDR's Folly*, but many fewer words are expended here providing the biographical background of the main figures. All five of those books are a bit dated, written before the advent of the Global Financial Crisis of 2008 and the ascendance of the World Economic Forum. Somewhat more recent but much lighter on details is Lawrence W. Reeds' 2011 pamphlet, *Great Myths of the Great Depression*.

Much of the scholarship on the 1930s is premised on the inaccurate notion that Presidents Nixon and Reagan and Chief Justice Rehnquist broke the New Deal, instead of merely braking some of its worst aspects for a time.[25] If this book seems to go too far in the other direction, it is only because the many claims about the New Deal's virtues that became well ensconced in public school and college curricula in the second half of the twentieth century need to be critically re-examined.[26]

If you think that America's 32nd president deserves a spot along with George Washington and Abraham Lincoln as one of the nation's saviors because he helped a troubled nation to get out of the Great Depression and win World War II, think again.[27] Biographer H.W. Brands branded FDR a "traitor to his class" but the wealthy New Yorker was much more than that.[28] FDR betrayed all classes and indeed the entire nation, at least as it was understood by its Founders and later classical liberals who stressed the importance of limited government and individual liberty. The only person ever elected to America's highest office more than twice hurt the nation, especially its poorest citizens, in ways large and small.[29] FDR's policies continue to cost the country today.[30]

Any favorable assessment of the FDR presidency by a twenty-first-century "Progressive"—somebody who wants to use the government to further goals like "equity" and "social justice"—is ironic because it fails to account for the victims of the New Deal, including African-Americans, American Indians, immigrants, minors, and women.[31] Although New Dealers rhapsodized about pluralism,[32] or "diversity" as they say today, New Deal policies injured America's most vulnerable denizens by creating something new—a large, powerful peacetime national government, along with precedents and taxes more than sufficient to fuel its postwar growth. Public Choice Theory explains the New Deal's unusual combination of economic failure and political success.[33] Improving economic conditions overall or for particular groups was not their goal, gaining and maintaining their own political power was. Americans lost so that Democrat leaders could win not just elections but the political sway necessary to implement a reform agenda designed to ensconce them in power.

The Long New Deal

In many ways, this book is about what might be termed the Long New Deal, 1929–1945, because analysis of Progressive influences and President Herbert Hoover's nostrums as well as the federal government's response to World War II are essential to understand the sea change that occurred during the New Deal proper, 1933–38.[34] By 1936, what Winston Churchill called "a new world order" based on the primacy of the state over the individual had already emerged, but it would take a world war to complete the transformation.[35] Economists have long understood that the New Deal "of course" constituted "the major turning point in the growth of the federal government."[36] John Q. Public also readily perceived that there was "a great deal of radical legislation being proposed in Washington," but most were too busy just surviving to fight it, and some wanted the government to try anything to get the economy back on its usual growth path.[37] In the end, then, the New Deal was not a victory for social equity or justice but, as legal historian David E. Bernstein put it, "more a triumph for government power as such."[38]

Labor Secretary Frances Perkins claimed that the New Deal was meant to be "radical, revolutionary and temporary." She was right about the first two, but very wrong about the third.[39] The New Deal, especially the "long" New Deal that began with Hoover[40] and ended with FDR's death in 1945, was part-socialist and part-corporatist/fascist, but always experimental.[41] Nobody knew what would work or not, so they tried everything under the Progressive sun, and then some, even though many New Deal programs blatantly contradicted or counteracted each other.[42] FDR knew nothing about economics, so if some policy proposal promised to increase the government's power, especially his power, he wanted to try it. None of the nostrums helped to alleviate the unemployment problem that provided cover for all the socioeconomic policy experimentation, much of which remains in place more than 90 years later.[43] Although the New Deal failed to improve employment or output,[44] it succeeded in increasing consumption and internal migration and reducing crime rates and some types of mortality.[45] More importantly from FDR's point of view, it succeeded politically, turning the Democratic Party into the "Party of the Laboring Man" by the end of 1933.[46]

Harry Hopkins, Head of the Works Progress Administration (later the Work Projects Administration, but always the WPA for short) and purportedly second in power only to FDR,[47] also tried to blind Americans to the permanent nature of the New Deal by claiming that "Whatever controls the people now want Government to exercise with relation to industry in behalf of a better and squarer deal for everyone, the people can take away at any time they feel industry does not need such controls."[48] Even when Hopkins uttered those words, many, perhaps most, Americans did not want the New Deal, they wanted an end to double digit (as high as one in three) unemployment and sky high investment uncertainty, goals that New Deal policies never achieved.[49] Egged on by egghead professors and ministers, Americans for the most part calmly acceded to "drastic government regulation" confident that it would end along with the economic crisis.[50]

Democrats, therefore, did not so much win the elections of 1932, 1936, and 1940 as they managed not to lose to Republicans so hapless that they got caught sending faking protest telegrams to Congress.[51] In 1935, Democrat James Warburg noted that "the vote of November, 1932, was in large measure a vote against rather than a vote for."[52]

Later, voting for FDR became a matter of self-preservation. After FDR's approval rating hit 50% in September 1935, he began to use the apparatus of the state to punish his critics while feeding the timid and persuadable with cash carrots. Republicans responded ineffectively, when they tried at all.[53]

The Republican Party had coalesced in 1856 as an antislavery party with strong appeal among the working classes and Jews, especially more affluent ones. Freedpersons voted for the "party of Lincoln" almost to a man, when they could vote that is. White Southerners were Democrats almost to a man. Both parties contained radical wings, Progressives starting circa 1905 in the case of Republicans and agrarian Populists starting in 1896 in the case of Democrats. And both contained conservative elements, including big business Republicans starting in 1896 and conservative Southern Democrats starting in 1860.[54]

With limited exceptions, Republicans dominated the federal government throughout the postbellum period and into the twentieth century. They held the White House all but 20 years between 1861 and 1932 and both the House of Representatives and the Senate most years. They lost control during Woodrow Wilson's first term but rebounded in the 1920s. Throughout that decade, though, Republicans eroded their base, driving out Jewish, immigrant, and African-American voters with policies that seemed too pro-big business if not outright anti-labor and anti-hyphenated American. In 1928, Democratic presidential candidate Al Smith lost to Republican presidential candidate Herbert Hoover but showed that a coalition of urban Catholics, including immigrant groups like Italians, could be wooed away from the GOP and into the open rhetorical arms of the Democrats, a swing that continued in 1930 when Republicans lost control of the House and saw their majority in the Senate dwindle to one.[55]

Prohibition and 3 years of depression, economic and emotional, and failed Hooverian policies did not help.[56] The Republican party, which remained largely locked out of the Solid South—"forced to think alike politically, many cease to think at all," a Richmond newspaperman once commented[57]—still contained (and arguably never lost) elements that considered themselves progressive in the sense of being willing to use state power to achieve what they believed to be laudable ends. They twice defeated the so-called "Old Right" wing of the party, which harbored remnants of the classical liberal view of limited government, first by allowing Hoover to be appointed Secretary of Commerce under President Harding and then allowing his nomination for the presidency. The old guard saw that Hoover was interventionist and technocratic, with progressive tendencies, but failed to squelch his ambition.[58] The Old Right still had articulate proponents, but they were better at critiquing interventions than proffering positive policies promoting hope.[59] That proved problematic because during the economic "emergency" simply being against the New Deal was not enough for most voters. They needed an alternative vision but found none worthy of their votes, which were being strongly pulled in the other direction by New Deal cash and promises. The GOP responded by dusting off the still reviled Hoover every 4 years to give a convention speech.

In 1936 and 1940, Republicans were in such disarray that they tried to create DINOs (Democrats in name only) in a desperate attempt to dampen the New Deal coalition forming within the Democratic Party.[60] Ironically, in 1940 it ran a RINO (Republican in name only), lifelong Democrat Wendell Willkie, against FDR—and lost despite Willkie's good looks, intelligence, and charming radio-friendly style, not to mention the sympathy he gained when the federal government forced him to sell Commonwealth & Southern to the Tennessee Valley Authority (TVA).[61] It helped that FDR, in the words of a biographer, straight up lied about everything from his polio prognosis to the likelihood of America's involvement in World War II.[62] Democrats also did everything in their power to instill fear and confusion in the electorate, hoping that incumbency would win the day, as it generally did.[63] And when or where in doubt, Democrats were not above buying votes or engaging in what today is called ballot harvesting.[64] With no interference from Washington, some even turned the police against black Republicans, as Edward H. Crump, the Democratic boss of Memphis did in 1940 to ensure the defeat of Willkie, who, unlike FDR, favored racial integration and antilynching legislation.[65]

Hopkins claimed that FDR and "the leaders of his party" restored "opportunity and a certain amount of security without the loss of personal liberty."[66] They did no such thing. Almost everything wrong with the American economy today, including a good part of its economic injustices, can be traced to FDR's New Deal and World War II policies.

The New Deal almost completely transformed everything economic, from agriculture to corporate governance to the meaning of the commerce clause to the extent and nature of regulation.[67] It also permanently raised the level of unemployment in the country throughout the rest of the twentieth century.[68] Especially in a country allergic to the policy spells spewed by the partisan purveyors of various "isms,"[69] change came quickly. At the beginning of 1933, a man with a gold coin in his pocket was a pillar of the community while a man with a bottle of whiskey was a scofflaw. By the end of that same year, the opposite was true.[70]

And 1933 was just the beginning of a dozen years of FDR-led transformation. By 1934, problems that in the past Americans would have handled with voluntary cooperation—like the immediate and effective nonprofit response to the tragic Johnstown, Pennsylvania flood of 1889 that killed over 2200 people—were turned over to the government without a second thought.[71] "The people," Ohio attorney Benjamin Roth lamented, "have gotten used to looking to the government for help." Worst of all was "that people are no longer worried about government spending" and had a "general indifference to increased spending."[72] By FDR's death in 1945, Americans had been transformed from citizens into subjects, from independent adults into wards of the state. Even though FDR himself once claimed "that government is ourselves and not an alien power over us,"[73] there was precious little Americans could do about the changes that he wrought.

As historian David M. Kennedy put it, "into the years of the New Deal was crowded more social and institutional change than in virtually any comparable compass of time in the nation's past."[74] Bruce Ackerman also saw the New Deal as a period of massive, rapid change but applauded it as an example of how electoral ratification of presidential leadership can cause de facto Constitutional change. His curious argument, if correct, is tacit admission of the New Deal's unconstitutional nature.[75] The Founders and Framers, the men who engineered the independence and establishment of a constitutional republic, never envisaged such fundamental changes being ratified outside of the amendment processes outlined in the Constitution itself and, in fact, would have seen the destruction of the American Republic in FDR's New Deal.

Contemporaries steeped in classical liberal thought they saw the same. Author and social theorist Albert Jay Nock considered the radical transformation of the American government under FDR a *coup d'état*, a rare example of one won through money rather than violence.[76] Journalist Garet Garrett also claimed that "in 1932 a bund of intellectual revolutionaries, hiding behind the conservative planks of the Democratic party, seized control of government."[77] Another journalist, Welshman Gareth Jones, proclaimed the New Deal a "revolution" that brought to America "a kind of Fascism."[78] Tellingly, communist Earl Russell Browder also found the early New Deal fascistic, though not yet a "developed fascism," and likened it to the "industrial slavery" of Benito Mussolini, the anti-communist dictator of Italy who entranced many pragmatic liberal American policymakers before he turned imperialistic and allied with Nazi Germany.[79] Other communists, however, openly embraced FDR and the New Deal and several New Dealers were Soviet agents.[80]

Hopkins retorted that criticism of the New Deal was acceptable in a democracy but that critics should answer the question "if you were called upon to replace the Administration tomorrow, what would *your* program be?"[81] Note the statist assumption implicit in the question. The answer of classical liberals, to protect individual life, liberty, and property through institutional arrangements like the retail gold standard, was no longer within the Overton Window, the set of possible policies acceptable to the New Deal power elite.

FDR's New Deal fundamentally changed the nature of the American nation state. As Garrett put it, FDR's policies replaced the venerable "The People" with an "administrative absolutism" cloaked in democratic-looking vestments. "Formerly government was the responsibility of the people," he noted, "now people were the responsibility of government,"[82] a government increasingly unaccountable to anyone, or anything.

FDR's New Deal was part of a global pattern of tumult.[83] It was not part of a plot or conspiracy, though Rexford Tugwell confided to his diary many of the behind-the-scenes machinations that went into preparing the public to accept radical policy proposals.[84] It was not even planned in great detail beforehand, although arguably roughly sketched after the 1932 election,[85] but rather flowed out of a heady mix of personality, pro-planning Progressive ideology, circumstance, and power greed.[86] In America, European-trained professors had spread the ideology and technique of revolution to, in Garrett's words, "writers, critics, analysts, advisers, administrators, directors of research, and so … prepared revolutionary intelligence in spectacles."[87] They stood ready to play revolutionary roles when the right crisis hit, an economic crisis so deep that many Americans acquiesced to the notion that, as journalist Gareth Jones put it, "We must plan our national life."[88] Or, as New Dealer Harold Ickes put it, "We are in the age of planning for the best of everything for all."[89] Thankfully, after a dozen years of failed interventions, many Americans again came to understand that "no man or group of men is smart enough to control prices or supply and demand or currency" so "the forces of competition and demand and supply" had to be allowed to "work things out in a natural way."[90]

The New Deal revolutionaries did not agree on everything but all believed that the power of the two voluntary sectors, nonprofit and commercial, needed trimming.[91] It ostensibly pitted individuals and Main Street businesses against Big Business,[92] but in the end Big Government sought to emasculate competition and render all businesses and charities appendages of the federal government instead of the independent political forces that they had been in the eighteenth and nineteenth centuries. Instead of the vigorous pursuit of happiness, forced "security"[93]—"security in democracy" as Hopkins put it[94]—became the organizing principle of a collectivized American society.[95]

This book lays out this Public Choice-inspired interpretation of the Long New Deal chronologically and thematically. Its conclusion could not be clearer—the New Deal moved America away from its classical liberal roots and toward a form of collectivism controlled, or at least steered, by power greedy politicians.[96] New Dealers indeed felt that they were "members of a distinct group or party," a vanguard, so to speak, devoted to the cause of revolutionary reset.[97]

Four Freedoms, No Liberty

Unlike America's Founders and Framers,[98] FDR did not believe in immutable natural rights but instead considered rights negotiable, tied to increasingly complex modern conditions.[99] To rely on the ideas of Adam Smith, he told the Young Democratic Clubs of America, would be to subject the economic structure to "confusion, destruction and paralysis."[100] His political philosophy pathos can best be understood by analyzing the so-called "four freedoms" that he sketched in his Annual Message to Congress on 6 January 1941, 2 months after his unprecedented third election to the presidency:

> The first is freedom of speech and expression – everywhere in the world.
> The second is freedom of every person to worship God in his own way – everywhere in the world.
> The third is freedom from want – which, translated into international terms, means economic understandings which will secure to every nation everywhere a healthy peace time life for its inhabitants – everywhere in the world.
> The fourth is freedom from fear – which, translated into world terms, means a world-wide reduction of armaments to such a point and in such a thorough fashion that no nation will be in a position to commit an act of physical aggression against any neighbor – anywhere in the world.
> That is no vision of a distant millennium.[101]

Despite the concluding claim, FDR's four freedoms were fanciful.

In the language of storied economist Thomas Sowell in his 1987 book *A Conflict of Visions: Ideological Origins of Political Struggles*, the four freedoms constitute a prime example of unconstrained, even utopian, thinking.[102] According to Sowell, the vision of some policymakers tends to be constrained by reality, or in other words by budgets, physical limitations, biological necessities, and other external constraints. Other policymakers, though, propose policies as though no real-world constraints exist, acting as if they can force their goals into existence through the passage of laws or the implementation of policies.

New Dealers were the latter, unconstrained, type of policymaker. FDR played the role of the all-knowing "self-anointed"leader who possesses ideal solutions to every problem,[103] "the Moses that leads his people out of the wilderness" as James Warburg put it.[104] Believing himself immune from self-interest and the intoxicating qualities of power, FDR thought that he should rule not just the nation, but everywhere in the world. A constrained or realist policymaker, by contrast, like Adam Smith or Alexander Hamilton, follows the scientific method, rule of law, logic, and custom.[105]

The American government then, now, and in every moment in between, did not, and does not, possess the power to achieve FDR's four freedoms even within the United States, much less everywhere in the world. As described in the pages below, FDR himself repressed speech, increased want, and spread uncertainty and fear—in America. As Amos Pinchot put it, FDR was like a flea. You never knew which way he was going to jump next, "thus leaving the country in a fog of doubt."[106]

FDR won his second, third, and fourth terms by using the mass media to hide the effects of his policies, which he also used to essentially bribe swing voters. And as army officer and political economist E.C. Harwood later noted, "every adult mind knows that there will never be freedom from fear in general."[107] Although generally affable enough to win over reporters, he was not beneath beating recalcitrant ones with the sticks at his disposal, including ignoring or deflecting their difficult questions and questioning their motivations or even their abilities. On at least one occasion, FDR instructed a journalist to put on a dunce cap and on another, he "awarded" a journalist critical of the war effort a German Iron Cross medal.[108]

The rest of the four freedoms speech shows how FDR had internalized a planning, statist approach to economic issues antithetical to liberty. As Harwood noted, people who are "free to dispose of their goods as they please can never be guaranteed freedom from want."[109]

Instead of helping individuals to achieve financial independence, FDR said "we should bring more citizens under the coverage of old age pensions and unemployment insurance," or in other words to make more Americans dependent on the government. He also said, "we should widen the opportunities for adequate medical care," which might have sounded innocuous at the time but ended up leading to the expensive, inefficient healthcare system that haunts the nation to this day. Finally, he said "we should plan a better system by which persons deserving or needing gainful employment may obtain it." But nobody can "plan" an employment "system." Only an economy free of fiscal, monetary, and regulatory distortions can ensure that all persons "deserving or needing gainful employment" will be able to find it.[110]

Other New Dealers also displayed a fundamental misunderstanding of the constrained genius of American institutions.[111] Hopkins, for example, believed that forming a bank somehow "deprived others of the right."[112] He claimed that when the American people saw "free markets and real competition ... slipping away, ... they turned for protection to the only agency to which a democratic people *would* turn—to their Government." Actually, however, Americans traditionally supported their Republic, not "democracy," and turned to self-help through voluntary associations, not the government, when they saw markets and competition slipping away.[113]

FDR was able to implement his radical agenda in part due to his spellbinding radio oratory and mastery of the media.[114] The collectivist leaders of Italy and Germany were also skilled communicators because they also needed to garner some popular support to rule. Unlike FDR, though, they preferred massive rallies where their wild gesticulations could fire their friends into a physical frenzy. The rulers of totalitarian Japan and the Soviet Union, by contrast, could rule more by force than by persuasion, so they were led by strongmen rather than propagandists.[115]

FDR also leveraged his status as a wealthy scion of an important family and a victim of polio.[116] Although he tried to prevent reporters from reminding people of his disability, especially in photographs, it was widely known that he could not walk unassisted. It worked, along with his patrician façade, to soften his image, making him seem less like a dictator than he literally was, in the Latin/Roman Republican sense of the word.[117] FDR also received help from a pack of young lawyers nicknamed the "happy hot dogs," ostensibly because they were apostles of Harvard Law professor Felix Frankfurter.[118]

Ironically, fear constituted the most important factor in FDR's success. Where the economy seemingly offered nothing but chaos, FDR offered seeming safety, which gave him the political space to inundate the country with government programs, all of which moved America toward state-directed collectivism. In 1930, the U.S. government remained devoted to negative liberty, to protect the natural rights of its citizens from foes foreign and domestic, including itself. Alexis De Tocqueville's words from a century earlier still held much force. All that an American wanted from his government was "not to be disturbed in his toil, and to be secure of his earnings."[119] By 1940, the U.S. government devoted itself to protecting and extending its own prerogatives and by freedom politicos like FDR meant freedom from individual responsibility, not individual autonomy.[120]

New Dealers covered the faults of their policies with a flood of misinformation, disinformation, and redefinitions, claiming, for example, that without the New Deal, "the American way would have become a mere memory," with "a concentration of feudal overlordship at the top and economic serfdom at the bottom."[121] That was a thinly veiled reference to the Great Depression, the complex causes of which are essential to understanding why Americans accepted the New Deal.

The Holy Grail

An economic depression is a recession, i.e., a reduction of real per capita output, coupled with deflation, i.e., a decline in the price level. By 1931, experts already called the economic downturn "a major depression" because "commodity prices continue to dribble downwards ... corporate net earnings are poor and often conspicuous in their absence."[122] Indeed, oil sank to a mere ten cents a gallon in 1932, down from $1.00 in 1928.[123] "It is almost unbelievable the ways prices have fallen in the past 2 years," Benjamin Roth noted early in the Depression. For what one would have paid for one "fairly good suit" in 1929, one could buy two suits in 1932.[124]

Before World War II, most recessions were depressions (recessions with deflation) because of the functioning of the gold standard. After World War II and the end of the classical gold standard, most recessions, with a few exceptions like Japan's 1990s downturn, were inflationary or had no trend effect on the price level. The Great Depression was "great" in the sense of being big and long-lived. It was not quite the depression to end all depressions, but it did spell the end of America's retail gold standard and the beginning of the current inflation-prone fiat monetary regime.[125]

At the broadest level, two types of books about the Great Depression exist, those that consider the economy inherently unstable and saved by government policy,[126] and those that consider the government inherently unstable and saved by the economy.[127] This book, with precious few others, falls into the latter category.[128] As economist H. Clark Johnson put it, "American policy set an unenviable standard for repeated bad judgement," and he was just talking about its monetary policy.[129]

As recently as the mid-1990s, the majority of New Deal scholars, including almost all the historians and half of economists, rejected the notion that the New Deal "served to lengthen and deepen the Great Depression."[130] But lengthen and deepen the downturn it did. To show that the economy saved the government rather than the converse, this book must help readers to understand the economics of the cataclysm, which is no mean feat. Labor economist Bob Margo considers the Great Depression akin to the Big Bang, an event that has haunted successive generations of economists.[131] Macroeconomist Ben Bernanke likened finding a satisfying explanation of the Great Depression to finding the Holy Grail, implying that the value is in the exploration rather than the inevitably disappointing result.[132]

Economists have yet to explain the Great Depression to their own satisfaction because they have failed to account fully for the Depression's deepest root cause, the rise of the Progressive agenda in the first few decades of the twentieth century.[133] Progressive policies made the economy less resilient by euthanizing portions of the proprietorship and small manufacturing classes and creating institutions, like the Internal Revenue Service (IRS—technically the Bureau of Internal Revenue until 1953) and Federal Reserve System (the Fed), that not only did not reverse the downturn but made the economy much worse.[134] Fed officials recently admitted the institution's complicity in the Depression and even James Warburg, son of one of the Fed's architects, argued that "a wiser business and political leadership could have done much to avoid some of the excessive manifestations of boom and collapse."[135]

Warburg also understood that after they came to power in March 1933, New Dealers implemented numerous policies that impeded economic recovery and prevented the U.S. economy from recovering its formerly robust path of growth and development until after World War II.[136] Instead of America's savior, FDR was its bane, plaguing the economy with inefficiencies, many of which last to this day, and some of which have compounded their ill effects over time.

The standard story, that the 1929 stock market crash caused the Great Depression and that New Deal programs kept the country together until global war in 1939 finally revivified the U.S. economy, is demonstrably untrue. A negative aggregate demand shock in 1929 (a Fed-induced recession and subsequent stock market crash) initiated a sustained aggregate demand contraction that, exacerbated by poor policy choices (tight monetary conditions, high tariffs, and high wage policies), lasted until the middle of 1931, when a series of aggregate supply shocks (bank failure waves left unchecked by the Fed, the Office of the Comptroller of the Currency, or state regulators) led to further decreases in output that was exacerbated by most New Deal policies.[137]

In other words, the U.S. economy traversed four distinct phases, each with different causes and effects.[138] The first was a contraction, foreseen by astute analysts like E.C. Harwood,[139] that began before the stock market decline and that would have ended, probably in late 1930 or early 1931, were it not for a series of policy blunders by the Fed, Hoover, and Congress. In 1933, the second phase began when FDR temporarily reversed the economic decline by stabilizing the banking sector and creating inflation (reflation) expectations.[140] Other New Deal policies, like the National Industrial Recovery Act (NIRA) and tax increases, though, soon created uncertainties and other economic headwinds that reversed the rebound, especially in terms of employment, leading by 1934 to what one unusually astute historian called "the first Roosevelt Depression."[141]

The third phase began in May 1937 when another series of policy blunders by FDR and the Fed induced another contraction, better understood as a second FDR depression than the admittedly more alliterative Roosevelt recession. The fourth phase began when the economy started growing again in the second half of 1938. The Depression finally faded as employment levels soared following the outbreak of global war in the late summer of 1939. In terms of personal consumption and private-sector per capita output, the economy did not really recover until after the world war but at least everyone who wanted a job could get one.[142]

Various statistics undergird this four-phase view of America's economy in the 1930s. Corporate profits (with inventory valuation and capital consumption adjustments) fell from 10.8% in 1929 to 7.5% in 1930 to a mere 2.9% in 1931. They went negative, but only slightly so, in 1932 (– 0.2) and 1933 (– 0.1), before turning positive again in 1934 (2.5) and then heading back up to 4% in 1935 and 6.2% in 1936. They even rose to 7.1% in the first year of the Roosevelt Recession (1937), before falling back to 5% in 1938. They rebounded to 6.6% in 1939, however, and then soared during World War II, topping out at 24.9% in both 1943 and 1944.[143]

Industrial production dropped from 1929 until early 1933 before roaring back temporarily before the imposition of the National Recovery Administration (NRA). It went up and down in 1934 and 1935 before heading upward again, finally exceeding 1929 levels just in time for the Roosevelt Depression of 1937. Similarly, new home construction by 1933 was just 10% of its 1925 level but thereafter slowly increased until the 1937 downturn.[144]

The expectation of increases in the money supply beginning in April 1933 was the main driver of the output turnaround. Roosevelt's "inflation program" increased inflation expectations, inducing consumers to buy before prices went up. It also brought real interest rates way down, into negative territory, through the Fisher effect (real interest rates equal nominal interest rates minus inflation expectations).[145] It also raised nominal incomes, which especially helped heavily indebted agriculturalists to pay their mortgages and even to buy automobiles and other consumer durables again, while lowering real wages a bit. That allowed banks to stabilize and some industrial workers to be rehired.[146]

If the Roosevelt or Hoover administration had allowed nominal wages to adjust to deflation or decisively devalued the dollar in terms of gold, or committed to minting silver or printing fiat dollars sufficient to keep the money supply growing at a predictable pace, the economy, including employment, would have rebounded and what we would call the Great Depression would have ended.[147] The Depression was indeed the shortest in countries, like Austria, Denmark, Germany, Japan, Sweden, and many Latin American nations, that abandoned the full gold standard in 1930 or 1931 and immediately or eventually reflated their money supplies.[148] Instead, both U.S. administrations tinkered with various economic policies, the power of which they barely understood, and which muted the full effects of the monetary policy adjustments that did take place.[149]

Sustained and high levels of policy uncertainty were particularly depressive. The stock market did not return to its pre-crash highs until 1954 because investors were reluctant to put more funds into a system that seemed to be faltering, not so much economically as politically. Just as businesses were finally recovering from the policy shocks imposed during the New Deal, including the imposition of high real wage policies and the SEC, they were hit by the Roosevelt recession. Then a world war broke out. War proved profitable for many corporations, but FDR taxed much of it away, and the postwar policy regime remained uncertain so long as "that man in the White House"[150] remained in power. Depression and war left individual investors battered and bereft of savings; some, like Roth, left investment diaries that provide blow-by-blow accounts of the difficulties they encountered.[151] In the postwar period, it took an end to arbitrary policies, courageous newcomers, like well-to-do PR legend Wilma Soss, and herculean publicity efforts by the New York Stock Exchange, to reinvigorate the stock market.[152]

Sketch of the Book

Instead of fearing fear itself, Americans should have feared FDR and his policies, which radically transformed America's policy landscape by creating the illusion that the government could improve matters.[153] During the New Deal, the federal government crowded out most forms of private initiative, including even coverage of private news events as journalists flocked to D.C., where most of the action occurred.[154]

The illusion of the primacy of government action was made possible by the rise of economic progressivism in the first two decades of the twentieth century and the singular ability of Progressive and New Deal politicians to double down on their policy mistakes. As the economy continued to struggle, Harry Hopkins simply became more convinced than ever "that the measures taken by this administration are only a beginning of what needs to be done."[155]

Chapter 2 details that sea change in American political thought, starting with America's unwritten economic constitution and the death of the last great nineteenth-century (classical) liberal, Edward Atkinson. It then proceeds to describe the rise of so-called police powers during the nineteenth and early twentieth centuries before tracing the adoption of the national income tax, the development of the Federal Reserve, the great ratchet effect of the Great War, and the inability of conservative forces in the 1920s to return the nation to the *status quo ante bellum*.

The causal importance of the stock market crash of 1929 has been exaggerated, Chapter 3 explains. It was simply the bearer of bad news. The Federal Reserve precipitated the downturn, then exacerbated it, by making money too cheap, then too expensive. Then it failed in its one true mission, to lend to struggling but salvageable banks. Its inaction, combined with the depressive trade and wage policies coming out of the

Hoover administration, ensured that a regular recession would turn into a deflationary depression.

The combination of the Fed's monetary and bank bailout fudge ups with international trade autarky and high wage bullying led to FDR's first presidential election victory in 1932, which helped to spark an acute economic crisis just as he took office in March 1933. That, in turn, made possible FDR's seizure of America's monetary and financial systems, described in Chapter 4.

Chapters 5 and 6 describe how the New Deal stymied recovery, especially a return to anything close to full employment. Five covers the four big bailouts for banks and railroads, homeowners, nonfinancial manufacturing and service industries, and agriculturalists. Six details how the federal government destroyed America's traditional system of private security, labor relations, and industrialization and electrification.

Critics tried to fight back, as described in Chapter 7, but they were outmatched by an administration that wielded public monies to great political effect. Even the U.S. Supreme Court (SCOTUS), Chapter 8 explains, could not withstand FDR's political machine. After some initial success slowing FDR's radical reforms, SCOTUS capitulated to political pressure, opening the floodgates to decades of rapid government growth.

The next Chapter 9, explains how New Dealers came to control the Fed and much of the political narrative surrounding the economy and the New Deal's alleged role in improving it. Thus began the long march through American institutions, first noted by President Dwight D. Eisenhower, that initially crested with the Great Society before surging again after the Reagan Revolution ran its course following the events of 11 September 2001. Although important in their own way, the Great Society, and the conservative periods that preceded and succeeded it, were in no way comparable to the New Deal in terms of scale, scope, or speed of change.[156] In fact, to some extent, the failures of the New Deal, especially in matters of race, made the Great Society necessary.[157]

Chapter 10 shows how FDR's wartime policies strengthened the New Deal's legacies while introducing new problems, especially in healthcare and insurance and the creation of a permanent surveillance state. Chapter 11 surveys the ways in which FDR's policies hurt the interests of women, minors, American Indians, immigrants, and people of color. The next and final chapter describes how the New Deal greatly weakened the American economy by saddling it with inefficient regulations, like employer-tied healthcare, and ineffective and costly regulatory regimes, like that of the SEC.

The afterword proffers concrete suggestions on how America could reverse the ill effects of the New Deal by returning to the principles of limited government upon which the nation was founded.

Notes

1. As quoted in David Beito, *The New Deal's War on the Bill of Rights: The Untold Story of FDR's Concentration Camps, Censorship, and Mass Surveillance* (Oakland: Independent Institute, 2023), 40.
2. Kiran Klaus Patel, *The New Deal: A Global History* (Princeton: Princeton University Press, 2016), 210; Garet Garrett, *The People's Pottage* (Caldwell, ID: Caxton Printers, 1953), 21.
3. Lauchlin Currie, "Lauchlin Currie's Memoirs," *Journal of Economic Studies* 31, 3/4 (2004), 212, 229.
4. James P. Warburg, *Hell Bent for Election* (New York: Doubleday, Doran & Company, 1935), 37–41.
5. Beito, *New Deal's War on the Bill of Rights*.
6. Marion Turner Sheehan, ed. *The World at Home: Selections from the Writings of Anne O'Hare McCormick* (New York: Alfred A. Knopf, 1956), 174.
7. Robert Mason, *The Republican Party and American Politics from Hoover to Reagan* (New York: Cambridge University Press, 2011), 58.
8. Richard Polenberg, *Reorganizing Roosevelt's Government: The Controversy Over Executive Reorganization* (Cambridge, Mass.: Harvard University Press, 1966), 50, 60, 68–69, 89, 127.
9. Burton Folsom, Jr. *New Deal or Raw Deal? How FDR's Economic Legacy Has Damaged America* (New York: Simon & Schuster, 2008), 233.
10. Philip Hamburger, *Is Administrative Law Unlawful?* (Chicago: University of Chicago Press, 2014), 1–7, 21–30, 508–11.
11. Robert H. Wiebe, *The Search for Order, 1877–1920* (New York: Hill and Wang, 1967), 34.
12. Folsom, *New Deal or Raw Deal?*, 41–42; T.H. Watkins, *The Great Depression: America in the 1930s* (New York: Little, Brown & Co., 1993), 137.

13. Amity Shlaes, *The Forgotten Man: A New History of the Great Depression* (New York: HarperCollins, 2007), 146.
14. JNF, Chairman of the SEC, 13 July 1940, Files of Chairmen Ganson Purcell and James J. Caffrey, and Commissioners Robert H. O'Brien and Robert K. McConnaughey, 1939–1948, Box 50, Records of the Securities and Exchange Commission, RG 266, National Archives and Records Administration, College Park, Maryland.
15. As quoted in Anthony J. Bolton, "'The Best Form of Assistance Always Is the Kind That Enables Folks to Help Themselves': Public Reaction to the New Deal in Hancock, Seneca, and Wood Counties of Ohio," (MA Thesis: Bowling Green State University, 2021), 107.
16. Garrett, *People's Pottage*, 8; Thomas Sowell, *Social Justice Fallacies* (New York: Basic Books, 2023), 96.
17. Garrett, *People's Pottage*, 6; Raymond Moley, "After Seven Years," in Amity Shlaes, ed. *New Deal Rebels* (Great Barrington, Mass.: American Institute for Economic Research, 2023), 249–51; Albion Small, "The Social Gradations of Capital," *American Journal of Sociology* 9, 6 (May 1914), 723.
18. Jean Edward Smith, *FDR* (New York: Random House, 2007), x.
19. David M. Kennedy, "What the New Deal Did," *Political Science Quarterly* 124, 2 (Summer 2009), 251; Paul Sabin, *Public Citizens: The Attack on Big Government and the Remaking of American Liberalism* (New York: W.W. Norton & Co., 2021); Jim F. Couch and William F. Shughart, *The Political Economy of the New Deal* (Northampton, MA: Edward Elgar, 1998), xiii, 1–2; Gary Dean Best, *Pride, Prejudice, and Politics: Roosevelt Versus Recovery, 1933–1938* (New York: Praeger, 1991), ix.
20. Folsom, *New Deal or Raw Deal?*, 253–54; John M. Jordan, *Machine-Age Ideology: Social Engineering and American Liberalism, 1911–1939* (Chapel Hill: University of North Carolina, 1994), 247–51; Roger G. Kennedy, "A New Deal for Nature – And Nature's People," in Henry L. Henderson and David B. Woolner, eds., *FDR and the Environment* (New York: Palgrave, 2005), 245.
21. G.Q. Flynn, "The New Deal and Local Archives: The Pacific Northwest," *The American Archivist* 33, 1 (Jan. 1970), 41–43.

22. I. Maurice Wormser, *Frankenstein, Incorporated* (New York: McGraw Hill Book Co., 1931), vi, 227; Richard K. Vedder and Lowell E. Gallaway, *Out of Work: Unemployment and Government in Twentieth-Century America*, updated ed. (New York: New York University Press, 1997), 129.
23. Currie, "Memoirs," 227.
24. Shlaes, *Forgotten Man*, 2–14; Folsom, *New Deal or Raw Deal?*, 1–15, 237; Couch and Shughart, *Political Economy*, 1–4; Jim Powell, *FDR's Folly: How Roosevelt and His New Deal Prolonged the Great Depression* (New York: Crown Forum, 2003), 1–26; Lawrence W. Reed, *Great Myths of the Great Depression* (Mackinac Center for Public Policy and the Foundation for Economic Education, 2011).
25. Mark C. Cairnes, "Editor's Preface," in Tony A. Freyer, *Hugo L. Black and the Dilemma of American Liberalism* (New York: Pearson, 2008), ix; Gary Gerstle, *The Rise and Fall of the Neoliberal Order: America and the World in the Free Market Era* (New York: Oxford University Press, 2022).
26. Jeremy Horpedahl, Phillip Magness, and Marcus Witcher, "Teaching the Causes of Great Depression to College Students: Evidence from History, Economic, and Economic History Textbooks," *Journal of Economics and Finance Education* 21, 2 (Fall 2023): 22–37.
27. Smith, *FDR*, ix; Jeremy K. Kessler, "The Political Economy of 'Constitutional Political Economy'," *Texas Law Review* 94 (2016), 1527–28.
28. H. W. Brands, *A Traitor to His Class: The Privileged Life and Radical Presidency of Franklin Delano Roosevelt* (New York: Anchor Books, 2008).
29. Paul Moreno, "An Ambivalent Legacy: Black Americans and the Political Economy of the New Deal," *Independent Review* 6, 4 (Spring 2002), 514.
30. Johan Norberg, *Financial Fiasco: How America's Infatuation with Homeownership and Easy Money Created the Economic Crisis* (Washington, DC: Cato Institute, 2009), 100–1.
31. Michael Schearer, "Batteryman vs. the New Deal: The Life of Fred C. Perkins," Working Paper (9 May 2021), 1.
32. Dalia Tsuk, "Pluralisms: The Indian New Deal As a Model," *University of Maryland Law Journal of Race, Religion, Gender*

and Class 1, 2 (2001): 408–12; Kristin S. Williams and Albert J. Mills, "Frances Perkins: Gender, Context, and History in the Neglect of a Management Theorist," *Journal of Management History* 23, 1 (2017), 37–38.

33. Moreno, "Ambivalent Legacy," 513–39.
34. John J. Wallis, "Lessons from the Political Economy of the New Deal," *Oxford Review of Economic Policy* 26, 3 (Autumn 2010), 442–43; Naomi Oreskes and Erik M. Conway, *The Big Myth: How American Business Taught Us to Loathe Government and Love the Free Market* (New York: Bloomsbury Publishing, 2023), 47, 397; Murray N. Rothbard, *America's Great Depression* 5th ed. (Auburn, Ala.: Ludwig von Mises Institute, 1963, 2000), 85–94, 185–320.
35. Winston Churchill, "What Good's a Constitution?," in Shlaes, ed., *New Deal Rebels*, 160.
36. Hugh Rockoff, "By Way of Analogy: The Expansion of the Federal Government in the 1930s," in Michael D. Bordo, Claudia Goldin, and Eugene N. White, eds., *The Defining Moment: The Great Depression and the American Economy in the Twentieth Century* (Chicago: University of Chicago Press, 1998), 125.
37. James Ledbetter and Daniel B. Roth, eds. *The Great Depression: A Diary by Benjamin Roth* (New York: Public Affairs, 2009), 105.
38. David E. Bernstein, *Only One Place of Redress: African Americans, Labor Regulations, and the Courts from Reconstruction to the New Deal* (Durham: Duke University Press, 2001), 106.
39. Williams and Mills, "Frances Perkins," 40.
40. Rothbard, *America's Great Depression*, 285–320.
41. FDR's critics from the Left were particularly worried about his administration's fascistic leanings. See, for example, Louis Adamic, *Dynamite: The Story of Class Violence in America*, rev. ed. (1934) (Oakland: AK Press 2008), 321. Fascism is authoritarianism from the Right of the political spectrum that relied upon co-opting private interests, especially large corporations, in service of the state.
42. Garet Garrett, "For Five Years, There Has Been No American System," in Shlaes, ed., *New Deal Rebels*, 223–38; Couch and Shughart, *Political Economy*, 19–20.
43. Powell, *FDR's Folly*, 1, 5.
44. Couch and Shughart, *Political Economy*, 25–26.

45. Price Fishback, "How Successful Was the New Deal? The Microeconomic Impact of New Deal Spending and Lending Policies in the 1930s," NBER Working Paper 21,925 (Jan. 2016), 62–64.
46. Ledbetter and Roth, eds. *Great Depression*, 130.
47. Couch and Shughart, *Political Economy*, 89.
48. Harry Hopkins, Works Progress Administration, The Works Program, Press Release, 16 Jul. 1938, FRASER.
49. Norberg, *Financial Fiasco*, 107–8.
50. Ledbetter and Roth, eds. *Great Depression*, 154–56.
51. Colin Gordon, "Rethinking the New Deal," *Columbia Law Review* 98, 8 (Dec. 1998): 2,047; Beito, *New Deal's War on the Bill of Rights*, 15.
52. Warburg, *Hell Bent*, 1.
53. Beito, *New Deal's War on the Bill of Rights*, 11.
54. Gerald H. Gamm, *The Making of New Deal Democrats: Voting Behavior and Realignment in Boston, 1920–1940* (Chicago: University of Chicago Press, 1989), 1–18, 57; Steve Fraser and Gary Gerstle, eds., *The Rise and Fall of the New Deal Order, 1930–1980* (Princeton: Princeton University Press, 1989), *ix-xii*; David Brady, Richard Brody, and David Epstein, "Heterogeneous Parties and Political Organization: The U.S. Senate, 1880–1920," *Legislative Studies Quarterly* 14, 2 (May 1989), 213–14.
55. Ryan J. Antonucci, "Building a New (Deal) Identity: The Evolution of Italian-American Political Culture and Ideology, 1910–1940," (Ph.D. diss.: University of South Carolina, 2021), 391–452.
56. Ledbetter and Roth, eds. *Great Depression*, 137.
57. As quoted in Sheehan, *World at Home*, 60. Antonucci, "Building a New (Deal) Identity."
58. Vedder and Gallaway, *Out of Work*, 70.
59. Justin Raimondo, *Reclaiming the American Right: The Lost Legacy of the Conservative Movement* (Wilmington, DE: ISI Books, 2008), xviii-xx; Gregory L. Schneider, ed., *Conservatism in America Since 1930: A Reader* (New York: New York University Press, 2003), 2.
60. Harry L. Hopkins, "The Essence of Democracy," The Works Program, Works Progress Administration, (30 Aug. 1938), 10, FRASER.

61. Jeremiah D. Lambert, *The Power Brokers: The Struggle to Shape and Control the Electric Power Industry* (Cambridge: The MIT Press, 2015), x, 54–80.
62. Smith, *FDR*, 452–56; Betty Houchin Winfield, *FDR and the News Media* (New York: Columbia University Press, 1994), 14.
63. Bolton, "“Best Form of Assistance’," 106.
64. Ralph Bunche, *The Political Status of the Negro in the Age of FDR* (Chicago: University of Chicago Press, 1973), 136.
65. Rachel S. Ferguson and Marcus M. Witcher, *Black Liberation Through the Marketplace: Hope, Heartbreak, and the Promise of America* (New York: Post Hill Press, 2022), 222–24; Folsom, *New Deal or Raw Deal?*, 206–11; Beito, *New Deal's War on the Bill of Rights*, 137–64.
66. Harry L. Hopkins, "The Essence of Democracy," The Works Program, Works Progress Administration, (30 Aug. 1938), 5, FRASER.
67. Smith, *FDR*, xii; Richard A. Epstein, *Forbidden Grounds: The Case Against Employment Discrimination Laws* (Cambridge: Harvard University Press, 1992), 140–41.
68. Vedder and Gallaway, *Out of Work*, 128.
69. Thomas Nixon Carver, *The Present Economic Revolution in the United States* (Boston: Little, Brown, and Co., 1925), 233.
70. Reed, *Great Myths*, 10.
71. Albert Jay Nock, *Our Enemy, the State* (New York: William Morrow & Co., 1935), 6.
72. Ledbetter and Roth, eds. *Great Depression*, 152, 162.
73. FDR, "Acceptance Speech for the Renomination for the Presidency, Philadelphia, Pa.," 27 June 1936 and "Address at Marietta, Ohio," 8 July 1938, American Presidency Project.
74. Kennedy, "What the New Deal Did," 251.
75. Gordon, "Rethinking," 2,029–54.
76. Nock, *Our Enemy*, 11–12, 24.
77. Garrett, *People's Pottage*, 6.
78. Gareth Jones, "Greater Tariffs – Chief Question at the World Conference," *The Western Mail* (14 June 1933): https://www.garethjones.org/unemployment/unemployment_10.htm.
79. John P. Diggins, "Flirtation with Fascism: American Pragmatic Liberals and Mussolini's Italy," *American History Review* 71, 2 (Jan. 1966): 487–506.

80. Harvey Klehr, *The Heyday of American Communism: The Depression Decade* (New York: Basic Books, Inc., 1984), 94; Beito, *New Deal's War on the Bill of Rights*, 123.
81. Harry L. Hopkins, "The Essence of Democracy," The Works Program, Works Progress Administration, (30 Aug. 1938), 6, FRASER.
82. Garrett, *People's Pottage*, 17–18, 9.
83. Patel, *New Deal Global History*, 1–9.
84. Rexford G. Tugwell, *The Diary of Rexford G. Tugwell: The New Deal, 1932–1935*, Michael Namorato, ed. (New York: Greenwood Press, 1992), 153.
85. Eric Rauchway, "The New Deal Was on the Ballot in 1932," *Modern American History* (2019): 1–13.
86. Jordan, *Machine-Age Ideology*, 232; George Selgin, *False Dawn: The New Deal and the Promise of Recovery, 1933–1947* (Chicago: University of Chicago Press, 2025).
87. Garrett, *People's Pottage*, 22.
88. Gareth Jones, "Greater Tariffs – Chief Question at the World Conference," *The Western Mail* (14 June 1933): https://www.garethjones.org/unemployment/unemployment_10.htm.
89. As quoted in Couch and Shughart, *Political Economy*, 66.
90. Ledbetter and Roth, eds. *Great Depression*, 210.
91. Garrett, *People's Pottage*, 22–24.
92. Schearer, "Batteryman," 16.
93. Garrett, *People's Pottage*, 56.
94. Harry L. Hopkins, "The Essence of Democracy," The Works Program, Works Progress Administration, (30 Aug. 1938), 5, FRASER.
95. Kennedy, "What the New Deal Did," 252–68.
96. Patel, *New Deal Global History*, 205–8.
97. Currie, "Memoirs," 209, 230.
98. Suzanna Sherry, "The Founders' Unwritten Constitution," *University of Chicago Law Review* 54, 4 (Fall 1987): 1133–34.
99. Bernstein, *Only One Place*, 4.
100. Bradley C.S. Watson, *Progressivism: The Strange History of a Radical Idea* (Notre Dame: University of Notre Dame Press, 2020), 30–32. Quotation at 31.
101. FDR, "Reading Copy," (Message to Congress, 1941), 20–21. https://www.fdrlibrary.org/four-freedoms.

102. Watkins, *Great Depression*, 138–63.
103. Thomas Sowell, *The Vision of the Anointed: Self-Congratulation as a Basis for Social Policy* (New York: Basic Books, 1995), 236.
104. Warburg, *Hell Bent*, 35.
105. Thomas Sowell, *A Conflict of Visions: Ideological Origins of Political Struggles* (New York: William Morrow & Co., 1987), Chapter 2.
106. As quoted in Best, *Pride*, 6.
107. E.C. Harwood, "The Full Significance of Freedom," *American Journal of Economics and Sociology* 4, 2 (Jan. 1945), 186.
108. Winfield, *FDR and the News Media*, 39, 67–69.
109. Harwood, "Full Significance of Freedom," 186–87.
110. FDR, "Reading Copy," (Message to Congress, 1941), 19. https://www.fdrlibrary.org/four-freedoms.
111. Warburg, *Hell Bent*, 48–50.
112. Harry Hopkins, Works Progress Administration, The Works Program, Press Release, 16 Jul. 1938, FRASER.
113. Works Progress Administration, The Works Program, Press Release, 16 Jul. 1938, FRASER; Robert E. Wright, *Liberty Lost: Rise and Demise of Voluntary Association in America Since 1700* (Great Barrington, Mass.: American Institute for Economic Research, 2023); David Beito, *From Mutual Aid to the Welfare State: Fraternal Societies and Social Services, 1890–1967* (Chapel Hill: University of North Carolina Press, 2000), 1–16.
114. Winfield, *FDR and the News Media*.
115. Patel, *New Deal Global History*, 104–12.
116. Reed, *Great Myths*, 16.
117. John Steele Gordon, *An Empire of Wealth: The Epic History of American Economic Power* (New York: HarperCollins, 2004), 333–34.
118. Otto Friedrich, "F.D.R.'s Dispute Legacy," *Time* (1 Feb. 1982): http://content.time.com/time/subscriber/article/0,33009,954983-6,00.html.
119. Alexis DeTocqueville, *Democracy in America*, Henry Reeve, trans. (New York: Pratt, Woodford & Co., 1848), 265–66.
120. Thomas Sowell, *Social Justice Fallacies* (New York: Basic Books, 2023), 82–83.
121. Works Progress Administration, The Works Program, Press Release, 16 Jul. 1938, FRASER.

122. Wormser, *Frankenstein*, vi, 230.
123. John Gunther, *Inside U.S.A.* (New York: Harper & Brothers, 1947), 878; E.C. Harwood, "The Automobile's Share of the Consumer's Income," (July 1928) Box 1, E.C. Harwood Archives, AIER, Great Barrington, Mass.
124. Ledbetter and Roth, eds. *Great Depression*, 65.
125. Saul Eslake, "The Difference Between a Recession and a Depression," *Economic Papers* 28, 2 (June 2009): 75–81.
126. See, most recently, Oreskes and Conway, *Big Myth*, 286.
127. The Great Recession of 2009 has been treated in a similar manner. Robert Hetzel, *The Great Recession: Market Failure or Policy Failure?* (New York: Cambridge University Press, 2012), 1–11.
128. Roger W. Garrison, "The Great Depression Revisited," *Independent Review* 3, 4 (Spring 1999): 596; Barry Eichengreen and Peter Temin, "The Gold Standard and the Great Depression," NBER Working Paper 6060 (June 1997), 37; Rothbard, *America's Great Depression*, xxxvii-viii.
129. H. Clark Johnson, *Gold, France, and the Great Depression, 1919–1932* (New Haven: Yale University Press, 1997), 183.
130. Robert Whaples, "Where Is There Consensus Among American Economic Historians? The Results of a Survey on Forty Propositions," *Journal of Economic History* 55, 1 (March 1995), 144.
131. Robert A. Margo, "Employment and Unemployment in the 1930s," *Journal of Economic Perspectives* 7, 2 (Spring 1993): 41–59.
132. Ben Bernanke, "The Macroeconomics of the Great Depression: A Comparative Approach," NBER Working Paper #4814 (August 1994), 1. The points made in Bernanke's sundry working papers generally can also be found in Ben S. Bernanke, *Essays on the Great Depression* (Princeton: Princeton University Press, 2000).
133. Margo, "Employment and Unemployment," 50–51.
134. Wiebe, *Search for Order*, 13.
135. Burton A. Abrams, *The Terrible Ten: A Century of Economic Folly* (Oakland: Independent Institute, 2013), 23; Warburg, *Hell Bent*, 1–2.
136. Yangyang Ji, "The Effect of New Deal Policies Revisited," *CESifo Economic Studies* (2021): 238–49.

137. Stephen Cecchetti and Georgios Karras, "Sources of Output Fluctuations During the Interwar Period: Further Evidence on the Causes of the Great Depression," NBER Working Paper 4049 (April 1992).
138. Thomas E. Hall and J. David Ferguson, *The Great Depression: An International Disaster of Perverse Economic Policies* (Ann Arbor: University of Michigan Press, 1998), 1–15.
139. E. C. Harwood, "The Underlying Causes of Our Recent Prosperity: Why the End Is Near," *The Annalist* (13 April 1928), 643, 650.
140. Hetzel, *Great Recession*, 65.
141. Best, *Pride*, 69–83, 175–202.
142. NBER, "US Business Cycle Expansions and Contractions," https://www.nber.org/research/data/us-business-cycle-expansions-and-contractions. Shughart, "New Deal and Modern Memory," 537; Robert Higgs, "Wartime Prosperity? A Reassessment of the U.S. Economy in the 1940s," *Journal of Economic History* 52, 1 (March 1992): 41–60.
143. Bureau of Economic Analysis, "Corporate Profits by Industry," rev. 9 Jan. 2004. Accessed 14 Jan. 2005.
144. Couch and Shughart, *Political Economy*, 83–84.
145. Hetzel, *Great Recession*, 68–69.
146. Joshua K. Hausman, Paul W. Rhode, and Johannes F. Wieland, "Recovery from the Great Depression: The Farm Channel in Spring 1933," *American Economic Review* 109, 2 (2019): 427–72.
147. Ledbetter and Roth, eds. *Great Depression*, 106; Harold L. Cole and Lee E. Ohanian, "The Great Depression in the United States from a Neoclassical Perspective," *Federal Reserve Bank of Minneapolis Quarterly Review* (Winter 1999), 2–3, 11–12.
148. Ben Bernanke and Harold James, "The Gold Standard, Deflation, and Financial Crisis in the Great Depression: An International Comparison"; Ben Bernanke and Ilian Mihov, "Deflation and Monetary Contraction in the Great Depression: An Analysis by Simple Ratios," in Bernanke, *Essays*, 70–71, 85–87, 108; Hetzel, *Great Recession*, 101–4.
149. Shughart, "New Deal."
150. Raimondo, *Reclaiming the American Right*, 112.
151. Ledbetter and Roth, eds. *Great Depression*.

152. Monika Ardelt, "Social Credit and Individual Growth: The Long-Term Effects of the Great Depression," *Journal of Aging Studies* 12, 3 (September 1998): 291–314; Janice M. Traflet, *A Nation of Small Shareholders: Marketing Wall Street After World War II* (Baltimore: Johns Hopkins University Press, 2013); Janice M. Traflet and Robert E. Wright, *Fearless: Wilma Soss and America's Forgotten Investor Movement* (New York: All Seasons Press, 2022).
153. Milton Friedman, "Why Government Is the Problem," *Essays in Public Policy* No. 39 (Stanford: Hoover Institution, 1993), 15.
154. Winfield, *FDR and the News Media*, 79.
155. Harry Hopkins, Public Works Administration, "Resurgent Democracy," 8 Oct. 1938.
156. Charles Murray, *Losing Ground: American Social Policy, 1950–1980* (New York: BasicBooks, 1984), 42.
157. Moreno, "Ambivalent Legacy," 528.

CHAPTER 2

Economic Progressivism Rises

Some historians see the New Deal as an aberration, a reaction, even an overreaction, to the Great Depression, the effects of which were largely gone or reversed by the 1980s.[1] Such treatments fail to distinguish cyclical ups and downs from long-term trends. Although true that the New Deal voter coalition finally gave way in 1980, many of its policy impacts continued.[2] As historian Eric Rauchway argues, the New Deal matters to us today because "evidence of the New Deal is everywhere even now, nearly a 100 years since it started. … it gives structure to our lives in ways we do not ordinarily bother to count or catalog."[3] It was the first time the nation shifted fundamentally from its traditional classical liberal path, which stressed small government, voluntarism, and individualism, to a "progressive," statist, collectivist government that increasingly substituted an increasingly powerful national government for private business, charity, and self-help.

That is not to argue that the transformation had no grounding in history or political incentives. The U.S. government and American people reacted to the Great Depression as they did because of what had come before. Other nations, like Canada, reacted less vigorously to the global downturn and recovered relatively quickly.[4] Yet others, like Germany, Japan, and the USSR, essentially sidestepped the downturn by moving their economies toward a wartime, command footing, replete with new

R. E. Wright, *FDR's Long New Deal*,
https://doi.org/10.1007/978-3-031-74141-8_2

money creation.[5] Until World War II, America took the most destructive path of all by decreasing economic freedom without restoring full employment or empowering the private sector to drive steady growth.[6] The destructive route lay open because of what came before and New Dealers took it because it provided the clearest path to electoral victory.

FDR's New Deal did not arise fully formed, like Athena from the forehead of Zeus, but rather evolved out of the so-called Progressive movement, which bequeathed FDR with old battle-hardened politicians like J.P. Morgan-foe Samuel Untermyer and progressive Republican George Norris of Nebraska.[7] Like the New Deal itself, historians have distorted the Progressive movement, giving it too much credit for economic improvements that occurred despite it, and not criticizing it enough for its dark origins in eugenics and Social Darwinism or its many socioeconomic costs.[8]

To batter down classical liberalism in a nation that took limited government for granted, putative reformers needed powerful rhetoric, like that inherent in the words "liberal" and "progress." Who could dare question progress or its inevitability in America, the land of the free and home of manifest destiny? To oppose Progressivism, and hence progress, was to position oneself on the "wrong side" of history, as slaveholders and Loyalists had done and paid dearly for it. It seemed un-American to oppose progress in a land dedicated to constant betterment.[9] That was why FDR always attacked the "old order" and likened his critics to holdovers from the "horse and buggy days," or "economic royalists," or "modern Torys."[10]

FDR's minions followed close behind. Because "conditions changed," New Deal employment practices administrator Malcolm Ross argued, so too should the relationship between the government and individuals, lest people suffer "because archaic opinions remained in force."[11] By the early postwar period, it was commonplace for textbooks to argue that change and development made it "necessary" for the government to go beyond "traditional types of government control" and to begin to "guide and channel economic actions."[12]

FDR learned to deprecate the past from his Democratic predecessor in the Oval Office, Woodrow Wilson, who also brought America a bigger government, a world war, racial segregationist policies,[13] and a new policy agenda, "The New Freedom." A new approach was needed, Wilson claimed, because "our life has broken away from the past. The life of America," he wrote in 1913, "is not the life that it was 20 years ago."

Economic conditions had changed "absolutely, from top to bottom." Old political debates over the meaning of the Constitution between liberals and conservatives "read now like documents out of a forgotten age." To ensure that the American people remained happy and prosperous, "governmental powers" had to be enlarged to keep up. America had entered a "new age" where few men own their own businesses and most were "the servant of a corporation," with nothing to protect them, except the government.

The old (classical) liberal order, Wilson claimed, had not kept up with the pace of business, economic, and technological change. Like the Red Queen in Alice in Wonderland, America's legal system needed to run faster just to keep up with the dizzying pace of change. Old time "liberal" thinking, though, prevented progress, keeping the law trailing the facts instead of the other way around. America had no choice; it must create a more powerful state or watch itself retrograde, its democracy overtaken by "an invisible empire" of "special interests." Despite the absence of crisis, Wilson saw "great discontent" with the status quo, a discontent well justified and empirically grounded. He needed more power to thwart the growing Socialist movement and smite the "do-nothingism" that threatened the nation's continued "progress."[14]

Liberal was the other rhetorically powerful word usurped by those interested in resetting the nation's baseline in favor of state power. Before the New Deal, it meant what we today must call "classical liberal," people who want to limit the government's power and thus maximize the ability of individuals to order their world through voluntary exchange and association. Today, and since the New Deal, liberal refers to people on the political Left, including Democrats, Progressives, and Socialists, who favor big government and mandatory collectivist solutions over voluntary individual ones.[15]

Whereas America's classical liberal Founders and Framers believed humans to be enlightened but flawed creatures, better than beasts but below angels, Progressives believed humans to be malleable entities that needed proper progressive guidance. Old notions like custom and property rights must be jettisoned lest progress, as they defined it, slow or stagnate. Another revolution remained unnecessary so long as progress toward undercutting the original Constitution could be made.[16]

In a sense, Progressives pushed for a sort of reset, though one arguably rooted in a more organic and empirically grounded crisis than the

New Deal or Covid resets. Immigration, the diminution of the proprietor classes (artisans, farmers, and shopkeepers), and rapid technological change did seem to pose a valid threat to social stability.[17]

Nevertheless, the claims of Progressives constituted little more than empty rhetoric. The American Republic's tremendous socioeconomic progress since the late eighteenth century rested on its (classical) liberal system of political economy, which sought to maximize the advantages of competition and minimize the costs of economic rent extraction, of using government power to get something for nothing.[18] British colonists in mainland North America had rebelled due to their fear of arbitrary power, commercial and political. They sought to rule themselves instead of taking orders from distant corporate monopolies and government officials who did not respect the rule of law because they were accountable to no one.[19] After securing their physical independence in the Revolution, the former subjects proclaimed themselves citizens, securing their individual autonomy with their state constitutions and an unwritten economic constitution, and their unity and might with the written U.S. Constitution. The economic freedom or "equality under liberty"[20] promised by those fundamental laws lasted largely intact for over a century, ensuring the new nation's rapid economic expansion, growth, and development.[21]

Progressives and New Dealers, the architects of FDR's plethora of policies, ironically leveraged that rapid change to quench an innate, conservative desire for "order."[22] Market processes and spontaneous order are inherently messy and often slow to change. They may even seem random or chaotic. The siren call sung by Progressive journalist Herbert Croly, who called for "collective education by means of collective action and collective discipline,"[23] and others held strong allure, even for some Republicans. Why not speed up progress by allowing an efficiently run democratically elected state to dictate it?[24] Only two national and scores of state constitutions stood in the way.

America's Lost Economic Constitution

Wilson and other Progressives also started the process of destroying constitutional barriers to increased governmental power. Wilson considered the U.S. Constitution "a living thing," and hence something that could adapt and evolve, instead of a set of timeless principles to be defended to the death.[25]

Worse, perhaps, Wilson only recognized the written Constitution. The notion of an unwritten U.S. economic constitution may be unfamiliar to some readers, but it is not a novel concept.[26] While America's state and federal political constitutions were written, the one on which they were all based, the British constitution, was not.[27] America's Founders and Framers believed that written political constitutions would best protect the people from government intrusions upon liberty. Economic change, though, was too rapid, nuanced, and important to protect with relatively rigid written constitutional strictures. Nobody from the founding generation expected national, state, or local governments to interfere with natural economic rights, like the right to make a living by engaging in lawful activities, the right to bodily autonomy, or the right to use the energy sources of one's choice. They expected reason combined with the traditions and institutions of the common law to check any legislative excesses and to slow the pace of legal change to minimize disruptions that might have untoward effects on economic incentives.[28]

The authority of custom in economic matters was strong and held, in the words of constitutional historian John Phillip Reid, that "whatever consciously had been abstained from in the nation or community from time immemorial was unconstitutional or illegal," whether a written document explicitly elucidated it or not. Custom was more pliable than legislation yet much less subject to the tyranny of the majority as its main function was to restrain government overreach into economic affairs, especially with respect to property broadly conceived. Americans believed that their economic rights were inviolable because they had been purchased with the blood, sweat, and tears of generations and because their unwritten economic constitution jived with Aristotelian natural rights and the Lockean social contract.[29] Moreover, governments were limited in extent and power, constrained by trust, consent, contract, constitution, liberty, and law.[30] As John Trenchard had explained in 1723, "Only the checks put upon magistrates make nations free; and only the want of such checks makes them slaves. They are free, where their magistrates are confined within certain bounds set them by the people."[31]

If a government were to deviate from the economic constitution, or other hoary and ingrained customs like trial by jury, the Framers believed that the Bill of Rights, especially the First, Second, and Fifth Amendments (speech/assembly, firearms, and due process, respectfully), would put a quick end to it, as would the next election. They, therefore, opted to leave economic rights, including basic natural rights like bodily autonomy and occupational and energy choice, out of the written national constitution, just as they almost left the prohibition against *ex post facto* laws implicit.[32] They soon allowed many explicit economic rights to pass from their state constitutions as well. Ergo, state constitutions and the Bill of Rights do not explicitly protect everyone's right to occupational choice, to make decisions about their own bodies, to protect themselves from bodily harm, or to use carbon-based fuels,[33] the way that they explicitly protect expression or firearms ownership. The federal Ninth Amendment and numerous similar state constitutional clauses, however, make clear the existence of such unenumerated rights, as does the Declaration of Independence and the written Constitution's Preamble.[34] As James Madison explained, the Ninth Amendment referred to areas of life so vast that they could not be minutely specified, obvious areas of personal discretion into which no government should tread.[35] Jurists once held the notion of an unwritten constitution sacrosanct, but it slowly faded, one death at a time, along with the rest of the classical liberal creed.

The American system of governance was imperfect but hardy, admitting hardly any substantive diminution until the uncivil war that began in 1861 ground down traditional restraints on the federal government until 1865. Like every big American war, it caused a ratchet effect, a permanent increase in the power and scope of the federal government.[36] The War of 1812, the Civil War, the Great War, and the Great Depression/ World War II all clearly permanently elevated government spending as a percent of GDP.[37]

While the federal government's power increased due to wars, the power of state and local governments crept up decade by decade, checked only occasionally by crises like the Panic of 1837, which exposed the folly of most government enterprise as overly ambitious taxpayer-funded public works projects faltered or were exposed as unnecessary or too expensive.[38]

The main concept underlying America's unwritten constitution was the presumption of individual liberty, as opposed to a presumption of governmental power. In other words, citizens did not have to prove that they had a right to this or that, the government had to prove that its diminution of individual liberty was both necessary and proper in each case. Before the New Deal, wars, and only wars, provided such proof. As Edmund Burke put it, the goal of government should be "to find out by cautious experiments, and rational, cool endeavours, with how little, not how much of this restraint, the community can subsist. For liberty is a good to be improved, and not an evil to be lessened."[39] The demise of the unwritten constitution, therefore, sped the growth of government power by removing one of the major checks against its growth.[40]

A book by Christopher G. Tiedeman published in 1890 entitled *The Unwritten Constitution of the United States: A Philosophical Inquiry into the Fundamentals of American Constitutional Law* reduced the unwritten constitution to "freedom from all legal restraint that is not needed to prevent injury to others; a right to do any thing that does not involve a trespass or injury to others ... a freedom from needless restraint" (76–77). But even before Tiedeman wrote, courts, like New York's Court of Appeals in *Bertholf v O'Reilly* (74 N.Y. 509), disavowed the unwritten constitution, arguing that "principles outside of the [written] Constitution" were not needed to protect Americans from government encroachment. Due process and other Constitutional precepts, broadly construed, sufficed. And, at first, they were, with the high court of New York in *Bertholf* arguing that taxes had to serve a "public purpose" and not just redistribute wealth. But as Progressives twisted concepts like due process and public purpose, the government established precedents that allowed for further incursions unchecked by the notion that it could tread only when and where absolute necessity summoned it.

"Police Powers" Run Amok

Over time, state and local governments came to assert increasing control over a broad swathe of the lives of everyday Americans. Occupations, for example, first became taxed, then subjected to health and safety regulations like fire codes, and finally licensed regarding education, experience, and expertise so that customers presumably would be less likely to suffer poor service. Municipalities also exerted other so-called "police powers," like the authority to ban public alcohol consumption, to restrict Sunday economic activities, and to prohibit gambling. Eventually, such police powers extended to the state and then the national level. Slowly, and then suddenly, America transformed from a nation of people skeptical of the ability of government to do anything useful to one peopled by the likes of Harry Hopkins, who believed "the Government can do a great many things."[41]

Classical liberals sought to minimize the government's coercive power over the individual. Initially, they limited the national government's role to military defense, safeguarding individual rights and contracts, and punishing *malum in se*, i.e., the very worst crimes, like treason.[42] They went by labels like Whig and Liberal in Britain, while in the United States all major parties and factions were composed of classical liberals, at least at first. Most ideological squabbles, like those between Thomas Jefferson and Alexander Hamilton, were matters of detail rather than principle, which is why Albert Gallatin's fiscal policies under Jefferson and Madison so closely resembled those of Hamilton.[43]

State and local governments exercised their so-called "police powers" ostensibly "to keep the peace" or to "maintain order." That clearly included their duty to quell riots and rebellions and to prevent violent and property crimes, a responsibility that grew along with the nation's cities, especially its "slums."[44] The exact extent of police powers, however, was never clearly delineated. They were thought relatively innocuous initially because of limitations on their geographical extent and the fact that into the early twentieth-century local government officials were largely accountable to their constituents.[45] Moreover, residents who disliked regulations in their town could move to another relatively easily if they could not sway elected officials to their views. Many municipal policing laws, even bad ones, however, eventually became state laws and federal statutes, considerably raising the cost of voting with one's feet.[46] Coalitions between "Baptists and bootleggers," i.e., between paternalists who thought they knew what was better for others and those seeking to profit by reducing competition, proved politically potent.[47]

Prohibitions on alcohol production, sale, and consumption constitute a major example of how do-gooders (literal Baptists) and rent seekers (literal bootleggers or illegal alcohol producers) combined to enlarge police powers at ever higher levels of government. Early on, most Americans concentrated on the individual benefits of sobriety and costs of addiction and so relied on moral suasion to reduce alcohol consumption. The negative externalities caused by excessive alcohol consumption combined with paternalism, the notion that prohibition laws were for the "own good" of the drunkard, to form the wedge that allowed alcohol consumption to move into the realm of local police powers. Those who sought to profit by supplying illegal alcohol then pushed for state, and later national, prohibition of alcohol because local codes were too easily subverted by simply buying or producing in nearby towns, counties, or states. By the 1850s, local bans on alcohol in scattered towns and counties had become statewide ones and, shortly after the Great War, national Prohibition. That would not be the last time that local laws eventually became the law of the land.[48]

Chattel slavery rendered paternalism especially common in the South but even in the North traditions like Puritanism conceived of freedom as the right to do as the righteous majority bade. North and South, religious folk were able to pass local ordinances and then statewide laws against Sunday travel or business activity, sometimes with exceptions for harvest seasons and slaves. Sabbatarianism never went national, though, likely because of a dearth of Sunday "bootleggers," as nobody turned a serious profit from restricting non-alcohol-related activities only on Sundays.[49]

Abolition of slavery also began at the local level before moving on to the state level and then going national with the adoption of the Thirteenth Amendment. Once again, religious folk teamed up with those who stood to profit to bring about change. Unlike alcohol and Sunday activity bans, which diminished everyone's liberty, banning slavery liberated some people while ending the theft of their labor and family members. Many freedpersons and their offspring still suffered horribly in the postbellum South, but do-gooders leveraged the nominal emancipation of slaves into a presumption that government reforms could further human progress. That gave them space in public discourse to push Progressive agendas.[50]

Despite some significant depressions and general stagnation in the South, the U.S. economy grew rapidly over the course of the late nineteenth century. Instead of focusing on improvements in the standard of living experienced by all, even lowly educated immigrants from southern Europe, many proto-progressives focused on wealth disparities. They argued that the social and economic injustices that they believed they saw could be reversed, as slavery had been, by augmenting state police powers. The most dangerous among them was a trio of economists—Thomas Sewall Adams, John R. Commons, and Richard T. Ely—from Wisconsin, the nation's intellectual center of European-trained Progressive thinkers.[51] Commons spoke for the group when he claimed that they were "trying to save capitalism by making it good," by which he meant moral according to their own moral precepts. In other words, Progressive economists, like all paternalists, believed that they knew what was better for Americans than Americans themselves did. Through collective action and government coercion, they believed, conflicting interests could be reconciled and the presumably powerless uplifted.[52]

Ely exploited the notion that wealth inequalities were a growing, bad thing to argue, in the name of God and democracy, against relatively unfettered markets and for more government involvement in the economy, a view shared by others, like Frank J. Goodnow.[53] In *Politics and Administration, A Study in Government* (1900), Goodnow claimed that the central state had only two functions, determining the will of the people, and then executing that will through government actions and programs. His book had nothing to say about Constitutional checks and balances, which Progressives came to see as impediments to "progress."[54]

By degrees, then, Americans came to ask what can government do about this *problem* rather than what can I do, in voluntary concert with my neighbors, about this *issue*? The New Deal finished the transformation. In 1933, Americans regularly gave alms to beggars but by 1935 they were more likely to refer them to a government relief agency instead.[55] Many Americans developed, in the words of New Deal critic Albert Nock, "the greatest nervous horror of freedom, the most inveterate and pusillanimous dread of contemplating the ideal picture of mankind existing in free and voluntary association."[56] Worse, most Americans failed to consider the aggregate effect of such changes in sentiment on the state of the nation and economy. From a nation of rugged individuals, America devolved by degrees into a nation of dependents, of people who even as adults needed help—from governments, therapists, and pills—just to live. The New Deal sped the infantilization of Americans, thereby fulfilling the prophecy of the paternalists.[57]

That process, though, began in the late nineteenth century. As great classical liberals died, few from the ranks of younger people, miseducated and misled by Progressives, could take their place. Left to fight FDR's New Deal were tattered and scattered remnants.[58] Nock was quite right when he wrote in 1928 that "the world is fast going away from old-fashioned people of my kind." Real American liberals, like Edward Atkinson, were a dead breed.[59]

Edward Atkinson, the Last Real Liberal

Classical liberalism's lodestone was negative liberty, the notion that the government shall not take the lives, liberty, or property of individuals without due process. Progressivism's lodestone was positive liberty. If an individual cannot "earn an honorable living,"[60] Progressives believed, then the government had a duty to step in to provide one, even if that meant denying the negative liberties of other individuals, as it usually did. If an individual cannot earn a living, classical liberals believed, family or community members should help to remove the underlying cause.

The classical liberal era of American history arguably ended in 1905 when Edward Atkinson died at the age of 78. (In Britain, the last real liberal was arguably G.K. Chesterton.[61]) In hindsight, journalists recognized that early in the new century, the average American "lost his early zest for citizenship" as he concentrated on business and technological change.[62] The assertion is impossible to prove but certainly the passing of eloquent defenders of classical liberalism like Atkinson made it more difficult for the busy businessman to insist on upholding negative liberty.

Born in 1827 in Brookline, Massachusetts, Atkinson ran a cotton mill and later a mutual fire insurance company. He was also a dietician and invented a kerosene lamp-powered cooking apparatus known as the Aladdin Oven. He also became a policy pundit who believed in limited government, individual autonomy, and the scientific method. He advocated for public policies—like the abolition of slavery, the reduction of tariffs and other barriers to free trade, and the denationalization of money—that enhanced individual liberty.[63]

Atkinson knew Abraham Lincoln and the importance of his insight that America needed a government of, for, and by the people. After Lincoln died, though, America increasingly became a government of, for, and by bureaucrats, and the process accelerated after Atkinson's death. By the end of FDR's reign, the new order was endemic.[64]

Classical liberalism allowed the U.S. Republic to thrive during its first tender century, but the Spanish-American War in 1898 signaled a new phase of expansion. Classical liberals like Atkinson abhorred imperialism and the economic and political exploitation of colonies or other vassal states. To protest the war, Atkinson joined the American Anti-Imperialist League and served as a vice president. He also published three short antiwar pamphlets, *The Cost of a National Crime, The Hell of War and Its Penalties*, and *Criminal Aggression: By Whom Committed?* The U.S. Postal Service seized all copies of Atkinson's pamphlets headed for the occupied Philippines. The free publicity that controversial policy generated enabled Atkinson to distribute 135,000 copies of his pamphlets and to call the members of President McKinley's cabinet graduates "from an asylum for the imbecile and feeble-minded."[65]

But as the last classical liberals like Atkinson aged out and passed to their reward, America's policy ranks filled with Progressives, people who believed in extensive government involvement in every aspect of life, including the economy. While classical liberals like Atkinson wanted to cut tariffs, they did not feel the need to replace any federal revenues lost in the process. Uncle Sam, like everyone else, would have to live within its means, which was fine because standards of living were improving for all, not just the rich. Atkinson admitted that in his "younger days" he "indulged in visions of the discovery of a panacea by which poverty might be abolished or very greatly alleviated," but with the experience he became what Thomas Sowell would later call a constrained thinker.[66] That led him to warn that policymakers should avoid "revolutionary changes which might bring in several devils in the place of the one which we might perhaps eject."[67]

Progressives, by contrast, were unconstrained thinkers who always assumed the worst possible outcomes from market forces and the best possible outcomes from government policies.[68] Unlike constrained classical liberal thinkers who sought to ameliorate social ills like poverty, Progressives believed that "social disorders are curable."[69] "Look at the new departments—Commerce, Agriculture, Internal Revenue," a journalist noted in 1931, "and you will read in massive, unmistakable headlines how the present intentions of this capital transcend its original intentions."[70] New Progressive departments needed increasingly large sums of cash to achieve their always ambitious and interventionist policy goals. They found it in a national income tax.[71]

The Federal Income Tax

With classical liberals a dying breed and hence an increasingly impotent intellectual and political force, Progressives, like members of the Wisconsin School, sought to increase revenue to feed government programs and to turn taxes themselves into instruments of social control. Ely, for example, believed that taxation could "diffuse wealth" and promote "equality of rights."[72]

In 1894, the federal government—with support from Progressive economists, farmers, workers, and others opposed to regressive excise taxes and tariffs—tried to impose a peacetime income tax on high-income individuals and corporations. Although an income tax largely jived with the views of classical liberal economists like Adam Smith and John Stuart Mill, SCOTUS proclaimed the tax unconstitutional.[73] It had little choice as the U.S. Founders and Framers had called taxation "the most important of any power that can be granted; it connects with all other powers." They had, therefore, proscribed "the great engine of tyranny and oppression" in narrow and confusing bounds.[74]

The Spanish-American War of 1898, though, increased pressure for a national income tax. Excise taxes and tariffs, the federal government's mainstays since the days of Hamilton, seemed too regressive, especially in wartime. By 1909, pressure for a federal income tax had swelled to the point that an income tax amendment resolution passed both houses of Congress by overwhelming majorities, ostensibly because nobody believed that enough states would ratify it.[75]

At the local level, real estate and capitation taxes have been mainstays since the colonial period.[76] In the eighteenth and nineteenth centuries, many Americans had also paid limited taxes on certain types of income, like that from professional work, via licensing requirements. The modest proceeds went to state or local governments or were emergency, wartime measures on high incomes. Taxes on personal property were also imposed but because such property was relatively easy to conceal, its total declared value grew slowly, or even shrank, even as incomes and real estate valuations increased steadily.[77] On those grounds, Progressives also sought state income taxes and managed to get one in Wisconsin that took effect in 1912. When its economy did not immediately come to a skittering halt, Progressives declared victory and redoubled efforts to ratify the Sixteenth Amendment.[78]

The Founders were predisposed against a federal income tax because it potentially rendered the Federal government far more powerful than they wished it to be. Moreover, income taxes were premised on the principle of ability-to-pay rather than on the traditional benefit principle, which held that people should pay taxes in proportion to the benefit they receive from the government, as with use fees and real estate taxes.[79]

In short, income taxes constituted a step toward socialism, the notion that "from each according to his abilities," at least abilities that were monetized, represented "social justice." One of the leading Progressive economists, Edwin R.A. Seligman, put the matter plainly: "Every one is equally interested in the State, because he cannot exist without the State. The principle of contribution becomes shifted from that of benefits to that of ability, of faculty, of capacity. Every man now must support the State to the full extent, if need be, of his ability to pay. He does not measure the benefits of State action to himself."[80]

Seligman's claim that individuals could not exist without the government was shockingly illiberal so Progressives usually started with the proposition that "government is and always will be necessary," hoping to win all but anarchists to their side before explaining why taxes had to be changed to make them fairer and more fecund.[81] Taxation, they argued, was a blessing because it funded "civilization," or at least those parts of civilization that were publicly funded, even those parts that could have been, or should have been, or used to be, privately financed. Taxes, they claimed, were not payment for services rendered but rather the "duty" of citizens to pay whether they received an equivalent in return or not. If taxes were made in proportion to the benefits received, Progressives pointed out, "then the maimed and the lame and the halt and the blind should pay the largest taxes,"[82] even though through most of the country's history to that point the physically impaired had been wards of their families, charities, and insurers, not government.[83]

To further enhance their power, Progressives also tried to pry open a door to nationalization by arguing that "the state may be regarded as a partner in all industrial undertakings, and is therefore entitled to a share in the proceeds."[84] The government most assuredly was not a partner in the usual sense of putting up risk capital or expertise but those who wanted more power and bigger government conveniently elided such counter-arguments while pushing what the populist masses wanted to hear, that corporate and income taxes would fall on the rich and alleviate the burden of excise taxes and tariffs and maybe even real estate levies.

Had populist voters realized that income taxes would within a few decades weigh heavily on all while creating a labyrinth of confusion and a mass of economic distortion, few would have supported state, let alone national, income taxes. But they were naïve, so Progressives managed to secure enough states for ratification of the 16th Amendment in February 1913. Legislation followed that October as part of a tariff bill. Only about 2% of taxpayers had to pay anything, and most just 1% of their income. The outbreak of the Great War a year later, though, would soon change that.[85]

America's classical liberal republic might have survived the national income tax alone, but it turned out to be just part of a panoply of Progressive reforms, built on belief in bureaucracy and technocracy, that would make FDR's New Deal possible.[86]

The Federal Reserve System

The Federal Reserve System emerged from a toxic stew of political interests. The proverbial "Baptists" believed that they could create an effective national lender of last resort (LLR) while the "bootleggers" came in two stripes, those who wanted to increase the power of New York bankers and those who wanted to increase the power of the federal government.[87] The resulting compromise was something of a Frankenbank, partly government controlled and centralized and partly banker controlled and decentralized. On paper, it was a formidable LLR that impressed many market observers.[88] In practice, however, it squelched clearinghouses and other private LLRs without replicating their abilities.[89]

Paul Warburg called the Federal Reserve Act "one of the greatest accomplishments ever recorded in the annals of Congress, an Act conferring untold benefits not only upon the United States but upon the entire world." His claim exceeded hyperbole but was to be expected from a man who thought that he had "devoted the best part" of his "life to the solution of our banking problem."[90]

America, though, had no more of a "banking problem" than it suffered from a taxation problem. Strictly speaking, the Federal Reserve, like state and national income taxes, was completely unnecessary. Warburg correctly noted that America's banking system was "inefficient" and "designed automatically to produce instability." But that does not mean that the Federal Reserve system was needed because reform of the existing system, especially the heavy reliance on tens of thousands of tiny, branchless "unit" banks, would have sufficed.[91] "The 1913 legislation," the most important historian of the Federal Reserve System concluded, "did not ensure that the new system would respond to crises better than the old." And until the passage of reforms in 1935, it clearly did not.[92]

Before the Fed, financial panics were frequent, and frequently disruptive, but private clearinghouses acted as local LLR that mitigated their effects at low cost.[93] In 1884, for example, the New York Clearing House Association issued clearinghouse loan certificates that banks could borrow to make payments to other banks. Only one bank failed during that short-lived panic and payments to depositors were not suspended.[94] That clearinghouse, along with two banking syndicates and the U.S. Treasury, also staved off a serious panic in 1890.[95] It was less successful in 1893 but the root problem was not with markets, or the adequacy of clearinghouses, but the systemically flawed correspondent banking network inherent in the unit bank-based dual banking system the United States adopted during the Civil War.[96] The New York clearinghouse functioned effectively, enabling banks to maintain credit levels even as deposits sharply declined. The clearinghouses in Atlanta, Baltimore, Birmingham,

Boston, Buffalo, Cincinnati, Detroit, New Orleans, Philadelphia, Pittsburgh, and Richmond also issued clearinghouse certificates during this significant panic.[97]

The Panic of 1907 allegedly proved the necessity of creating a central bank with the authority to act as an LLR during financial crises. Some claimed that J.P. Morgan and other private interests had quelled the panic, and that proved they had too much power and hence had to be replaced by a public institution. Others claimed that private lenders failed to stop the 1907 Panic well enough, thus proving the need for a national LLR under government auspices.[98] Many banks throughout the nation, even in relatively financially solid places like Sioux Falls, South Dakota, had to limit withdrawals or pay out with cashiers' checks stamped "payable only through the clearinghouse." Such expedients, though, were ingenious and only had to work a few weeks.[99]

While Progressives laid plans for a central bank, Congress in the 1908 Aldrich-Vreeland Act addressed the LLR issue directly by authorizing the Treasury to issue special temporary currency during emergencies. When the Great War broke out in 1914, many European investors sold stocks to buy gold to repatriate. To reduce pressure on financial markets, the U.S. Treasury authorized the emission of over $385 million of the Aldrich-Vreeland emergency currency, mostly issued through national banks. No widespread banking panics occurred.[100] The Federal Reserve later claimed that it had staved off catastrophe when it became operational in late 1914 but that appears to have been hyperbole. Only about a third of the total emergency currency authorized was issued and all of it was retired by July 1915. Clearinghouses also provided aid, as usual, to the tune of $212 million.[101]

Progressives, though, brushed emergency currency and clearinghouse associations aside as too few, too ineffective, and too reactive. Central bank advocates like Warburg thought they could stop panics before they got started. What was needed, Warburg claimed, was an authority "that had actual power to put on the brakes if the car were moving too fast and heading for the precipice."[102] They just needed a break big and strong enough for the job. So instead of reforming the existing unit bank-based correspondent banking system, they sought to superimpose a new system, one that they controlled, over the old. That system soon revealed itself as a hodgepodge of conflicting ideas and interests, privately owned by member banks but ultimately controlled by politicians and technocrats.[103]

What Progressives ultimately sought was monetary policy discretion, which the founders of the Fed discussed in terms of making the money supply more "elastic." But giving the Fed significant discretion to increase or decrease the money supply or interest rates necessarily entailed giving up fixed exchange rates or the free international flow of capital.[104] Both were core aspects of the gold standard that nobody would publicly declare that they wanted to abandon. So, Progressives set up the Fed with the gold standard intact and bided their time. Thanks to the Great War, they would not have to wait long.

Great War Ratchet Effects

Woodrow Wilson was a Progressive through and hoped to use his presidency to advance the Progressive agenda of fundamentally changing the nature of the relationship between the U.S. federal government and the American people.[105] The Great War that broke out in Europe in 1914 provided him with a major opportunity to do so as all Americans conceded the importance of national defense and the federal government's prime role in it.[106] Wilson used the war, for example, to justify building a dam and power plant in Muscle Shoals, Alabama, which FDR later expanded into the Tennessee Valley Authority (TVA).[107]

Most Americans rightly believed that "progress is directly dependent upon our ability to work together." It was, as a future Federal Reserve leader Marriner Eccles put it, "an age of organization."[108] (One New Dealer described Eccles as being "with" the New Dealers, but not "of" them.[109]) But while classical liberals like Atkinson valued voluntary cooperation and organization, Progressives valued telling Americans that they had better cooperate, or else. Progressive legitimacy stemmed from their victory in elections; they rejected the classical liberal notion that majorities could tyrannize minorities. Progressive America was conceived of as a democracy, not a republic, so the slimmest majority could rule pretty much as it saw fit, at least until the next election. On top of that, Wilson believed that public administration was a science applicable to all nations equally, so he purported to believe that he could adapt European-style bureaucratic controls without injuring a republican government like that of the United States. In fact, though, he initiated the process, completed by FDR, of turning America's general government into a national government, i.e., from a government that directly influenced citizens in only a few, Constitutionally proscribed realms into one that inserted itself into every aspect of every citizen's life.[110]

War made it even easier to ignore checks and balances and dissenting voices and the Great War, which America finally entered in 1917, was no exception. As Albert Nock later put it, wars always bring about "savage governmental coercions of all kinds" because it is generally assumed better to be coerced by one's own government than by foreign troops.[111] As a result, the American people acquiesced to another ratcheting up of government influence on the economy and another ratcheting down of civil liberties with the passage of Espionage Act and the Trading With the Enemy Act in 1917 and the Sedition Act in 1918. Some two thousand Americans were arrested and over 1200 imprisoned under those and other acts before the Great War ended in November 1918. Shortly after, in *Schenk v. United States*, SCOTUS upheld such restrictions on free speech and free trade when the nation faces "a clear and present danger," though many of those arrested were soon released as part of a general amnesty.[112]

At the same time, the Great War brought into prominence or soft power a slew of New England intellectuals and paternalists who would influence the New Deal 15 years later. Victorious in the combined quest for women's suffrage and Prohibition, they eagerly awaited conditions that would allow them to force others to conform and do their bidding. Out of this same milieu grew the *New Republic*. Founded in 1914 as a Progressive organ, the magazine waxed powerful with help from J.P. Morgan money and the pens of Herbert Croly, Walter Lippmann, Walter Weyl, Felix Frankfurter, and, especially, Columbia University professor John Dewey.[113] Like most of the others, Croly deprecated the Constitution whenever it conflicted with Progressive goals because righteous ends justified even the meanest means, a lesson not lost on FDR as he rose through the Democratic Party ranks in the 1910s and 1920s.[114]

The Great War also gave Progressives the policy space to run a command economy and, fortunately for Americans alive then but unfortunately for those alive during and since the New Deal, not enough time to screw up too seriously. The War Finance Corporation, War Labor Board, the Food Administration, the Shipping Board, and, most importantly, the War Industries Board engaged in unprecedented levels of regulation, including quantity and price controls, in the name of the war effort.[115] Though never rigorously shown, the rationale for wartime central planning became *de rigueur* and was repeated during the Second World War, the UN police action in Korea, and the end of the Vietnam conflict. As one early economic policy textbook writer put it, "the market works well as an allocator in normal times, when changes are small and gradual. But it works badly in an emergency, when they must be large and sudden."[116]

As the war ended, thanks to their control of the economy Progressives told themselves, that a pandemic killed millions globally. Then a sharp postwar adjustment recession struck and America went back into its isolationist shell. By the time the dust cleared, Republicans were again in the Oval Office and nobody in power seriously studied the real results of the wartime command and control economy. Instead, all eyes turned toward the new communist Soviet Union, which appeared to be an economic success that most Americans did not wish to emulate. Meanwhile, Progressives prepared for a new war or another crisis that would allow them to seize economic power once again.[117]

America circa 1910 was imperfect but far better than at any time since. Taxes were low and the national debt was only a token. Inflation was unheard of and the police state was unthinkable. The Great War changed that, but not permanently. The 1920s brought peace and prosperity but also Prohibition, increased private debt, and, eventually, a more powerfully flawed state apparatus.[118]

The Lost Roaring Twenties

Republicans controlled the White House from March 1921 through February 1933 and while they took some steps to reclaim ground given up to the Progressives in the first two decades of the new century—taxes were slashed and wartime economic controls dropped—their reforms proved insufficient to return the country to its classical liberal roots. The Supreme Court of the United States (SCOTUS) successfully fought off challenges to economic freedom and classical liberal interpretations of the Constitution but established no major new precedents or doctrines as the *Lochner* case had in 1905 when it shot down "police power" laws that favored special interest groups.[119] Moreover, it provided support for government-owned and run businesses in *Green v. Frazier*, held that taxpayers had no standing in disputes over how their taxes were spent and failed to reign in the growing administrative state.[120]

By extending regulatory control over the emerging radio industry in the Radio Act of 1927, for example, President Coolidge and the power hungry "undersecretary of everything" Herbert Hoover set the stage for FDR's legendary control of the crucial new mass communications medium.[121] Similarly, the federal government put the Wilson Dam at Muscle Shoals up for sale but balked at the offers.[122] It paid off the national debt a bit but could have gone much further, as Garet Garrett urged, to prepare the federal government fiscally for any future challenges.[123]

Coolidge correctly noted that Progressivism remained inherently reactionary because the pinnacle of political thought had been achieved in the Declaration of Independence, but like SCOTUS, he did not try to squelch the very notion that America's governance or political systems needed to be, or indeed could be, improved.[124] The Republican presidents, especially Herbert Hoover, also failed to question technocracy, the Progressive belief that experts could and should efficiently guide resources to their most highly valued uses. Some so embraced technocracy that they even rejected majoritarian democracy for fascistic corporatism or other forms of elite rule.[125] Science and technology had transformed private material living conditions in just a few decades and promised to do likewise for public services, but its haughty self-assurance countenanced distinctly non-classical liberal modes of thought, including paternalism and even eugenics.[126]

Progressive economists and other social scientists, meanwhile, found in foreign countries what they took to be empirical evidence for the efficacy of state intervention in the economy. A few independent thinkers, like E.C. Harwood, understood the logical fallacies in their unscientific approach to the question of state size but for the most part, their views remained uncontested, in part because many economists wanted grants that flowed most easily to those with Progressive bona fides, and then to those who at least kept silent their critiques of minimum wages, social insurance, government make-work, and other ideas floating in American policy circles by the 1920s.[127]

At the heart of the matter, the Republicans in control of the country believed that politicians should not try to fix that which does not appear broken. By the 1920s, most Americans believed their country was the best in the world and maybe the best of all time. In 1925, Marriner Eccles told bankers in Utah that America had some problems but added that its "problems are problems of life and growth, not of death and decay." Despite their "follies and failures," Americans were "slowly but surely getting ahead" and the economy sped along at almost 6% per year, twice the long-run average. Peace and technological progress in automobiles, radios, and other consumer durables were widely believed to have fueled the roaring economy, but Austrian economists Ludwig von Mises and Friedrich Hayek were right to point out that cheap credit kept it growing at an artificially high rate.[128]

Another wave of the industrial revolution that had been driving higher productivity for over a century took place in the 1920s, which witnessed a boom in new technology and the widespread adoption of existing technologies, like electric motors, in the nation's factories.[129] Higher productivity meant higher incomes for industrial workers. Real wages increased while hours worked decreased and unemployment remained low, averaging just 3.3% during the 1923–29 period.[130]

With the opportunity costs of obtaining more education high, however, educational attainment did not keep up. "Not so long ago," Harry Hopkins reminded Americans, even "college boys were not expected to bother about public questions, and most of them were pretty vague about economics."[131] So most Americans had little understanding of the economic pressures building due to the Fed's policies, and those who eventually would, like Columbia University-educated financial journalist Wilma Soss, did not persuade policymakers that something was amiss.[132]

The main problem was that during the post-Great War recession of 1919–21, the Federal Reserve eased monetary conditions and subsequently kept real interest rates relatively low for fear of causing a recession if it tightened, which it finally began to do in a credible way only in 1928. The ensuing recession led to a global goods glut because the Fed again made poor policy decisions.[133] By the time it became clear that the economy was in serious trouble, a Republican technocrat named Herbert Hoover was in the Oval Office. With unemployment soaring and production plummeting, he could not have done much to restore the American government to its classical liberal roots even if he had wanted to. By the time he came up for re-election in 1932, the American people were ready for a change and the Progressives stood ready to deliver it.

Notes

1. Jefferson Cowle and Nick Salvatore, "The Long Exception: Rethinking the Place of the New Deal in American History," *International Labor and Working-Class History* 74, 1 (Fall 2008): 3–32.

2. Gerald H. Gamm, *The Making of New Deal Democrats: Voting Behavior and Realignment in Boston, 1920–1940* (Chicago: University of Chicago Press, 1989), 18.
3. Eric Rauchway, *Why the New Deal Matters* (New Haven: Yale University Press, 2021), 4–7. See also John Steele Gordon, *An Empire of Wealth: The Epic History of American Economic Power* (New York: HarperCollins, 2004), 343–44.
4. Jim F. Couch and William F. Shughart, *The Political Economy of the New Deal* (Northampton, MA: Edward Elgar, 1998), 26; Richard K. Vedder and Lowell E. Gallaway, *Out of Work: Unemployment and Government in Twentieth-Century America*, updated ed. (New York: New York University Press, 1997), 129.
5. Kiran Klaus Patel, *The New Deal: A Global History* (Princeton: Princeton University Press, 2016), 41–43, 66–69, 89, 93, 101–3, 124–25, 134–37, 243–47.
6. William F. Shughart, "Bending Before the Storm: The U.S. Supreme Court in Economic Crisis, 1935–1937," *The Independent Review* 9, 1 (Summer 2004), 56.
7. H. W. Brands, *A Traitor to His Class: The Privileged Life and Radical Presidency of Franklin Delano Roosevelt* (New York: Anchor Books, 2008), 334–37; Jim Powell, *FDR's Folly: How Roosevelt and His New Deal Prolonged the Great Depression* (New York: Crown Forum, 2003), 142.
8. Bradley C.S. Watson, *Progressivism: The Strange History of a Radical Idea* (Notre Dame: University of Notre Dame Press, 2020).
9. Matthew W. Slaboch, *A Road to Nowhere: The Idea of Progress and Its Critics* (Philadelphia: University of Pennsylvania Press, 2017).
10. Garet Garrett, *The People's Pottage* (Caldwell, ID: Caxton Printers, 1953), 45.
11. Malcolm Ross, *All Manner of Men* (New York: Harcourt, Brace, & World, 1948), 289.
12. Glenn W. Miller, *Problems of Labor* (New York: Macmillan Co., 1951), 512.
13. Nancy J. Weiss, "The Negro and the New Freedom: Fighting Wilsonian Segregation," *Political Science Quarterly* 84, 1 (March 1969), 61–79.

14. Woodrow Wilson, *The New Freedom: A Call for the Emancipation of the Generous Energies of a People* (New York: Doubleday, Page & Co., 1913), 3–7, 33–36.
15. Amity Shlaes, *The Forgotten Man: A New History of the Great Depression* (New York: HarperCollins, 2007), 11.
16. Charles R. Kesler, "Foreword," in Watson, *Progressivism*, x–xi.
17. Robert H. Wiebe, *The Search for Order, 1877–1920* (New York: Hill and Wang, 1967); Lenore Ealy and Steven D. Ealy, "Progressivism and Philanthropy," *The Good Society* 15, 1 (2006): 35–42; Albion Small, "The Social Gradations of Capital," *American Journal of Sociology* 9, 6 (May 1914), 721.
18. G.Q. Flynn, "The New Deal and Local Archives: The Pacific Northwest," *The American Archivist* 33, 1 (Jan. 1970), 44–45.
19. Albert Jay Nock, *Our Enemy, the State* (New York: William Morrow & Co., 1935), 31, 65–145.
20. Thomas Nixon Carver, *The Present Economic Revolution in the United States* (Boston: Little, Brown, and Co., 1925), 64–65.
21. John Phillip Reid, *Constitutional History of the American Revolution*, abridged ed. (Madison: University of Wisconsin Press, 1995), ix, xiii–xvii; Robert E. Wright, *One Nation Under Debt: Hamilton, Jefferson, and the History of What We Owe* (New York: McGraw-Hill, 2008); E.C. Harwood, "The Winning Plans in the Pabst Postwar Employment Awards," (Dec. 1944), Box 2, E.C. Harwood Archives, AIER, Great Barrington, Mass.
22. Wiebe, *Search for Order*.
23. As quoted in Ealy and Ealy, "Progressivism and Philanthropy," 37.
24. Powell, *FDR's Folly*, 1–2.
25. Wilson, *New Freedom*, 47.
26. Suzanna Sherry, "The Founders' Unwritten Constitution," *University of Chicago Law Review* 54, 4 (Fall 1987): 1,127–77; Thomas C. Grey, "The Uses of an Unwritten Constitution," *Chicago-Kent Law Review* 64, 1 (April 1988): 211–38.
27. Reid, *Constitutional History*, 3.
28. Paul G. Mahoney, "The Common Law and Economic Growth: Hayek Might Be Right," *Journal of Legal Studies* 30 (June 2001): 503–25; Sherry, "Founders' Unwritten Constitution," 1, 129–30.

29. Thomas C. Grey, "Origins of the Unwritten Constitution: Fundamental Law in American Revolution Thought," *Stanford Law Review* 30, 5 (May 1978), 843–45, 891–93; Reid, *Constitutional History*, 5–15, 39–40.
30. Reid, *Constitutional History*, 51–59; E.C. Harwood, *The Counterrevolution* (Great Barrington, Mass.: AIER, 1951), 21.
31. John Trenchard, "Cato's Letters," No. 115, 9 Feb. 1723: https://oll.libertyfund.org/title/gordon-cato-s-letters-vol-4-december-8-1722-to-december-7-1723-lf-ed.
32. Sherry, "Founders' Unwritten Constitution," 1, 157–58.
33. Randy E. Barnett, "Introduction: James Madison's Ninth Amendment," in Randy E. Barnett, ed. *The Rights Retained by the People: The History and Meaning of the Ninth Amendment* (Fairfax, Va.: George Mason University Press, 1989), 37–38 n.98; Kermit L. Hall, ed. *Collected Works of James Wilson* (Indianapolis: Liberty Fund, 2007), 1082–83; Randy E. Barnett, *Restoring the Lost Constitution: The Presumption of Liberty* (Princeton: Princeton University Press, 2004), 253–54.
34. Anthony B. Sanders, *Baby Ninth Amendments: How Americans Embraced Unenumerated Rights and Why It Matters* (Ann Arbor: University of Michigan Press, 2023).
35. Barnett, "Introduction," in Barnett, ed. *Rights Retained by the People*, 3, 11–29; Barnett, *Restoring*, 259.
36. Robert Higgs, *Crisis and Leviathan: Critical Episodes in the Growth of American Government* (New York: Oxford University Press, 1987).
37. Robert Hormats, *The Price of Liberty: Paying for America's Wars* (New York: Henry Holt, 2007); John J. Wallis, "Lessons from the Political Economy of the New Deal," *Oxford Review of Economic Policy* 26, 3 (Autumn 2010): 445–48.
38. Milton Friedman, "Why Government Is the Problem," *Essays in Public Policy* No. 39 (Stanford: Hoover Institution, 1993), 15.
39. Edmund Burke, *On Empire, Liberty, and Reform: Speeches and Letters*, ed. David Bromwich (New Haven: Yale University Press, 2000), 170.
40. Barnett, *Restoring*, 253–73, 354–58.
41. Harry L. Hopkins, *The Realities of Unemployment* (Washington, DC: WPA, 1937), 12.

42. Albert Nock, "Liberalism, Properly So Called," Working Paper, (1943).
43. Wright, *One Nation Under Debt*.
44. Wiebe, *Search for Order*, 38–39.
45. Garrett, *People's Pottage*, 65.
46. Thomas R. Dye, *Understanding Public Policy* 14th ed. (New York: Pearson, 2013), 85–86.
47. Adam Smith and Bruce Yandle, *Bootleggers & Baptists: How Economic Forces and Moral Persuasion Interact to Shape Regulatory Policies* (Washington, DC: Cato Institute, 2014), vii–x.
48. Nock, "Liberalism"; Albert Nock, *On Doing the Right Thing, And Other Essays* (New York: Harper and Brothers, 1928), 161–78; Robert E. Wright, *Liberty Lost: Rise and Demise of Voluntary Association in America Since 1700* (Great Barrington, Mass.: American Institute for Economic Research, 2023).
49. Smith and Yandle, *Bootleggers*, 77.
50. Robert E. Wright, *The Poverty of Slavery: How Unfree Labor Pollutes the Economy* (Cham, Switzerland: Palgrave, 2017).
51. Marianne Johnson, "Taxation in the Early Progressive Era: From Revenue to Social Policy," SSRN Working Paper, 14 June 2022; Jeffrey Paul, *Winning America's Second Civil War: Progressivism's Authoritarian Threat, Where It Came From, and How to Defeat It* (New York: Encounter, 2024).
52. As quoted in William M. Dugger, "The Reform Method of John R. Commons," *Journal of Economic Issues* 13, 1 (Jun. 1979), 369.
53. Lenore Ealy, "Philanthropy and Civil Society: An Ethic of Beneficence for the Modern Age," Acton University Working Paper, (2015).
54. Ralph L. DeFalco III, "Was There Ever a Neoliberal Order?" *Law and Liberty*, 18 Oct. 2022.
55. Nock, *Our Enemy*, 7.
56. Nock, *On Doing the Right Thing*.
57. Garrett, *People's Pottage*, 56.
58. Nock, "Liberalism."
59. Nock, *On Doing the Right Thing*.
60. Works Progress Administration, The Works Program, Press Release, 16 Jul. 1938, FRASER.
61. Daniel Betti, "G.K. Chesterton on the Fundamentals of Liberalism," *AIER Daily Economy* (27 September 2022).

62. Marion Turner Sheehan, ed. *The World at Home: Selections from the Writings of Anne O'Hare McCormick* (New York: Alfred A. Knopf, 1956), 116.
63. Harold F. Williamson, *Edward Atkinson: The Biography of an American Liberal, 1827–1905* (Boston: Old Corner Book Store, Inc., 1934), 230–31.
64. Friedman, "Why Government Is the Problem," 11.
65. Williamson, *Edward Atkinson*, 229.
66. Thomas Sowell, *A Conflict of Visions* (New York: William Morrow & Co., 1987).
67. Edward Atkinson, "Remarks," in F.B. Sanborn, ed. *The Single Tax Discussion* (Concord, Mass.: American Social Science Association, 1890), 61.
68. Powell, *FDR's Folly*, 26.
69. Ealy and Ealy, "Progressivism and Philanthropy," 36.
70. Sheehan, ed., *World at Home*, 70.
71. Atkinson, "Remarks," in Sanborn, ed. *Single Tax*, 55.
72. Richard Ely, "Taxation in American States and Cities," *Baltimore Sun* (3 March 1888), 2.
73. Javier San Julian Arrupe, "When Lawmakers Met Progressives: Debating the American Federal Income Tax of 1894," University of Barcelona School of Economics Working Paper No. 418 (March 2022).
74. As quoted in Jack N. Rakove, *Original Meanings: Politics and Ideas in the Making of the Constitution* (New York: Vintage 1996), 183–84.
75. Hormats, *Price of Liberty*, 94–95, 102–3.
76. Alvin Rabushka, *Taxation in Colonial America* (Princeton: Princeton University Press, 2008).
77. Benjamin Sherman Asquith, "Some Substitutes for the General Property Tax," (MA Thesis: University of Iowa, 1912), 41–42.
78. Johnson, "Taxation in the Early Progressive Era."
79. Arrupe, "When Lawmakers Met Progressives."
80. Seligman, "Address," in Sanborn, ed. *The Single Tax Discussion*, 42.
81. See, for example, Asquith, "Some Substitutes," iv.
82. Asquith, "Some Substitutes," 6.

83. Dora L. Costa, *The Evolution of Retirement: An American Economic History, 1880–1990* (Chicago: University of Chicago Press, 1998), 25.
84. "Taxation," *Encyclopaedia Britannica* 9th ed. (1888): https://en.wikisource.org/wiki/Encyclop%C3%A6dia_Britannica,_Ninth_Edition/Taxation.
85. Arrupe, "When Lawmakers Met Progressives"; Hormats, *Price of Liberty*, 104–21.
86. Wiebe, *Search for Order*, 145–63.
87. Smith and Yandle, *Bootleggers*, 31, 69.
88. E. C. Harwood, "The Underlying Causes of Our Recent Prosperity: Why the End Is Near," *The Annalist* (13 April 1928), 643.
89. John Milton Cooper, Jr. *Woodrow Wilson: A Biography* (New York: Random House, 2009), 224–26.
90. Paul M. Warburg, *The Federal Reserve System: Its Origin and Growth, Reflections and Recollections* Vol. 1 (New York: Macmillan Co., 1930), 9.
91. Warburg, *Federal Reserve System*, 16.
92. Allan Meltzer, *A History of the Federal Reserve: Volume I: 1913–1951* (Chicago: University of Chicago Press, 2003), 4; Robert Hetzel, *The Great Recession: Market Failure or Policy Failure?* (New York: Cambridge University Press, 2012), 23–25.
93. Robert Craig West, *Banking Reform and the Federal Reserve, 1863–1923* (Ithaca: Cornell University Press, 1974), 27; O.M.W. Sprague, *History of Crises Under the National Banking System* (Washington: General Printing Office, 1910), 319; Hetzel, *Great Recession*, 15.
94. Benjamin Hoffner, "United States: New York Clearing House Association, the Panic of 1884," *Journal of Financial Crises* 4, 2 (2022): 1,278–99.
95. Benjamin Hoffner, "United States: New York Clearing House Association, the Panic of 1890," *Journal of Financial Crises* 4, 2 (2022): 1300–21.
96. Christopher Cotter and Peter L. Rousseau, "Correspondent Banking, Systematic Risk, and the Panic of 1893," MPRA Paper No. 113340, (May 2022).

97. Natalie Leonard, "United States: New York Clearing House Association, the Crisis of 1893," *Journal of Financial Crises* 4, 2 (2022): 1222–40.
98. Robert F. Bruner, *The Panic of 1907: Lesson Learned from the Market's Perfect Storm* (Hoboken, N.J.: Johne Wiley & Sons, 2007), 57–64, 71–88, 121–33, 141–47.
99. Sprague, *History of Crises*, 434–59.
100. Meltzer, *History of the Federal Reserve*, 82–83.
101. Sean Fulmer, "United States: Aldrich-Vreeland Emergency Currency During the Crisis of 1914," *Journal of Financial Crises* 4, 2 (2022): 1156–79.
102. Warburg, *Federal Reserve System*, 12, 16.
103. Meltzer, *History of the Federal Reserve*, 2–5.
104. Maurice Obstfeld, Jay C. Shambaugh, and Alan M. Taylor, "The Trilemma in History: Tradeoffs Among Exchange Rates, Monetary Policies, and Capital Mobility," NBER Working Paper 10,396 (March 2004).
105. Murray Rothbard, "World War I as Fulfillment: Power and the Intellectuals," *Mises Daily* (9 Nov. 2018).
106. Watson, *Progressivism*, 14–16.
107. Clair Wilcox, *Public Policies Toward Business* rev. ed. (Homewood, Ill., Richard D. Irwin, Inc., 1960), 829–30.
108. Marriner Eccles to the Utah Bankers Association, June 1925. FRASER: https://fraser.stlouisfed.org/archival-collection/marriner-s-eccles-papers-1343/speech-utah-bankers-association-460005.
109. Lauchlin Currie, "Lauchlin Currie's Memoirs," *Journal of Economic Studies* 31, 3/4 (2004), 209.
110. Vincent Ostrom, *The Intellectual Crisis in American Public Administration*, 3rd ed. (Tuscaloosa: University of Alabama Press, 2008), 23–25, 156–57.
111. Nock, "Liberalism."
112. Christina L. Boyd, "Sedition Act of 1918," *The First Amendment Encyclopedia* (Washington, DC: CQ Press, 2009); David Asp, "Espionage Act of 1917," *The First Amendment Encyclopedia* (Murfreesboro, TN: Free Speech Center, 2024).
113. Rothbard, "World War I as Fulfillment."

114. David T. Beito, *The New Deal's War on the Bill of Rights: The Untold Story of FDR's Concentration Camps, Censorship, and Mass Surveillance* (Oakland: Independent Institute, 2023), 5.
115. Powell, *FDR's Folly*, 2.
116. Wilcox, *Public Policies*, 721.
117. Powell, *FDR's Folly*, 2–3, 76.
118. Garrett, *People's Pottage*, 90.
119. David E. Bernstein, *Only One Place of Redress: African Americans, Labor Regulations, and the Courts from Reconstruction to the New Deal* (Durham: Duke University Press, 2001), 4.
120. William M. Wiecek, *The Lost World of Classical Legal Thought: Law and Ideology in America, 1886–1937* (New York: Oxford University Press, 1998), 152–54, 162–64.
121. Beito, *New Deal's War on the Bill of Rights*, 89–99.
122. Wilcox, *Public Policies*, 830.
123. Garet Garrett, *A Bubble That Broke the World* (Boston: Little, Brown, and Company, 1932), 11.
124. Watson, *Progressivism*, vii.
125. John P. Diggins, "Flirtation with Fascism: American Pragmatic Liberals and Mussolini's Italy," *American History Review* 71, 2 (Jan. 1966): 491.
126. John M. Jordan, *Machine-Age Ideology: Social Engineering and American Liberalism, 1911–1939* (Chapel Hill: University of North Carolina, 1994), 88, 155–84, 243.
127. Hugh Rockoff, "By Way of Analogy: The Expansion of the Federal Government in the 1930s," in Michael D. Bordo, Claudia Goldin, and Eugene N. White, eds., *The Defining Moment: The Great Depression and the American Economy in the Twentieth Century* (Chicago: University of Chicago Press, 1998): 125–54.
128. Marriner Eccles to the Utah Bankers Association, June 1925. FRASER: https://fraser.stlouisfed.org/archival-collection/mariner-s-eccles-papers-1343/speech-utah-bankers-association-460005. Roger W. Garrison, "The Great Depression Revisited," *Independent Review* 3, 4 (Spring 1999): 599.
129. Robert F. Bruner and Scott C. Miller, "The Great Crash of 1929: A Look Back After 90 Years," *Journal of Applied Corporate Finance* 31, 3 (Fall 2019), 46.

130. Robert VanGiezen and Albert E. Schwenk, "Compensation From Before World War I Through the Great Depression," *Compensation and Working Conditions* (Fall 2001).
131. Harry Hopkins, Public Works Administration, "Resurgent Democracy," 8 Oct. 1938.
132. Janice M. Traflet and Robert E. Wright, *Fearless: Wilma Soss and America's Forgotten Investor Movement* (New York: All Seasons Press, 2022).
133. Garrison, "Great Depression Revisited," 599–600.

CHAPTER 3

The Great Crisis

Although the tax treatment of stock market gains helped to drive up prices by discouraging sales during bull markets,[1] the economic boom of the 1920s was primarily premised on the promise that a "New Era" had arrived.[2] The Federal Reserve and government regulators had forever ended the boom-and-bust cycle of the nineteenth century, except in the wake of massive upheavals like a Great War followed by a Great Pandemic.[3] This boom was truly different from earlier ones, pundits exclaimed, because new technologies, better governance, and never-ending peace were bound to bring inexorable progress.[4] As the young Army engineer E.C. Harwood explained in 1928, though, the "seeming invulnerability and capacity for unlimited progress is a marked feature of all such speculative periods as they near an end."[5] Even into 1931, most Americans expected the economy to rebound into a period of glorious growth. It would, but not for another 15 years. In the meantime, they looked to journalist Anne O'Hare McCormick much "like that fat comedian in the movies who sits in heavy contemplation after he gets tangled up in his own gear."[6]

When exaggerated confidence in the new era shattered in 1931 following troubles in Japan, Germany, Britain, and elsewhere, investors came to have an exaggerated fear of macroeconomic instability, unemployment, and stagnation.[7] That fear, that reassessment of risk, kept many investors, like Wilma Soss and Benjamin Roth, out of the stock

R. E. Wright, *FDR's Long New Deal*,
https://doi.org/10.1007/978-3-031-74141-8_3

market until after the next global war and the inflation that followed it.[8] Facing higher taxes and few new infusions of investor cash, companies were starved for the capital they needed to reorganize, retool, and re-hire workers, which of course kept America's macroeconomy in the doldrums.

Overall, the recession became a depression when enough people realized that the government did not have a clue about the real causes of the downturn or the proper policy path out of it. They expected this time to be different, and it was, but in the wrong direction. They blamed Hoover and Republicans more generally, an outcome eerily predicted by Harwood in May 1928, before Hoover even became President. "The occurrence of another depression with no better solution being offered than 'muddle on' may well," he warned, "prove unforgivable, so far as the average working man is concerned."[9]

Blaming the Messenger, the Stock Market

Since the New Deal, or at least the 1954 publication of John Kenneth Galbraith's *The Great Cash: 1929*,[10] school children across America have been told that a malfunctioning stock market caused the Great Depression and that bold intervention by the federal government and a global war saved the economy.[11] (Income and wealth inequality get blamed too, but mostly in history books too obviously partisan to discuss further here.[12]) That the Great Depression was payback for an "orgy of speculation" became a stock Democratic talking point.[13] Slightly more detailed versions of the story blame the stock market crash of October 1929 and President Hoover's alleged do-nothing or laissez-faire response for the unprecedented depth and duration of the Depression.[14]

In a yet more sophisticated view, Progressive lawmakers proclaimed that securities prices were "frequently" manipulated, leading to "excessive speculation" and "sudden and unreasonable fluctuations." That, in turn, caused "alternately unreasonable expansion and unreasonable contraction of the volume of credit available" for the producers of real goods, transportation services, and trade. It also prevented "the fair valuation of collateral for bank loans."[15] In short, the stock market caused the Depression and its attendant "widespread unemployment and the dislocation of trade, transportation, and industry."[16]

Those standard stories, though, cannot withstand the slightest scrutiny. For starters, Hoover was an engineering technocrat, not a free market classical liberal. His policy responses were unprecedented in American history,[17] a fact acknowledged by FDR himself. In late September 1932, in a campaign speech in Sioux City, Iowa, FDR accused Hoover of heading "the greatest spending administration in peace time in all our history" and of piling the cost of "bureau on bureau" and "commission on commission" onto Americans ill positioned to pay for it all.[18] FDR's New Deal was built on the back of policies implemented by Hoover, including the Reconstruction Finance Corporation (RFC), higher taxes, business bashing, immigrant restriction, public works and relief programs, and high wage policies.[19]

Some economists deny the existence of a stock market bubble in 1929.[20] They probably underestimate the cost of short selling stocks, but they could still be correct.[21] Evidence of widespread fraud or price manipulation before the market break remains scant. Bulls (longs) and bears (shorts) had tussled for control in the world's financial markets for centuries and the U.S. stock market had suffered similar declines many times before without triggering anything like the Great Depression.

Most tellingly of all, the U.S. economy was in recession before the stock market fell that fateful Fall.[22] Stocks fell in the fall of 1929 because of financial fundamentals. The return on assets for America's biggest corporations, for example, dropped from an average of 9 to 1% that year.[23]

The major difference was that earlier downturns had been allowed to work themselves out. Only with the ascendance of Progressivism and its interventionist mindset did the federal government intercede so deeply in the economy, and it erred in several major ways. Between the Crash and the 1932 presidential election, the stock market revived at least eight times, only to fall again to new lows, but that only shows that there were moments when investors believed expansion was imminent. The stock market is never a perfect predictor, but the rollercoaster suggests that policies, not economic fundamentals, held the economy back at crucial junctures.[24] Those policies have been long since identified.

The Federal Reserve allowed the economy to grow too fast in the 1920s by keeping interest rates too low, i.e., lower than they would have been in the pre-Fed period under the classical gold standard.[25] It also let credit standards become too lax, leading to a large number of poor investments that could not withstand even a normal downtick in the business cycle.[26] Even tiny unit banks, for example, were allowed to purchase high yield, high risk, and low liquidity foreign bonds.[27] Moreover, by not explaining to banks and borrowers that it no longer felt strictly constrained by the rules of the prewar gold standard, the Fed induced banks to lend, and borrowers to borrow, more than they otherwise would have. Borrowers and lenders both believed that the Roaring Twenties was a sustainable expansion driven by productivity enhancements and technological advancements. So, they took on increasingly greater risks, as evidenced by the increase in legitimate consumer durables finance lenders but also a plethora of scams and flim-flams. Cheap, easy credit made some sectors of the U.S. economy boom for a time. As Harwood explained, by 1929 money "could have been, and was, obtained in almost any amounts for almost any project. Financing was never easier."[28] The cost of easy credit was a harder fall when everyone learned that "this time" was not "different"[29] and that much business investment was unwarranted except when interest rates were artificially low. The policy-induced misallocation of resources would help to drag the economy down when the business cycle turned in 1929.[30]

According to Federal Reserve architect Paul Warburg, the Great Crash would have been much worse were it not for "the country's unbounded confidence in the unequalled strength of the Federal Reserve System and the availability of its vast resources to the country's banks."[31] Knowledgeable observers like Harwood conceded "that the public today is apt to conceive of the Federal Reserve System as an all-wise, all-powerful institution which, by its very existence, guarantees sound banking."[32] Warburg knew, though, that future historians would wonder why the "financial authorities" stood by "so long while unheard-of quantities of inflammable material were massed in an unsafe structure, and while cool observers had been warning the public of the threatening, indeed, inevitable catastrophe?"

In 1927, the Fed reduced its discount rate from 4 to 3% and purchased U.S. and British government securities "on a large scale," in order, according to Warburg, to aid Britain and other European countries "in their efforts to establish or reestablish their gold standards."[33] Once it became clear that inflation and speculation were on the rise, the Fed reversed course on interest rates but without, Warburg admitted, "sufficient vigor and persistency." Desirous of deflecting blame, Warburg argued the Fed wavered due to push back from businesses. The Fed was ultimately in charge of America's monetary policy, though, and clearly blundered several times, whether due to its own weaknesses or its lack of independence from business interests.[34]

When the Federal Reserve increased the money supply and lowered the discount rate in 1927, it, according to Federal Reserve Board member Adolph Miller, committed "one of the most costly errors" of any central bank over the previous three-quarters of a century. Miller thought "that a different policy at that time would have left us with a different condition" during the Depression because leverage levels and stock prices would have been lower. He was likely right.[35]

The Federal Reserve raised its discount rate from 3.5 to 5% in early 1928, while also engaging in open market securities sales that took enough dollars out of circulation to raise bankers' acceptance rates from 3% in January 1928 to 4.5% that July and later to 5%. Output began contracting in 1929. In late May 1929, the stock market, likely in response to the softening economy, suffered several downside breaks. The Fed, though, allowed big New York banks to back up the securities market in a way that created moral hazard, emboldening the longs (bulls) instead of encouraging an orderly liquidation back toward rational valuations.[36]

"The [Federal Reserve] Board, in these fateful months," Warburg admitted, "sat still" as stock prices surged over the summer of 1929 to levels likely well above fundamental values. As the Federal Reserve Bank of New York (FRBNY) belatedly raised its discount rate to 6%, 6 months or a year too late to do any good, a bitter battle broke out between two camps, one blaming the Fed "for meddling too much, the other for not meddling enough."

Warburg was right that "everybody concerned acted to the best of his knowledge and ability," but missed that the fact that the Fed possessed that much policy discretion constituted the main problem.[37] The Fed had tasked itself to do the impossible, to maintain the veneer of the gold standard while giving itself enough policy discretion to smooth out business cycles. In the process, it lost sight of its main job, acting as a national LLR when bank depositors panicked and pulled their money out of the banking system. Little wonder that since the mid-1990s, most historians and economist historians agree that the Fed's actions and inactions to some extent caused, exacerbated, and extended the Depression.[38]

The Real Culprit, the Federal Reserve

If the stock market did not cause the greatest economic downturn in history, what did? Macroeconomists have been trying to get the story right for almost a century now. Some stymie themselves by searching for a single leading cause and coming up econometrically empty. Clearly, the proximate cause was the large decrease in the money supply experienced in the early 1930s, but why did the money supply drop drastically? Was it due to the gold standard or policy decisions by the Fed, some combination of the two, or something else entirely?

One thing is for sure, the drop in the money supply was a cause rather than an effect of the downturn. Although it is true that *demand* for money will decrease as economic activity falls, its *supply* under market conditions will never drop to the point that physical cash becomes scarce. Yet that is exactly what occurred in the early years of the Great Depression, when Americans began to sound like colonial merchants notoriously short of cash. As attorney Benjamin Roth put it in several times during the late Summer and Fall of 1931, "there is (simply) no money in circulation."[39]

Americans responded to the dearth of physical money by spot bartering or mixing barter with credit, like in colonial "bookkeeping barter" where goods and services were credited/debited in account books in money terms but settled only annually in cash.[40] Labor cooperatives sprang up in dozens of cities, from Rochester, New York to Portland, Oregon, "where the carpenter builds a porch for a suit of clothes and the cobbler mends shoes for a crate of garden truck."[41]

Others shorn of exchange media created and used non-federally sanctioned forms of money. Several hundred different municipalities, businesses, and cooperatives issued close to a billion dollars worth of their own bearer notes, or "scrip" in the parlance of the day. For example, in Massillon, Ohio, Jacob Coxey, leader of the (in)famous Coxey's "Army of Peace" that invaded Washington, D.C. in 1894,[42] issued "$100 city bonds to be used as money."[43] It was not the first nor last time Americans resorted to such "local currencies," but it was their deepest excursion since the Civil War. Scrip came in a wide variety of forms, from notes made of spruce wood backed by the assets of failed banks to paper notes backed by reserves of sauerkraut. Some of the scrip was quite odd but worked anyway, suggesting just how dire the need for liquid cash had become. Most authorities suffered scrip to circulate despite their often ambiguous legality. The Fed, though, remained hostile because it feared that scrip might cause inflation, as if scraps of wood and sauerkraut issued by small towns and local delicatessens were close substitutes for bank notes and deposits.[44]

Tellingly, simulations show that the Great Depression would not have occurred if the Fed had kept the money supply growing at about 3.3%, its pre-Crash trend, instead of allowing it to decrease so markedly.[45] It could have done so as it owned plenty of gold. In fact, until September 1931 the Fed's biggest "problem" was limiting gold inflows, so up to that point it could have increased the money supply without endangering the gold-dollar tether.[46] The government could also have printed fresh fiat money, or minted new silver dollars, to meet the increasingly strident demands of Great War veterans for early payment of their pensions.[47] (Such a policy passed in 1936 over FDR's objection but was funded with borrowed rather than new money, rendering it a fiscal rather than a monetary stimulus.[48])

The decrease in the money supply alone could not have been the sole cause of the downturn, however, because a money supply contraction of similar magnitude in the early 1920s did not lead to anything like the massive downturn in output and employment experienced in the 1930s. "If the 20% deflation of the 1930s caused the Great Depression," two Federal Reserve economists asked, "why didn't the 20% deflation of the 1920s also cause a major depression?"[49] The most concrete answer is that real wages fell precipitously in the 1920s but not in the 1930s.[50]

A more complicated answer is that the post-World War I deflation represented an automatic and expected reversal of a large wartime inflation. The 1930s deflation, by contrast, came after a long period of prosperity and high levels of borrowing stimulated by Federal Reserve policies. Although abetted by the remnants of the gold standard, the 1930s deflation was policy induced and economically irrational and hence not fully anticipated by borrowers.[51]

In other words, not all deflations are equal. Some are due to central bank policies and some, like those after the inflations of the Revolutionary, Civil, and Great War, occur naturally under the classical gold standard. As described by David Hume in the eighteenth century, the classical gold standard was self-equilibrating, i.e., automatic. When domestic gold stocks are high, so too are all domestic prices, except interest rates, which are low. That hurts exports because domestic goods look expensive to foreigners and encourages imports because foreign goods look inexpensive to domestic consumers and businesses. Moreover, relatively low domestic interest rates encourage investment abroad. To pay for increased imports when exports are down, the domestic country must ship some of its gold abroad, which eventually brings down the domestic price level and raises interest rates, which also will attract gold inflows. People and institutions do not borrow too much during the inflationary period, though, because they know that deflation will *certainly* occur at some point, increasing the real economic burden of their debts as prices fall.[52]

Other deflations, though, are policy induced and hence to some degree may be unexpected, leaving borrowers with higher-than-expected real debts.[53] High real debts led to personal, farm, and nonfarm business bankruptcies and eventually bank runs that further decreased the money supply due to lost or suspended deposits. Velocity, the frequency with which money changes owners, also declined as physical cash fled into hoards because people feared more bank runs and/or a dollar devaluation. Moreover, cash earns superior risk-free returns in deflationary periods.[54]

All those shocks decreased not only the number of banks, but the willingness of remaining banks to lend.[55] Debt deflation also reduced aggregate consumption by making credit not only more difficult to obtain for households struggling under higher real debt burdens, but also less desirable for anyone to seek.[56] As the market price of assets dropped, so too did the net worth of individuals and businesses, making them riskier borrowers, all else equal. Moreover, financial institutions and markets became less efficient due to the economic situation, making them less eager to make loans, especially to individuals and small firms.[57] Debt deflation was most severe in countries, like the United States, where leverage had been high when the stock market broke in late 1929.[58]

All the shocks associated with debt deflation also increased uncertainty, especially given the synergistic effects of several other bad policies discussed in more detail in subsequent sections of this chapter.[59] All that showed up in lower total factor productivity, which by one estimate would have risen 11% between 1929 and 1933 if it followed its 1920s trend. Instead over those 4 years, it declined by 14%.[60]

In other words, the early 1920s deflation was expected to be short-lived and was, while the 1930s deflation caught policymakers and many people and businesses off guard and over leveraged.[61] Although market participants in the late 1920s could personally recall four serious periods of deflation,[62] they were all predictable outcomes of the automatic functioning of the classical gold standard. The 1930s deflation, by contrast, would not have occurred under a fully functioning classical gold standard. The large deflation of 1932, in particular, cannot be modeled *ex post* (after the fact) with the same equations that predict the degree of deflation in other Depression years.[63]

What happened in 1932? Britain went off gold in September 1931, perhaps somewhat unexpectedly because it was the first time it ever did so in peacetime.[64] Astute observers, however, already knew that restoration of the gold standard after the Great War was fragile because it had been done in a haphazard way that was unsustainably asymmetric. Use of the term "gold standard" in the 1920s, economist Murray Rothbard noted, "was more of a deception than anything else. It was an attempt to draw to the government the prestige of being on the gold standard, while actually failing to abide by the limitations and requirements of that standard."[65] Under the new gold bullion or gold exchange system, central banks counted foreign exchange reserves as substitutes for gold even though such reserves did not flow automatically to places where they were most needed like gold did. Unlike during the classical prewar gold standard, central bankers in the 1920s and 30s could choose to "sterilize" gold inflows by decreasing other forms of money, like bank notes and deposits.[66] The Humean or self-equilibrating market mechanism undergirding the longtime success of the classical gold standard briefly described above could not work in those circumstances. U.S. public and private loans to help Germany pay its Great War reparations further muddled matters, as did the Fed's overall incompetence.[67] That incompetence found root in the Fed's fundamental misunderstanding of the gold standard as an automatic adjustment to international trade and capital flows that it might help along, but not permanently contravene, with domestic interest rate adjustments.[68] As E.C. Harwood noted in June 1928, the Fed had been "a step in the right direction" but the "fundamental principles" underlying the institution remained "not fully understood."[69] Unfortunately, few others understood the extent of the new institution's weak intellectual undergirding.[70]

Some countries, in particular the United States and France, were able to stockpile gold without suffering from corrective domestic price inflation. At the end of 1924, the U.S. Treasury held $4.575 billion in gold, half of the world's gold supply.[71] Under a functioning classical gold standard, Americans would have exchanged some of that gold for relatively inexpensive foreign goods while finding it difficult to sell their own relatively expensive wares abroad. That did not happen to the extent it would have because Americans were able to pay for imports with foreign reserves, or in other words U.S. financial securities, instead of gold. When the trade flow reversed, the Federal Reserve sterilized gold inflows to reduce big fluctuations in the domestic price level.

Later, France managed to accumulate gold while driving its domestic price level lower, an impossibility under the classical gold standard.[72] France alone absorbed almost every ounce of new gold produced globally from 1927 through 1932.[73] Even though they did not account for half of the world's output, the United States and France held half the world's gold reserves, thereby squeezing the money supplies of any country that remained on gold.[74] India played an underappreciated role, too, by absorbing large quantities of gold for nonmonetary uses.[75]

In other words, the Fed over the course of the 1920s effectively removed America from the automatic mechanisms of the gold standard. It essentially determined the domestic money supply through the purchase or sale of gold and financial securities. At a key moment in mid-1930, when the Fed should have been purchasing securities, and thus increasing the money supply, it again dithered, with some of its leaders suggesting staying the course while others argued for securities sales, which would have contracted the money supply yet more.[76]

It seems that the Fed did not yet fully comprehend that it, not the gold standard, determined the domestic money supply. For example, it defended the nation's gold stockpile when gold outflows began to occur in the fourth quarter of 1931 by raising the domestic interest rate. The tactic stemmed the gold outflow, but higher real (price-level adjusted) interest rates were the last thing the American economy needed in 1931. Instead of the automatic adjustments of the gold standard, America's money supply and hence the price level largely depended on Fed policy, which was uneven at best and hence unpredictable.

Fed officials also seem not to have understood the difference between nominal and real interest rates.[77] As contemporary economist Irving Fisher explained, nominal interest rates seemed low but due to deflation real interest rates remained much too high to stimulate economic recovery. (The Fisher Equation, where the real interest rate is equal to the nominal interest rate minus inflation, explains why. Deflation is negative inflation and subtracting a negative number is the same as adding. The real interest rate is 10%, for example, if the nominal interest rate is at 6% and *deflation* is running at 4%. It is just 2%, though, if the nominal interest rate is at 6% and *inflation* is running at 4%. Real interest rates in America were indeed at 10% in 1930 and 1931.[78])

Ergo, the Fed wrongly interpreted low nominal interest rates as a sign that monetary policy was easy, a belief bolstered by its misreading of "excess" reserves, i.e., cash in bank vaults and deposits with the Fed that exceeded the legal minimum. Reserves remained high because banks did not have many people or businesses to lend to because they either didn't want to borrow or because they were not good credit risks given the deteriorating economic situation. Banks themselves did not want to borrow from the Fed, which it also mistook as a sign that monetary policy was easy, even "sloppy." That mistaken belief allowed Fed officials to justify raising interest rates to maintain the nation's gold stock when the actual effect was to further dampen output and cause yet more loan defaults and bank failures.[79]

Bank failures were problematic for several reasons. Foremost, the Fed did little to stop increasingly severe and frequent bank runs even though it was ostensibly created for the sole goal of tamping down on financial crises by acting as an LLR.[80]Due to pressure from member banks, which hoped to gain branching privileges, the Fed soon after the Great War fell into the habit of allowing banks, especially small unit banks in rural areas, to fail.[81] From 1921 until 1929, deposits of failed banks totaled $1.6 billion, with depositor losses of about $565 million. Instead of taking the lead on changing policies to discourage unit banks and encourage statewide or interstate branching, the Fed allowed market forces, to wit bank failures, to do the job for it. It didn't even block the 1927 McFadden Act, which empowered states to restrict the branching of Federal Reserve member banks.[82]

The Fed's "let them fail" policy continued during the Depression,[83] when deposits of failed banks between 1930 and 1933 hit $6.8 billion, with $1.3 billion in depositor losses.[84] Those failures meant that the money supply sank yet more and that less bank credit was available to finance business investment and consumption, which caused yet more failures and defaulted loans, which spurred yet more bank runs. Similar negative feedback loops wrecked the economies of other countries with ineffective LLRs too.[85]

The drop in the stock market, the failure of banks, and the dearth of money also increased what financial economists called asymmetric information, or adverse selection and moral hazard. Increased moral hazard meant that borrowers in trouble had increased incentives to strategically default on what they owed, and to extract as many resources as possible from the firms they controlled before they went bankrupt, thus ensuring and speeding their demise. Higher adverse selection meant that it became more difficult for banks and investors to tell the difference between good and bad investments. Therefore, many reduced lending, leading to the increases in excess reserves that the Fed misread as easy monetary conditions. In 1929, bank loans totaled 85% of total deposits but by January 1933 loans constituted just 58 percent of deposits.[86]

Economist Ben Bernanke later argued that "central banks could do little in the face of combined banking and exchange-rate crises, as the former seemed to demand easy money policies while the latter required monetary tightening."[87] But the Fed could have, and indeed should have, implemented Hamilton nee Bagehot's Rule to stop bank runs.[88] That means it should have lent to all borrowers that could post sufficient good collateral at a penalty rate, thus saving solvent banks without subsidizing bankrupt ones or inducing moral hazard, which is to say creating incentives for banks to take big risks.[89]

I can safely say that the Fed *should* have acted as an LLR because that was its ostensible reason for existing.[90] And we know it *would* have worked because some Federal Reserve districts lent more freely to banks than others did. In states like Mississippi overseen by two different Federal Reserve district banks, a natural experiment took place. Turns out that banks, holding all else constant, failed much less frequently in the area under the control of more proactive Federal Reserve district banks, especially Atlanta, and failed most often in districts overseen by St. Louis and other noninterventionist district banks.[91]

The Fed's own Benjamin Strong knew the importance of aiding sound institutions during liquidity crises as he had helped JP Morgan during the Panic of 1907.[92] Even Lauchlin Currie, a member of FDR's so-called Freshman Brain Trust, later admitted that "the Government should have underwritten all of the banks that survived to 1932" as that would have entailed "no loss" to taxpayers and would have "avoided the unnecessary distress and retardation of the recovery that the locking up of billions of dollars of checking and time deposits caused."[93]

The Fed was not well led after Strong, who provided the institution with strong leadership until his death in 1928. Whether Strong would have pushed for the Fed to act more aggressively as an LLR, or at least engaged in countercyclical monetary policy, we can never know. Clearly, however, he did not prepare his colleagues for what was to come.[94] The Fed was not the only central bank to misread the monetary situation. In 1931, for example, Germany's central bank failed to act as an LLR and it was not alone.[95] "Central bankers continued to kick the world economy while it was down," two economist historians once wrote, "until it lost consciousness."[96]

Even without following Hamilton's Rule, the Fed could have greatly aided the economy in 1932 by engaging in open market operations of sufficient magnitude to counteract the decrease in the money supply since 1929, including the $1.5 billion worth sitting in currency hoards according to Harwood's estimate.[97] Instead it bought only $1 billion of securities between April and August 1932.[98]

In the end, what ended the first phase of America's Great Depression was not the Fed, but the new Roosevelt administration's decision to increase the money supply, first by buying gold and then by substantially devaluing the dollar in terms of gold. To get out of their own depressions, other nations took similar paths, abandoning gold altogether when necessary. Output immediately began to grow and trade revived. If FDR had stopped there, as many other nations did, America's Depression would have ended in 1934, and perhaps sooner if he also reversed two of Hoover's worst policies, high tariffs and high wages. Instead, FDR allowed the latter to continue largely unimpeded and implemented numerous additional new policies that exacerbated unemployment and undermined business investment.[99]

Awful Autarky

President Hoover was far from a free market classical liberal or a do-nothing type. New Dealers like Harry Hopkins who could not explain why Hoover's economic interventions failed while the almost identical ones of FDR would succeed perpetrated that myth.[100] Hoover "issued statements about rugged individualism," Hopkins claimed, and "wooed prosperity by all the magic spells of the economic soothsayers." In sooth, Hoover, "the Great Engineer,"[101] just listened to other inexpert experts, socialist ones who believed that "it is only by the combined effort of business, labor and government to increase production that an effective rise in the national income can be attained."[102] Currie also claimed that Hoover retained a "dogged adherence to erroneous economic theories [that] permitted the economy to slide deeper and deeper into depression, almost to the point of general bankruptcy," whatever that means.[103]

In fact, though, Hoover was in thrall to almost as many economic fallacies as his successors would be. Hoover was so interventionist, in fact, that FDR smeared him as a "socialist" in the 1932 presidential campaign. That claim was factually hyperbolic and probably a projection of FDR's own socialistic views.[104] It was not, however, without basis as federal government expenditures as a share of GNP increased from 16.4 to 21.5% between 1930 and 1931. Some of that was from a growing numerator (higher expenditures) and some from a shrinking denominator (lower GNP).

Hoover's response to the Great Crash and the Great Slump that followed was not to do nothing, but to pass various orders and laws, many of which FDR extended, expanded the scope of, or enlarged.[105] One of the first, and worst, was a very high protective tariff called Smoot-Hawley, a beggar-thy-neighbor tariff passed in June 1930, right when the economy likely would have begun to pull out of its recession had the Fed not allowed the money supply to dry up. Thanks to ample input from manufacturers, like the Pennsylvania Manufacturers Association's President Joseph R. Grundy,[106] the new tariff, considered dead in some circles in November 1929,[107] ended up being the highest in a century.[108] It was also broad and cut deep by slapping duties on formerly free goods, including resources like linseed oil and tungsten, used as inputs in manufactured goods. Henry Ford called it "an economic stupidity." Graeme K. Howard of General Motors predicted that the tariff "would spell economic isolation ... and the most severe depression ever experienced."[109] Some 1024 economists agreed in a strongly worded missive, but Hoover signed the tariff into law anyway.[110]

While the Smoot-Hawley Tariff's direct effect on the largely self-sufficient U.S. economy was not large, it clearly increased uncertainty, spurred retaliatory tariffs that hurt exports, especially farm exports, and damaged the free flow of capital internationally.[111] Financial journalist Garet Garrett called high tariffs "this stupid way of all wanting to sell without buying" but of course, policymakers were not swayed by mere economic logic.[112]

Tariffs were as old as the nation itself. Protective tariffs, though, were not. They came and went in waves starting in the run-up to the War of 1812. Protective tariffs were also not a form of "pump priming" as some Progressives believed, but they were certainly a form of rent extraction, and a much more controversial one than patents or copyrights.[113] Tariffs were politically tricky because concentrated interests, the owners and employees of the manufacturers or growers of protected goods, earned rents (unearned profits) in proportion to the size of the taxes they could induce the federal government to place on the wares of their foreign competitors. Consumers, though, were hurt by the higher prices that tariffs brought. As Alexander Hamilton had explained in his *Report on Manufacturers* over a century earlier, what tariffs gave to manufacturers and the government, it took from consumers and from overall efficiency by keeping inefficient domestic producers afloat.[114]

Thanks to the recession and the struggling stock market, however, the Smoot-Hawley Tariff became a relatively easy sell, a mechanism for keeping up profits, employment, and wages. Some policymakers also thought it would help the monetary situation. Rather than abandon the gold standard or devalue the dollar in terms of gold, policymakers hoped the tariff would reduce imports and thus, holding exports constant, slow or reverse gold outflows.[115]

It was unrealistic to expect exports to hold up, though, when retaliation, which took the form of higher tariffs, lower quotas, and exchange controls, was easy and the world's supply of monetary gold was being hoarded by France and the United States. The Smoot-Hawley Tariff was so steep that foreign governments felt the need to retaliate with tariffs of their own large enough to cut demand for U.S. exports, in real terms, to just 57% of its 1923–25 level by 1932.[116] Even Great Britain, which had been free trade for a century, passed a general tariff in retaliation. Peeved at the tariff on their watches, the Swiss called for a boycott of all American goods.[117] "There has never before been such a wholesale and widespread retreat from international economic co-operation," the League of Nations proclaimed that year. The trade war that Hoover started caused about half of the 25% decline in world trade that occurred between 1929 and 1932.[118]

Moreover, the tariffs reduced any remaining effectiveness of the gold standard.[119] Deflation gave nominal tariffs additional bite, reducing both trade levels and productivity yet further. Up to 10% of the output decline in the first phase of the Great Depression is attributable to Hoover's high tariff regime.[120] Furthermore, when the world's economies began to rebound, trade restrictions hampered recovery.[121]

American farmers were particularly hard hit as demand for wheat and other staples plummeted, further reducing prices already driven down by deflation. Sweet corn dropped to two dozen for 15 cents while tomatoes, peaches, apples, and potatoes sank to 20 cents for a half-bushel basket, which cost farmers a nickel to buy.[122] At those prices, many succumbed to bankruptcy, leading to the failure of thousands of small community banks across the nation. Those bank failures, in turn, negatively impacted depositors and small nonfarm business borrowers. Big banks liked the loss of putative competitors, but branching and other regulatory restrictions prevented them from doing business in small locales now bereft of effective financial intermediation. Meanwhile, the Federal Reserve, captive to big bank interests, let the carnage continue. Instead of trying to keep the financial sector intact, Hoover concentrated his efforts on keeping real wages high.

The tariff debacle also established a pattern wherein many countries tried to emulate America's anti-Depression policies, even the dumber ones. As a result, the global downturn was also exacerbated and extended, which meant, aside from the tariffs themselves, world trade could not help to lift the U.S. economy out of its slump.[123]

Hoover's High Wage Hallucination

The interventionist Hoover made other policy blunders, like subsidizing agricultural production instead of aiding the orderly liquidation of the least efficient farmers and ranchers. But his biggest blunder by far stemmed from the fact that he believed, as other respectable policymakers also mistakenly did, that high wages cause prosperity. Actually, prosperity causes high wages.[124] Reversing the causality tricked him into chasing prosperity through high wage policies instead of inducing prosperity through economic freedom and sound money, even though common investors understood, as Benjamin Roth noted on 19 September 1932, "the depression can't end until wages come down."[125] Yet Hoover cajoled and coerced employers into maintaining, and even in some cases raising, nominal wages by threatening to strengthen labor unions if they did not comply.[126]

Workers eager to maintain their employment did accept some nominal wage cuts but policies kept them up as everyone just tried to hang on until the economy "turned the corner" and money came out of hoards and prices started upward again.[127] High tariffs helped keep wages up, at least in protected industries. Economists Richard Vedder and Lowell E. Galloway estimate that those higher wages led to 3.8 percentage points higher unemployment and drastically reduced profits, both of which fed the first wave of bank failures and subsequent drop in the money supply.[128]

Another autarkic policy, reducing the number of foreign laborers, also kept real wages up.[129] Hoover restricted new immigration and expelled foreign nationals already in the country because they depressed wages when employed and depleted precious community resources when not, a cruel policy that FDR continued. In the early 1930s, some 400,000 undocumented Mexicans living and working in America were repatriated under orders from the Department of Labor's Bureau of Immigration and with the aid of local law enforcement officers.

First, officials came for those suspected of criminal activity, then they came for the masses who had entered the United States before it tried to control immigration at its southern border.[130] The southwest was most directly affected but Mexicans working industrial jobs in high unemployment areas like Chicagoland were no longer needed as strikebreakers, so they were also harassed and finally officially ousted. Sending a Mexican family to the border by rail cost an estimated $37.50, far less than schooling their children, feeding them when unemployed ($336 per year), and so forth.[131]

Contrary to legend, Hoover was a planner, an economic interventionist who believed that he could "fix" the economy. He had rationed Americans' food at the end of the Great War so successfully that his last name had become a verb, to Hooverize, or in other words to economize or conserve. As head of the Department of Commerce under presidents Harding and Coolidge, Hoover also had successfully brought manufacturers and construction contractors together to standardize the size of bricks. Like most technocrats, though, he was prone to focus on his wins rather than his losses, and the benefits of his policies rather than their costs. President Coolidge kept "Wonder Boy" on at Commerce even though he later noted that Hoover had offered him "unsolicited advice for 6 years, all of it bad."[132] Others derided Hoover as the Secretary of Commerce and the Undersecretary of Everything Else.[133]

Within a month of the Great Crash, Hoover tried to convince business leaders to keep wages high even though prices, and profits, were falling. This great economic planner didn't seem to understand that higher real wages did not mean more purchasing power in aggregate, it meant lower profits for business owners and/or fewer employees.[134] John Maynard Keynes and Harvard economist Edward Chamberlin made that point clearly, and the latter pointed out that high wages induced employers to substitute machinery for workers, a trend slowed only by depressed financial conditions.[135] Decades later, Vedder and Gallaway would create a model that accurately predicted annual unemployment rates over decades based on productivity-adjusted real wages.[136]

Hoover, however, continued to jawbone in favor of high wages throughout his presidency and to back his words with legislation like the Davis-Bacon Act of 1931, which required that workers on federally financed construction projects receive a "prevailing wage" padded by unions.[137] Hoover also defended nominally denominated or "sticky" union wage contracts. In the Norris-LaGuardia Act of 1932, Congress outlawed "yellow dog" contracts that prohibited workers from belonging to unions.[138] Where unions were strongest, real wages were highest, but so too was unemployment.[139] Some economists, including Ben Bernanke and Michael Bordo, argue that high real wages created unemployment levels high enough to explain the bulk of the 1929–33 downturn.[140] During the initial deflationary phase of the Great Depression, real wages increased (from an index of 100 in 1929 to 113 in 1931), squeezing profits and hence output.[141]

Market self-equilibration did not occur, so the most widely held view of the macroeconomy at the time, so-called liquidationist theory, did not hold, although it often had before and has done so since. When Treasury Secretary Mellon infamously said that all the government had to do was allow the liquidation of labor, stocks, farmers, and real estate, he was not being cruel, he was relating the classical economic view of downturns: recessions are simply mechanisms for eliminating the weakest businesses and repurposing their human, financial, and physical resources into new fields of endeavor. The choice was never between recession or no recession but between slight recession now or big recession later.[142]

The big question is why the economy proved the liquidationists wrong, at least during the early 1930s.[143] Real wages did not increase across all sectors, but they did display a significant degree of "stickiness."[144] "In the increasingly structured and politicized labor markets of the interwar period," economist historians Peter Temin and Barry Eichengreen explained, "wages lacked the flexibility they once possessed."[145] More than in previous downturns, most people were employees instead of proprietors.[146] They worked under nominal wage contracts, some, like union contracts, quite formal and impossible to break without government support. Unlike proprietors, whose incomes automatically fell when the overall price level did, employees under contracts did not have to accept wage cuts. It was literally easier to fire workers than to decrease their pay.

Many economists have wondered why employees about to be fired did not voluntarily agree to a lower wage, contract or not. Rational people, though, might rather be unemployed than accept a lower nominal wage.[147] They might have nominally denominated debts to repay but they might expect some leniency if unemployed. Also, the formally unemployed could not have their wages garnished. Individuals might have been better off working in the informal sector and keeping all their wages rather than keeping their formal sector jobs at a lower nominal wage while laboring under big debts, as many Americans were, for the first time in the nation's history, by the late 1920s and early 1930s.[148] As Garrett pointed out, after the Great War Americans began to borrow so they could have the good things in life before they could afford to buy, by traditional metrics.[149]

Interestingly, many employers were not eager to impose nominal wage cuts on their employees. In the 1910s and 1920s, many had come to believe that efficiency wages, or in other words paying more than equilibrium wages, improved profitability by rendering workers hard working and more loyal, a lesson taught by Henry Ford's famous wage increase. Better to cut the least productive workers entirely than to decrease wages across the board.[150]

Moreover, due to upward trends in productivity thanks to technological advances large and small, nominal wage cuts sufficient to keep workers employed would have to have been substantial in some industries. Productivity in beet sugar production, for example, increased dramatically due to mechanization just as demand for sugar fell due to recession, inducing employers to throw workers out of work and to replace them with machines when demand later increased.[151] Substituting relatively inexpensive and unregulated physical capital for relatively expensive and highly regulated labor appears to have occurred across many industries. That might have helped the economy in the long run but worked to deepen the Depression short term.[152]

In some industries, a dearth of bank credit and short-term debt market access would have also necessitated large nominal wage decreases because companies with pinched cash flows could not have financed their operations otherwise. So, they laid off workers instead and workers accepted that rather than *de minimis* wages.[153]

That is not to say that workers were content. On 6 March 1930, deemed International Unemployment Day by Comintern, unemployed workers protested across the Western world, including in some 30 American cities. The biggest protests erupted in New York and Detroit, but Baltimore, Boston, Buffalo, Chicago, Cleveland, Denver, Los Angeles,

Philadelphia, San Francisco, Seattle, and some smaller industrial cities in the Midwest also saw workers turn out by the thousands and tens of thousands. The Communist Party of the United States of America (CPUSA) estimated that 1.25 million people turned out, all told, but rival communist organizations thought that an overestimate by a factor of ten. Whatever the number of protestors, clashes with police led to about 250 arrests nationwide. The worst violence occurred in Manhattan where protesters decided to march from Union Square to City Hall without a parade permit. The police broke up the procession with their nightsticks and blackjacks and a fire hose dousing supplied by the fire department. Organizers received 6 months in jail.[154]

Throughout the 1930s, various socialist and communist organizations and parties tried to mobilize the unemployed masses with slogans like "Fight!—Don't Starve" and "Socialism in Our Time" and the creation of "Unemployed Councils," locally organized communist cells that drew inspiration from the St. Petersburg soviets of 1905.[155] In addition to aiding the March 1930 protests, the Councils organized hunger marches, rent strikes, and other types of direct action, but they never attracted a large following and eventually petered out.

The Councils were also involved, along with the CPUSA, in the 7 March 1932 Ford Hunger March that turned deadly.[156] The march began on the outskirts of Detroit and ended at Ford's largest plant, the River Rouge facility in Dearborn, where Dearborn police and Ford security guards shot pistols and even machine guns at workers, five of whom, including 3 communists, eventually died of their wounds. Three score others[157]—of the 3000 or so unemployed men outside the gates calling for jobs for themselves and taxes for the rich—were injured by gunfire, tear gas, or blasts of freezing water before the marchers dispersed.[158]

Authorities dealt with the more radical elements of the labor movement harshly because some workers had shown a penchant for violence themselves, especially blowing things up with dynamite, and one of their intellectual leaders, Louis Adamic, openly wondered if "more dynamite" would be necessary to achieve worker aims during the Depression.[159] Harwood and others worried about violence too, citing the "ugly mood" that had swamped the country during "the last depression period" following the Great War. "Radicalism, bolshevism, the spirit that overthrew Russia, grows apace at such times," he warned.[160]

Other threats to the peace also surfaced as the Depression dragged on. By May 1932, 20,000 unemployed Great War veterans were also fed up and camped out near Washington, D.C., while demanding that their veteran benefits, due in 1945, be paid immediately. About half of the so-called Bonus Army dispersed after Congress rejected their pleas but those who remained were forcibly removed by the actual Army in the summer of 1932. The incident, more than anything else, sealed Hoover's fate that November.[161]

Although unemployed Americans enjoyed a First Amendment right to protest, demonstrations ultimately did not help their cause because it fed a vicious cycle wherein bad news generated negative sentiment and expectations, which then generated additional negative economic performance and worsening sentiment and more dire expectations. The cycle can be followed in newspapers, diaries, and other sources and became more difficult to slow or reverse as the economy worsened throughout Hoover's first, and only, term in office.[162]

Notes

1. Murray N. Rothbard, *America's Great Depression* 5th ed. (Auburn, Ala.: Ludwig von Mises Institute, 1963, 2000), 164.
2. James Ledbetter and Daniel B. Roth, eds., *The Great Depression: A Diary by Benjamin Roth* (New York: Public Affairs, 2009), 4.
3. Robert Craig West, *Banking Reform and the Federal Reserve, 1863–1923* (Ithaca: Cornell University Press, 1974), 227.
4. Carmen M. Reinhart and Kenneth S. Rogoff, *This Time Is Different: Eight Centuries of Financial Folly* (Princeton: Princeton University Press, 2009), 15–17.
5. E.C. Harwood, "Stock Speculation Versus Florida Memories," (May 1928), Box 1, E.C. Harwood Archives, AIER, Great Barrington, Mass.
6. Marion Turner Sheehan, ed. *The World at Home: Selections from the Writings of Anne O'Hare McCormick* (New York: Alfred A. Knopf, 1956), 75.
7. Timothy Cogley and Thomas J. Sargent, "The Market Price of Risk and the Equity Premium: A Legacy of the Great Depression?" UC Davis Department of Economics Working Paper Series #05-22 (March 2005); Ledbetter and Roth, eds., *Great Depression*, 69.

8. Janice M. Traflet and Robert E. Wright, *Fearless: Wilma Soss and America's Forgotten Investor Movement* (New York: All Season Press, 2022).
9. E.C. Harwood, "The First Step Toward Reform of the Money-credit System," (May 1928), Box 1, E.C. Harwood Archives, AIER, Great Barrington, Mass.
10. William Shughart, "The New Deal and Modern Memory," *Southern Economic Journal* 77, 3 (2011), 515 n2.
11. Lawrence W. Reed, *Great Myths of the Great Depression* (Mackinac Center for Public Policy and the Foundation for Economic Education, 2011).
12. Jeremy Horpedahl, Phillip Magness, and Marcus Witcher, "Teaching the Causes of Great Depression to College Students: Evidence from History, Economic, and Economic History Textbooks," *Journal of Economics and Finance Education* 21, 2 (Fall 2023): 22–37.
13. For examples, see Robert F. Bruner and Scott C. Miller, "The Great Crash of 1929: A Look Back After 90 Years," *Journal of Applied Corporate Finance* 31, 3 (Fall 2019), 49; Paul M. Warburg, *The Federal Reserve System: Its Origin and Growth, Reflections and Recollections* Vol. 1 (New York: Macmillan Co., 1930), 505.
14. Pierre-Cyrille Hautcoeur, "Financial Crisis and Depression: Are There Lessons to Draw from the Great Depression?" *Realities Industrielles* (August 2018); Jean Edward Smith, *FDR* (New York: Random House, 2007), ix.
15. "The Securities and Exchange Act of 1934," Title 1, Sec. 2, para. 3.
16. "The Securities and Exchange Act of 1934," Title 1, Sec. 2, para. 4.
17. Johan Norberg, *Financial Fiasco: How America's Infatuation with Homeownership and Easy Money Created the Economic Crisis* (Washington, DC: Cato Institute, 2009), 101–5.
18. As quoted in James P. Warburg, *Hell Bent for Election* (New York: Doubleday, Doran & Company, 1935), 9.
19. Rothbard, *Great Depression*, 285–320.
20. Stephen G. Cecchetti, "Understanding the Great Depression: Lessons for Current Policy," NBER Working Paper #6015 (April 1997).

21. E.C. Harwood, "Should the Investor Sell Short?" (July 1928) Box 1, E.C. Harwood Archives, AIER, Great Barrington, Mass.
22. Bruner and Miller, "Great Crash," 44–45; Jim F. Couch and William F. Shughart, *The Political Economy of the New Deal* (Northampton, MA: Edward Elgar, 1998), 8.
23. Efraim Benmelech, Carola Frydman, and Dimitris Papanikolaou, "Financial Frictions and Employment during the Great Depression," NBER Working Paper No. 23216 (March 2017).
24. Ledbetter and Roth, eds., *Great Depression*, 73.
25. E.C. Harwood, "In Justice to the Federal Reserve Board," (July 1928) Box 1, E.C. Harwood Archives, AIER, Great Barrington, Mass.
26. Rothbard, *Great Depression*, 85–87, 159–62.
27. Garet Garrett, *A Bubble That Broke the World* (Boston: Little, Brown, and Company, 1932), 48, 52.
28. E.C. Harwood, "A Criticism of Stimulated Construction As a Cure for Business Depression," *The Annalist* (30 May 1930), 1,155.
29. Barry Eichengreen and Kris Mitchener, "The Great Depression as a Credit Boom Gone Wrong," BIS Working Papers No. 137, (September 2003).
30. Shughart, "New Deal," 524–25.
31. Warburg, *Federal Reserve*, 501.
32. E.C. Harwood, "Review: The Federal Reserve System by Paul M. Warburg," (June 1930) Box 1, E.C. Harwood Archives, AIER, Great Barrington, Mass.
33. Warburg, *Federal Reserve*, 502; Jim Powell, *FDR's Folly: How Roosevelt and His New Deal Prolonged the Great Depression* (New York: Crown Forum, 2003), 28–29.
34. Warburg, *Federal Reserve*, 504; E.C. Harwood, "In Justice to the Federal Reserve Board," (July 1928) Box 1, E.C. Harwood Archives, AIER, Great Barrington, Mass.
35. David C. Wheelock, "Monetary Policy in the Great Depression: What the Fed Did, and Why," *St. Louis Federal Reserve Review* (March/April 1992), 7–8.
36. Powell, *FDR's Folly*, 29.
37. Warburg, *Federal Reserve*, 507–8, 512.
38. Robert Whaples, "Where Is There Consensus Among American Economic Historians? The Results of a Survey on Forty

Propositions," *Journal of Economic History* 55, 1 (March 1995), 143.

39. Ledbetter and Roth, eds., *Great Depression*, 14–15, 24, 38, 40.
40. Amity Shlaes, *The Forgotten Man: A New History of the Great Depression* (New York: HarperCollins, 2007), 139; Ron Michener, "Money in the American Colonies," *EH.Net Encyclopedia* (2003/11).
41. Sheehan, ed. *The World at Home*, 124.
42. Robert E. Wright, "Elites Gone Wild," *AIER Daily Economy Blog* (19 Feb. 2021). https://www.aier.org/article/elites-gone-wild/
43. Ledbetter and Roth, eds., *Great Depression*, 46–47, 82–84, 99–100, 142.
44. Loren Gatch, "Local Money in the United States During the Great Depression," *Essays in Economic & Business History* 26 (2008): 47–61.
45. Bennett McCallum, "Could a Monetary Base Rule Have Prevented the Great Depression?" NBER Working Paper No. 3162 (November 1989); George Selgin, *False Dawn: The New Deal and the Promise of Recovery, 1933–1947* (Chicago: University of Chicago Press, 2025); Shughart, "New Deal, 522.
46. Powell, *FDR's Folly*, 30.
47. Ledbetter and Roth, eds., *Great Depression*, 50–52, 58–59.
48. Bill White, *America's Fiscal Constitution: Its Triumph and Collapse* (New York: PublicAffairs, 2014), 192–93; John F. Cogan, *The High Cost of Good Intentions: A History of U.S. Federal Entitlement Programs* (Stanford: Stanford University Press, 2017), 68.
49. Harold L. Cole and Lee E. Ohanian, "Re-examining the Contributions of Money and Banking Shocks to the U.S. Great Depression," *NBER Macroeconomics Annual* 15 (2000): 183–227.
50. Lee E. Ohanian, "What—or Who—Started the Great Depression?" *Journal of Economic Theory* 144 (2009): 2310–35.
51. Barry Eichengreen and Peter Temin, "The Gold Standard and the Great Depression," NBER Working Paper 6060 (June 1997); Larry White, *Better Money: Gold, Fiat, or Bitcoin?* (New York: Cambridge University Press, 2022), 34.
52. West, *Banking Reform*, 163.

53. Charles W. Calomiris, "Financial Factors in the Great Depression," *Journal of Economic Perspectives* 7, 2 (Spring 1993), 75–76; White, *Better Money*, 47–50.
54. E.C. Harwood, "Effects of Currency Hoarding," *Barron's* (15 Feb. 1932), 3, 11.
55. Richard G. Anderson, Michael Bordo, John V. Duca, "Money and Velocity During Financial Crises: From the Great Depression to the Great Recession," NBER Working Paper 22,100 (March 2016).
56. Calomiris, "Financial Factors," 68.
57. Ben S. Bernanke, "Non-Monetary Effects of the Financial Crisis in the Propagation of the Great Depression," NBER Working Paper Series 1054 (Jan. 1983).
58. Calomiris, "Financial Factors," 70–73.
59. Robert Higgs, "Regime Uncertainty: Why the Great Depression Lasted So Long and Why Prosperity Resumed After the War," *Independent Review* 1, 4 (1977): 561–90; Couch and Shughart, *Political Economy*, 29–30.
60. Cole and Ohanian, "Re-examining," 222.
61. James D. Hamilton, "Was the Deflation During the Great Depression Anticipated? Evidence from the Commodity Futures Market," *American Economic Review* 82, 1 (1992): 157–78.
62. Stephen G. Cecchetti, "Prices During the Great Depression: Was the Deflation of 1930–32 Really Unanticipated?" NBER Working Paper No. 3174 (November 1989).
63. Allan Meltzer, "Monetary and Other Explanations of the Start of the Great Depression," *Journal of Monetary Economics* 2 (1976): 455–71; White, *Better Money*, 76–96.
64. Eichengreen and Temin, "Gold Standard," 29.
65. Rothbard, *Great Depression*, 149.
66. H. Clark Johnson, *Gold, France, and the Great Depression, 1919–1932* (New Haven: Yale University Press, 1997), 3.
67. Eichengreen and Temin, "Gold Standard"; Garrett, *Bubble*, 58–98.
68. West, *Banking Reform*, 163.
69. E.C. Harwood, "Co-ordination of National and State Banks with Money-credit Reform," (June 1928) Box 1, E.C. Harwood Archives, AIER, Great Barrington, Mass.

70. Richard Timberlake, *Constitutional Money: A Review of the Supreme Court's Monetary Decisions* (New York: Cambridge University Press, 2013), 225.
71. Marriner Eccles to the Utah Bankers Association, June 1925. FRASER: https://fraser.stlouisfed.org/archival-collection/marriner-s-eccles-papers-1343/speech-utah-bankers-association-460005.
72. Johnson, *Gold*, 3–4.
73. Ben Bernanke, "The Macroeconomics of the Great Depression: A Comparative Approach," NBER Working Paper #4814 (August 1994), 8–10; Douglas A. Irwin, "Did France Cause the Great Depression?" NBER Working Paper 16350 (September 2010).
74. Barry Eichengreen, "The Gold-Exchange Standards and the Great Depression," NBER Working Paper No. 2198 (March 1987).
75. Johnson, *Gold*, 7, 178, 182.
76. Meltzer, "Monetary," 466; Johnson, *Gold*, 188.
77. Meltzer, "Monetary"; Christina D. Romer and David H. Romer, "The Missing Transmission Mechanism in the Monetary Explanation of the Great Depression," NBER Working Paper 18746 (Jan. 2013); Shughart, "New Deal," 524.
78. Wheelock, "Monetary Policy," 3, 10–11; Allan Meltzer, *A History of the Federal Reserve: Volume I: 1913–1951* (Chicago: University of Chicago Press, 2003), 52–53; Burton A. Abrams, *The Terrible Ten: A Century of Economic Folly* (Oakland: Independent Institute, 2013), 31; Robert Hetzel, *The Great Recession: Market Failure or Policy Failure?* (New York: Cambridge University Press, 2012), 52.
79. Calomiris, "Financial Factors."
80. Abrams, *Terrible Ten*, 25–32; Ross Robertson, *The Comptroller and Bank Supervision: A Historical Appraisal* (Washington, D.C.: Officer of Comptroller of the Currency, 1968), 118.
81. Wheelock, "Monetary Policy," 15–16.
82. Powell, *FDR's Folly*, 30–32.
83. Wheelock, "Monetary Policy," 4.
84. Calomiris, "Financial Factors," 69.
85. Ben Bernanke and Harold James, "The Gold Standard, Deflation, and Financial in the Great Depression: An International Comparison," NBER Working Paper No. 3488 (October 1990).

86. Calomiris, "Financial Factors," 69.
87. Bernanke, "Macroeconomics of the Great Depression," 11.
88. Cecchetti, "Understanding."
89. Thomas E. Hall and J. David Ferguson, *The Great Depression: An International Disaster of Perverse Economic Policies* (Ann Arbor: University of Michigan Press, 1998), 100–2.
90. Hall and Ferguson, *Great Depression*, 81; Hetzel, *Great Recession*, 24.
91. Gary Richardson and William Troost, "Monetary Intervention Mitigated Banking Panics During the Great Depression: Quasi-Experimental Evidence from the Federal Reserve District Border in Mississippi, 1929 to 1933," NBER Working Paper No. 12591 (October 2006); Andrew J. Jalil, "Monetary Intervention Really Did Mitigate Banking Panics During the Great Depression: Evidence Along the Atlanta Federal Reserve District Border," *Journal of Economic History* 74, 1 (March 2014): 259–73.
92. Wheelock, "Monetary Policy," 13; Robert F. Bruner, *The Panic of 1907: Lesson Learned from the Market's Perfect Storm* (Hoboken, N.J.: Johne Wiley & Sons, 2007), 186–87.
93. Currie, "Memoirs," 206.
94. Wheelock, "Monetary Policy," 4.
95. Johnson, *Gold*, 5, 8, 181, 188.
96. Eichengreen and Temin, "Gold Standard," 2.
97. Harwood, "Time for Bold Action," 12, 18.
98. Michael Bordo and Arunima Sinha, "A Lesson from the Great Depression that the Fed Might Have Learned: A Comparison of the 1932 Open Market Purchases with Quantitative Easing," Working Paper (September 2015).
99. Eichengreen and Temin, "Gold Standard," 19.
100. Shlaes, *Forgotten Man*, 148–49.
101. Powell, *FDR's Folly*, 39.
102. Harry L. Hopkins, "The Essence of Democracy," The Works Program, Works Progress Administration, (30 Aug. 1938), 7, FRASER.
103. Currie, "Memoirs," 228.
104. Warburg, *Hell Bent*, 65.
105. Reed, Great Myths, 5–7.
106. John Gunther, *Inside U.S.A.* (New York: Harper & Brothers, 1947), 611.

107. Sheehan, ed. *World at Home*, 11.
108. Abrams, *Terrible Ten*, 37.
109. Shlaes, *Forgotten Man*, 96–97.
110. Rockoff, "By Way of Analogy," in Bordo, Goldin, and White, eds., *Defining Moment*, 133.
111. Douglas A. Irwin, "The Smoot-Hawley Tariff: A Quantitative Assessment," *Review of Economics and Statistics* 80, 2 (May 1998): 326–44.
112. Garrett, *Bubble*, 7.
113. Harry Hopkins, Works Progress Administration, The Works Program, Press Release, 16 Jul. 1938, FRASER.
114. Richard E. Sylla and David J. Cowen, *Alexander Hamilton on Finance, Credit, and Debt* (New York: Columbia University Press, 2018), 196–222.
115. Barry Eichengreen and Douglas A. Irwin, "The Slide to Protectionism in the Great Depression: Who Succumbed and Why?" NBER Working Paper No. 15142 (July 2009/Feb. 2010).
116. Meltzer, "Monetary," 460.
117. Powell, *FDR's Folly*, 43–44.
118. Quoted in Eichengreen and Irwin, "Slide to Protectionism," 12–13.
119. Meltzer, "Monetary: 460; Johnson, *Gold*, 181.
120. Mario J. Crucini and James Kahn, "Tariffs and the Great Depression Revisited," Federal Reserve Bank of New York Staff Report No. 172 (September 2003).
121. Eichengreen and Irwin, "Slide to Protectionism."
122. Ledbetter and Roth, eds., *Great Depression*, 71.
123. Kiran Klaus Patel, *The New Deal: A Global History* (Princeton: Princeton University Press, 2016), 34–37.
124. Powell, *FDR's Folly*, 42, 40.
125. Ledbetter and Roth, eds., *Great Depression*, 73.
126. Lee E. Ohanian, "Great Depression?"
127. E.C. Harwood, "Is This Recovery? Why So Long Postponed?," (Feb. 1932) Box 1, E.C. Harwood Archives, AIER, Great Barrington, Mass.
128. Richard K. Vedder and Lowell E. Gallaway, *Out of Work: Unemployment and Government in Twentieth-Century America*, updated ed. (New York: New York University Press, 1997), 97, 113–24.

129. Richard J. Jensen, "The Causes and Cures of Unemployment in the Great Depression," *Journal of Interdisciplinary History* 19, 4 (Spring 1989): 559–60.
130. Abraham Hoffman, *Unwanted Mexican Americans in the Great Depression* (Tucson: University of Arizona Press, 1974).
131. Neil Betten and Raymond A. Mohl, "From Discrimination to Repatriation: Mexican Life in Gary, Indiana, During the Great Depression," *Pacific Historical Review* (Aug. 1973) 42, 3:370–88.
132. Shlaes, *Forgotten Man*, 16, 36–38; Ethel H. Triebel, "The Department of Commerce Under Herbert Hoover, 1921–1928," (MA Thesis: Loyola University, 1939).
133. C. Donald Johnson, *The Wealth of a Nation: A History of Trade Politics in America* (New York: Oxford University Press, 2018), 188.
134. Reed, *Great Myths*, 7.
135. Powell, *FDR's Folly*, 118.
136. Vedder and Gallaway, *Out of Work*, 31–58.
137. Couch and Shughart, *Political Economy*, 16; David E. Bernstein, *Only One Place of Redress: African Americans, Labor Regulations, and the Courts from Reconstruction to the New Deal* (Durham: Duke University Press, 2001), 6.
138. Powell, *FDR's Folly*, 41; Vedder and Gallaway, *Out of Work*, 137.
139. Robert A. Margo, "Employment and Unemployment in the 1930s," *Journal of Economic Perspectives* 7, 2 (Spring 1993): 52 n.15.
140. Michael D. Bordo, Christopher J. Erceg, and Charles L. Evans, "Money, Sticky Wages, and the Great Depression," NBER Working Paper 6071 (June 1997); Vedder and Gallaway, *Out of Work*, 112–27.
141. Ben Bernanke and Harold James, "The Gold Standard, Deflation, and Financial Crisis in the Great Depression: An International Comparison," in Ben Bernanke, ed., *Essays on the Great Depression* (Princeton: Princeton University Press, 2000), 87.
142. J. Bradford DeLong, "'Liquidation' Cycles: Old-Fashioned Real Business Cycle Theory and the Great Depression," NBER Working Paper 3546 (December 1990).

143. Ben S. Bernanke and Kevin Carey, "Nominal Wage Stickiness and Aggregate Supply in the Great Depression," NBER Working Paper 5439 (January 1996).
144. Bernanke, "Macroeconomics," 2–3.
145. Eichengreen and Temin, "Gold Standard," 3.
146. Ledbetter and Roth, eds., *Great Depression*, 4.
147. Bernanke, "Macroeconomics," 34–36.
148. Robert E. Wright, *Financial Exclusion: How Competition Can Fix a Broken System* (Great Barrington, Mass.: AIER 2019), 44–47.
149. Garrett, *Bubble*, 4.
150. Ranjit Dighe, "America's High Wage Economy in the 1930s," (Ph.D. diss., Yale University, 1997), Chapter 4.
151. "Labor Requirements Cut in Half in Beet Sugar Manufacturing," Works Progress Administration, 4–1819 (5–6 Nov. 1938), FRASER.
152. Alexander J. Field, *A Great Leap Forward: 1930s Depression and U.S. Economic Growth* (New Haven: Yale University Press, 2011), 48, 155, 297.
153. Benmelech, Frydman, and Papanikolaou, "Financial Frictions."
154. Harvey Klehr, *The Heyday of American Communism: The Depression Decade* (New York: Basic Books, 1984), 33–34.
155. Daniel J. Leab, "'United We Eat': The Creation and Organization of the Unemployed Councils in 1930," *Labor History* 8, 3 (1967): 300–15; Roy Rosenzweig, "'Socialism in Our Time': The Socialist Party and the Unemployed, 1929–1936," *Labor History* 20, 4 (1979): 485–509.
156. Klehr, *Heyday*, 58–60.
157. "Four Killed in Riot at Main Ford Plant as 3,000 Idle Fight," *New York Times* (8 March 1932).
158. Ledbetter and Roth, eds., *Great Depression*, 48.
159. Louis Adamic, *Dynamite: The Story of Class Violence in America*, rev. ed. (1934) (Oakland: AK Press 2008), 283.
160. E.C. Harwood, "The First Step Toward Reform of the Money-credit System," (May 1928), Box 1, E.C. Harwood Archives, AIER, Great Barrington, Mass.
161. Powell, *FDR's Folly*, 52.
162. Ali Kabiri, Harold James, John Landon-Lane, David Tuckett, and Rickard Nyman, "The Role of Sentiment in the US Economy: 1920 to 1934," *Economic History Review* 76, 3 (2022): 1–28.

CHAPTER 4

A Hundred Days Later

The Great Depression did not affect the entire country equally. California and the South Atlantic region fared better, with milder and shorter downturns and much less unemployment. Other parts of the country were devastated, partly due to the structure of regional economies.[1] FDR and his New Dealers, however, cared not about those variations. They wanted to implement radical reforms and, like some other leaders in Europe at the time, were happy to use the Great Depression to acquire power.

On the eve of the 1932 election, Americans were of two minds: they wanted the government to do something about economic conditions, but they were unsure what, exactly. Politicians complained that they were deluged with mail blaming them "if we act and if we don't act."[2] During his 1932 campaign against Hoover, FDR deftly leveraged this unprecedented split in the psyche of the American voter by promising to reduce federal spending, defend gold "at all hazards," remove the federal government from services better provided by private enterprise, and overall end Hoover's "extravagance."[3]

FDR also vaguely alluded to a "New Deal" and some policies, like a minimum wage, eventually enacted. Some of the allusions were so daft that they could not have been taken as serious policy proposals, including his promise to make securities issuers provide a statement of "true earnings," as if the calculation of profits was a mere matter of calculation instead of assumptions about depreciation, the cost of capital, and risk.

R. E. Wright, *FDR's Long New Deal*,
https://doi.org/10.1007/978-3-031-74141-8_4

Unlike Hoover, who usually hit the same talking points in all his speeches, FDR spoke to specific audiences, basically telling each group what it wanted to hear. That made his messaging less focused but more effective at swaying voters. More policy details came after his election but only his inauguration made clear the radical extent of his vision.[4]

The economic situation was so bad by the time FDR took office in March 1933 that many Americans wanted him to do something, anything really, in the hopes of reviving their fortunes.[5] Comedian Will Rogers claimed that everyone would cheer if FDR "burned down the Capitol" because "we at least got a fire started anyhow."[6] After his election, FDR quietly fanned the flames, hoping to enter the White House during a crisis so he would have a mandate for sweeping change under the guise of an emergency.[7] Hoover obliged by telling bank supervisors and examiners to engage in forbearance, or in other words to allow insolvent banks to remain open. They complied,[8] but insolvent banks tend to perform poorly, so all forbearance did was to make matters worse. The crisis culminated in yet another wave of bank holidays and closures just as FDR took office in early March 1933.[9] Thus began a long campaign of dividing the American people into favored and disfavored groups or classes so that they could be more easily controlled during the Constitutional upheavals to follow.[10]

The Bank Holiday and the FDIC

The usual story is that FDR came into office during a crisis and responded with the best policy option at his disposal, temporarily shuttering all the nation's banks beginning on 6 March 1933. Few mention the Pecora Investigation, a Senate Banking Committee probe that exposed some unsavory tactics used by Wall Street firms, and FDR's post-election policy proposals precipitated the crisis. Fewer still note that the euphemistic "holiday" caused massive disruptions in the payment system that pushed thousands of companies, including many banks, into bankruptcy. Most of the banks were tiny branchless "unit" banks that existed solely because of regulatory restrictions against branching. California allowed branching, so it had fewer, larger, stronger banks and hence fewer bank failures.[11] Those banks made loans to small local businesses, keeping the California economy relatively vibrant.[12] The state, therefore, fared relatively well during the Depression, which is why displaced Okies and Arkies fled to California instead of other states.[13] (Canada allowed nationwide branch banking and it, too, fared relatively well during the Depression despite the fact that its two biggest stock exchanges, in Toronto and Montreal, suffered losses as devastating as those of New York.[14])

Bank supervision, then largely the purview of the Office of the Comptroller of the Currency and state regulators, remained lax and the Fed did not yet have the power to shut shaky banks down.[15] Most failures, therefore, were not triggered by regulators but rather by stockholders facing double liability in the face of deposit runs often initiated by large depositors or stockholders with inside information about the bank's condition.[16] In early 1933, fears that FDR would devalue the dollar spurred depositors to make withdrawals, touching off a fourth and final wave of bank failures. State after state responded by declaring a bank holiday, which only induced depositors in states where banks remained open to withdraw their deposits while they still could.[17]

FDR naturally followed suit at the national level and in the process started the process of confiscating gold by outlawing gold exports.[18] He then relied on general ignorance of the weakness of bank regulators to induce the public to believe that all the bad banks had been shut down and only the solvent ones allowed to reopen, starting on 13 March.[19] By 15 March, 70% of the banks in operation on 3 March had reopened.[20] Announcement of the formation of the Federal Deposit Insurance Corporation (FDIC) and its consumer deposit guarantee, along with FDR's masterful press conference and famously reassuring fireside chat, added credibility to the claim.[21] Deposits flowed back into banks and hoarding, long a major bane to monetary policymakers, decreased, increasing velocity and/or the effective money supply.[22]

Thus, America came to be burdened by the first of many unnecessary federal New Deal agencies. Another set of regulators, the depositor insurers at the FDIC and soon FSLIC (Federal Savings and Loan Corporation), imposed additional costs on banks (and hence their customers) without making anyone's money any safer. States that required higher bank capital (owner equity) and lower reserve requirements, that placed fewer restrictions on branching, and that gave supervisors more power to shutter troubled banks, experienced fewer bank failures, all else constant. Forcing banks to hold high reserves proved counterproductive because to compensate for lost revenue, banks took bigger risks on their loans.[23] Most regulators and informed market participants could distinguish failing banks at least six months before runs finished them off. One key sign was that they suffered from higher borrowing costs.[24]

As mentioned previously, four waves of bank runs occurred because Hoover had prevented regulators from closing troubled banks, leaving depositors and stockholders to do the work, but only after additional losses had been incurred. Under forbearance, bankers who knew their banks were in trouble took high risks in the hopes of returning them to profitability with a big score or two. And when all was lost, a few pilfered what they could. The same pattern repeated itself fifty years later during the Savings and Loan Crisis.[25]

Apologists for the FDIC bashed the efficacy of double liability, claiming that it had obviously failed as 38 states had implemented it by 1930 yet waves of bank failures occurred anyway.[26] But failures occurred under deposit insurance schemes, too, including the FDIC and especially its thrifty sister the FSLIC, which had to be shuttered after the Savings and Loan Crisis of the 1980s. The key issue is the ability to make the threat of imposing double, triple, or unlimited liability credible, and only the government can do that. If shareholders know that they will have assets seized if the banks they own shares in fail, they will monitor those banks carefully and force them to close before they suffer negative capitalization. If shareholders believe that the government will not enforce double liability, they have much less incentive to monitor or call for closure.[27]

Bank failures did not become a major problem again until the 1970s but that long spell had little to do with the FDIC and much to do with what economists call financial repression. Banking became highly regulated due to interest rate and entry restrictions. Specifically, the FDIC, Comptroller of the Currency, and the Federal Reserve worked with state regulators to minimize the formation of new banks and to encourage solid banks to open branches in under-banked areas. Unit banking would not officially die until the 1990s, but the Great Depression marked the beginning of its end.[28]

Gold Confiscation and Dollar Devaluation

Less than a week in office, FDR slew the second putative cause of the Great Depression, the retail gold standard, by starting the process of confiscating most of the public's gold money.[29] Withdrawing the United States on 3 July from the London Economic Conference (LEC), which was slated to reduce tariffs and restore the gold standard, sealed what the events of March 1933 started.[30] Calling the gold standard an "old fetish," as FDR lectured at the LEC,[31] helped to bolster expectations that reflation would soon occur. With real interest rates suddenly lower and prices expected to increase, economic activity jumped appreciably in anticipation. The air was again "thick with smoke" in industrial cities like Youngstown, Ohio.[32] The economy soon crashed again, though, because the monetary base remained stagnant, and other New Deal policies nipped the nascent momentum in the bud.[33]

Gold confiscation proceeded under Section 3 of the "Act to Provide Relief in the Existing National Emergency in Banking" passed on 9 March. The law, which amended Section 11 of the Federal Reserve Act of 23 December 1913, stated that the Treasury Secretary *could* require "any or all individuals, partnerships, associations and corporations to pay and deliver to the Treasurer of the United States, via their Federal Reserve district bank, any or all gold coin, gold bullion, and gold certificates" in their possession in exchange for Federal Reserve notes at $20.67 per ounce. Those found guilty of hoarding gold could be subject to "a penalty equal to twice the value of the gold or gold certificates" thus withheld.

On 5 April, FDR ordered all gold holdings, with a $100 per person exemption, sold to the Federal Reserve on those terms.[34] In a presser on 19 April, he signaled his desire to allow the dollar to depreciate against foreign currencies.[35] On 6 May, a joint declaration of Congress abrogated gold clauses in all public and private contracts. The next day, FDR announced on the radio his intention to abrogate the gold clause in all contracts. On 5 June, Congress made gold clause abrogation official, which initiated a flurry of lawsuits finally settled by the Supreme Court in 1935.[36]

Ten days later, an MGM film entitled "Inflation" provided political cover for those moves by extolling the benefits of expanding the money supply to a dubious public that liked low prices.[37] Prices increased by 15% on the expectation that the administration was committed to increasing the money supply. Industrial activity also picked up, with steel mills operating at 63% of capacity in June 1933 compared to just 17% that March. But the money supply did not increase and in mid-July the stock market tanked yet again as the dollar strengthened in international markets.[38]

On 28 August, a new executive order outlawed the holding or exportation of gold, with four minor exceptions for jewelry, coins of numismatic value, and industrial uses.[39] When some "small holders" and a "relatively few large holders" failed to comply with FDR's gold order of 28 August, Henry Morgenthau, Jr., the Acting Secretary of the Treasury, reiterated the decree on 28 December.[40] It maintained the fiction that it was merely holding the gold until the emergency passed and Americans could buy it back at $20.67 an ounce. That would never happen, at any price.

As recently as 1932, there had been no market evidence that anyone thought the U.S. government would devalue the dollar.[41] Nevertheless, on 12 May 1933, the (Elmer, not Norman) Thomas Amendment to the Agricultural Adjustment Act authorized FDR to increase the official price of gold, i.e., to devalue the dollar, up to $41.34 per ounce. But it did not mandate devaluation, a policy on which FDR dithered because, ever the politician, he wanted to appease those who wanted to increase the money supply with silver and/or fiat money "greenbacks" like those issued by the Union during the Civil War.[42]

The 1939 movie *The Wizard of Oz*, which was based on a 1900 children's book by L. Frank Baum entitled *The Wonderful Wizard of Oz*, can be interpreted as a monetary allegory. Political tensions over gold (yellow bricks), silver (slippers, changed to ruby in the movie), and greenbacks (Emerald City) had persisted since Baum wrote.[43] FDR decided to use the authority granted him by the Thomas Amendment to experiment with the price of gold, purchasing newly mined or foreign gold with fiat dollars to drive up its market price, and selling it for fiat dollars to decrease its market price. The gyrations he made up each morning, choosing an increase of 21 cents one day because it was three times seven, a "lucky number." The dollar indeed depreciated in foreign exchange markets, some 30–45% depending on the currency, by July.[44] Under FDR's arbitrary control the policy was perfect for increasing uncertainty, slowing private lending to a trickle, and keeping the world economy in the doldrums, a point readily made by John Maynard Keynes, O.M.W. Sprague and other U.S. economists, and even random investors.[45] In more economically adroit hands, though, it could have become a mechanism for initiating a fiat, floating exchange-rate monetary system constrained by gold.[46]

Perhaps instead of likening FDR's policies to the "gold standard on the booze," Keynes should have referenced the poppy field outside the Emerald City.[47] Either way, FDR eventually sobered up enough to return to the yellow brick road, sort of. In addition to authorizing the Treasury Secretary to engage in gold market open operations through the Federal Reserve Bank of New York (FRBNY) to maintain the foreign exchange value of the dollar at $35 an ounce, the Gold Reserve Act passed on 30 January 1934 amended the Federal Reserve Act to provide that Federal

Reserve Notes (FRN) would henceforth be redeemable in other FRN instead of gold. The next day, FDR officially devalued the U.S. dollar to $35.00 per ounce (Oz, get it?) of gold. The transition from a retail gold standard to a domestic fiat currency and gold exchange standard was complete, to the chagrin of all except those hoping to receive federal jobs or other largesse in return.[48]

Gold already turned over to the Fed was then officially confiscated, i.e., made the property of the federal government, at $20.67 per ounce. The discrepancy between that price and the new $35 valuation produced several billion dollars of windfall profits for the U.S. government. The federal government also announced that it would no longer pay any price for any old gold turned in anymore, but rather would credit the sum brought in as partial payment of the "double the value" fine that it began to enforce.[49] To avoid that fine should their hoards be discovered, people began to surrender old gold anonymously, without remuneration. By the end of January 1934, Americans had turned over to FDR an additional $58.8 million of gold certificates, coins, and bars.[50]

The administration glossed over the confiscation and the devaluation with a saccharine word salad. Confiscation was necessary so that the Treasury can "protect and maintain the value of our money," a necessary step to create "a new and sounder money system … that will serve better the needs of a modern nation." Devaluation was unimportant too because "changing the amount of gold in the dollar does not mean any change in the number of dollars you hold or the dollars you owe … and there will still be one hundred cents in every dollar." Every cent represented less actual money, gold, but Americans could rest assured that FDR remained wedded to a decimalized currency. FDR also assured Americans that "the dollar will be backed by the full credit and resources of the United States government and the American people," so "a more steady purchasing power for your dollar will be maintained."[51] That claim was a non sequitur, though, because the gold value of the U.S. dollar was now determined by fiat and Federal Reserve monetary policies and proved much less stable than under the classical gold standard.[52]

Many Americans were unhappy with the monetary aspects of the New Deal. Some, apparently, held onto their gold despite the risk. Others hoarded precious metals the only legal way possible, through exclusions for jewelry and coins of numismatic value. Most, though, discovered that the easiest route available was to hoard fiduciary coins, which is to say coins that contained some precious metal, though with a market value below that of their face value. Treasury reported the problem in June 1934 without explaining the underlying cause. "An extraordinary demand for subsidiary coins, which has almost completely exhausted the supplies in the Federal Reserve banks, the United States Treasury and the mints, has sprung up within the last few months," it reported. "The demand is far out of proportion to any that has ever occurred before at this time of the year in the whole history of the mints."

Americans hoarded fiduciary coins in case the government devalued the dollar yet again.[53] They need not have gone through the trouble, though, because the dollar would maintain its nominal $35 per ounce peg until the nation went entirely off gold in the early 1970s and again legalized private gold holdings. FDR's devaluation, and his gold buying experiments, reversed the Fed-induced reduction in the money supply enough to jumpstart the U.S. economy. Unemployment remained high and business investment remained at low levels, though, because FDR's New Deal was far from complete. Americans had to suffer through many more economic experiments, almost all of which proved detrimental to their material well-being.

Bashing Investment Banks and Brokerages

Americans have never been enamored of banks, especially big ones. The nation's earliest and largest chartered commercial banks, the Bank of North America and both institutions called the Bank of the United States (1791–1811; 1816–1836) found themselves attacked from multiple quarters. Many also mistrusted "Wall Street" and other financial centers, even while themselves gambling on stock fluctuations directly or indirectly in so-called bucket shops. For decades, Americans had worried about the accumulation of financial power by J.P. Morgan and the mammoth trusts that had formed during the Great Merger Movement around the turn of the century. Books like John Moody's *The Truth About the Trusts* (1904), Woodrow Wilson's *The New Freedom* (1913), Louis Brandeis' *Other People's Money* (1914), and I. Maurice Wormser's *Frankenstein, Incorporated* (1931) had convinced Americans that corporate economic concentration was a fact and a disturbing one at that.[54] Revelations that J.P. Morgan had not paid any income tax in 1931 or 1932 did not sit well with the public, especially after the failure of the Insull utilities empire in 1932 cost investors over $85 million.[55]

Progressives were not about to let such scandals go to waste,[56] preferring what James Madison in 1794 had called "the old trick of turning every contingency into a resource for accumulating force in the government."[57] According to New Dealer Harry Hopkins, "trustful workers ... lost their savings in bad securities or bad banks," and they needed the government to protect them from such things forevermore.[58] When the stock market fell and refused to get back up, and many voters clamored for vengeance against anyone involved in finance, New Dealers, including Brandeis himself, saw a chance to regulate bankers, brokerages, and stockbrokers from D.C., though they were already under the jurisdiction of state securities regulators.[59]

Observers like MIT professor E.C. Harwood and journalist Anne O'Hare McCormick saw that the American people wanted revenge and would not be "over-cautious" in their search for scapegoats. Harwood urged the banking sector to reform from within and self-govern, much as the New York Stock Exchange did.[60] Yet, as McCormick understood, "the tendency is to blame the bankers for almost everything."[61] New Dealers, therefore, met little resistance when they rammed through Congress a series of banking regulations and a securities act, colloquially known as the 33 Act or the Truth in Securities Act. It was the federal government's first foray into securities regulation, which had traditionally been the purview of state regulators. So-called Blue-Sky Laws were Progressive measures enacted by 47 of the then 48 states between 1911 and 1931, ostensibly to protect small investors. The Blue-Sky Laws of many states, though, did more to protect small unit banks by limiting competition for both loans and deposits than it did to protect investors.[62] Harry Hopkins argued that New Deal securities regulation was needed to outlaw the sale of "worthless securities,"[63] a tacit admission that Progressive Blue-Sky laws had proven ineffective. Outside of the context of FDR's New Deal, it was an odd admission given that fraudulent issues were not a major problem thanks to longstanding laws against fraud.[64] Nevertheless, devoted statists like Olga M. Steig rose to the defense of government securities regulation by calling critics careless and uninformed. Fraud laws were not enough, she claimed, because of "countless unfair practices which, although they do not constitute legal fraud, are quite as potent in the toll they take."[65]

Passed by voice vote with little discussion, the 33 Act was largely toothless until bolstered by an additional act the next year that replaced the Federal Trade Commission (FTC) with a new, dedicated enforcement bureau, the Securities and Exchange Commission (SEC). Although unappreciated at the time because the devil lay in arcane procedural details, the 33 Act benefitted the larger, more prestigious investment banks by protecting them from competition from newer and smaller entrants.[66] At the same time, it satiated FDR's desire to avenge himself after having lost big bucks in the securities markets in the 1920s.[67]

New Dealers, however, also passed the Banking Act of 1933, which contained a section colloquially known as Glass-Steagall that forced banks to become either commercial banks, i.e., depository institutions that made loans, or investment banks, i.e., banks that dealt in financial securities like stocks and bonds. After 16 July 1934, banks could no longer do both, so they had to choose one business or the other, or split into distinct corporations, as J.P. Morgan would do.

Why Washington sought to break up arguably the strongest banks in the nation remained an open question, especially because most failed banks were tiny unit banks that did not engage in investment banking.[68] When some of the big banks affected by Glass-Steagall tried to extend the deadline, Treasury Secretary Morgenthau shut them down by asserting that "it seems no useful purpose would be served by further postponing the consummation of this reform" beyond the original deadline.[69] The enforced divorce of commercial and investment banks proceeded according to plan, with costly results covered in the conclusion. Subsequent research shows that large banks that engaged in either commercial or investment banking activities pushed for the "reform" to reduce competition from J.P. Morgan and other universal banks. New Dealers were happy to egg on the rivalry so they could appear to be engaging in meaningful reform.[70]

The Baptist politicians and banker bootleggers were not yet done. In the Securities Exchange Act of 1934, Progressives asserted that securities transactions were a form of interstate commerce and that regulating financial markets was necessary "to protect and make more effective the national banking system and Federal Reserve System, and to insure the maintenance of fair and honest markets."[71] That was ironic given that Fed policy was, as we have seen, the main cause of macroeconomic instability.

The 34 Act, as it came to be known in financial circles, created the SEC and charged it with protecting investors from Wall Street firms by mandating margin requirements, or in other words the percent of securities purchases that could be borrowed.[72] Most of the details, though, the New Deal Congress delegated to the SEC. For example, Section 11 required the SEC to "prescribe such rules and regulations as it deems necessary or appropriate in the public interest or for the protection of investors ... to prevent such excessive trading." That massive delegation of power allowed the SEC to pander to the needs of larger banks and brokerages while limiting competition from smaller enterprises and startups.

The 34 Act also empowered the SEC to enforce the 33 Act and further moved the securities markets from a regime of selective disclosure to one of mandated disclosure. In other words, it forced companies that wanted to issue publicly traded securities to provide information about their respective businesses to everyone, at the same time. Issuers complied by providing only low-quality, pro forma information. While that might sound "fair," it was inferior to the system that had evolved organically since the 1790s wherein securities issuers provided high-quality information to a relatively few important investors, to whom other investors looked for signals to buy, hold, or sell. So-called "dumb money" knew it was best to follow investors in the know, who had access to high-quality information precisely because it did not have to be shared with everyone. The selective disclosure regime also induced most investors to do what they wanted to do anyway, buy, hold, and collect dividends until the market moved higher.[73]

Scholars like David M. Kennedy claim that "Wall Street before the 1930s was a strikingly information-starved environment."[74] In fact, data proves that the selective disclosure regime of the 1920s was palpably better than the SEC's misnamed full disclosure regime, which legal scholar Paul Mahoney has called a secrecy regime because it forbids information flows at crucial moments, like the period just before businesses issue shares for the first time.[75] From 2001 to 2020, the mean first-day return on stocks issued in initial public offerings (IPOs) was 18.6%. In other words, newly issued stocks ended their first trading day almost a fifth higher in price on average even though it was in the best interests of the issuing corporations to sell their shares for as many dollars as possible. Issuers, though, sold shares almost twenty percent lower than they could have. During the 1920s, IPO underpricing was much lower, an average of just 8.2%. Moreover, in the 1920s high-risk companies were no more underpriced on average than low-risk companies were. During the SEC's full disclosure regime, however, high-risk companies were more highly underpriced than low-risk ones, suggesting that full disclosure particularly harmed high-risk companies, for which possession of accurate information is crucial to make a reasonable valuation.[76]

Long-Term Heartburn from Short-Term Relief

New Dealers also misunderstood the economic roles of wages and prices, which led to yet more disastrous policy decisions. Depression-era Americans needed food and cash but instead of directly providing those necessities, New Dealers instead destroyed food and wasted time and resources with economically unnecessary make-work jobs doled out more for partisan political purposes than economic need.[77]

Hopkins, an unconstrained thinker, conflated productive work with jobs. He thought jobs of any sort were key because he could manufacture and measure them. What the economy needed, though, was productive work, something that was in short supply due to the Fed's and Hoover's policy mistakes.[78]

The New Deal had many disparate components, each with different effects. Agricultural Adjustment Administration (AAA) payments to farmers, for example, managed to *reduce* county-level retail sales, likely by reducing work for farm workers by removing land from cultivation. In addition to wasting food, the federal government wasted money, spending more than a million dollars to kill crop pests while simultaneously spending millions to destroy crops or pay farmers not to plant.[79]

Between 1933 and 1939, about half of New Deal grant spending went to relief, about 20% to public works, about 20% to veterans, and about 10% to farmers.[80] Each additional dollar of public works (PWA, PBA, PRA, i.e., the public works, buildings, and roads administrations) and relief spending (WPA, FERA, CWA, and SS ADC and OAA) expended between 1933 and 1939 increased retail spending in 1939 over 1929 levels by about 44 cents. Because a little over half of income was spent on retail purchases, that means that every dollar of New Deal relief and public works spending raised income in 1939 by 85 cents.[81] That was pretty good but bear in mind that FDR could have reversed deflation and lifted nominal incomes a full dollar *immediately* by convincing the Fed to engage in another, larger round of open market purchases[82] or a crop duster drop[83] (helicopters were invented in 1939 but not widely used until the 1950s) without devaluing the dollar, confiscating gold, or implementing a confusing array of new regulations and programs. On 6 March 1933, Harwood, by then a professor at M.I.T., broached the idea of issuing "federal reserve notes without limit" in a private telegram to FDR confidante Raymond Moley and similar ideas were publicly discussed several times throughout the first half of 1933.[84]

In early 1934 Treasury Secretary Morgenthau rejected Senate Bill 2949, "To promote resumption of industrial activity, increase employment, and restore confidence by fulfillment of the implied guaranty by the United States Government of deposit safety in national banks." If passed, the bill would have made whole the depositors in failed national and state-chartered banks that were members of the Federal Reserve System, thus immediately restoring a good portion of the lost money supply. Morgenthau argued that the bill would establish a dangerous precedent, "the principle of guaranty by the United States of bank deposits, past, present, and future," which was an odd claim given the recent establishment of the FDIC. He also argued that the bill would not "stimulate recovery by promoting industrial activity and employment" because most of the funds would go to a very small number of very rich people "and this group may in large part place comparatively little thereof in circulation by purchase of commodities or in industry activity productive of employment."[85] The claim was also odd given the fact that most depositors were owed relatively small sums but crucial to their survival. The bill would have been less random than an indiscriminate crop dusting but still re-inflated the money supply.

Given that the administration would not consider making whole the depositors in the banks that the federal government itself regulated, it may seem that giving out cash for nothing would have been politically impossible. Many Americans, though, would have seen it as better than relief work, which they believed only taught men how to "lean on a shovel" and become "bums" who lived off the hard labor of others while pretending otherwise.[86] Better to create and distribute money that the Fed should have created anyway than to have millions of men wasting years learning how to shirk at work. The real problem for FDR was that a quick infusion of new cash would have ended the Depression quickly, rendering his New Deal politically unpalatable, if not impossible.

So instead, FDR created the Federal Emergency Relief Administration (FERA), which provided aid to states on a matching basis as well as direct and work relief between the summer of 1933 and June 1935 as a stopgap to augment strained household budgets.[87] About half of its expenditures, which totaled $4.12 billion, Hopkins could spend where he saw fit, which was not always, as presumed, where it was most needed.

Whereas FERA primarily provided direct relief (cash), the Civil Works Administration (CWA) provided work relief during its brief existence from November 1933 through March 1934. Even FDR admitted most of the work was of the "leaf-raking variety," i.e., unskilled, unimportant, and, in the South, grossly overpaid. Nobody was going to work a mule for fifty cents when he could get a buck thirty for pretending to repair a ditch.[88]

The Works Progress Administration (WPA) and PWA (Public Works Administration) replaced the CWA and FERA in summer 1935 to give New Deal bureaucrats more control over the distribution of funds, while aid to the hardcore unemployed returned to the exclusive control of state and local governments until Social Security for dependent spouses and children came online later in 1935.[89] Hopkins at the WPA and Ickes at the PWA frequently squabbled over budgets and projects, a struggle that Hopkins appears to have won for the most part.[90]

New Dealers tried to make the PWA and its close cousins, the Public Buildings Administration (PBA) and the Public Roads Administration (PRA), appear like the nation's savior although, due to planning and approval delays, the PWA did not fully gear up until the summer of 1934. When it was needed most, in early 1933, the PWA could only take over some road work projects already mapped out. Its architects, engineers, and skilled construction workers built the Grand Coulee Dam, the Florida Keys causeway, the Triborough Bridge, and two aircraft carriers crucial to the early war in the Pacific, the *Yorktown* and the *Enterprise*. Most were overpaid, though, meaning more public goods could have been built, or those could have been built at less taxpayer expense.[91]

In 1938, Labor Secretary Frances Perkins and the Commissioner of the Bureau of Labor Statistics Isador Lubin published a pamphlet called *P.W.A. and Industry: A Four-Year Study of Regenerative Employment*. It began and ended with lies and contained mostly half-truths in between. "The construction of public works," it began, "has long been a first line of defense against unemployment in periods of severe depression." In fact, just a century before, numerous states, from New York to Illinois, responded to a market panic and depression (recession plus deflation) by *stopping* their public works programs.

The pamphlet then invoked the myth of the multiplier, noting that every public works construction worker needed inputs from many more men working in factories and on trains and trucks. What the pamphlet did not explain was that artificially created demand reallocated resources away from taxpayers' preferred uses of their money to the government's preferred uses of taxpayers' money. Modern estimates put the multiplier at one, meaning that a dollar paid to workers and for materials increased economic output by a dollar, which again could have been achieved by simply giving an American a newly created dollar.[92] Rather than increasing aggregate demand, public works projects displaced private decisions with government-chosen winners and losers. In the case of the Grand Coulee and Hoover dams, Indians who lost tribal lands and various inundated environmental niches lost while construction contractors and their employees won, as did New Deal politicians. As the PWA itself admitted, all approved public works projects "were required to have specific social value and to be conducted in such a way as to relieve unemployment (p. 8)." In other words, its projects were purposely economically inefficient too.

It is true, as the pamphlet stated, that "contractors and builders, workers in the building trades, and employees normally at work in factories fabricating building materials were widely unemployed (p. 7)." But two wrongs do not make a right. The economically and morally best way to re-employ those men was not to take money from taxpayers to put them to work on projects that FDR thought best for his re-election efforts but to cure the root of the unemployment disease, which was the high real wages caused by government and Federal Reserve policies. After dipping from 113 in 1931 to 107.9 (1929 = 100), the index of real wages jumped to 115.8 in 1934, then stayed relatively constant until it jumped to 121.9 in 1937 and a whopping 130.0 in 1938.[93]

The PWA, PBA, and PRA all competed directly with private employers for workers and wages.[94] Because they paid high wages relative to the work done,[95] the PWA had to hire through unions or the United States Employment Service to minimize "kick-backs" from workers to the men who made employment decisions about them (p. 8). As noted previously, real wages could have been reduced quickly by increasing the money supply, thereby stimulating employment in companies that created goods demanded by consumers. But that would have been beside the point, which was to impress the public and spread taxpayer money to constituents who could be persuaded to vote for FDR.[96]

Repealing Prohibition and Raising Taxes

Instead of repealing Smoot-Hawley, FDR pushed through a law that allowed the secretary of state to negotiate reciprocal trade agreements. Average rates came down but in 1940 they remained among the highest in the nation's history.[97]

In his first 100 days in office, FDR also began the process of ending Prohibition, the nationwide ban on the production and sale of alcohol that had begun in January 1920. Repeal proved a salubrious policy as the unholy alliance between Baptists and bootleggers had caused massive economic distortions and aided in the rise of organized crime and violent crime, which allegedly necessitated the enactment of stricter gun laws, like the 1934 act limiting ownership of fully automatic "machine" guns.[98] Ending Prohibition was perhaps the New Deal's finest hour, although unintentionally so.[99]

As Treasury records make clear, the federal government's main goal was not to liberate Americans to make their own decisions, or even to reverse a bad policy, it was to collect alcohol excise taxes and to increase (taxable) employment. In both particulars, it succeeded.[100] It regularly boasted of the sums it collected while simultaneously reminding Americans of the stiff penalties they faced for selling alcohol products without the proper tax stamps.[101] In other words, FDR did not end the alcohol ban because it was bad policy that caused greater injury than it prevented, he did it to redirect the economic rents being extracted by bootleggers and organized crime bosses to his radical reform agenda. Treasury's tactics were not much different from the tactics of those bosses. In late May 1934, for example, Treasury stated that "vineyardists in many sections of the country" would *benefit* from its decision to tax "farmers who possess home-made natural wine ... produced from salvaged grapes," because if the government got its dime per gallon cut, it would forego raiding and seizing farms.[102]

Between December 1933 and the end of February 1934, Treasury collected almost $13 million in liquor, wine, and sparkling wine duties.[103] But the trend was downward, which set off alarm bells. Assistant Treasury Secretary Stephen B. Gibbons called it "a very unhealthy condition," even though the end of the Christmas holiday and the initial re-stocking of wine cellars and bar shelves could well have explained the decline.[104] Gibbons need not have worried as America's many drinkers soon lifted the alcohol excise to the fourth most important federal tax, just behind the tobacco excise, by 1935.[105]

The taxes created incentives for evasion, so FDR's bureaucrats went on a still seizing bender, taking by 23 April 1934, 148 stills, 17,800 gallons of spirits, almost 432,000 gallons of mash, and 29 automobiles and trucks. The actions were legally justified, but the total value of seized assets was, at just over $213,000, barely an offset for the costs associated with the 187 arrests also made. Seizures continued unabated nevertheless, with weekly arrests and stills seized numbering in the hundreds.[106]

In June of that year, Treasury went after retailers who sold beer by the glass because some of them had the bright idea of reusing barrels and the affixed excise stamps. "Heavy penalties" were threatened against retailers unless they drove their spigots through the stamps when tapping their beer barrels for sale.[107]

Maybe New Dealers also thought it prudent to allow the unemployed masses to self-medicate with alcohol so that they would be less likely to oppose America's radical restructuring. They did not, however, seriously contemplate legalizing opium, morphine, heroin, or cocaine, all of which remained tightly controlled. Or perhaps the hard drug dealers were simply more respectable than booze bootleggers. With wholesale prices at $100 an ounce, and retail as much as $1.00 a grain ($387 an ounce), opium proved a highly profitable commodity. Treasury officials purported not to understand why so many doctors and pharmacies kept their hard drugs and prescription pads in unlocked wooden cabinets.[108] Obviously, many of the reported thefts doctors reported were illicit sales, with perhaps some insurance fraud also in the mix.

In any event, Treasury also began to pay more attention to cigarette taxes. In March 1934, it revoked Internal Revenue's previous Class B classification of the 11-inch cigarettes of Axton-Fisher Tobacco Company of Louisville, Kentucky because somebody finally stumbled upon the company's tax arbitrage scheme. Per the Revenue Act of 1926, Class A cigarettes weighed not more than 3 pounds per thousand and were taxable at $3 per thousand. Class B cigarettes weighed more than 3 pounds per thousand and were taxed at $7.20. Axton-Fisher's produce was "so marked and perforated as to be easily divisible with a knife into four packages of the standard length of 2–3/4 inches at each bearing the brand label." In other words, consumers were not interested in smoking 11-inch long (filter-less) cigarettes, Axton-Fisher and its customers were interested in paying $7.20 instead of $12.00 per thousand in taxes, or 3.6 instead of

6 cents per the standard 20-cigarette pack. It was a clever ruse to exploit a dumb tax (why not just tax by weight?) but it could not be countenanced and hence was ruled "a manifest evasion of the Revenue Act." New Dealers needed the cash![109]

But Americans could not drink and smoke enough to satiate the demands of the New Deal, so in May 1934 Treasury seized the *Soyo Maru*, a silk-laden Japanese ship, and held it as security until its owner, Japanese steamship company Toyo Kisen Kaisha, paid over $370,000 in back taxes and interest to Uncle Sam.[110] More importantly, the government began to add new excise taxes, many of them highly regressive, on automobiles, cameras, furs, long-distance telephone calls, gasoline, jewelry, movie tickets, phonographs, radios, stock transfers, and telegrams.[111] New taxes, like one on food distributors, were also enacted, presumably to punish middlemen for hurting farmers, though no serious attempt to understand the incidence of such taxes was made.[112]

In early 1934, Treasury bragged that even though tax receipts were up a whopping 68%, its operating expenses were down thanks to "reduction of wages and salaries ... failure to fill vacancies" and "filling vacancies at lower pay grades." Those and other savings decreased tax collection costs from 1.853% in FY 1933 to 1.084% in FY 1934.[113] Those efficiency reforms were great, but it was more than a little ironic that at the same moment, the administration blasted private businesses that tried to cut their expenses via fewer jobs and lower pay.

Federal income tax rate increases began under Hoover and continued under FDR. The Revenue Act of 1932 increased tax rates, doubling the income, corporate, and estate rates. Tax revenue increased from 11.6% of national income in 1929 to 21.1% in 1932, or in other words from $4.7 to $11.8 billion.[114] New Dealers also raised income tax rates in 1936 and 1940, with marginal rates topping out at 79%,[115] while exemption reductions slowly turned what was once a "class" tax on the wealthy into a "mass" tax on almost all, a process that Social Security's payroll tax and the introduction of withholding during World War II completed.[116] State income tax rates went up too.[117] Although some tax increases may have temporarily allayed fears about the deteriorating federal budget, overall, they clearly hurt the economy by diminishing aggregate demand.[118]

More stringent enforcement measures were also enacted.[119] In early January 1934, FDR closed a major tax loophole by requiring tax preparers to sign, and take responsibility for, the tax returns that were paid to complete. "The purpose of these regulations," Treasury noted, "is to enable the taxpayer to fix the responsibility for the return where it belongs" and "to insure a higher degree of accuracy" in tax returns.[120] Overall, Treasury treated taxpayers in unbelievably heavy-handed ways. For example, Guy T. Helvering, Commissioner of Internal Revenue, told taxpayers in April 1934 "that the additional information form which taxpayers will be required to file with their returns for the calendar year 1934 will not be available for public inspection until after March 15, 1935."[121]

Clearly, New Dealers felt they needed cash to fund the New Deal, including its bailouts, relief programs, and a 100,000 person increase in the number of federal employees by 1935.[122] So they tripled taxation and doubled down on tax collection efforts, prompting poet Ogden Nash to close one of his poems: "I pray the Lord my soul to take/If the tax-collector hasn't got it before I wake."[123]

When receipts slowed in 1937, Treasury Secretary Morgenthau lambasted "fascists" engaging in tax avoidance and evasion, "rich men" who refused to "bear their burdens" in support of FDR's version of democracy. Ironically, the dip in revenue was due more to the depression-within-a-depression caused by federal policies than to tax dodging.[124]

Not yet followers of John Maynard Keynes, New Dealers wanted to balance the federal budget, seemingly unaware that taking a dollar from a distiller to provide a meaningless job to an unemployed worker was more redistributive than additive.[125] That point was obvious to others, though, including U.S. Senator from Oklahoma Thomas Gore. Though physically blind, Gore clearly saw that no depression could "be ended by gifts … handed out by the Federal Treasury, and extorted from taxpayers that are bleeding at every pore."[126] In other words, only by borrowing and spending did the federal government have a chance of increasing aggregate demand, something that it never came close to trying at sufficient scale to end the Great Depression.[127] Or, it could have just paid for its programs with new money, which was the one thing the macroeconomy needed more than anything else between 1930 and 1933.

Notes

1. Joshua L. Rosenbloom and William A. Sundstrom, "The Sources of Regional Variation in the Severity of the Great Depression: Evidence from U.S. Manufacturing, 1919–1937," NBER Working Paper No. 6288 (November 1997); Jim F. Couch and

William F. Shughart, *The Political Economy of the New Deal* (Northampton, MA: Edward Elgar, 1998), 125–29.
2. Marion Turner Sheehan, ed. *The World at Home: Selections from the Writings of Anne O'Hare McCormick* (New York: Alfred A. Knopf, 1956), 113.
3. Lawrence W. Reed, *Great Myths of the Great Depression* (Mackinac Center for Public Policy and the Foundation for Economic Education, 2011), 8.
4. Eric Rauchway, "The New Deal Was on the Ballot in 1932," *Modern American History* (2019): 1–13.
5. William Shughart, "The New Deal and Modern Memory," *Southern Economic Journal* 77, 3 (2011), 539.
6. Amity Shlaes, *The Forgotten Man: A New History of the Great Depression* (New York: HarperCollins, 2007), 150; Otto Friedrich, "F.D.R.'s Dispute Legacy," *Time* (1 Feb. 1982): http://content.time.com/time/subscriber/article/0,33009,954983-6,00.html.
7. Shlaes, *Forgotten Man*, 142–43.
8. H. W. Brands, *A Traitor to His Class: The Privileged Life and Radical Presidency of Franklin Delano Roosevelt* (New York: Anchor Books, 2008), 288.
9. Peter Conti-Brown and Sean H. Vanatta, "The Logic and Legitimacy of Bank Supervision: The Case of the Bank Holiday of 1933," *Business History Review* 95, 1 (Spring 2021): 87–120.
10. Mary Grabar, *Debunking FDR: The Man and the Myths* (New York: Regnery, 2024).
11. Reed, *Great Myths*, 10.
12. Sarah Quincy, "Loans for the 'Little Fellow': Credit, Crisis, and Recovery in the Great Depression," NBER Working Papers, 31779 (October 2023).
13. Reed, *Great Myths*, 10.
14. Robert E. Wright, "Banking System Stability/Fragility: The Roles of Governance and Supervision in Canada and America," in Mark S. Bonham, ed., *Becoming 150: 150 Years of Canadian Business History*, (Toronto: Canadian Business History Association, 2018): 226–38; Joe Martin, "The 1929 Stock Market Crash, A Tale of Two Cities," *Prospectus* (18 October 2022); Jim Powell, *FDR's Folly: How Roosevelt and His New Deal Prolonged the Great Depression* (New York: Crown Forum, 2003), 32.

15. Joseph R. Mason, "The Evolution of the Reconstruction Finance Corporation as a Lender of Last Resort in the Great Depression," in Robert E. Wright, ed. *Bailouts: Public Money, Private Profit* (New York: Columbia University Press, 2010), 71.
16. Lauchlin Currie, "Lauchlin Currie's Memoirs," *Journal of Economic Studies* 31, 3/4 (2004), 206; James Ledbetter and Daniel B. Roth, eds., *The Great Depression: A Diary by Benjamin Roth* (New York: Public Affairs, 2009), 30, 39, 45.
17. Powell, *FDR's Folly*, 32–33; Ledbetter and Roth, eds., *Great Depression*, 91–97.
18. Robert Hetzel, *The Great Recession: Market Failure or Policy Failure?* (New York: Cambridge University Press, 2012), 68.
19. Conti-Brown and Vanatta, "Logic and Legitimacy"; Hetzel, *Great Recession*, 74–75.
20. Mason, "Evolution" in Wright, *Bailouts*, 91.
21. Brands, *Traitor*, 300–5, 327.
22. E.C. Harwood, "Effects of Currency Hoarding," *Barron's* (15 Feb. 1932), 3, 11.
23. Kris James Mitchener, "Bank Supervision, Regulation, and Instability During the Great Depression," NBER Working Paper 10475 (May 2004).
24. Charles W. Calomiris and Joseph R. Mason, "Contagion and Bank Failures During the Great Depression The June 1932 Chicago Banking Panic," NBER Working Paper #4934 (Nov. 1994).
25. Ledbetter and Roth, eds., *Great Depression*, 26; Ross Robertson, *The Comptroller and Bank Supervision: A Historical Appraisal* (Washington, D.C.: Officer of Comptroller of the Currency, 1968), 118.
26. Ralph W. Marquis and Frank P. Smith, "Double Liability for Bank Stock," *American Economic Review* 27, 3 (Sep. 1937): 490–502.
27. Alexander W. Salter, Vipin Veetil, and Lawrence H. White, "Extended Shareholder Liability as a Means to Constrain Moral Hazard in Insured Banks," *Quarterly Review of Economics and Finance* 63 (Feb. 2017): 153–60.
28. Robertson, *Comptroller and Bank Supervision*, 125–43.
29. Reed, *Great Myths*, 10.
30. Sebastian Edwards, *American Default: The Untold Story of FDR, the Supreme Court, and the Battle Over Gold* (Princeton:

Princeton University Press, 2018), 92–94; Shlaes, *Forgotten Man*, 161–63.

31. James P. Warburg, *Hell Bent for Election* (New York: Doubleday, Doran & Company, 1935), 20.
32. Ledbetter and Roth, eds., *Great Depression*, 121.
33. Gareth Jones, "The Dollar Inflation: Higher Prices and Revival in Trade," *The Western Mail* (5 May 1933): https://www.garethjones.org/unemployment/unemployment_5.htm; Hetzel, *Great Recession*, 68–70.
34. Ledbetter and Roth, eds., *Great Depression*, 105.
35. Hetzel, *Great Recession*, 68; Ledbetter and Roth, eds., *Great Depression*, 106–7.
36. Edwards, *American Default*, xxii-xxiv; Warburg, *Hell Bent*, 24.
37. Hetzel, *Great Recession*, 67; Ledbetter and Roth, eds., *Great Depression*, 162.
38. Ledbetter and Roth, eds., *Great Depression*, 113–14, 117, 122–23.
39. Edwards, *American Default*, xxi-xxv.
40. "Order of the Secretary of the Treasury Requiring the Delivery of Gold Coin, Gold Bullion, and Gold Certificates to the Treasurer of the United States," U.S. Treasury Press Releases, Vol. 11, 1933–34, FRASER.
41. Chang-Tai Hsieh and Christina D. Romer, "Was the Federal Reserve Constrained by the Gold Standard During the Great Depression? Evidence from the 1932 Open Market Purchase Program," *Journal of Economic History* 66, 1 (March 2006): 140–76.
42. Brands, *Traitor*, 327.
43. Ranjit S. Dighe, ed., *The Historian's Wizard of Oz: Reading L. Frank Baum's Classic as a Political and Monetary Allegory* (Westport, CT: Praeger Publishers, 2002), 1–9.
44. Hetzel, *Great Recession*, 68.
45. Garet Garrett, *The People's Pottage* (Caldwell, ID: Caxton Printers, 1953), 35–36; Powell, *FDR's Folly*, 73; Ledbetter and Roth, eds., *Great Depression*, 132, 140.
46. Scott Sumner, "Roosevelt, Warren, and the Gold-Buying Program of 1933," *Research in Economic History* 20 (2001): 135–72; Burton Folsom, Jr. *New Deal or Raw Deal? How FDR's*

Economic Legacy Has Damaged America (New York: Simon & Schuster, 2008), 105.
47. Shlaes, *Forgotten Man*, 170.
48. "Memorandum for the Press," 30 Jan. 1934, U.S. Treasury Press Releases, Vol. 11, 1933–34, FRASER; Ledbetter and Roth, eds., *Great Depression*, 151–53.
49. "For Immediate Release," 15 Jan. 1934, "Release to Morning Papers," 18 Jan. 1934, U.S. Treasury Press Releases, Vol. 11, 1933–34, FRASER.
50. "For Release to Morning Newspapers," 23 Jan., 5 Feb., 1934, U.S. Treasury Press Releases, Vol. 11, 1933–34, FRASER.
51. "Secretary Morgenthau Address,"16 Jan. 1934, U.S. Treasury Press Releases, Vol. 11, 1933–34, FRASER.
52. Hetzel, *Great Recession*, 70–71.
53. "For Release, Morning Papers," 12 Jun. 1934, U.S. Treasury Press Releases, Vol. 11, 1933–34, FRASER.
54. Robert M. Abrams, "Brandeis and the Ascendancy of Corporate Capitalism," in Louis Brandeis, *Other People's Money and How the Bankers Use It* (New York: Harper Torchbooks, 1974), vii–xvi, xxxiv–xxxviii.
55. Shlaes, *Forgotten Man*, 190.
56. David M. Kennedy, "What the New Deal Did," *Political Science Quarterly* 124, 2 (Summer 2009), 251–68.
57. James Madison to Thomas Jefferson, 14 March 1794: https://founders.archives.gov/documents/Madison/01-15-02-0179. This quotation may be the origin of the pithier, but unsourced, claim that Madison said: "Crisis is the rallying cry of the tyrant." Quoted many places on the internet and in Couch and Shughart, *Political Economy*, 223.
58. Works Progress Administration, The Works Program, Press Release, 16 Jul. 1938, FRASER.
59. Ledbetter and Roth, eds., *Great Depression*, 157–58.
60. E.C. Harwood, "What Is a Sound Money-Credit System?" (February 1933), Box 1, E.C. Harwood Archives, AIER, Great Barrington, Mass.
61. Sheehan, ed., *World at Home*, 97.
62. Paul G. Mahoney, "The Origins of the Blue-Sky Laws: A Test of Competing Hypotheses," *Journal of Law and Economics* 46 (April 2003): 229–51.

63. Harry L. Hopkins, "The Essence of Democracy," The Works Program, Works Progress Administration, (30 Aug. 1938), 5, FRASER.
64. Powell, *FDR's Folly*, 108; Watson Washburn, "Anti-Fraud Legislation," *Michigan Law Review* 31 (1933): 768–75.
65. Olga M. Steig, "What Can the Regulatory Securities Act Accomplish?," *Michigan Law Review* 31 (1933), 776.
66. Paul G. Mahoney, "The Political Economy of the Securities Act of 1933," *Journal of Legal Studies* 30 (Jan. 2001): 1–31.
67. Gary Dean Best, *Pride, Prejudice, and Politics: Roosevelt Versus Recovery, 1933–1938* (New York: Praeger, 1991), 4.
68. Powell, *FDR's Folly*, 57–62.
69. "Secretary Morgenthau to Duncan U. Fletcher," 9 May 1934, U.S. Treasury Press Releases, Vol. 11, 1933–34, FRASER.
70. Powell, *FDR's Folly*, 62–64.
71. "The Securities and Exchange Act of 1934," Title 1, Sec. 2.
72. "The Securities and Exchange Act of 1934," Title 1, Sec. 4, Sec. 7.
73. Robert E. Wright, *Corporation Nation* (Philadelphia: University of Pennsylvania Press, 2014), 137–47, 195–96, 207–12.
74. Kennedy, "New Deal," 255.
75. Mahoney, "Political Economy."
76. Jie Gan, Paul Mahoney, and Jianping Mei, "IPO Underpricing: A Tale of a Different 1920s," SSRN Working Paper (20 Apr. 2022).
77. Couch and Shughart, *Political Economy*, 125–46.
78. Harry L. Hopkins, "The Essence of Democracy," The Works Program, Works Progress Administration, (30 Aug. 1938), 5, FRASER.
79. Anothony J. Bolton, "'The Best Form of Assistance Always Is the Kind That Enables Folks to Help Themselves': Public Reaction to the New Deal in Hancock, Seneca, and Wood Counties of Ohio," (MA Thesis: Bowling Green State University, 2021), 87; Warburg, *Hell Bent*, 13.
80. Price Fishback, "The Newest on the New Deal," *Essays in Economic and Business History* 36, 1 (2018), 3.
81. Price V. Fishback, William C. Horrace, and Shawn Kantor, "Did New Deal Grant Programs Stimulate Local Economies? A Study of Federal Grants and Retail Sales During the Great Depression," *Journal of Economic History* 65, 1 (March 2005): 36–71.

82. Michael Bordo and Arunima Sinha, "A Lesson from the Great Depression that the Fed Might Have Learned: A Comparison of the 1932 Open Market Purchases with Quantitative Easing," Working Paper (September 2015).
83. W.N. Stokes, Jr. *Credit to Farmers: The Story of Federal Intermediate Credit Banks and Production Credit Associations* (Washington, DC: Farm Credit Administration, 1973), 98.
84. E.C. Harwood to Raymond Moley, 6 March 1933, E.C. Harwood Archives, Great Barrington, Mass.; Ledbetter and Roth, eds., *Great Depression*, 85, 106.
85. H. Morgenthau, Jr. to Duncan U. Fletcher and Memorandum, 13 Apr. 1934, U.S. Treasury Press Releases, Vol. 11, 1933–34, FRASER.
86. Bolton, "'Best Form of Assistance'," 83–84.
87. Grace Abbott, *From Relief to Social Security: The Development of the New Public Welfare Service* (Chicago: University of Chicago Press, 1941), 227–28.
88. Couch and Shughart, *Political Economy*, 89, 91–94.
89. Fishback, "Newest," 3–4.
90. Couch and Shughart, *Political Economy*, 118.
91. Powell, *FDR's Folly*, 91–92.
92. Fishback, "Newest," 4–5; Price Fishback, "How Successful Was the New Deal? The Microeconomic Impact of New Deal Spending and Lending Policies in the 1930s," NBER Working Paper 21925 (Jan. 2016), 19–20.
93. Bernanke and James, "Gold Standard," in Bernanke, ed., *Essays*, 87.
94. Fishback, "Newest," 4.
95. Richard J. Jensen, "The Causes and Cures of Unemployment in the Great Depression," *Journal of Interdisciplinary History* 19, 4 (Spring 1989): 558.
96. Powell, *FDR's Folly*, 92–95.
97. Folsom, *New Deal?*, 241.
98. Gary Kleck, *Targeting Guns: Firearms and Their Control* (New York: Aldine DeGruyter, 1997), 108; Best, *Pride*, xv.
99. Burton A. Abrams, *The Terrible Ten: A Century of Economic Folly* (Oakland: Independent Institute, 2013), 1–21.
100. Eline Poelmans, Jason E. Taylor, Samuel Raisanen, and Andrew C. Holt, "Estimates of Employment Gains Attributable to Beer

Legalization in Spring 1933," *Explorations in Economic History* 84 (April 2022).

101. "For Release, Morning Newspapers," 6 Feb., "Memorandum for the Press," 7 Feb. 1934, U.S. Treasury Press Releases, Vol. 11, 1933–34, FRASER.
102. "For Immediate Release," 28 May 1934, U.S. Treasury Press Releases, Vol. 11, 1933–34, FRASER.
103. "Distilled Liquors and Wines Importations, Duties Collected, and Stocks in Customs Bonded Warehouses, December 1933, January and February 1934," U.S. Treasury Press Releases, Vol. 11, 1933–34, FRASER.
104. Stephen B. Gibbons to Secretary Morgenthau, 7 Mar. 1934, U.S. Treasury Press Releases, Vol. 11, 1933–34, FRASER.
105. Abrams, *Terrible Ten*, 19.
106. "Activities of Regulative Inspectors, Bureau of Industrial Alcohol, For Week Ending April 21, 1934," 30 Apr. 1934, passim, U.S. Treasury Press Releases, Vol. 11, 1933–34, FRASER.
107. "For Immediate Release," 13 June 1934, U.S. Treasury Press Releases, Vol. 11, 1933–34, FRASER.
108. "Immediate Release," 15 Jun. 1934, U.S. Treasury Press Releases, Vol. 11, 1933–34, FRASER.
109. "For Release, Afternoon Newspapers," 29 Mar. 1934, U.S. Treasury Press Releases, Vol. 11, 1933–34, FRASER.
110. "Immediate Release," 1 May 1934, U.S. Treasury Press Releases, Vol. 11, 1933–34, FRASER.
111. Folsom, *New Deal?*, 122–23.
112. Shlaes, *Forgotten Man*, 154.
113. "For Release, Morning Papers," 30 Apr. 1934, U.S. Treasury Press Releases, Vol. 11, 1933–34, FRASER.
114. Reed, *Great Myths*, 8; Powell, *FDR's Folly*, 48–49; Shughart, "New Deal", 529 n.34.
115. Tax Foundation data, www.taxfoundation.org. Accessed 10 May 2023.
116. Bill White, *America's Fiscal Constitution: Its Triumph and Collapse* (New York: PublicAffairs, 2014), 208–12.
117. Donald Ray Escarraz and Thomas Yirak, "The Evolution of Georgia's Tax Structure," *Georgia Government Review* 1, 2 (Summer 1968): 1–6.

118. David A. Zalewski, "A Reconsideration of the Revenue Act of 1932," *Essays in Economic and Business History* (2006): 56–68.
119. Alan Reynolds, "The Economic Impact of Tax Changes, 1920–1939," *CATO Journal* (Winter 2021).
120. "For Release to Morning Newspapers," 16 Jan. 1934, U.S. Treasury Press Releases, Vol. 11, 1933–34, FRASER.
121. "For Immediate Release," 28 May 1934, U.S. Treasury Press Releases, Vol. 11, 1933–34, FRASER.
122. Warburg, *Hell Bent*, 6. Nock counted only 90,000. Albert Jay Nock, *Our Enemy, the State* (New York: William Morrow & Co., 1935), 13.
123. Ogden Nash, "One from One Leaves Two," in Amity Shlaes, ed. *New Deal Rebels* (Great Barrington, Mass.: American Institute for Economic Research, 2023), 84.
124. Powell, *FDR's Folly*, 77–8.
125. Best, *Pride*, x.
126. As quoted in Folsom, *New Deal?*, 91.
127. George Selgin, *False Dawn: The New Deal and the Promise of Recovery, 1933–1947* (Chicago: University of Chicago Press, 2025).

CHAPTER 5

The Big Four Bailout Regulators

New Dealers repealed Prohibition more to increase taxes than to advance individual liberty. Almost every other aspect of the New Deal greatly reduced individual liberty by turning decision-making over to agencies in the federal government's executive branch. Harry Hopkins claimed that regulations simply laid out "the rules of fair play"[1] or mitigated malfunctioning markets suffering from "excessive competition" or other made-up maladies.[2] In fact, New Deal regulations reduced liberty and economic incentives to work harder, longer, smarter, and faster by increasing the power of unelected bureaucrats.

Many New Dealers admired the Soviet Union and wanted to bring communism to America. At the same time, America's diehard Communists, the ones who had organized the march on Ford's plant in 1932, saw in the New Deal a political opportunity that they could exploit. After being open about their goals in earlier years, many Communists starting in 1935 tried to hide their intentions by blending into the Left, and the New Deal in particular. They were so successful that one chronicler labeled the decade communism's American heyday.[3]

Both New Dealers and devoted Communists knew that the harder they pushed for collectivism, the harder the pushback would be. So, they decided instead to push for power instead of ideological gains per se and to let communism evolve as the government usurped the scope of private economic decision-making by degrees, much as economist

R. E. Wright, *FDR's Long New Deal*,
https://doi.org/10.1007/978-3-031-74141-8_5

Friedrich Hayek warned in his postwar best-seller, *The Road to Serfdom*. FDR's incremental strategy resulted in an abuse of regulation, the "police power," unprecedented in peacetime America.

Historian David M. Kennedy claims that the New Deal was only "supposedly regulation-mad" because it created just four new regulatory bodies, the SEC, the National Labor Relations Board (NLRB), the Civil Aeronautics Authority (now the Federal Aviation Administration), and the Federal Communications Commission (FCC), while greatly strengthening just four others, the Federal Power Commission, the FTC, the Interstate Commerce Commission (ICC), and the Federal Reserve.[4] Others abounded, but the number of new or enhanced agencies created by FDR was less important than the scale and scope of those eight.

Some of those regulators possessed enormous powers that they often wielded destructively. The Federal Reserve, for example, had enough power to cause the first phase of the Great Depression and prevent a natural recovery by overseeing the failure of over ten thousand banks. As discussed below, it also caused a depression-within-a-depression in 1937. As described in the conclusion, the SEC helped to foment the Global Financial Crisis and Great Recession of 2008–9.

The Civil Aeronautics Act of 1938 created a Civil Aeronautics Board that regulated the routes and rates of airlines until dismantled during the Carter administration. Like most other New Deal regulations, it was based on faulty economic assumptions and rent seeking and hence imposed net costs on the nation. The same could be said of common carrier regulations that assumed that the public interest was benefited "when transportation is provided at times and between localities at nonremunerative rates."[5] Those regulations raised consumer costs for four decades before being overturned by Carter.

The ICC and the Motor Carrier Act of 1935 managed to destroy the private passenger rail industry in the United States and almost ended private freight as well. They did so by subsidizing trucks while burdening rail with excessive regulations. Again, it would be Carter, not Reagan, who helped with the deregulation of both trucks and freight rail.[6]

The FCC ostensibly prevented costly battles over broadcast spectrum, but in the process, it favored lower-quality local programming over national networks. Moreover, it could be, and was, used to squelch political dissent.[7] By the end of the 1930s, almost all of FDR's critics had been forced from the airwaves.[8]

The growth of the national administrative state raised important questions about the traditional separation of powers between the three main branches of government because often Congress delegated authority to the Executive, which then delegated authority to unelected bureaucrats who implemented law-like rules and then adjudicated them when questions inevitably arose. Those problems threatened to stop FDR's reform agenda in its tracks, but FDR and his New Dealers prevailed with help from SCOTUS and scholars. For example, James M. Landis, dean of Harvard's law school, in his 1938 book *The Administrative Process* argued that the courts should not be so quick to interfere with the power of administrators to adjudicate rules of their own creation. What was needed, he argued, was improvement of administrative methods, not juridical oversight.[9]

FDR's new regulators and regulations caused less dramatic damage than the Fed or the SEC but also precious little in the way of benefits. The same could be said of the main subjects of this chapter, the big four bailout "bailouts" regulators, the Reconstruction Finance Corporation (RFC) for banks and railroads, HOLC (Home Owners' Loan Corporation) for mortgage lenders and borrowers, the National Industrial Recovery Administration (NIRA) and its "Blue Eagle" campaign for industry, and the Agricultural Adjustment Administration (AAA) for farmers and ranchers.

A bailout (noun) occurs when a government or private entity bails out (verb) a financially distressed business or industry, generally by providing it with cash, credit, or insurance. Bailouts come in many forms. Some types of bailouts, like Hamilton or Bagehot's Rule, are salutary because they stop financial panic from spreading at low cost. Other types of bailouts are quite destructive because they socialize losses while privatizing profits and thus redistribute resources from taxpayers to businesses or industries that take big risks.[10] Until the New Deal, bailouts in America had been infrequent and inconsequential,[11] but FDR normalized them, and moved them away from Hamilton's Rule and toward more economically costly, redistributive varieties. They were, however, a great way to win votes and to increase dependency on Washington. "Anyone wanting credit for any purpose," journalist Garet Garrett explained, "went no longer to Wall Street but to Washington."[12] Some people may have liked that until they learned that dealing with a competitive industry was far preferable to dealing with a compulsory monopolist with the power to tax.

The Reconstruction Finance Corporation

The first big bailout regulator, the Reconstruction Finance Corporation, or RFC for short, began operations in February 1932 under Hoover. The U.S. Treasury bought all $500 million of its initial shares but mostly allowed its board of directors to run it as they saw fit.[13]

At first, the RFC followed Hamilton's Rule by making loans to financially distressed corporations at a relatively high rate of interest on the security of good, liquid collateral. Private lenders still willing to lend on such terms complained, however, so the RFC began to make longer, riskier loans at lower rates of interest. As far as anyone can tell, all it did was to delay some bank failures.[14]

Most of the RFC's loans went to banks and building and loan associations but about 10% went to the railroad sector.[15] Between 1932 and 1939, the RFC (and the PWA, which pitched in about 10% by value) lent over two score railroads a total of $800 million at below market interest rates. The program failed to achieve its stated goal of preventing railroad defaults and may have increased the likelihood of default by encouraging wage and investment bloat. Years later, then Assistant Attorney General Robert H. Jackson admitted that "when the Government through the RFC saved ... big business from going through the wringer it also saved many incompetent managements."[16] Ironically, though, RFC loans did not help overall railroad employment because they hurt competitors that did not receive any bailout funds.[17]

The railroad bailout was justified by the claim that banks wanted to charge troubled railroads 8 or 9% to refinance maturing bonds with 4% coupons, which obviously would have created considerable cash flow problems that cheaper refinancing would not. But railroads that had to borrow so dearly would have sold off assets, shuttered unprofitable lines, or found other ways to cut costs or increase revenues. Railroads that received cheap RFC financing remained afloat but bloated. Almost 98% of the loans had been repaid by 1939 but the sector remained overregulated and its competitors highly subsidized.[18] In the 1970s, it would face a crisis necessitating new bailouts.

Late in the Hoover administration, Congress enlarged the RFC's capital and remit, empowering it to make loans to state and municipal governments, public infrastructure projects, and new agricultural and rural lenders including the Federal Intermediate Credit Banks and Federal Home Loan Banks (FHLB).

After FDR took over, the RFC began buying special preferred shares in troubled banks, essentially partially nationalizing them. The shares paid guaranteed 6% per year dividends and were senior to common shares in the event of bankruptcy. The shares also enjoyed limited liability and voting rights that amounted to de facto control rights. Although the RFC could not lawfully control more than 49% of voting shares, it often owned the largest bloc of voting shares and hence it could choose most if not all members of the board.

FDR's RFC also became much more aggressive in its lending program, further extending maturities and relaxing collateral requirements so that it could rehabilitate troubled banks, finance the sale of the good assets of deeply troubled institutions, and make depositors whole while liquidating banks that were too far gone to save. By June 1935, the federal government owned a third of the nation's total banking capital. The next month, it stopped buying banks' preferred shares and many banks began to redeem the shares. Flush with cash, the RFC began lending to nonbank businesses, at first ostensibly to further aid recovery and then to aid military production during World War II. The Small Business Administration replaced it in 1953 after credible accusations of influence peddling were made against it. It was an ignominious ending for a regulator that, while far from optimal, was part of a series of reforms that eventually stopped the banking panics that ravished the money supply and disrupted the financial system during the Depression's first phase.[19]

HOLC Housing Bailout

As stock prices increased in the 1920s, so too did the price of real estate, by at least 45% on average across the country.[20] One careful study showed that real estate prices in Manhattan, which constituted 4% of the total U.S. real estate market by value, peaked in the third quarter of 1929 before plummeting by two-thirds by the end of 1932. Like stock prices, real estate prices thereafter rose modestly some years only to suffer setbacks the next. They did not return to earlier valuations during the 1930s, with the average price per square foot in 1939 estimated at $2.29 compared to $6.91 in 1929.[21] Real estate price movements in the rest of the country were broadly similar and were still almost 50% below their 1930 level a decade later.[22] In Chicago, for example, prices fell 50% between 1928 and 1932 and did not recover much for the rest of the decade.[23] Florida experienced a "spectacular" real estate bubble in the mid-1920s that in the words of political economist E.C. Harwood attracted speculators "as molasses draws flies."[24] Prices there did not recover until World War II.[25] By August 1931, a particular house in Youngstown, Ohio purchased for $11,000 in 1929 could not be sold for $4,400.[26]

Housing prices declined during the first phase of the Depression because the prices of everything else, except for labor, did as well due to the drop in the money supply discussed in Chapter 4. High real interest rates also meant low real present values. Matters did not improve much after 1933 because unemployed men couldn't qualify for mortgages and most banks and other mortgage lenders could not, or did not want to, lend anyway. Price decreases led to foreclosures because refinancing became more difficult and resale almost impossible. Most mortgages ran three to five years and were interest-only, with balloon payments for the principal due at the end. In good times, they were safely renewed when they fell due with a seemingly ample 50% loan-to-value on average. Over half of all homeowners, however, borrowed some of that 50% on second mortgages, often from individual lenders, and always at much higher rates of interest.[27]

As real estate prices plummeted during the Depression, lenders were understandably reluctant to lend on slim positive, no, or even negative equity due to increased economic and policy uncertainty, even after some economic indicators turned upward. In one documented case, a lender flat out stated of heavily indebted widower Joshua Clark, "We are not willing to carry him." Better to be safe than to be sorry, especially in an era when over half of all states passed mortgage payment moratoria.[28] Even when and where lenders could foreclose, one real estate investor explained, "they had to face the uncertainties of the rental market or book a loss." In addition, high real estate taxes killed many marginal deals.[29]

The mortgage market changed radically during the early years of the New Deal. Prior to its implementation, even in the early years of the Depression, individual lenders accounted for between a third and half of all mortgages by volume in rural states like South Dakota. Beginning in 1933, their share of the market plummeted to single digits. Life insurers, savings institutions, and commercial banks also almost completely stopped originating new mortgages, crowded out by federal land banks, the market share of which increased from single digits to 83% in 1934.[30]

In the nonfarm residential portion of the mortgage industry, savings and loans, insurers, mutual savings banks, commercial banks, and individuals also reduced new lending. Hoover created the FHLB system in 1932 to staunch lender losses caused by the flood of foreclosures, a quarter of a million nonfarm residential and commercial properties annually by 1932, caused by plummeting incomes, rents, and real estate prices.[31] In the worst years, 1931–1936, lenders foreclosed more than 10 in 1,000 mortgages.[32] The FHLB advanced funds to lenders, primarily building and loans (savings and loans) on the collateral of home mortgages under certain maturity and loan-to-value restrictions and with a super-lien, i.e., first call on any failed mortgage lender's remaining assets.[33]

As a further aid to both homeowners and lenders, FDR established the HOLC during his first one hundred days in office in 1933. HOLC sold bonds to financial institutions and the public to finance the purchase of just over one million distressed and even defaulted nonfarm mortgages from lenders. Instead of foreclosing, it then refinanced the mortgages on relatively easy terms, 5% interest on a 15- to up to a 25-year amortizing loan with 80% loan-to-value based on a generous valuation. (For example, an $8000 mortgage on a home valued at $10,000 but perhaps worth only $9000 given the depressed market conditions.) HOLC also paid any tax arrears and for necessary repairs, folding the extra costs into the mortgage.[34]

HOLC's efforts did not end the mortgage crisis as total foreclosures by all lenders remained in six figures through 1939. It also did not help real estate prices overall, but it did support the housing market in some smaller counties with populations under 50,000 and relatively little private financial intermediation. Specifically, it kept housing prices about 21% higher in those places than they would have otherwise fallen to. That benefit came at a cost, however. HOLC eventually foreclosed on 20% of its modified mortgages, at an average loss of 33% and total loan losses of $338 million.

Due to those foreclosures, HOLC came to own roughly 2% of America's housing stock. Like many other New Deal programs, HOLC avoided embarrassment and bankruptcy due to the outbreak of World War II and the postwar boom. It shut down after receiving the last payment on its last outstanding mortgage in 1951, having cost taxpayers an estimated $53 million, plus the implicit cost of the federal government's guarantee of its bonds. It was, therefore, neither "profitable," as sometimes later claimed, but neither was it the expensive boondoggle that some New Deal critics feared it would be.[35]

Like the RFC, then, HOLC helped some Americans at the direct expense of others. It also indirectly hurt Americans by creating or abetting an economically distorted regulatory environment replete with racist practices extended by the Federal Housing Administration (FHA) created by the National Housing Act of 1934.[36] To stimulate lending, the FHA insured mortgages that met its underwriting requirements. It made mortgage terms more uniform while essentially cartelizing mortgage origination. Also formed by the National Housing Act of 1934 was the Federal National Mortgage Association, which later morphed into the infamous "Fannie Mae" that played a leading role in the global financial crisis of 2008.

Another New Deal reform was the establishment of Federal Savings and Loan Associations (FSLA) to fill the savings and mortgage functions of traditional Building and Loans, many of which were moribund. By August 1939, 1392 federal savings and loan institutions boasted assets of $1.473 billion. Although successful at first, the FSLA system caused major financial problems in the 1980s, the Savings and Loan Crisis.[37]

Housing starts increased from their 1933 nadir, but it is difficult to parse the effect of the FHA or other New Deal housing bailouts from the improvement in general economic conditions between 1934 and 1937.[38] Even if they were entirely responsible for the uptick, the downstream costs to the American people and economy from the crises created by New Deal-era mortgage institutions rendered them a raw deal indeed.

Retarding Recovery with the Blue Eagle

The National Industrial Recovery Act (NIRA) formed the NRA and tasked it with increasing prices through the cartelization of various industries, from producers of cement to macaroni makers. That means it allowed businesses to collude to fix production shares, a practice anathema to America's open access market system and unwritten constitutional principles like the right to earn a living.[39] It also encouraged union formation, strikes, and high wages, and thus unemployment and production disruptions.[40] Despite the fact that industrial nominal wages rose by over 20% when they should have continued falling to match the lower price level, hundreds of strikes were in progress by mid-summer 1934.[41]

Despite its name, the NRA "retarded recovery," in the words of contemporary Brookings Institute economists and Ohio investors.[42] The program made no sense economically, except under some extreme assumptions about the elasticity of demand, especially during a depression.[43] More recently, scholars like Harold Cole, Lee Ohanian, and Jason E. Taylor count the NIRA and other New Deal cartelization policies as major inhibitors of recovery.[44] Many businesses supported the NIRA, though, because cartelization proved profitable for some.[45] Supporters of big government rejoiced at the formation of an agency that in its first year alone created more pages of regulations than the entire legislative output of the U.S. government since its founding.[46] Moreover, critics and skeptics were kept off the airwaves while FDR received carte blanche to pitch his policies during Fireside Chats and more formal addresses.[47]

Businesses that complied with the NRA codes (and its presidential precursor) were allowed to put the Blue Eagle emblem on their advertising and signage. Those who broke the agreements had to surrender their Blue Eagles or suffer fines and even imprisonment. Rather than submit to selling bread for six cents a loaf instead of the five cents it wanted to charge, one bakery, ironically called Liberty Baking, was run out of business in Washington, D.C. in November 1934. Yes, the U.S. federal government shut down a bakery for selling bread too *cheaply* during the Depression. In another case, the government was poised to put another business out of business, and thereby put men out of work entirely, because the owner paid willing workers less than the code wage.[48] By October 1933, violations started flooding courts even in smaller cities in the heartland.[49]

The idea was that cartelization and empowerment of labor would create the expectation of higher prices and wages, thus breaking expectations of the deflationary downward spiral that had come to dominate thinking by 1933. Virtually all economists concede that the policy, which lasted almost two full years before being killed by the Supreme Court, was daft. Some, though, have supported it in the topsy-turvy world of the Depression, as an example of a "second best" policy.[50] Such a view might be justifiable theoretically, but the economic reality proved far different, and far more complex than most realize because the codes worked out for each industry varied greatly in terms of their length, detail, and enforcement.

Because FDR believed in the so-called under-consumption view of the Depression, his administration thought that higher nominal prices would encourage higher nominal wages, leaving workers with more money with which to buy things. Increased aggregate demand would end the Depression. All that the NRA did, though, was to encourage a weird form of central planning, like that begun under Hoover and presaged by the Great War's War Industries Board.[51]

What the New Dealers missed was that to maintain employment levels, nominal wages had to *fall*, not increase. When wages are forced higher by policies, like the NIRA and minimum wage laws, employers have incentives to automate. Those who cannot automate can afford to retain only the most productive workers, those who produce more than they take home in wages and fringe benefits.[52] Employers seek to discover the marginal worker, the one whose value added matches his or her total compensation, and to let go of all their less efficient workers while retaining their more efficient workers. In a free market, though, less efficient workers can retain their jobs by accepting lower pay, thus rendering them profitable to keep employed. If regulations artificially force wages up, the formerly marginal worker becomes one of the less efficient workers and, lawfully unable to negotiate a lower wage, becomes a net cost to the employer and hence expendable. In other words, although the NRA's industrial cartelization helped some workers, it did so at the expense of others, the ones forced out of work and into bread lines.

To reduce the negative effect of higher hourly wages on employment, Hoover and Democrat Senator Hugo Lafayette Black of Alabama pushed for reducing the work week. The same pay for fewer hours of work, though, was simply an increase in hourly compensation, not a way of "sharing" work because employers still had an incentive to shed their least efficient workers. The only upside of artificially high real wages was that it induced companies to invest in new technology, especially technologies associated with mass production, which some managed to do despite financial constraints.[53]

One would think that a program like NIRA that kept unemployment high, the major economic problem after 1933, would have failed to pass into law. In many industries, though, larger companies wanted cartelization because it protected them from competition from smaller upstarts. Larger companies could also more easily absorb the administrative costs of the Blue Eagle.[54] That is why in 1931, Gerard Swope, President of General Electric, proposed an eponymous plan that would have allowed industry trade associations to fix market shares and enforce them. Hoover swatted down the Swope plan, but FDR fell under the spell of Rexford Tugwell, whose book *The Industrial Discipline and the Governmental Arts* offered a blueprint for relaxing antitrust laws, purportedly to allow for the more efficient coordination of resources. Tugwell was a planner through and through who threw around oxymorons like "intelligent state control."[55]

With support from New Dealer "Baptists" and big business "bootleggers," the NIRA easily passed both houses of Congress and became law. Details proved difficult to negotiate in many industries, however, so FDR in July 1933 implemented the President's Reemployment Agreement as a stopgap. The agreement cajoled employers into promising to reduce the average workweek and to raise hourly wage rates. The first indeed worked to increase employment by inducing employers to hire two part-timers instead of one full-time worker putting in 45, 50, or more hours per week. Such work sharing allowed almost 2.5 million additional Americans to draw paychecks, albeit at the expense of the formerly full-time workers who lost hours. The higher hourly wage rates, though, spelled fewer jobs overall, reducing the agreement's overall effect to just 1.34 million jobs on net.[56] But even that exaggerates its effect because employers could have split jobs on their own if they believed it would benefit their respective bottom lines.

Like the NRA, the presidential agreement allowed companies to credibly signal to consumers that they were compliant with FDR's diktat by using Blue Eagle insignia and emblems. They lost the right to display the Blue Eagle if they reneged or did not sign on to their industry's NRA code once adopted. Ford Motor Company refused to sign; Henry Ford reportedly referred to the Blue Eagle as "that Roosevelt Buzzard."[57] Nevertheless, his company maintained its market share, perhaps because consumers knew that it exceeded the automobile industry NRA guidelines, but more likely because his cars were often the best available value. Many less iconic or less competitive businesses, though, felt as though they had to sign on, just as many would sign on to scientifically dubious policies during the Covid pandemic of 2020–22, or lose market share.

The presidential agreement and the NRA restricted employment to those 16 years and older and set maximum workweeks and minimum wages, with variations across industries, regions, and city size. As noted, they also encouraged cartelization, which reduced output and hence recovery, creating what economists call a negative supply shock that sent prices higher, as intended, but quantities consumed lower.[58]

FDR made Hugh "Iron Pants" Johnson, one of a surprising number of Mussolini admirers in the U.S. government,[59] the main man when it came to forcing the Blue Eagle on companies that saw it more as a Red Soviet duck. Johnson used his bully pulpit as head of the NRA to threaten noncompliant companies with boycotts and even a literal "punch in the nose." He sent Jacob Maged to jail for pressing a suit for 35 cents instead of the 40 cents specified in the Tailor's Code.

The presidential agreement and NRA certainly did raise hourly wages, by 25 to almost 43% in 13 major industries, but most of that gain was offset by fewer hours of work. Output increased in some industries, primarily due to Blue Eagle advertising. In others, output fell due to the collusion encouraged by cartelization. Goods prices increased but stopped rising after about four months. That was all a small benefit compared to the high costs of regulatory compliance. Many smaller businesses violated the minimum wage and maximum hours codes, which cost them their Blue Eagles. An outsized number of violations occurred in New York City, ostensibly due to the lower monitoring costs there.

Underground markets for less expensive goods soon sprang up, forcing Johnson and other bureaucrats into calling the police on hardworking Americans.[60] So-called "hot oil" out of Texas was particularly worrisome, as were cheap chickens.[61] All had to be suppressed. No wonder Albert Jay Nock called the New Deal "a nation-wide, State-managed mobilization of inane buffoonery and aimless commotion."[62] The absurdity of fining bakers and jailing tailors for charging too little was just what FDR's New Deal needed to re-educate Americans to follow orders instead of their common sense.

Support for the NIRA peaked in September and October of 1933 but declined in November and December because the economy headed downward once again, in large measure due to the Blue Eagle.[63] Even after SCOTUS ruled the codes unconstitutional in the *Schechter* decision, many companies continued to follow them. Moreover, many components of the NIRA made comebacks in other guises, like the National Labor Relations Act (NLRA) and the Fair Labor Standards Act of 1938, which mandated a $0.40 per hour federal minimum wage, a 40-hour work-week, and a ban on 16-year-olds working during school hours. Even cartelization continued in industries that could self-enforce price and quota agreements. For the most part, however, the period of relative economic freedom between the Schechter decision and the implementation of the NLRA witnessed the best economic performance of the entire 1930s because output rose, as did employment and hours worked.[64]

Bailing Dust from the Bowl

Farmers, ranchers, and other agriculturalists were hit by all the same problems as other Americans: less demand for their labor and goods, mortgage refinancing difficulties, and a dearth of cash and credit. Mother Nature whacked many of them with another, a major, multi-year drought that decimated their topsoil, primarily through wind erosion. Much of it landed on other people's property but only after losing most of its agricultural value. Longstanding government policies were complicit, by encouraging agricultural overproduction in general and by encouraging westward expansion of small farms into the arid west, but ultimately less important than the natural hydrological cycle.[65]

Although the Dust Bowl devastated some farms and ranches, it was not as widespread, long-lived, unusual, or important as many believe. A retrospective report on ranch profitability in western South Dakota during the Depression published in 1941 mentioned cyclical waterfall variations but stressed business factors, like achieving minimum efficient scale and minimizing losses, as the key to financial success. Even during the driest and wettest years, ranch income varied significantly with the quality of management and improvements, like stock ponds and fodder sheds.[66]

The Dust Bowl mostly affected the Great Plains but not all of it equally. Some places with more rain or lucky geography suffered not at all while other places nearby were severely negatively impacted.[67] Much of Oklahoma, for example, was spared but it was said that in one day three of its western counties lost 50 million tons of topsoil.[68]

Detailed county-level maps created by the Soil Conservation Service are now available digitally.[69] They show, among other things, that much of what people think they know about the Dust Bowl reflects New Deal propaganda—or "communication artistry"[70] as defenders call it—told through song, fiction, and dramatic photographs, sometimes staged ones. In sum, agricultural activities per se did not cause dust storms, droughts did. The storms in the 1930s were unfortunate but not a crisis, but that did not prevent policymakers and journalists from turning them into one.[71]

In 1932, the National Land-Use Planning Committee responded to arid conditions in the west by suggesting that the government return 6.5 million acres to grassland and relocate the agriculturalists trying to make a living on them.[72] The plan died at the time but it was even considered as a tacit admission that the federal government's nineteenth-century bison, Indian, and homesteading policies had been failures.

FDR, however, would implement a similar policy. Even before becoming president, FDR promised to lock farm leaders in a room "and tell them not to come out until they have agreed on a plan."[73] But what he really wanted was to impose programs on the farmers, and did so, forcing or cajoling many to give up their land and lifestyles.[74] As in other economic sectors, New Dealers sought to swamp rural agricultural areas with change, most of it of dubious value.[75] All of the programs were designed, in one way or another, to limit competition in favor of central planning in the agricultural sector and thereby to destroy farmer autonomy.[76]

New Dealers first disastrously tried to raise farm prices by killing livestock, including piglets and baby chicks, plowing up planted crops, and allowing fruit to rot on the tree while millions of Americans went hungry.[77] Economist Irving Fisher beseeched FDR to simply increase the money supply instead of destroying "food and clothing when many are starving and half naked!"[78] The common man also had difficulty understanding "how the destruction of basic foods supplies can bring back prosperity when so many people are hungry." That is because it couldn't and didn't.[79]

Later, New Dealers paid farmers not to grow certain crops or raise certain livestock in the first place.[80] That was a shade better than wasting resources but not by much because the least productive agriculturalists were the ones most eager to sign up and to take their least productive land out of cultivation. Many farmers then worked their remaining land more intensively, by applying fertilizer for example.[81] Little wonder that agricultural prices remained well below the level of August 1929, regardless of the dollars and policies thrown at what was misleadingly called the "farm problem."[82]

Were that not enough, the subsidy programs were unnecessary because farmers and ranchers who earned negative returns per acre, or per animal, cut back production if for no other reason than they could not afford to plant or raise as much as previously.[83] They could also use excess corn for fuel and surplus wheat and other grains to feed livestock.[84] Moreover, food for human consumption could be imported, and much was. That directly kept domestic prices down and slowed money growth because gold had to be exported given the low state of U.S. exports due to the retaliatory tariffs other countries put in place following Smoot-Hawley.[85]

Such seemingly irrational programs were rational, though, because the real goal was to implement the New Deal rather than to end the Depression or to help agriculturalists. President Coolidge vetoed wheat and cotton price-fixing bills in 1927 and 1928 because he "knew the difference between common sense and nonsense."[86] The bills, called McNary-Haugen after their sponsors, tried to raise the prices of farm produce by requiring the government to buy large quantities of the commodities at above market prices and then sell it overseas at a loss to taxpayers.

Despite the obvious economic irrationality of the idea, New Dealers revived the idea in a farm subsidy program that provided farmers with so-called "nonrecourse loans." Farmers only had to repay loans collateralized with grain or other agricultural goods if the collateral's market price exceeded a price determined by a government bureaucrat. If it didn't, the government forgave the difference between the sum due on the loan and the sum the collateral sold for at market, essentially creating a price floor. By 1934, fully two-thirds of farm income came from the government, i.e., taxpayers, through such nonrecourse loans and other transfer payments.[87]

In his movie *The Plow That Broke the Plains*, Pare Lorentz suggested that the New Deal could end the Dust Bowl, but his stories were as artificial as his staged image of a cow skull on parched earth. The Dust Bowl forced more than a million farmers off parched farms in the Central Plains. Many moved to California, where the agricultural sector was doing relatively well, as was the banking sector.[88] Most moved of their own accord, but in 1934 some lucky ones received a taxpayer subsidy when the Land Utilization Program bought 11 million acres of privately owned submarginal land and relocated the residents. The program aided the residents but not the environment as most of the land had remained grassland and hence did not need natural restoration. Two years later, New Dealers formed the "Great Plains Committee," but its basic premise proved flawed. Agricultural activity had not made the Badlands of the Dakotas worse, as federal land grabbers claimed, because landowners had strong incentives to engage in conservation.[89]

With the passage of the Farm Credit Act in June 1933, New Dealers built upon the federal farm credit infrastructure created by President Wilson in the 1916 Farm Loan Act and extended by William G. Harding in 1923.[90] Most of the joint stock mortgage lenders formed under those acts failed early in the Depression. The institutions established after 1923 to provide the intermediate-term loans that many farmers needed from season to season also fared badly, largely because the entire system was politicized and forced into operation from the top. The Farm Credit Act established a Farm Credit Administration (FCA) and 12 Production Credit Corporations that capitalized, supervised, and trained the employees of local Production Credit Associations. The act also established 12 district Banks for Cooperatives headed by a Central Bank for Cooperatives. By April 1934, more than 600 Production Credit Associations had formed in the 48 states and Puerto Rico.[91]

The FCA also tried to revivify other components of the complex system, many of which were moribund. Federal Land Banks, for example, remained open but lent little. Federal Intermediate Credit Banks were in good shape financially but only because few retail agricultural lenders wanted to borrow from them. The RFC also made agricultural loans, especially to ranchers, through 12 regional credit corporations. Congress also authorized the Secretary of Agriculture to make emergency seed loans. In May 1933, Congress passed the Emergency Farm Mortgage Act, which provided resources, and the government's credit, to the Federal Land Banks so they could refinance farm mortgages at 4.5%. When news of the act hit the airwaves, some 43,000 distressed farmers contacted the FCA seeking aid.

Early in 1934, Congress established the Farm Mortgage Corporation (FFMC) to buy the bonds of Federal Land Banks, thus allowing them to continue refinancing operations, to make new loans, and to buy privately held mortgages, generally at a 30% discount or "haircut." By the end of 1935, Federal Land Banks and the FFMC owned 48% of farm mortgage debt nationally in the process of saving tens of thousands of farms from foreclosure and commercial banks, insurers, and other mortgage lenders from defaults and write downs.[92]

Despite all that aid, many farmers still struggled to make payments. Farm foreclosures topped out at 38.8 per 1,000 in 1933 but by 1937 it was down to only 18.1, barely below the 18.7 foreclosed in 1931, and well above peak nonfarm foreclosure rates.[93] That, even though the Federal Land Banks were slow to foreclose and often lengthened the mortgage amortization period to lower annual payments. Nevertheless, by 1939 the Federal Land Banks had acquired 44,000 farms through foreclosure and voluntary deeds. Until the war drove up prices, some Federal Land Bank officers, like the vice president of the Omaha Federal Land Bank, spent much of their time "begging member-borrowers to stay on their farms rather than hand over the deed and leave their farms."[94]

In 1938, federal policymakers including H.R. Tolley, A.G. Black, and Henry A. Wallace decided that farmers needed "all-risk" crop insurance, a product that overregulated private insurance companies could not profitably provide.[95] FDR's men saw the program as a way to win votes in rural areas, which had supported Republican Alf Landon in the 1936 presidential election. If they could not win the votes of the farmers themselves, they could at least win over farmers' bankers and other creditors. So they created a farm insurance program that served more like a social safety net than as a bona fide insurance policy. Unlike Social Security, however, coverage remained voluntary.

Because farmers could opt in or out of the program, adverse selection and moral hazard ran high. In other words, the farmers most likely to suffer crop losses signed up and once they did they had little incentive to mitigate risks. Smarter than the bureaucrats running the Federal Crop Insurance Corporation (FCIC), most farmers stayed away from the government's crop insurance entirely. Although federal crop insurance subsidized the riskiest, most marginal farmers, the ones that should have been allowed to exit for greener pastures in other industries, FDR's men pushed the program. To increase signups, they equated government crop insurance with freedom itself. "Be free … be sure … Insure!" read its 1942 propaganda pamphlet on the subject. Most farmers knew, however, that "freedom from worry" was a sales gimmick that would limit their political freedom. After that word chicanery failed to win over enough farmers to allow FCIC to break even, regulators forced financial institutions to make crop insurance a precondition for agricultural credit, yet another costly and unnecessary New Deal regulation.[96]

Notes

1. Harry L. Hopkins, "The Essence of Democracy," The Works Program, Works Progress Administration, (30 Aug. 1938), 6, FRASER.
2. Daniel J. Gifford, "The New Deal Regulatory Model: A History of Criticism and Refinements," *Minnesota Law Review* 68 (1983), 302–3.
3. Harvey Klehr, *The Heyday of American Communism: The Depression Decade* (New York: Basic Books, Inc., 1984), xi.
4. David M. Kennedy, "What the New Deal Did," *Political Science Quarterly* 124, 2 (Summer 2009), 256.

5. Gifford, "New Deal Regulatory Model," 303–4.
6. Naomi Oreskes and Erik M. Conway, *The Big Myth: How American Business Taught Us to Loathe Government and Love the Free Market* (New York: Bloomsbury Publishing, 2023), 315–25.
7. Gifford, "New Deal Regulatory Model," 304–5.
8. David T. Beito, *The New Deal's War on the Bill of Rights: The Untold Story of FDR's Concentration Camps, Censorship, and Mass Surveillance* (Oakland: Independent Institute, 2023), 6.
9. James M. Landis, *The Administrative Process* (New Haven: Yale University Press, 1938).
10. Robert E. Wright, ed. *Bailouts: Public Money, Private Profit* (New York: Columbia University Press, 2010).
11. Robert E. Wright, "Government Bailouts," in Robert Whaples and Randall Parker eds., *Handbook of Major Events in Economic History* (New York: Routledge, 2013): 415–27; Bill White, *America's Fiscal Constitution: Its Triumph and Collapse* (New York: PublicAffairs, 2014), 187; Burton Folsom, Jr. *New Deal or Raw Deal? How FDR's Economic Legacy Has Damaged America* (New York: Simon & Schuster, 2008), 77.
12. Garet Garrett, *The People's Pottage* (Caldwell, ID: Caxton Printers, 1953), 37–38, 72.
13. Joseph R. Mason, "The Evolution of the Reconstruction Finance Corporation as a Lender of Last Resort in the Great Depression," in Wright, ed. *Bailouts*, 83; Jim Powell, *FDR's Folly: How Roosevelt and His New Deal Prolonged the Great Depression* (New York: Crown Forum, 2003), 47–48.
14. Mason, "Evolution," in Wright, ed. *Bailouts*, 82–86.
15. Jim F. Couch and William F. Shughart, *The Political Economy of the New Deal* (Northampton, MA: Edward Elgar, 1998), 84.
16. As quoted in Garet Garrett, "For Five Years, There Has Been No American System," in Amity Shlaes, ed. *New Deal Rebels* (Great Barrington, Mass.: American Institute for Economic Research, 2023), 229.
17. Lydon Moore and Gertjan Verdickt, "Railroad Bailouts in the Great Depression," Working Paper, 2022.
18. Moore and Verdickt, "Railroad Bailouts."
19. Mason, "Evolution," in Wright, ed. *Bailouts*, 86–97.
20. Price Fishback, Alfonso Lagunes, William Horrace, Shawn Kantor and Jaret Treber, "The Influence of the Home Owners' Loan

Corporation on Housing Markets During the 1930s," NBER Working Paper Series 15824 (March 2010), 5; James Ledbetter and Daniel B. Roth, eds., *The Great Depression: A Diary by Benjamin Roth* (New York: Public Affairs, 2009), 4.
21. Tom Nicholas and Anna Scherbina, "Real Estate Prices During the Roaring Twenties and the Great Depression," *Real Estate Economics* 41, 2 (2013): 278–309.
22. Fishback, Lagunes, Horrace, Kantor, and Treber, "Influence," 6.
23. Homer Hoyt, *One Hundred Years of Land Values in Chicago: The Relationship of the Growth of Chicago to the Rise of Its Land Values, 1830–1933* (Chicago: University of Chicago Press, 1933).
24. E.C. Harwood, "Stock Speculation Versus Florida Memories," (May 1928), Box 1, E.C. Harwood Archives, AIER, Great Barrington, Mass.
25. Kenneth Ballinger, *Miami Millions: The Dance of the Dollars in the Great Florida Land Boom of 1925* (Miami, Fl.: Franklin Press, 1936), 5; Ledbetter and Roth, eds., *Great Depression*, 4, 63; William Frazer and John J. Guthrie, Jr., *The Florida Land Boom: Speculation, Money, and the Banks* (Westport, Conn.: Quorum Books, 1995), xiii.
26. Ledbetter and Roth, eds., *Great Depression*, 11.
27. Price Fishback, Jonathan Rose, and Kenneth Snowden, *Well Worth Saving: How the New Deal Safeguarded Home Ownership* (Chicago: University of Chicago Press, 2013), 12–16.
28. Fishback, Rose, and Snowden, *Well Worth Saving*, xi, 1–3, 17–19, 23.
29. Ledbetter and Roth, eds., *Great Depression*, 9, 15, 159.
30. South Dakota State Planning Board, *Mortgage Status of Farm Land in South Dakota* (1938), 9–10.
31. Fishback, Rose, and Snowden, *Well Worth Saving*, 11, 22.
32. Natalie Leonard, "United States: Federal Home Loan Bank Advances, 1932–1941," *Journal of Financial Crises* 4, 2 (2022), 1182–83.
33. Powell, *FDR's Folly*, 45–46.
34. Couch and Shughart, *Political Economy*, 84–85; Fishback, Rose, and Snowden, *Well Worth Saving*, 3–4.
35. Nicholas and Scherbina, "Real Estate Prices"; Fishback, Rose, and Snowden, *Well Worth Saving*, 7–8, 107–11, 113–19, 128.

36. Kristen B. Crossney and David W. Bartelt, "The Legacy of the Home Owners' Loan Corporation," *Housing Policy Debate* 16, 3/4 (2005): 547–74.
37. Couch and Shughart, *Political Economy*, 85–87.
38. Gail Radford, "The Federal Government and Housing During the Great Depression," in John F. Bauman, Roger Biles, and Kristin M. Szylvian, eds. *From Tenements to the Taylor Homes: In Search of an Urban Housing Policy in Twentieth Century America* (University Park: Pennsylvania State University Press, 2000), 107–8.
39. Jason E. Taylor, *Deconstructing the Monolith: The Microeconomics of the National Industrial Recovery Act* (Chicago: University of Chicago Press, 2019).
40. Ledbetter and Roth, eds., *Great Depression*, 129–33, 155–56.
41. Louis Adamic, *Dynamite: The Story of Class Violence in America*, rev. ed. (1934) (Oakland: AK Press 2008), 317; Richard K. Vedder and Lowell E. Gallaway, *Out of Work: Unemployment and Government in Twentieth-Century America*, updated ed. (New York: New York University Press, 1997), 138–42.
42. Powell, *FDR's Folly*, 127; Ledbetter and Roth, eds., *Great Depression*, 156.
43. Gifford, "New Deal Regulatory Model," 301; Powell, *FDR's Folly*, 119–20.
44. Harold L. Cole and Lee E. Ohanian, "The Great Depression in the United States from a Neoclassical Perspective," *Federal Reserve Bank of Minneapolis Quarterly Review* (Winter 1999), 2–24; Harold L. Cole and Lee E. Ohanian, "New Deal Policies and the Persistence of the Great Depression: A General Equilibrium Analysis," *Journal of Political Economy* 112, 4 (August 2004): 779–816.
45. Colin Gordon, "Rethinking the New Deal," *Columbia Law Review* 98, 8 (Dec. 1998): 2,038.
46. Amity Shlaes, *The Forgotten Man: A New History of the Great Depression* (New York: HarperCollins, 2007), 202.
47. Beito, *New Deal's War*, 113.
48. Taylor, *Deconstructing the Monolith*, 1–3.
49. Ledbetter and Roth, eds., *Great Depression*, 135.
50. Gauti B. Eggertsson, "Was the New Deal Contractionary," *American Economic Review* 102 (2012): 524–55.
51. Taylor, *Deconstructing the Monolith*, 5–6, passim.

52. David E. Bernstein, *Only One Place of Redress: African Americans, Labor Regulations, and the Courts from Reconstruction to the New Deal* (Durham: Duke University Press, 2001), 6–7, 102.
53. Robert A. Margo, "Employment and Unemployment in the 1930s," *Journal of Economic Perspectives* 7, 2 (Spring 1993): 44–50.
54. Lawrence W. Reed, *Great Myths of the Great Depression* (Mackinac Center for Public Policy and the Foundation for Economic Education, 2011), 11.
55. Folsom, *New Deal?*, 69.
56. Jason E. Taylor, "Work-sharing During the Great Depression: Did the 'President's Reemployment Agreement' Promote Reemployment?" *Economica* 78, 309 (Jan. 2011): 133–58.
57. Powell, *FDR's Folly*, 120, 126.
58. Taylor, "Work-sharing?"
59. David F. Schmitz, *The United States and Fascist Italy, 1922–1940* (Chapel Hill: University of North Carolina Press, 1988); Powell, *FDR's Folly*, 76–77; John P. Diggins, "Flirtation with Fascism: American Pragmatic Liberals and Mussolini's Italy," *American History Review* 71, 2 (Jan. 1966): 487–506.
60. Reed, *Great Myths*, 12.
61. Shlaes, *Forgotten Man*, 203.
62. Reed, *Great Myths*, 12.
63. Jason E. Taylor and Todd C. Neumann, "Recovery Spring, Faltering Fall: March to November 1933," *Explorations in Economic History* 61 (July 2016): 54–67.
64. Jason E. Taylor and Todd C. Neumann, "The Effect of Institutional Regime Change Within the New Deal on Industrial Output and Labor Markets," *Explorations in Economic History* 50 (2013): 582–98.
65. Amity Shlaes, *Great Society: A New History* (New York: HarperCollins, 2019), 94.
66. Aaron G. Nelson and Gerald E. Korzan, *Profits and Losses in Ranching, Western South Dakota, 1931–1940 Bulletin 352* (Brookings, S.D.: South Dakota State College, 1941).
67. Theresa A. Glanz, "Federal Land-Use Policy and Resettlement in the Great Plains: An Experiment in Community Development During the New Deal Years, 1933–1941," (Ph.D. Diss., University of Nebraska, 2020), 37.

68. John Gunther, *Inside U.S.A.* (New York: Harper & Brothers, 1947), 879.
69. Geoff Cunfer, "The Southern Great Plains Wind Erosion Maps of 1936–1937," *Agricultural History* 85, 4 (Fall 2011): 540–59.
70. Betty Houchin Winfield, *FDR and the News Media* (New York: Columbia University Press, 1994), xi.
71. Geoff Cunfer, "Scaling the Dust Bowl," in Anne Kelly Knowles, ed. *Placing History: How Maps, Spatial Data, and GIS are Changing Historical Scholarship* (Redlands, CA: ESRI Press, 2008), 95–121.
72. Glanz, "Federal Land-Use Policy," 41.
73. As quoted in H. W. Brands, *A Traitor to His Class: The Privileged Life and Radical Presidency of Franklin Delano Roosevelt* (New York: Anchor Books, 2008), 325.
74. Karl Hess, *Visions Upon the Land: Man and Nature on the Western Range* (Washington, DC: Island Press, 1992), 87–88.
75. Glanz, "Federal Land-Use Policy," 39.
76. Brands, *Traitor to His Class*, 324–26.
77. Powell, *FDR's Folly*, 134.
78. Shlaes, *Forgotten Man*, 167.
79. Ledbetter and Roth, eds., *Great Depression*, 129.
80. Brands, *Traitor to His Class*, 329.
81. Folsom, *New Deal?*, 66.
82. Theodore Saloutos, "New Deal Agricultural Policy: An Evaluation," *Journal of American History* 61, 2 (Sept. 1974), 397–98.
83. See, for example, the data in Tables 1–5 in Nelson and Korzan, *Profits and Losses*, 25–26; James P. Warburg, *Hell Bent for Election* (New York: Doubleday, Doran & Company, 1935), 52.
84. Ledbetter and Roth, eds., *Great Depression*, 81.
85. Folsom, *New Deal?*, 66–67.
86. Lawrence W. Reed, "What Calvin Coolidge's 'Common Sense' Vetoes of Two Farm Bills Can Teach about Price Controls," *FEE* (23 Sept. 2022): https://fee.org/articles/what-calvin-coolidge-s-common-sense-vetoes-of-two-farm-bills-can-teach-about-price-controls/.
87. Gary Libecap, "The Great Depression and the Regulating State: Federal Government of Agriculture, 1884–1970," in Michael D. Bordo, Claudia Goldin, and Eugene N. White, eds. *The Defining Moment: The Great Depression and the American Economy in the*

Twentieth Century (Chicago: University of Chicago Press, 1998), 189, 195.

88. Alan Brinkley, *Culture and Politics in the Great Depression* (Waco: Baylor University Press, 1998), 17, 33–34.
89. Glanz, "Federal Land-Use Policy", 38, 41–42.
90. Couch and Shughart, *Political Economy*, 85.
91. W. Gifford Hoag, *The Farm Credit System: A History of Financial Self-Help* (Danville, Ill.: Interstate Printers & Publishers, Inc., 1976), 237–38; W.N. Stokes, Jr. *Credit to Farmers: The Story of Federal Intermediate Credit Banks and Production Credit Associations* (Washington, DC: Farm Credit Administration, 1973), 2.
92. Hoag, *Farm Credit*, 231–37.
93. Powell, *FDR's Folly*, 138.
94. Hoag, *Farm Credit*, 246–47.
95. Robert E. Wright, "Reinsurance in America: Regulatory Regimes and Markets," in Leonardo de las Cagigas and Andre Straus, eds. *Role of Reinsurance in the World* (Cham, Switz.: Palgrave, 2021), 23–43.
96. Shane Hamilton, "Crop Insurance and the New Deal Roots of Agricultural Financialization in the United States," *Enterprise & Society* 21, 3 (Sept. 2020): 648–80.

CHAPTER 6

Raw Alphabet Soup Deal

Historian Burton Folsom was on to something when he asked if the New Deal was really a Raw Deal. It was, because its goal was not to end the toxic stew of recession, deflation, and unemployment, for which getting the money supply back to its trend growth line would have sufficed. Instead, FDR sought to reformulate the role of the federal government in the lives of individual Americans and to secure re-election in the process. The New Deal programs described in Chapters 4 and 5 could perhaps be explained away as mistakes made by economically challenged policymakers desperate to aid the American people in unprecedented times. Everyone from bankers to borrowers and agriculturalists to the unemployed received aid, some of it substantial, if poorly conceived and delivered. But the programs described in this chapter were unmistakably not mistakes. For the first time in American history, the federal government began extending "entitlements," in the form of cash or overpaid employment, to people who had not performed specific services for said government. Most of the programs, though, aggrandized Washington by crowding out nonprofits and state and local governments with no clear net benefit for Americans.[1]

Unsatisfied with their other policy failures, New Dealers pushed for an alphabet soup of three-letter agencies, several of the most egregious of which are described in this chapter. As with the reforms and programs of the First Hundred Days and the First New Deal, the programs of the

R. E. Wright, *FDR's Long New Deal*,
https://doi.org/10.1007/978-3-031-74141-8_6

Second New Deal were not entirely bad but not one of them passed a basic cost–benefit test then, or now, and some even exacerbated unemployment and other aspects of the Depression. They passed into law, as Public Choice Theory predicts, in part because their effects could be hidden and in part because they enticed key constituencies to join, or stay loyal to, the Democratic Party, especially the Progressive wing of it.

Social Over Private Security

Some scholars say that radical plans like that of Francis E. Townsend forced FDR to accept the formation of Social Security as a lesser evil.[2] Townsend's Plan did gain rapidly in popularity, in part due to its unique structure, which created significant monetary incentives to form new chapters, in part due to its slick marketing efforts, and partly because of its generous terms.[3] The initial Plan promised to pay $200 a month to every unemployed, un-incarcerated American aged 60 or more on the condition that they spend it all before their next check arrived. A new 2% tax on all transactions allegedly would have funded it. Some 25 million Americans supported the Plan.[4]

The popularity of a big special interest giveaway proposal does not explain why FDR opted for a permanent program instead of short-term relief. Even if FDR believed, as Edith Abbott did, that "other depressions will come, with new waves of unemployment and destitution,"[5] he could have created a program that activated only in dire times. Moreover, Townsend's Plan survived passage of the Social Security Act (SSA), only to be killed off by the war, postwar economic prosperity, and the reforms made to the old-age pension program in 1939.[6]

FDR correctly predicted that due to the payroll taxes funding the program, along with lies about it being insurance or an investment account, Social Security would become politically untouchable.[7] He also believed, following the dictum of nineteenth-century German chancellor Otto von Bismarck, that a government-provided old-age pension program made citizens less radical because it gave them something to look forward to and a vested interest in the success of the state.[8]

Perhaps more than any other New Deal policy, then, Social Security revealed FDR's underlying agenda. Townsend's Plan, which would have amounted to a geriatric universal basic income (UBI),[9] was unacceptable to New Dealers because it would have indiscriminately given all the elderly, regardless of their color, gender, or political affiliation, significant economic and political power.[10]

The Social Security Act became law in August 1935. In addition to "old-age insurance," the act also created means-tested welfare programs for the aged, the blind, the unemployed, and families with dependent children.[11] It also contained minor provisions for vocational rehabilitation and healthcare for mothers and children.[12] (Disability insurance came in the 1950s.[13]) Many of Social Security's programs have changed, some quite radically since the Act's passage. The creation of a national welfare state was disastrous, especially for people of color, a subject taken up in Chapter 11. The focus here is on the life annuity and survivorship program.[14]

The need to make changes to the original Social Security system was perceived almost immediately. Huey Long helped to slow the program's launch by filibustering funding for the Social Security Administration in the Senate. A torrent of criticism and legal challenges followed but Justice Harlan Stone tipped Frances Perkins that "you can do anything under the taxing power."[15] That was incorrect under classical liberal ideas of the nation's written and unwritten constitutions but helped the Act to pass constitutional muster in 1937 in a High Court by then firmly controlled by New Dealers.

In 1939, the government amended the Social Security Act so that the retirement portion became a "pay-as-you-go" redistribution program instead of the original "full reserve" public retirement pension, which Keynesians despised.[16] The reformed law allowed the first annuity payments to be made the following year and at a higher level than originally stipulated. It also changed the benefit formula from one based on lifetime cumulative earnings to one based on average monthly earnings. It increased payments to spouses and added child survivor benefits, too, but cut the lump sum payment down to a paltry funeral expense allowance.[17] Increases in the payroll tax were also postponed. Overall, the idea was to redistribute more wealth, but devils lurked in the demographic details.[18] After additional changes later, including forcing new groups of workers into it to help fund it, Social Security little resembled its original form, prompting two scholars of the program to employ the metaphor about boiling a frog slowly by degrees.[19]

None of the reforms, though, changed the program's problematic premise. In the 1936 presidential campaign, Republican presidential candidate Alf Landon called Social Security a "fraud on the working man.

The saving it forces on our workers is a cruel hoax."[20] Indeed, one big problem with Social Security was that by forcing Americans to contribute to a quasi-pyramid scheme, decisions about investment and work that should be personal ones under America's unwritten economic constitution became politicized, a plaything for policy pundits to ponder and pontificate about.[21] But the logic of the New Deal demanded that the paternalist state must strike down the fraternal order that had preceded it.[22]

Although the payroll taxes were low at first, they grew over time, until most workers paid more in Social Security than in income taxes. The payroll taxes, which are regressive and in most instances de facto entirely paid by workers, are unavailable for investment, forcing many people to become entirely dependent on the government for their retirement income.[23] Even pro-social insurance researchers understood that workers, even in good years, were not able to save much, if at all, after paying their Social Security taxes.[24]

FDR, much as he did with farmers, essentially paid older workers not to work. In line with the radical agenda of the New Deal, Social Security also created an expectation of retirement upon achievement of a given age, a novel concept in America. Since the nation's formation, some Americans have "retired" due to superannuation or disability or because they had saved sufficient assets to eliminate the need to work. As incomes increased, labor force participation at older ages declined. But workers had always made the choice, in conjunction with employers, about how much to work, and at what tasks.[25] Even mandatory company pensions had not stopped older Americans from taking other work if they saw fit and could find it. Social Security, by contrast, provided strong incentives to stop working entirely once a certain age had been achieved, regardless of the individual's ability and willingness to continue working.[26]

Social Security also distorted investment decisions by forcing Americans, through the Social Security payroll tax, the nation's first mass tax on income,[27] to buy the government's life annuity instead of private annuities, life insurance, real estate, business equity, or financial securities. Americans had always owned corporate stocks and corporate and government bonds in greater numbers than typically assumed but ownership levels increased dramatically during the Liberty Bonds drives of the Great War and in the Roaring Twenties.[28] Magazines ran stories about how members of various occupations could invest to best build future income.[29]

Apologists for social insurance tend to claim that by the 1930s such investments had become much less common than previously and that was certainly true in the case of business equity.[30] The traditional system of private security, however, was not broken. Calvin Coolidge had described an important aspect of it, insurance, in a 1923 speech.[31] A 1929 study showed that only 4% of New York's elderly were reliant upon charity or public assistance,[32] in part because some fraternals provided homes for their aged members.[33] Although the percentage of elderly living in poverty allegedly hit 50% in 1935,[34] the percentage of Americans aged 65 or older who were institutionalized doubled during the Depression, but only 1.5–3%, which was lower than that of 1910.[35] Most families, especially immigrant families, thought it shameful to allow family members to be institutionalized, so they supported their aged members, as families, nuclear and extended, traditionally had.[36]

The Depression and the New Deal, though, still strained the traditional system. Holding gold had become illegal in 1933 and the real estate and stock markets were down, but both would eventually roar back.[37] Moreover, equity in small businesses, whether proprietorships or partnerships, became less common mainly due to New Deal regulatory policies skewed in favor of bigger farms and bigger businesses. By the early postwar period, knowledge of the old system of private security was seemingly forgotten, replaced instead by horror stories of destitution, miserly state old-age pensions and poor houses, and adult children forced to care for their aged parents, even though more than 75% of men 65 or older remained head-of-household even in the depths of the Depression.[38] Ironically, many families today would be better off if adult children, like in the pre-Depression era, supplemented the income of their own elderly parents in lieu of Social Security.[39]

Another big problem with Social Security was its one-size-fits-all nature. It may have worked for long-lived couples with no children, but it failed families with children, especially couples that had children who matured before the parents passed. Unlike most of the assets acquired under the traditional system of private security, Social Security annuity payments died with the parents, leaving no assets for the next generation (except that paltry burial payment).[40] Most of the income of the poorest-aged Americans comes from Social Security because the payroll taxes FDR made them pay eats up funds they otherwise could have invested in real estate or other assets to greater effect.[41] Moreover, due to numerous oddities in its benefits formula and differential longevity, Social Security also tended to aid old white women at the expense of people of color, an important topic returned to in the conclusion.[42]

FDR insisted that Social Security payroll taxes be set on the high side so that the program would never be threatened politically by having to tap into general revenues.[43] That security for Social Security, though, came at a cost. Even the few semi-economic literate New Dealers, like Lauchlin Currie, understood that Social Security "made more difficult the problem of achieving recovery and led to less production and consumption than would otherwise have occurred. It was a prime example of how faulty economic reasoning can cost a people billions of dollars in loss of income."[44] Currie complained because the payroll taxes were unnecessarily high, leading to surpluses that the Federal government until recently "borrowed" to fund other expenditures. Had he known more about the system of private security that had evolved over American history, he would have also realized that Social Security was completely unnecessary as individual Americans knew better than any government how to save to provide for their families and future selves.

The Progressive Workplace

Just as Social Security tried to win the votes of seniors, the Civilian Conservation Corps (CCC) and the National Youth Administration (NYA) sought to secure the youth vote. The brainchild of FDR's wife Eleanor (ER), and one of her pet projects,[45] the NYA's stated purpose was to aid "four million youth who are eager, ready, and willing to work!" Like all New Deal bureaucrats, NYA administrator Aubrey Williams (after the departure of African-American educator Mary McLeod Bethune) purported to believe that his program created purchasing power by providing jobs to people without considering where the money originated. He bragged about the 5149 athletic fields built by his young workers without questioning whether the fields were needed, and if they were, why they were not constructed by private initiative. "It *is* spending [emphasis in original]," he conceded at one point, "but it is spending which should be chalked upon the credit rather than the debit side of the government's ledger." Quoting FDR, "the yield on this investment should be high."[46] The yield was indeed high, for the Democratic Party.

ER, who was a master of media in her own right, claimed that FDR went along with the NYA despite potential political opposition due to the program's fascistic overtones.[47] FDR said he would personally suffer all criticism if the program was the right thing to do for the nation's youths. That was posturing as the program was clearly a way to win the lifelong support of young voters. Betty and Ernest Lindley, the authors of *A New Deal for Youth* (1938), admitted as much when they dedicated their book to ER "because in mining towns, in beet sugar villages, in mountain back-washes, in city slums, on isolated farms, in high schools, in colleges, in universities where we have been—youth speak of her as their friend."[48] The poor, miseducated youth concentrated on that which is seen, not the opportunity costs of the NYA's projects, or in other words what else might have been done with the more than $330 million the NYA expended. Likely, it would have been more or better ballfields because, like its parent, the WPA, NYA projects cost more than they would have if put out to private bid.[49] ER tried to get her pet established "on a permanent basis" but World War II saw the program folded into the mobilization effort and shuttered in 1943 along with its parent, the WPA.

The other major program for young people, the CCC, was built upon a program called the Temporary Emergency Relief Administration created by FDR as governor of New York in 1932. As its name implied, the CCC concentrated on forestry, soil erosion, flood control, park improvements, and similar natural resource-related projects. At any one time, up to 500,000 young men aged 17–28, plus an additional 15,000 American Indians, veterans, and local experienced men, worked for the CCC, which employed a total of about 3 million over its 9-year existence. Begun in 1933, the CCC ended in 1942 as priorities shifted to military recruitment and industrial production. Unlike most New Deal programs, the CCC was run like a military camp, and in fact, received logistical aid from the Army. Moreover, it inspired many similar programs at the state level.

Like some other New Deal programs, the CCC was accused of fascistic overtones, in part because of its militaristic veneer, and in part because it was segregated by race. Had news leaked that its leaders looked to Nazi Germany's Reicharbeitsdienst ("National Labor Service") for both inspiration and even administrative guidance, it might have been early to the chopping block, though it must be recalled that the regime was not yet fully reviled and Germany had been a leading source of Progressive social thought.[50] One historian found the CCC and its Nazi doppelganger "strikingly similar" and believed that they shared "a special closeness."[51]

Left in the dark about such details, the American public generally lauded the CCC for creating employment and training young men for private-sector jobs.[52] There is no evidence that the CCC did anything to improve the U.S. economy[53] but by the 1980s many Americans looked back on the CCC "as one of the most successful New Deal programs."[54] "Roosevelt's Tree Army," as it was sometimes called, may have been because it helped to increase physical fitness and prepare men for military life during World War II[55] while simultaneously indirectly aiding hard-hit rural communities.[56]

An amalgamation of various New Deal programs like the NYA, the WPA was no CCC. It was huge, at its apex operating "in practically every county in the United States."[57] According to Currie, WPA head administrator Harry "Hopkins year after year forced a reluctant Congress to give him larger appropriations for relief than originally provided for."[58] The WPA's remit was as broad as its geographical extent, from public works projects to recreation.

Yes, recreation. New Dealers believed that Americans, especially those from the "wrong side of the tracks," were so hapless that they needed a federal bureaucracy to provide recreational activities for them. In 10,000 communities across the nation, 40,000 "WPA recreation leaders" turned vacant stores and schoolrooms into rec centers so that depressed people could engage in "dramatics, swimming, dancing, baseball, music, puppetry, weaving, festivals, woodworking, metal craft, camping and a hundred other activities." For example, 19 states ran 162 music projects that employed some 8000 musicians in bands, orchestras, operas, and quartets. The WPA also employed music copyists, conductors, librarians, tuners, binders, and 900 music teachers.[59] The goals of the program were "the employment of the unemployed" but also to seed out of "permanent budgets" more government-based entertainment "with the coming of more stable times."[60]

Many Americans, though, were not amused by the WPA. So at 7:30 pm on Thursday, 16 May 1935, just ten days after FDR created it by executive order, Hopkins assumed control of the NBC, CBS, and MBS (Mutual Broadcasting System, a consortium of independents) radio networks to tell listeners that his WPA would not countenance corruption as it quickly geared up to get 3.5 million unemployed Americans off the dole and back to work. He promised that the projects carried out locally but with oversight from Washington, would be "not only in the best interests of the unemployed, but as a great national endeavor, the results of which will be of benefit to the Nation and all of its citizens."[61]

Nevertheless, many Americans believed that the WPA promoted neither "work" nor "progress," in part because about 40% of the WPA's budget went to overhead.[62] Even after it was renamed to the Work Projects Administration in 1939, skeptics claimed that WPA stood for "We Piddle Around" or "We Poke Around" because the workload was generally light, especially for the high wages it paid. In some places, politicos padded payrolls with their pals. In others, those who seemed too Republican were discharged or cowed into voting Democrat, or at least contributing to the Democratic Party's campaign coffers.[63] Hundreds collected contributions on behalf of Democrat candidates for office, while untold others did "work" like cataloguing ways to cook spinach. Others, like researchers in the WPA Historical Records Survey, published puffy propaganda pieces for the president.

In 1938, for example, WPA researchers "disclosed that in 1851, Mrs. James John Roosevelt" joined 64 other "eminent ladies of society and wealth" to petition the New York Common Council to aid unemployed seamstresses through the establishment of a "Female House of Industry," ostensibly because "all assistance from Charitable Societies is withdrawn."[64] But the WPA historians did not point out that the aid was withdrawn because the crisis had passed and charities were busy building up their coffers for the next downturn instead of wasting resources on unemployable seamstresses. They also did not note how government money crowded out private charity, which held out well, especially in places where it had a long history, like New England, until inundated with New Deal dollars.[65] Or how it crowded out fraternals, which contrary to New Deal propaganda held up well during the Depression.[66] Or how it outlawed Americans' traditional social safety net, the right to work for room and board.

Hopkins was one of the unconstrained thinkers that Thomas Sowell later identified as the root cause of inane government policies. In 1937, Hopkins, apparently blissfully unaware of the tradeoffs between job stability, wages, and hours, wrote that the WPA worker's "job must be as stable as possible, his hours short enough to let others also have jobs, and his buying power must be high."[67] Ironically, he entitled his unconstrained pamphlet *The Realities of Unemployment*. "Our aim," he aimlessly continued, "is to supply to industry as many physically strong, mentally alert, skilled workers as we can." He never explained why employers could not find, or create, such great workers on their own, but he did assert that "the Federal Government cannot refuse responsibility for providing jobs to those whom private industry does not hire."

Then, he claimed that "America will win this fight" against unemployment "because it has the brains and the wealth and the leadership." Well, it had the wealth.

Hopkins claimed that Americans "should have been discussing it [unemployment] for at least 20 years." But why? Hopkins did not understand that business, economic, and technological change would create not just new jobs, but new types of jobs. Like many fearful of AI and robots today, he saw a future filled with more workers and less need for them due to automation. And like many environmentalists today,[68] he saw mass unemployment "in the sections where soil or natural resources have been exhausted," as if natural resource exhaustion was possible without meddling from people like himself.[69]

Thankfully, the WPA finally finished the last of its projects in 1943 and was shut down because high wartime employment rendered it indefensible.[70] A rational government would never have implemented it in the first place. Unemployment did not cause the Great Depression, the Great Depression caused unemployment. Employing people only to put money in their pockets so they could buy stuff did not make things, at least not the things that consumers definitively wanted. It was no coincidence that We Piddle Around workers were variously described as Boondogglers and Dingbat Makers.[71]

Businesses did not want to make things because workers' wages were too high given what they could produce. Ironically, Hopkins argued that the high price of goods in monopolized industries led to production cuts and hence unemployment. He could or would not apply the same analysis to wages because the WPA did not help to solve the high wage problem, but rather exacerbated it by crowding out private employers. (Earlier relief programs like the CWA, though, aided private employment by stimulating the economy at its lowest point in 1933–34.)[72]

New Deal central planners never could figure out a way to pay workers the right wage. Workers resented wages based on familial need because determining "need" required constant monitoring of family situations by bureaucrats. Low, so-called "security wages" were supposed to induce workers to take higher-paid work in the private sector whenever possible but the differentials, which were roughly based on geographical location and skill level, were vast and seemingly arbitrary. When pay was pegged at near market wages, private employers complained that they could not find workers because, with wage constant, everyone preferred relatively secure and easy government to more exacting and riskier private work.[73]

In 1938, New Dealers passed the Fair Labor Standards Act (FLSA). It mandated a federal minimum wage and time and a half-pay for hourly workers who clocked more than 40 hours a week. It also prohibited a broad swathe of child labor. Like the presidential agreement, NRA, and WPA, it kept workers unemployed by elevating real wages.

Labor unions also kept wages high and unsurprisingly were another New Deal darling. The National Labor Relations Act, or Wagner Act, of 1935 put labor relations under the control of a National Labor Relations Board, a bureaucracy filled with union sympathizers who everywhere saw "unfair labor practices" where others saw companies in difficult times trying to stay afloat while fiercely competing for consumer dollars.[74] Specifically, the act made it illegal for employers to influence workers trying to join a union, to create a company union (one controlled by the employer), to discriminate against workers on the basis of union membership, to seek retribution against whistleblowers, or to not bargain collectively. Employers could, however, discriminate against workers who were not union members, effectively creating a "closed shop" regime where unions could force employees into membership.

The Wagner Act also restored some of the NIRA's labor regulations even on companies located entirely in a single state under the theory that all companies of any size affect interstate commerce, if only indirectly through aggregate supply conditions. SCOTUS upheld the constitutionality of the Wagner Act in general in several cases and in *Fruehaf Trailer* (1937) and *Friedman-Harry Marks Clothing Co.* (1937) because both companies sourced raw materials or sold finished products across state lines.[75]

Moreover, to move out of the economic emergency, New Dealers argued, wages had to be high, and by necessity that meant supporting unions and protecting the jobs of striking workers. The Wagner Act undoubtedly helped unions to wax larger and stronger,[76] emboldening many to call strikes in 1936–37, when unemployment was still in double digits.[77] So real wages increased yet more, but productivity slumped. During the Great Depression, the total hours worked per laborer dropped by 21%. Some of that decrease was due to job-sharing arrangements but a big hunk of it, according to Nobel laureate Ed Prescott, was due to people wanting to work less, at least in formal markets, due to Hooverian and New Deal policies.[78] Using dynamic general equilibrium modeling, other economists have also shown that "the slowness of the recovery from the Depression was due to a shock that increased the market power of workers."[79] The Wagner Act fits that description.

Hopkins tried to justify Wagner by claiming that "unions are designed to protect and improve the conditions of labor—the interest of the common man, which bulks very large in the general welfare."[80] Problem is that unions are designed to protect unions, first their leadership and then their rank and file, at the expense of non-union workers and consumers. Moreover, Wagner forced workers to join unions and pay their dues. That limited "free riding" on union contracts by non-dues-paying workers but at the very high cost of not allowing workers to say "no," essentially turning workers into "forced riders" and unions into compulsory monopolies willing and able to ignore the wishes of their members.[81]

Socialist Light: The TVA and Rural Electrification

In his movie *The River*, Pare Lorentz suggested that the TVA had saved the Tennessee Valley and that a program like it could help the entire Mississippi Valley. Many New Dealers would have loved to extend the TVA's collectivist model to the entire country. The TVA was essentially socialism lite, the federal government's first foray into large-scale peacetime economic planning and the ownership of some of the means of production.[82] Many other New Deal programs, like Social Security and rural electrification, also possessed significant collectivist undertones.

While true that New Dealers did not nationalize a bunch of industries,[83] even though some wanted to, it is not hyperbole to describe the New Deal as collectivist.[84] FDR's Resettlement Administration, for example, created eight rural resettlement communities in Alabama, where residents, the most vulnerable people in the country essentially, were (re)educated in the progressive values of John Dewey.[85]

Some of the resettlements were essentially industrial. Others, especially in the South, were agricultural and just as communitarian. The Division of Subsistence Homesteads and the Resettlement Administration were key players, but several other agencies tried to control the program. They all wanted to claim it should the social experiment work, but nobody wanted to be responsible if it failed because it was so patently un-American.[86] The idea was to get unemployed people off the roles by giving them a bit of land to work by resettling them in small communities with others in the same situation. The experiments, which went about as well as the many private rural communes, religious and secular, attempted in America in the nineteenth century, i.e., not well at all, were tried in every U.S. state and all the major territories (Alaska, Hawaii, Puerto Rico, Virgin Islands).[87] Ak-Sar-Ben, twenty miles west of Omaha, proved as dreadful as its name (Nebraska spelled backward) and was soon deserted, just as local observers predicted.[88]

At one point, New Dealers hoped to purchase over 75 million acres of "submarginal" land nationwide upon which to resettle the inhabitants, who were incapable of determining the best place to live themselves. Urbane urbanites like Hopkins and Tugwell would decide what was best for them in what the former called "a rational resettlement of America."[89] It was nothing short of the central planning of lands that earlier forms of government planning had screwed up. It was completely unnecessary, as demonstrated by the subsequent success of areas like Nebraska's sand hills that resisted federal incursions and relied on market signals to determine landholding patterns.[90]

Tugwell, though, believed that America's "peasants" were no better than Russia's and hence would only stop wasting their lives and lands if he intervened.[91] They needed to learn a better way of farming, Tugwell's way. Born and raised in a small mountain town in western New York, Tugwell's experiences with agriculture were limited to his father's small-time cattle outfit and later his small orchard.[92] Tugwell, who spent his twenties and thirties studying economics with socialists like Scott Nearing in the agricultural heartlands of Philadelphia and Manhattan universities, somehow fancied himself an expert at cotton farming. Tellingly, Tugwell's only agriculture paper of note published before he joined Roosevelt's team was a book chapter on "Russian Agriculture," the fruit of his visit to the Soviet Union in 1927.[93] Another keen New Deal agricultural expert, Lee Pressman, wondered what could be done for the "macaroni growers."[94]

Tugwell's great insight was that people who worked a job and grew their own food would be materially better off than those who just worked.[95] Americans, though, already knew this commonsense fact. Even before FDR took office, many Americans started backyard gardens. In fact, in some places gardens had replaced office buildings torn down due to a dearth of cash to pay the taxes on them.[96] In Gary, Indiana, 20,000 families gardened on vacant lots, just to get by.[97] But New Dealers knew better than everyday people and began to instruct them on *how* to garden and preserve food.[98] Yet they also made anyone growing more than five bushels of potatoes obtain a special license or suffer a $1000 fine and/or a year in prison.[99]

Passed in part thanks to Tugwell's departure from the administration in 1936, which followed the 1935 purge of radical AAA administrators at the behest of Southern Democrats, the Bankhead-Jones Farm Tenant Act of 1937 ended Tugwell's unpopular and ill-conceived central planning fiasco by converting marginal agricultural lands into national and state parks and by lending poor tenant farmers the money they needed to buy the land that they worked on a subsidized basis. The credit program was administered under the Farm Security Act, which replaced the Resettlement Administration with the Farm Security Administration (FSA).[100] Tugwell's resettlement experiments had worked at cross purposes with other New Deal programs, which sought to limit agricultural production and to liquidate smaller, less efficient farms, not multiply them. In 1982, the federal government destroyed many of the records associated with the forced cooperatives, presumably out of embarrassment.[101]

The farm tenant purchase program was less embarrassing. All but $71,575 of the $23.7 million lent was repaid and the tenants it aided became if not Democratic Party stalwarts, then lifelong statists, loyal wards of the state instead of paternalist plantation owners.[102] Within a decade, though, "in an era of high employment, rising national income, and rapid technological progress in agriculture," Bankhead-Jones had become obsolete and perhaps too effective at diminishing the power of plantation owners. By the postwar period, most loans under the program were simply too small to fund the acquisition of farms of viable size. All told, by 1945 the program had helped only about 47,000 tenant families to achieve ownership, leaving almost 1.9 million people still in tenancy. It is unclear the extent to which the low program utilization rate was due to a dearth of borrowers or too stringent underwriting requirements.[103] The FSA itself was also dismantled in the 1940s, and its remaining functions parceled out between other alphabet agencies, including the Extension Service, the Farm Credit Administration, and the Farmers Home Administration.[104]

The TVA, which created, owned, and operated hydroelectric and fertilizer plants and flood control systems in parts of seven southern states, was, aside from some PWA low-income housing projects, the only nonfinancial New Deal project to be directly government owned.[105] Progressives loved to laud it, based mostly on the TVA's own propaganda claims.[106] What they conveniently forgot is that the government's achievements were necessary only because the government itself prevented private industry from engaging in such projects at such scale.[107] As Albert Jay Nock put it, "the State can arrange the terms of competition to suit itself."[108] The federal government enjoyed both scale economies denied private entities and the power to bend state governments to its will at low to no cost. It paid no taxes and had lower borrowing costs because it was backstopped by taxpayers.[109] Moreover, it frequently failed to factor taxpayer subsidies into project cost estimations.[110] And the fact that existing power generation in Tennessee exceeded average consumption by 60% proved no barrier to its implementation.[111]

The TVA turned into a major polluter too. Ten of its 12 power plants in 1977 violated the Federal Clean Air Act. It alone was responsible for 14% of the entire nation's sulfur emissions in 1973. It simply stonewalled the Environmental Protection Agency (EPA) by arguing that one federal agency had no power over another.[112] Proponents also forgot that the dams and hydroelectric plants, like the Pick-Sloan Missouri Basin Program began at the end of World War II, destroyed numerous communities and ecosystems.[113] All told, the TVA flooded an area bigger than the state of Rhode Island and forced over 15,000 people from their homes.[114] Moreover, the flood control systems forced farmers to rejuvenate their soils with artificial fertilizers instead of the naturally occurring river floods that TVA dams largely prevented.

Most telling of all, though, was that in subsequent decades Tennessee, which received all its electrical power from the TVA, did not thrive relative to comparable states, like Georgia, which received hardly any of its power from the TVA. Eventually, Tennessee even fell behind, as did Mississippi, which also received much of its power from the TVA. That was likely because cheap TVA electricity and fertilizer subsidized small farmers, keeping them on the land instead of inducing them to move to higher-productivity occupations and areas.[115]

FDR sought to bring state-subsidized electricity to the rest of rural America as well. He sought to crush opposition by passing the Wheeler-Rayburn bill, which would have authorized the SEC to abolish private utilities that were not part of a "geographically or economically integrated system," i.e., rural utilities. Congress squelched it after over 800,000 letters opposing the bill hit their mailboxes by the end of June 1935.[116]

But that could not stop FDR from signing Executive Order No. 7037 in May 1935. The order added to the New Deal alphabet soup the Rural

Electrification Administration (REA) and tasked it with initiating, formulating, administering, and supervising "a program of approved projects with respect to the generation, transmission, and distribution of electric energy in rural areas." A year later, Congress formally created the agency and authorized a decade-long program that allowed local non-commercial organizations, including cooperatives, municipalities, and nonprofits, to finance the construction of centralized generation plants and grids with 10-year loans from the REA at the same rate of interest that the REA paid on the bonds it sold of the same maturity. The subsidized loan was perhaps fair because the REA burdened would-be rural electricity providers with regulations like spending at least 25% of their budgets on wages and hiring at least 90% of their workers from relief rolls, as if jobs were completely fungible and hiring an already employed man would not eventually lead to the employment of an unemployed worker somewhere.

The restrictions were later loosened to secure enough skilled workers experienced in electrical utilities work,[117] but nevertheless, Richardson Trading Company in Alabama had to constantly seek rule regulation relaxation from REA administrators in Washington on hours and wages. Its request to increase its work week to 48 hours, though, met a flat denial from Washington bureaucrats who thought it could easily just hire more men and run two shifts without considering the state of the local skilled labor market or the poor state of the state's rural roads.[118]

The REA also fudged up some basic public administration that led to higher costs. On most public works projects, the government reimbursed contractors 90% of their materials costs upon delivery at the worksite, which allowed contractors to buy in bulk, pay lower "cash" prices, and stockpile materials to ensure steady work. The REA, though, would pay only after the materials, like wires and transmission poles, were installed. That induced contractors to order materials as needed, which led to considerable delays at times and higher unit costs. As one befuddled contractor put it, he could not understand the REA's policy as "we understand that all such jobs are set up more, or less for the general relief of the country" and were already budgeted.[119]

The REA found that it had to further subsidize electrification efforts by sending its own expert engineers and lawyers to help rural cooperatives to form, create viable business plans, and sign contracts reasonable enough to ensure that they could service the REA's loans. It also ran "farm tours," which were also called "the REA circus," wherein it helped local community organizers to convince farmers that they needed grid electricity. By 1937 it had formed a permanent Utilization Division tasked with educating farmers on the "benefits of [grid] electricity." That alone would have told rational administrators that something was amiss, but again the New Deal was about transforming American life, in this case by making rural folk use grid transformers.[120]

In addition to being tasked with encouraging the production of aluminum and other electricity-intensive war materiel during World War II, the REA increased the percentage of U.S. farms connected to a centralized grid from about 11–78 in 15 years.[121] New Dealers claimed victory, but all the REA did was change the way that farmers used electricity, or substitute electricity for other power sources. It is patently untrue that prior to the REA, farmers had "no washing machine, no power with which to operate pump or well or provide hot water."[122]

Prior to the construction of expensive transmission grids, farmers heated water with wood, coal, or gas, lighted their homes with kerosene, chilled food in root cellars and/or with harvested ice, produced their own electricity with windmills, mechanical energy, and diesel or gasoline generators, or they bought it in town on weekends and stored it in large batteries,[123] rendering untrue the babblings of a New Dealer who claimed that "one doesn't go into a retail store and buy a package of electricity over the counter."[124] To take advantage of the grid, farmers had to wire their entire houses and buy new electric appliances, by no means an inexpensive proposition.

Yet another agency, the Electric Home and Farm Authority, Inc. (EHFA), subsidized the home appliance part of the transformation. Led by David E. Lilienthal out of the TVA's office in Chattanooga but chartered in Delaware, the EHFA was a wholly owned subsidiary of the U.S. government with branches in numerous states. Formed by Executive Order Number 6514 on 19 December 1933, its main goals were:

> To advance the general economic welfare of the nation by developing and fostering the increased use of electrical power through the reduction of the cost thereof to the consumer and through the reduction of the cost and price of electrical equipment and appliances; to aid in the distribution of electrical appliances and equipment by financing the purchase thereof through the lending and advancing of money, extending of credit and guaranteeing of obligations of individuals, firms, corporations and others, upon the security of mortgage or other liens upon or claims against electrical appliances and equipment, and in general to carry on in connection

> with such financing a chattel mortgage-loan business; to cooperate with any Federal agency or branch of the Federal Government or with any of the several States, or subdivisions or agencies of such States, or with cooperative of other organizations, or with private corporations or associations, and to make such studies, experiments or demonstrations as may be necessary and suitable to advance and foster an orderly and proper physical, economic and social development in any of the several States by means of the use of electricity or electrical power.[125]

In other words, not only did FDR subsidize the generation and redistribution of electricity but he also tried to increase consumer demand by subsidizing the electrical appliance industry. Despite the EHFA's subsidies, many farmers cut corners by installing only a few drop cords[126] themselves or using "jack-leg" electricians who cut corners. REA officials understood the importance of safety because fires would have dampened demand, but they stressed the need to induce customers to install numerous "outlets and base plugs in each room so as to encourage the fullest possible use of electricity."[127]

The greatest effect of the REA, in fact, may have been to induce commercial electricity companies to begin to service more rural customers, something the misunderstood Samuel Insull had been doing for over a decade before the Great Mess began in 1929.[128] The growth of electrical power plants and grids in the 1920s had been amazing, almost doubling the capitalization of the much older railroad industry.[129] Insull led the way by forming holding companies that specialized in raising the funds necessary to buy, modernize, and combine numerous electrical utilities companies. He also pushed for, and got, state regulation, as opposed to the hodgepodge of municipal regulators that had hampered the industry from its earliest days.

Insull's growing empire of electricity ran on cash, much of it raised by its investment banker, Halsey, Stuart & Co., selling securities to small investors. After the market for electricity sagged year after year along with the rest of the economy, Insull found that he could no longer raise new equity and his empire collapsed. Numerous small bondholders suffered losses and they joined up with FDR, who wanted municipal power companies, to take it out on Insull and the rest of the commercial electricity sector. Charged with various state and federal crimes in 1933, Insull was apprehended while vacationing in Istanbul and returned to the United States to stand trial. He admitted that he had made errors of business judgment but denied any criminal wrongdoing. A jury of his peers acquitted him of all charges, but years of litigation took its toll on his reputation and health. Although his holding companies failed, leaving security holders with pennies on the dollar, none of his operating companies went under.[130]

In the 1930s, despite the hubbub over Insull, commercial electrical utility companies moved much more quickly to bring electricity to previously unserved areas than the REA did by being smart about it, extending generation plants and distribution lines only to areas where demand was relatively high and costs relatively low. They would have continued to spread their lines when economically feasible had not New Deal attorneys Felix Frankfurter, Thomas Corcoran, and Benjamin Cohen impeded their growth with the Public Utility Holding Company Act of 1935 and the Federal Power Act of 1935, which were both direct outgrowths of the administration's outrage over the failure of Insull's holding companies.[131] Due to such legislation, the SEC added a public utilities division that scrutinized the securities issuance of electric and other utility companies.[132]

Nonprofit local initiatives were also capable of expanding grids without FDR's help. In Oregon and Washington State, PUDs (public utility districts) brought power to rural areas starting in 1930.[133] Noncommercial entities were happy to fill in some of the gaps if subsidized by the REA, but even with its aid a fifth or so of farmers continued to supply their electricity needs the old-fashioned ways until they, too, joined the grid in subsequent decades as costs naturally dropped.[134]

What the REA accomplished was helping to electrify rich people's summer homes in places like Baldwin County, Alabama, on the east side of Mobile Bay, sooner than they otherwise would have been. The Baldwin County Power Company already supplied 52 cottages but did not find it cost-effective to service the more remote ones. It also served farmers.[135] There were some additional farmers in Baldwin that might benefit from cheap electricity, for sure, but many of the homeowners who signed up for the REA project there were the wealthy owners of vacation cottages, apparently including the state's governor,[136] who ran fans, radios, and lights for a few months each summer. "The slump in consumption at this time," the local superintendent explained to the head of Alabama's REA, "was due to practically all of the summer cottages being closed, a number of which were very good customers." Of the 1000 Baldwin County customers the REA expected,[137] only 453 signed up on net after persistent power problems caused multiple disconnects.[138] Persistent problems with the firm contracted to do the business, which apparently was chosen for political reasons,[139] led to numerous delays and other difficulties.[140]

Overall, most of the REA's loans were eventually repaid and farm output and productivity increased. The subsidy was large but the initial cost to taxpayers was relatively low.[141] Subsidies for rural grid electricity have, however, continued to this day under the Rural Utilities Service and have become considerably more costly.[142] Moreover, rural electrification slowed the development of small-scale wind, solar, hydroelectric, and other renewable energy sources, as well as batteries.

Notes

1. John F. Cogan, *The High Cost of Good Intentions: A History of U.S. Federal Entitlement Programs* (Stanford: Stanford University Press, 2017), 6.
2. Colin Gordon, "Rethinking the New Deal," *Columbia Law Review* 98, 8 (Dec. 1998), 2045.
3. Edwin Amenta, *When Movements Matter: The Townsend Plan and the Rise of Social Security* (Princeton: Princeton University Press, 2006), 35–51.
4. Sylvester J. Schieber and John B. Shoven, *The Real Deal: The History and Future of Social Security* (New Haven: Yale University Press, 1999), 23–24.
5. Edith Abbott, "Editor's Preface," Grace Abbott, *From Relief to Social Security: The Development of the New Public Welfare Service* (Chicago: University of Chicago Press, 1941), v.
6. Schieber and Shoven, *Real Deal*, 77–78; Amenta, *When Movements Matter*, 176–96.
7. Schieber and Shoven, *Real Deal*, 8.
8. Jim Powell, *FDR's Folly: How Roosevelt and His New Deal Prolonged the Great Depression* (New York: Crown Forum, 2003), 173–74.
9. Abbott, *Relief*, 236.
10. On the effects of UBI generally, see Robert E. Wright and Aleksandra Przegalinska, *Debating Universal Basic Income: Pros, Cons, and Alternatives* (Cham, Switzerland: Palgrave, 2022).
11. Abbott, *Relief*, 228–29.

12. Jim F. Couch and William F. Shughart, *The Political Economy of the New Deal* (Northampton, MA: Edward Elgar, 1998), 98.
13. Dominick Pratico, *Eisenhower and Social Security: The Origins of the Disability Program* (New York Writers Club Press, 2001).
14. Schieber and Shoven, *Real Deal*, 26.
15. As quoted in Schieber and Shoven, *Real Deal*, 44 and Amity Shlaes, *The Forgotten Man: A New History of the Great Depression* (New York: HarperCollins, 2007), 229.
16. Couch and Shughart, *Political Economy*, 99.
17. Dora L. Costa, *The Evolution of Retirement: An American Economic History, 1880–1990* (Chicago: University of Chicago Press, 1998), 173–74.
18. Schieber and Shoven, *Real Deal*, 57–59; Burton A. Abrams, *The Terrible Ten: A Century of Economic Folly* (Oakland: Independent Institute, 2013), 55–57.
19. Schieber and Shoven, *Real Deal*, 93, 107–13.
20. As quoted in Schieber and Shoven, *Real Deal*, 53.
21. Abrams, *Terrible Ten*, 52; Michael J. Graetz and Jerry L. Mashaw, *True Security: Rethinking American Social Insurance* (New Haven: Yale University Press, 1999), 4–7; Benjamin M. Friedman, ed., *Should the United States Privatize Social Security?* (Cambridge, Mass.: MIT Press, 1999).
22. David Beito, *From Mutual Aid to the Welfare State: Fraternal Societies and Social Services, 1890–1967* (Chapel Hill: University of North Carolina Press, 2000), 137–60.
23. John B. Shoven, "Social Security Reform: Two Tiers Are Better Than One," in Friedman, ed., *Should?* (Cambridge, Mass.: MIT Press, 1999), 1, 16, 18.
24. Glenn W. Miller, *Problems of Labor* (New York: Macmillan Co., 1951), 271–72.
25. Costa, *Evolution of Retirement*, 1–3, 23.
26. Schieber and Shoven, *Real Deal*, 20; Miller, *Problems*, 260–62; Costa, *Evolution of Retirement*, 19–20.
27. Bill White, *America's Fiscal Constitution: Its Triumph and Collapse* (New York: PublicAffairs, 2014), 197–98; Powell, FDR's Folly, 83.
28. Robert E. Wright, *Financial Exclusion: How Competition Can Fix a Broken System* (Great Barrington, Mass.: AIER 2019), 52–55;

William Z. Ripley, *Main Street and Wall Street* (Boston: Little, Brown and Co., 1929), v-vii, 16–54.

29. See, for example, E.C. Harwood, "How the Army Officer Builds His Future Income," *Magazine of Wall Street* (29 Aug. 1928), 1116, 1150–51.
30. Schieber and Shoven, *Real Deal*, 18–20.
31. Calvin Coolidge, "The Modern Method by Which men Make the Uncertain Certain," in Amity Shlaes, ed. *New Deal Rebels* (Great Barrington, Mass.: American Institute for Economic Research, 2023), 7–8.
32. Powell, *FDR's Folly*, 175.
33. Beito, *Mutual Aid*, 2.
34. See, e.g., Seymour Moskowitz, "Adult Children and Indigent Parents: Intergenerational Responsibilities in International Perspectives," *Marquette Law Review* 86, 3 (Winter 2002), 414.
35. Costa, *Evolution of Retirement*, 112–13.
36. Beito, *Mutual Aid*, 26.
37. Schieber and Shoven, *Real Deal*, 21.
38. Miller, *Problems*, 273–76; Costa, *Evolution of Retirement*, 107–8.
39. Robert J. Barro, "Comments," in Friedman, ed., *Should?*, 114; Costa, *Evolution of Retirement*, 25–26.
40. Shoven, "Social Security Reform," in Friedman, ed., *Should?*, 21–22.
41. Lawrence A. Frolik and Alison M. Barnes, *Elder Law: Cases and Materials*, 4th ed. (Newark, N.J.: Lexis-Nexis, 2007), 153.
42. Robert J. Barro, "Comments," in Friedman, ed., *Should?*, 114.
43. Schieber and Shoven, *Real Deal*, 42.
44. Lauchlin Currie, "Lauchlin Currie's Memoirs," *Journal of Economic Studies* 31, 3/4 (2004), 221.
45. Mildred W. Abramowitz, "Eleanor Roosevelt and the National Youth Administration 1935–1943—An Extension of the Presidency," *Presidential Studies Quarterly* 14, 4 (Fall 1984): 569–80.
46. Aubrey Williams, "The Work of the National Youth Administration," *Living* 1, 4 (Nov. 1939): 65–66.
47. Betty Houchin Winfield, *FDR and the News Media* (New York: Columbia University Press, 1994), 81–82.
48. As quoted in Abramowitz, "Eleanor Roosevelt," 570.
49. Couch and Shughart, *Political Economy*, 116–17.

50. Lenore Ealy and Steven D. Ealy, "Progressivism and Philanthropy," *The Good Society* 15, 1 (2006), 40.
51. Kiran Klaus Patel, *Soldiers of Labor: Labor Service in Nazi Germany and New Deal America, 1933–1945* (New York: Cambridge University Press, 2005), 4, 398.
52. Kiran Klaus Patel, *The New Deal: A Global History* (Princeton: Princeton University Press, 2016), 85–90.
53. Patel, *Soldiers of Labor*, 395.
54. John C. Paige, *The Civilian Conservation Corps and the National Park Service, 1933–1942: An Administrative History* (Washington, DC: U.S. Department of the Interior, 1985).
55. Charles Tocci and Ann Marie Ryan, "Conserving the American Man: Gender, Eugenics and Education in the Civilian Conservation Corps," *History of Education* 51, 2 (2022): 224–43.
56. Michael Sherraden, "The Local Impact of the Civilian Conservation Corps, 1933–1942," *Journal of Sociology & Social Welfare* 10, 3 (December 2014).
57. F. C. Harrington, "Misconceptions Concerning the WPA Program," WPA, 4-1901, (26 Feb. 1939), 7, FRASER.
58. Currie, "Memoirs," 228.
59. The Works Progress Administration, The Works Program, Press Release, 16 Dec. 1935, FRASER.
60. "WPA Provides Leisure-Time Activities for Millions: 10,000 Communities Participate," Works Progress Administration, 4-1824, (13 Nov. 1938), FRASER.
61. The Works Progress Administration, The Works Program, Press Release, 17 May 1935, FRASER.
62. The Works Progress Administration, The Works Program, Press Release, 16 Dec. 1935, FRASER.
63. The Works Progress Administration, The Works Program, Press Release, 16 Jul. 1938, FRASER.
64. The Works Progress Administration, The Works Program, Press Release, 21 Jun. 1938, FRASER.
65. Burton Folsom, Jr. *New Deal or Raw Deal? How FDR's Economic Legacy Has Damaged America* (New York: Simon & Schuster, 2008), 78–81; Robert E. Wright, *Liberty Lost: The Rise and Demise of Voluntary Association in America Since Its Founding* (Great Barrington, Mass.: American Institute for Economic Research, 2023).

66. Beito, *Mutual Aid*, 224–30.
67. Harry L. Hopkins, *The Realities of Unemployment* (Washington, DC: WPA, 1937), 1, 12.
68. Brian Black, "Reference on Planning: Imaging River Conservation in the 1938 TVA Hearings," in Henry L. Henderson and David B. Woolner, eds., *FDR and the Environment* (New York: Palgrave, 2005), 182–83.
69. Hopkins, *Realities*, 10.
70. Lawrence W. Reed, *Great Myths of the Great Depression* (Mackinac Center for Public Policy and the Foundation for Economic Education, 2011), 13.
71. Couch and Shughart, *Political Economy*, 109–10, 114–15.
72. Todd C. Neumann, Price V. Fishback, and Shawn Kantor, "The Dynamics of Relief Spending and the Private Urban Labor Market During the New Deal," *Journal of Economic History* 70, 1 (March 2010): 195–220.
73. Neumann, Fishback, and Kantor, "Dynamics of Relief Spending," 200.
74. Reed, *Great Myths*, 14–15.
75. Miller, *Problems*, 444–49.
76. Miller, *Problems*, 450; Shlaes, *Forgotten Man*, 330.
77. Powell, *FDR's Folly*, 195–206.
78. Edward C. Prescott, "Some Observations on the Great Depression," *Federal Reserve Bank of Minneapolis Quarterly Review* 23, 1 (Winter 1999): 25–31.
79. Lawrence J. Christiano, Roberto Motton, Massimo Rostagno, "The Great Depression and the Friedman-Schwartz Hypothesis," NBER Working Paper 10255 (2004), 1, 8.
80. Works Progress Administration, The Works Program, Press Release, 16 Jul. 1938, FRASER.
81. George Leef, *Free Choice for Workers: A History of the Right to Work Movement* (Ottawa, Illinois: Jameson Books, 2005), xiii–xiv, 32–35.
82. John Gunther, *Inside U.S.A.* (New York: Harper & Brothers, 1947), 734.
83. David M. Kennedy, "What the New Deal Did," *Political Science Quarterly* 124, 2 (Summer 2009), 252–53.
84. James P. Warburg, *Hell Bent for Election* (New York: Doubleday, Doran & Company, 1935), 26–27.

85. Rebecca K. Duke, "From Dewey to Skyline Farms: Progressive Education in New Deal Resettlement Communities," (Ph.D. Diss., Middle Tennessee State University, 2020).
86. Patel, *New Deal*, 210–11.
87. Theresa A. Glanz, "Federal Land-Use Policy and Resettlement in the Great Plains: An Experiment in Community Development During the New Deal Years, 1933–1941," (Ph.D. Diss., University of Nebraska, 2020), 51–52; Patel, *New Deal*, 211–12.
88. Folsom, *New Deal?*, 70.
89. As quoted in Patel, *New Deal*, 211.
90. Karl Hess, *Visions Upon the Land: Man and Nature on the Western Range* (Washington, DC: Island Press, 1992), 84–96.
91. Duke, "From Dewey to Skyline Farms," 63–64; Warburg, *Hell Bent*, 53.
92. Powell, *FDR's Folly*, 15.
93. Lee J. Alston and Joseph P. Ferrie, *Southern Paternalism and the American Welfare State: Economics, Politics, and Institutions in the South, 1865–1965* (New York: Cambridge University Press, 1999), 77.
94. Couch and Shughart, *Political Economy*, 19.
95. Glanz, "Federal Land-Use Policy," 62.
96. James Ledbetter and Daniel B. Roth, eds., *The Great Depression: A Diary by Benjamin Roth* (New York: Public Affairs, 2009), 11, 44, 63.
97. Couch and Shughart, *Political Economy*, 7.
98. Patel, *New Deal*, 212.
99. Warburg, *Hell Bent*, 42.
100. Alston and Ferrie, *Southern Paternalism*, 45, 75.
101. Glanz, "Federal Land-Use Policy," 54–55.
102. Alston and Ferrie, *Southern Paternalism*, 87–88.
103. Edward C. Banfield, "Ten Years of the Farm Tenant Purchase Program," *Journal of Farm Economics* 31, 3 (Aug. 1949): 469–86.
104. Alston and Ferrie, *Southern Paternalism*, 76.
105. Patel, *New Deal*, 185; Garet Garrett, *The People's Pottage* (Caldwell, ID: Caxton Printers, 1953), 72; Gail Radford, "The Federal Government and Housing During the Great Depression," in John F. Bauman, Roger Biles, and Kristin M. Szylvian, eds. *From Tenements to the Taylor Homes: In Search of an Urban Housing Policy*

in Twentieth Century America (University Park: Pennsylvania State University Press, 2000), 104–6.

106. William U. Chandler, *The Myth of TVA: Conservation and Development in the Tennessee Valley, 1933–1983* (Cambridge, Mass.: Ballinger Publishing Co., 1984), 53, 66.
107. Paul Sabin, *Public Citizens: The Attack on Big Government and the Remaking of American Liberalism* (New York: W.W. Norton & Co., 2021), 27–28; Gunther, *Inside U.S.A.*, 185.
108. Albert Jay Nock, *Our Enemy, the State* (New York: William Morrow & Co., 1935), 9.
109. Shlaes, *Forgotten Man*, 272, 350.
110. Warburg, *Hell Bent*, 28.
111. Powell, *FDR's Folly*, 143–44.
112. Chandler, *Myth of TVA*, 135.
113. Clair Wilcox, *Public Policies Toward Business* rev. ed. (Homewood, Ill., Richard D. Irwin, Inc., 1960), 839–40.
114. Powell, *FDR's Folly*, 151.
115. Chandler, *Myth of TVA*, 43–53.
116. David T. Beito, *The New Deal's War on the Bill of Rights: The Untold Story of FDR's Concentration Camps, Censorship, and Mass Surveillance* (Oakland: Independent Institute, 2023), 12.
117. H.S. Person, "The Rural Electrification Administration in Perspective," *Agricultural History* 24, 2 (April 1950), 70–74.
118. I.B Richardson to Richard J. Beamish, Jr., 1 Jan. 1938, Gordon Persons to Richardson Trading Co., 10 Sept. 1937, Richardson Trading Co. to Gordon Persons, 1 Sept. 1937, Richard J. Beamish to Gordon Persons, 9 Sept. 1937, Gordon Persons to M.O. Swanson, 2 Sept. 1937, Richardson Trading Co. to Gordon Persons, 1 Sept. 1937, Gordon Persons to Richardson Trading Co., 2 Aug. 1937, Folder 11, Baldwin County Electric Membership Corporation, Rural Electrification, SG51083, Alabama Department of Archives and History, Montgomery, Alabama.
119. Richardson Trading Co. to John M. Carmody, 28 Sept., 8 Oct. 1937, Folder 11, Baldwin County Electric Membership Corporation, Rural Electrification, SG51083, Alabama Department of Archives and History, Montgomery, Alabama.
120. Person, "Rural Electrification," 78–79.
121. Chandler, *Myth of TVA*, 57.

122. Gunther, *Inside U.S.A.*, 131.
123. Richard Willis, *Long Gone* (New York: Greenpoint Press, 2007), 17–18, 21, 43–44, 131–34.
124. As quoted in Person, "Rural Electrification," 76.
125. Corporation Records, SG 005461, Volume Domestic C-M, 1868–1934, Alabama Department of Archives and History, Montgomery, Alabama.
126. Willis, *Long Gone*, 107.
127. Gordon Persons to Frank Earle, 5 Aug. 1937, Folder 5, Baldwin County Electric Membership Corporation, Rural Electrification, SG51083, Alabama Department of Archives and History, Montgomery, Alabama.
128. Jeremiah D. Lambert, *The Power Brokers: The Struggle to Shape and Control the Electric Power Industry* (Cambridge: The MIT Press, 2015), 22–28.
129. William Z. Ripley, *Main Street and Wall Street* (Boston: Little, Brown and Co., 1929), 276–92.
130. Lambert, *Power Brokers*, 18–47.
131. Powell, *FDR's Folly*, 23–24; Lambert, *Power Brokers*, 47–49.
132. For its detailed reports in the latter half of the 1930s, see Accession Number 57A153, Box 321, Records of the Securities and Exchange Commission, RG 266, National Archives and Records Administration, College Park, Maryland.
133. Gunther, *Inside U.S.A.*, 131–32.
134. Person, "Rural Electrification," 75; Chandler, *Myth of TVA*, 57.
135. C.D. Papadeas to Gordon Persons, 24 Aug. 1937, Folder 23, Baldwin County Electric Membership Corporation, Rural Electrification, SG51083, Alabama Department of Archives and History, Montgomery, Alabama.
136. Press Release, n.d., Folder 2, Baldwin County Electric Membership Corporation, Rural Electrification, SG51084, Alabama Department of Archives and History, Montgomery, Alabama.
137. Press Release, n.d., Folder 2, Baldwin County Electric Membership Corporation, Rural Electrification, SG51084, Alabama Department of Archives and History, Montgomery, Alabama.
138. Carl Schlich to Gordon Persons, 21 Nov. 1938, Folder 5, Baldwin County Electric Membership Corporation, Rural Electrification, SG51083, Alabama Department of Archives and History, Montgomery, Alabama.

139. The head of the Alabama REA flat out told the REA in Washington that the contractor was “not qualified either financially or technically to handle a job the size of the Baldwin County project.” Its request to use the “next lowest qualified bidder” instead was, however, denied. Gordon Persons to Guy W. Thaxton, 19 July 1937, Folder 11, Baldwin County Electric Membership Corporation, Rural Electrification, SG51083, Alabama Department of Archives and History, Montgomery, Alabama.
140. Gordon Persons to Frank Earle, 14 Nov., 21 July, 21 Apr., 5 Mar. 1938, Frank Earle to Gordon Persons, 20 Apr. 1938, Folder 5, Richardson Trading Company to Graybar Electric Co., n.d., Graybar Credit Manager to Richardson Trading Company, 17 Aug. 1938, Gordon Persons to I.B. Richardson, 31 Mar., 21 June 1938, Folder 11, Baldwin County Electric Membership Corporation, Rural Electrification, SG51083, Alabama Department of Archives and History, Montgomery, Alabama.
141. Carl Kitchens and Price Fishback, “Flip the Switch: The Impact of the Rural Electrification Administration, 1935–1940,” *Journal of Economic History* 75, 4 (December 2015): 1,161–95.
142. Richard P. Keck, “Reevaluating the Rural Electrification Administration: A New Deal for the Taxpayer,” *Environmental Law* 16, 1 (Fall 1985): 39–89.

CHAPTER 7

Crushing Dissent

Harry Hopkins believed that "only the power of the government can start the golden stream flowing again."[1] He undoubtedly referred to prosperity, but other "golden" imagery undoubtedly streamed into the minds of many Americans opposed to the New Deal when they heard such blatant statist propaganda. Contrary to myth, FDR faced much criticism, especially at the street level. His machine could not control individual communications, so historians must excavate such resistance from private diaries and correspondence.[2] Most journalists, including many accomplished ones like Anne O'Hare McCormick, gushed over FDR's New Deal. McCormick proved especially adept at deflecting damning accusations from FDR's most vocal critics, like claims that he sought to establish a dictatorship and led a quiet revolution demolishing traditional American values and governance. She twice characterized the New Deal as just "a little left of center."[3] Dissenters just did not properly "understand" the importance of the New Deal agenda.[4]

Hopkins claimed that in a republic like the U.S. policy decisions are made "in the full light of day, amid the freest sort of criticism, with the help of all the people."[5] But instead of conceding the problem of putting tens of millions of people on the dole, Hopkins assumed the dole was necessary and then argued that without the dole, all those people would become communists or fascists.[6] Americans, in other words, had to choose between the New Deal and a worse form of collectivism, perhaps

R. E. Wright, *FDR's Long New Deal*,
https://doi.org/10.1007/978-3-031-74141-8_7

one brought about by violence.[7] Many Americans knew that was a false dichotomy and struggled to slow, stop, and reverse the New Deal and its top architect, "Franklin 'double-crossing' Roosevelt."[8]

Many people in rural northwest Ohio, for example, accepted relief out of desperation but within a few years came to see that the New Deal was resetting American values, especially the relationship between citizens and their governments. As federal budget deficits soared, even conservative Democrats noted how far the party had strayed from the principles of Thomas Jefferson and Andrew Jackson.[9] Critics, like *Chicago Daily News* editor Frank Knox (who sought the Republican presidential nomination in 1936 but ended up being Alf Landon's running mate), wanted to know not only where New Deal money was going, but where it was coming from. Many concluded that it was coming from honest, hardworking people and going to political cronies and bums.[10]

Hopkins shot back that all the New Deal's critics could come up with was "raising frightful bugaboos—of revolution, of dictatorship, of the collapse of our social institutions." He claimed that they were "eugenicists" like Harvard economist Thomas Nixon Carver, "Tories" (an FDR favorite[11]) because they were like the loyalists to the British crown who "could not stand the New Deal of 1776," and Civil War-era "Copperheads" who would rather see the nation split asunder than to pay their fair share of taxes. And he said all that in a speech entitled "The Essence of Democracy!" given before a woman's group in Boston.[12]

As the Depression continued, loonies came out of their closets and caves to push all sorts of agendas. As Ohio attorney Benjamin Roth noted, "the depression has loosed all the radical thinkers."[13] New Deal dissidents like Huey Long, Father Coughlin, and Francis Townsend saw some of the failings of FDR's policies but sought to double down on them rather than thwart the New Deal. Long, for example, wanted massive taxes on millionaires to fund the agenda laid out in his 1933 autobiography *Every Man a King*, which included old-age pensions, free college education, free homesteads, and veterans' bonuses.[14] FDR wanted federal old-age pensions so he could take credit for them but did not think that free farms and degrees would garner sufficient votes on net. And he disliked veterans, arguing in his 1934 veto of a bonus bill for them that "the fact of wearing a uniform does not mean that he can demand and receive from his Government a benefit which no other citizen receives." For FDR, military service was a duty, like paying taxes, so only those physically disabled by war were eligible for government aid. Veterans sought compensation for putting their lives at risk and suffering emotional trauma, not for wearing certain clothes, a position that U.S. policymakers had repeatedly respected since the republic's founding. But because veterans wanted to be paid as a right, not as a present, FDR could not be certain that his support would lead to sufficient votes on the net to warrant the outlay, which of course would reduce the amount he could spend on purple voters in swing states.[15]

Every nation that the Depression struck long and hard developed dissenting parties, most anti-establishment or from the Right side of the political spectrum.[16] America was no exception. A new Union Party formed but gained little traction in the 1936 election, in part due to counterattacks, literal assassination in Long's case, and character assassination in the cases of Coughlin and Townsend.[17] When Coughlin tried to make a comeback in 1937, the FCC employed "every resource" to trounce his radio show and eventually prevailed with the aid of new regulations regulating broadcast speech.[18] That same year, the SEC would not allow Townsend to claim registration exemption under the 1933 Act when he tried to sell $5 million worth of his personal promissory notes to supporters.[19]

As the nation descended into Depression, dissent grew, becoming louder after the New Deal began in 1933. FDR tried to crush all dissent, using every legalistic means at his disposal, from regulatory and tax coercion to propaganda and vituperation. Before turning against the administration in 1937, for example, New Dealer Hugh S. Johnson called Long and Coughlin a "pair of political termites," accused Coughlin of "pious flubdub," and alluded to the vehement anti-Catholicism of the second Klan. Townsend was threatened with an investigation for running a pension racket.[20]

This chapter sketches out the ideology of dissent, along with major instances of direct action, before concluding with some of the ways in which FDR counter-attacked. The president employed many tactics but the overall strategy of turning America's Fifth Estate, its watchdogs in newspapers and radio, into his personal lapdog, largely worked.[21]

The Great Dissenters

Corporations and trade associations aided by the New Deal, like some banks and businesses that benefited from regulations like the NIRA, did not oppose FDR's policy agenda. Others fought it at almost every turn.

The National Association of Manufacturers (NAM), for example, opposed 31 of 38 major New Deal proposals between 1933 and 1941. It rightly understood that if the government would encourage private enterprise instead of bashing it at every turn, then temporary "pump priming" jobs would be unnecessary.[22] Many leaders of fraternals and commercial insurers also opposed the New Deal because they realized that social insurance invaded their turf, arguably unfairly.[23]

Several great newspapers attacked the New Deal whenever, and however, possible. It was said that White House staffers assiduously avoided contact with New Dealers depicted in the biting political cartoons on the front page of the *Chicago Tribune*, a high-circulation daily published by Robert McCormick that put the interests of the American heartland ahead of all else. Labeling FDR the "American Kerensky," the *Tribune* gave FDR credit for ending Prohibition and cutting government waste but excoriated him and his followers on just about everything else. The NRA especially inflamed McCormick because it smacked so much of fascist corporatism and because it threatened to turn newspapers into state-controlled media. Only under intense pressure from McCormick did FDR back down and build first amendment protections into the NRA codes for newspapers and other publishers.[24]

Most dissent, though, came from the pens and typewriters of individuals. Not all were effective. Some resorted to ad hominem attacks, while others spouted ideas even more inane than those of the administration. Many, though, provided trenchant analysis of the costs of the New Deal.[25]

Much of that analysis came from what has come to be called "the Old Right," from people who harbored some classical liberal ideas about limited government and states' rights but wrapped them in veneration of family, religion, and tradition. They distrusted and disliked rapid change of any sort and so often evoked the common law and other vestiges of America's unwritten constitution.[26] At the fringes, some, like the "Twelve Southerners," wanted America to move back toward its agricultural, preindustrial roots. Others, like Seward Collins of *The American Review*, argued for monarchy and openly admired FDR's power grab because the ends justified the means. Collins, though, preferred a monarch "in whom all governmental responsibility of a State is vested," as the only power sufficient to end America's plutocracy.[27]

At the other end of the spectrum of New Deal dissidents was Albert Jay Nock (1870–1945), an erstwhile Progressive mugged by the reality of the Great War ratchet who became a staunch advocate for individual liberty. After his *The Freeman* folded in 1924, Nock began writing for *The American Mercury*, edited by Henry Louis (H.L.) Mencken, a literary libertarian known for his acerbic wit.[28] The so-called "Sage of Baltimore" was also one of FDR's toughest critics.[29] He called the President an "obvious demagogue" who made "whoopee out of the pathetic hopes and illusions of poor and miserable people."[30]

A former Episcopal minister, Nock in 1935 published *Our Enemy, the State*, which can be seen as a sort of bridge between the classical liberalism of Edward Atkinson and the modern libertarian movement that emerged shortly after the end of World War II.[31] Nock clearly saw the radical nature of the New Deal, dismissing "matters like price-fixing, wage-fixing, inflation, political banking, 'agricultural adjustment,' and similar items of State policy" as shiny baubles hiding the fundamental change underlying all, "an increase in State power and a corresponding decrease of social power."[32] Like Mencken and others, Nock saw, and disavowed, the parasitical tendencies of modern governments. The voluntary association he saw as the great bulwark of the ruled against the exploitation of rulers.[33]

Garet Garrett was another of the prolific voices of the Old Right who found a distinctive voice in opposition to the New Deal.[34] A home-schooled farm boy, he ran off to the big city where he fell in with the wrong crowd, printers. By 1894, he covered the formation of Coxey's Army in Ohio and the Pullman Strike for the Cleveland *Press*. Over the next several decades, he covered financial news for the *New York Times Annalist*, the *New York Times* proper, the *Wall Street Journal*, the *New York Evening Post*, the *New York Tribune*, and the *Saturday Evening Post*. He wrote novels in his spare time, including one that may have influenced *Atlas Shrugged*.

Garrett also wrote nonfiction, including *The Bubble That Broke the World*, which presaged Murray Rothbard's 1963 book, *America's Great Depression*, on the causes of the Great Depression. He attacked virtually every aspect of the New Deal, from the FDIC to Social Security, so often and so vehemently that Sinclair Lewis in his 1935 dystopian novel *It Can't Happen Here* listed him as one of the first people who would be arrested if America went full fascist. Garrett's 1938 essay "The Revolution Was" proved too controversial to publish until 1945. In 1953, Garrett repurposed it to lead off *The People's Pottage*, his most popular nonfiction work. Like the Biblical Esau, Garrett showed, the American people had sold their liberty for a bowl of bean soup (mess of pottage).[35]

Garrett at first opposed America's entry into both world wars, which made him persona non grata even during the "all hands on deck" phase of the Second World War. FDR blacklisted him, as Mencken feared he would all his political opponents, although Garrett became eager to support the cause after realizing the systemic threat posed by Germany and Japan.[36]

Cathrine Curtis also opposed U.S. involvement in the early stages of World War II by forming the Women's National Committee to Keep the U.S. Out of War. Called "the most dangerous woman in America," Curtis was also a staunch critic of the New Deal. Born to wealthy parents and encouraged to engage in business and financial endeavors, Curtis gained fame after the Great War as an actor and one of the lone female movie producers in the 1920s. In 1934, Curtis began hosting "Women and Money," a biweekly radio program on New York's WMCA. The show soon died, though, because of what she called a "Radio Gag Rule" that limited both female voices and those critical of the New Deal. She wasn't wrong as the Federal Radio Commission (FRC) had denied radio frequency licenses to so-called "propaganda" stations even under Republican presidents. Sometimes, the FRC killed a station's profitability by limiting its wattage (geographical reach) or airtime (daytime only), both of which hurt advertising revenue.[37]

Not one to back down from a fight, in 1935 Curtis formed the Women Investors Research Institute and Women Investors in America. By 1939, Women Investors boasted almost 300,000 members from 28 states and lobbied against legislation that threatened women's financial independence, which of course included a good deal of the New Deal. Curtis focused on females because she feared that most American women were shockingly susceptible to the New Deal and internationalist propaganda.[38]

In 1951, the founder of the American Institute for Economic Research (AIER), Colonel E.C. Harwood, lamented that "there are many Americans who no longer have confidence in freedom; they may pay it lip service, but their actions belie their words."[39] Harwood formed AIER in 1933 specifically to combat the New Deal. An engineer with significant Army experience, Harwood believed that one could plan a bridge or other construction project but, unlike technocrats like Hoover, did not believe that entire economies could be successfully centrally planned.

A student of economic policy history and a professor at M.I.T., Harwood so clearly saw the path that the federal government was likely to take that he was, in a sense, a critic of the New Deal even before Hoover became president.[40] His critiques of the monetary system, the Fed's lack of independence, and federal policymaking more generally were more detailed and trenchant than most because he paid careful attention to details and incentives.[41] Already in June 1928, he had proclaimed that if anyone ever had "the power accompanying control of the dollar" it would signal "a return to despotism."[42] He predicted an economic downturn and financial market troubles in January and February 1929[43] and had already noted that Hoover's pump priming plan showed little promise.[44] In April 1929, he argued that "tariff retaliations must likewise be reckoned on."[45] In November 1929, right after the stock market debacle began, an editor cut his warning that a wave of bank failures was likely.[46] Already in May 1930, he chastised those who believed that the way out of depression was to spend funds "which would not be spent on the basis of business considerations."[47] Little wonder that the prolific engineer turned political economist created AIER almost immediately upon FDR's ascendance to power.

Another U.S. Army officer with engineering experience opposed to the New Deal was Henry O. Flipper. Born in slavery in Georgia in 1856, Flipper learned through his intensive study of history that the United States did not invent slavery, which was a ubiquitous institution dating back to at least antiquity. He was a staunch proponent of the Constitution as understood by Edward Atkinson and the Founders and Framers. His critique of the New Deal was similar to that later espoused by prominent African-American conservatives like Thomas Sowell, Walter Williams, and Clarence Thomas. He died in 1940, presumably because his old heart could not stomach the news that FDR was running for a third term.[48]

Another cogent critique of the New Deal came from Senator Josiah Bailey of North Carolina. The Conservative Manifesto he penned along with some other Southern lawmakers argued that the ongoing transformation of Americans' relationship with the federal government had destroyed private incentives to invest in new business activities and to hire workers. Depression would continue to stalk the land until the federal government's anti-business policies and attitudes reversed.[49]

Washington Post columnist Mark Sullivan frequently criticized the New Deal agenda, including FDR's alliance with Hollywood. He had also criticized Hoover for trying to bring glitz into politics. "To assume that glamour and wisdom go hand and hand," he warned, "is a serious fallacy—the two qualities are more often divided than together."[50]

African-American attorney and activist John P. Davis also criticized the New Deal, especially its many negative effects on blacks. "Federal relief officials themselves admit," he wrote in 1935, "that grave abuses exist in the administration of rural relief to Negroes." The NRA did not bring increased employment or wages for black industrial workers because they were either exempted from minimum wage regulations or not employed at all. He also indicted other major New Deal programs, including the AAA, PWA, and TVA, for injuring the interests of African-Americans, while revealing many lesser programs as "lily-white social planning."[51]

New Dealers "secured so little support or help from economists as a class," one New Deal economist claimed, because "the penalties for non-conformity were harsh," and included being ousted from university positions.[52] That may have occurred but there is an even bigger reason why many economists eschewed the New Deal, because it was economically nonsensical.[53] Plus, there was some ambiguity in the firings. An associate professor of statistics was fired, for example, not because he showed that 94% of industrial life policies lapsed but for criticizing the industrial insurance (life insurance for poor people) industry based on that misleading statistic. The lapse rate, insurance experts knew, was largely a function of government regulations that gave industrial life policyholders who no longer wanted their policies no other exit path. The stat prof also missed the fact that industrial life was extremely competitive, meaning that it was offered on the best terms then technologically possible.[54]

Former high-ranking New Deal officials also criticized the New Deal. FDR's Director of the Bureau of the Budget, Lewis W. Douglas, resigned after only a year on the job because he understood that America stood at a crossroads, and under FDR would head down the wrong path. "This great country," he warned in May 1935, was subjecting itself "to the despotism of bureaucracy, controlling our every act, destroying what equality we have attained, reducing us eventually to the condition of impoverished slaves of the state."[55]

Similarly, James Warburg, the son of Fed architect Paul Warburg and an early FDR financial advisor, wrote a book explaining that the election of 1936 would not be a vote for or against a man or a political party, but rather "for the continuance or discontinuance of the freedom we have enjoyed under what for want of a better name we call the American scheme of life." He argued, in no uncertain terms, that "the present administration is doing more harm than good." He likened America to "an express train" headed for "a broken culvert," i.e., a massive wreck.[56] He and his wife followed up with additional anti-FDR screeds.

Alfred E. Smith, the Democrat's presidential candidate in 1928 and a reluctant supporter of FDR in 1932, vocally turned against the New Deal in 1936. He joined the American Liberty League of conservative Democrats eager to thwart the ongoing radical transformation of America by taking out FDR. Although his switch is often depicted as sour grapes or a political ploy, Smith had principled reasons to join the opposition, including an abiding belief in states' rights.[57] The Democratic Party, he explained, was inciting class warfare while not fulfilling its 1932 campaign promises. The federal government had grown, not shrunk, and its budget remained in deficit. Worse, FDR's alphabet agencies did nothing to help recovery. Smith called the NRA "a vast octopus set up by government, that wound its arms around all the business of the country, paralyzed big business, and choked little business to death." He also said that FDR's "young Brain Trusters caught the Socialists in swimming and they ran away with their clothes."[58]

The Democrat's 1924 presidential nominee, John W. Davis, also rejected FDR in 1936. The incumbent president was no Democrat, he explained, because the Democratic Party had always "stood for a faithful observance of the Constitution, of the limitations it puts upon the powers of government and the distribution which it makes of those powers between the nation and the States and between the departments of the Federal Government itself." Foremost, he reminded readers, "it has opposed centralization in government as the sure road to tyranny." And even though he helped to bring about the graduated federal income tax, Davis called its use for merely redistributive purposes a form of theft and "communism in all but name."[59]

Radical labor activist and author Louis Adamic also chastised FDR from the Left, calling his early labor policies as effective as talking "nicely to the crew of a speeding train urging them not to crush the ants on the rails." According to Adamic, "society must always *compel* business to function for the social good." FDR exaggerated the strength of the labor provisions in the NRA, Adamic asserted, noting the president's desire not to alienate his "yacht-owning friends."[60] Given his later incessant business bashing and the passage of the Wagner Act, FDR may have taken Adamic's criticism to heart.[61]

FDR also faced dissent from others on the Left. Muckraking financial journalist John T. Flynn turned against the New Deal during the

First Hundred Days when FDR began breaking most of his most important campaign promises. The NRA really stuck in Flynn's craw, so he denounced it as "the gravest attack upon the whole principle of the democratic society in our political history."[62]

Many leading writers and intellectuals, from Ernest Hemingway to Richard Wright (no relation), were communist sympathizers if not card-carrying members. They wanted to use the economic crisis to make sweeping reforms immediately and chastised the administration for being too timid. But FDR knew that radical change would not play politically and that only about 100,000 were radical enough to join America's Communist Party. Most Americans were still traditionalists, if no longer dyed-in-the-wool classical liberals. They were more voluntary communalists, as depicted in the 1933 film *Our Daily Bread*, than communists. When the Lynds returned to "Middletown" (Muncie, Indiana) in 1935, they expected to find dramatic change in the residents' outlook on life and the government's role in it. Instead, they discovered that most Muncieites continued to live by the same values that they had a decade earlier. Most other Americans did too, so they remained ashamed of receiving government handouts, and angry that their once mighty communities had been laid so low.[63]

Direct (In)Action

Some dissenters displayed a blatant disregard for New Deal regulations. York, Pennsylvania battery manufacturer Fred C. Perkins, for example, spent 18 days in jail to protest the NRA's minimum wage provision. A graduate of Cornell University in 1901, Perkins protested other New Deal nostrums as well because they conflicted with his classical liberal view of the government and its limited role in the economy and people's day-to-day lives.[64] Others, as noted above, also went to jail rather than submit to the dictates of the Blue Eagle.

Dissent also took the form of tax avoidance and even outright tax "strikes." In Manhattan, the West Side Taxpayers' Association resolved in March 1932 that taxpayers should withhold their 1932 taxes until the municipal government adjusted government salaries and reduced assessments to reflect current market values. Tax collections were suspended for 2 years in Chicago and held up by litigation for years afterward thanks to the efforts of the Chicago Association of Real Estate Taxpayers. The strike faded, though, because Mayor Anton Cermak convinced the local papers to stop advertising tax protestors and to donate space for "Pay Your Taxes Savings Clubs." SCOTUS helped by refusing to hear any of the cases.[65]

Tax avoidance stemmed from the tax increases FDR's New Deal agenda demanded. The New Deal had to be fed and the economic crisis continued, and higher taxes fulfilled both goals. Apologists noted that only John D. Rockefeller paid the highest marginal tax rate, but most other Americans paid more taxes than ever before.[66] Harry Hopkins revealed the attitude of many Progressives when he claimed that "it is stupid for the top one-tenth of 1% of the people to be getting as much income as the entire bottom 40%,"[67] no matter how the uber-wealthy acquired their high incomes. Little wonder that critics claimed that the unofficial motto of FDR's New Deal was soak-the-rich, especially after the president announced in 1935 that the tax system had done too "little to prevent an unjust concentration of wealth and economic power."[68]

New Dealers did not often argue that businesses should not earn any profit, but they often qualified profit-making with ambiguous terms like "reasonable."[69] Reasonable to whom, business owners and leaders rightly wondered. Asymmetric treatment meant that the government would not help if profits were "too low" but that it would surely intercede if they were "too high," a premonition that proved especially prescient during World War II. "Business is now hesitant about making long term plans," Marriner Eccles explained in 1937, "partly because it feels it does not know what the rules of the game are going to be."[70] Business owners large and small made the case clearly that "lack of confidence" in the administration and policy uncertainties held back business investment.[71] In a 1939 survey, 54% of respondents agreed that FDR's attitude toward business impeded recovery, while only 26% demurred.[72]

Lamont du Pont, for example, noted that "uncertainty rules the tax situation, the labor situation, the monetary situation, and practically every legal condition under which industry must operate."[73] Little wonder that businesses dramatically reduced investment, spurring what some called a "capital strike." Business investment fell 80% between 1929 and 1933 while consumption only fell from 65 to 50% of GDP over those same years.[74] Net investment during the Depression was zero[75] because, as one Ohioan put it, "all sense of value, optimism and initiative seems to have disappeared."[76]

Businesses did not really "go on strike" like workers did, but the government's pro-labor policies, including its support of sit-down strikes, made business leaders think twice or thrice before investing in more physical capital that could be shuttered by unions for weeks or months at a time.[77]

Not that it was easy to raise funds for expansion anyway. Due to high levels of policy and macroeconomic uncertainty,[78] most individuals refused to invest in anything but sure bets, which were few and far between.[79] For evidence, just look at the spread in yields between presumed safe government bonds and the bonds of the riskiest classes of corporations. AT&T's bond prices stayed up while those of second-class issuers, like Youngstown Sheet and Tube, dropped below 50% of par even though they continued to pay interest.[80] The spread jumped dramatically, indicating that investors needed a lot of extra money to hold assets that might go bad at any moment.[81] So investors, especially wealthy ones, bought tax-exempt government bonds and bided time.[82]

As the diary of Ohio attorney Benjamin Roth makes clear, many common investors simply did not have sufficient cash to invest in anything and were glad that they had not jumped back into the stock market, which continued to spiral further downward than anyone could believe.[83] When members of America's 15 million-or-so person investor class did get their hands on some money, they kept it out of the market for fear of losing it, if not to bankruptcy then to FDR's constant policy experimentation. Others sought to divest as soon as FDR expressed interest in a sector. As one female investor told ER, "we expect to be tramped on but we do wish the stepping would be a little less hard."[84]

Fear of the seemingly all-encompassing power of FDR's New Deal even affected politically favored sectors. Not even the Great Beer Bubble of 1933 revivified the economy or the stock market, as many had hoped based on historical precedent.[85] Early that year, before the total abandonment of Prohibition in December, the federal government amended the Volstead Act by making 3.2% alcohol beer legal. Many states followed suit over the course of 1933, spawning waves of new entry into the market along with the return of former brewers that had switched to brewing legal cognates like ginger, root, and non-alcoholic hop-based beer. Unable to obtain sufficient financing from troubled banks, hundreds turned to the securities markets to try to raise sufficient financial capital to take advantage of the reopening market. Securities law and regulatory uncertainty, however, proved a barrier for burgeoning beer firms as well as the few other businesses looking to start or expand.[86] Investor Benjamin

Roth correctly predicted that the "whole thing" was "over-rated and that the excitement will die down in a few months."[87]

Instead of listening to what businesses and their bankers had to say, New Dealers decided to attack them with a new tax, an undistributed profits surtax in effect in 1936–37.[88] The idea was to force companies to put profits to work by paying dividends, investing them in new business activities, or having them taxed away.[89] Forty percent of firms opted for the tax,[90] in part because, as investment guru Benjamin Graham noted, the law was full of so many loopholes and easily devised workarounds that its main effect was to injure the interests of small stockholders.[91] Officials ended it after the 1937 tax year, as the depression-within-a-depression that the law may have helped to bring about meant that even fewer corporations than usual had any profits, distributed or otherwise, to tax.[92]

The tax acted as a barrier to entry by reducing the return on new endeavors in a period when risks were obviously elevated. Even expansion of existing enterprises made little sense so long as the tax remained in place.[93] The undistributed profits tax also hurt corporations trying to pay down debt. Due to the Fed's easy monetary policy and talk of a new era where old rules did not apply, many big corporations went into the Depression laden with debt, much of it in the form of long-term bonds. Some succumbed to bankruptcy but even those that survived could not afford to borrow more or would not even consider seeking additional funds. Most treaded water until their leadership retired or conditions improved after World War II.[94]

The Depression's bank failure waves hurt innovation, especially at smaller companies that relied on bank financing. Banking was such a local business before the advent of widespread branching that the effects of bank failures can be measured. The quantity and quality of new patents by smaller firms more reliant on bank financing fell by about a quarter relative to larger, publicly traded firms.[95]

Help from abroad was not forthcoming. America was not yet seen as an ironclad haven, especially after the gold confiscation. Moreover, the Smoot-Hawley tariff limited the availability of dollars abroad. As the interwar gold exchange system broke down, many countries imposed capital controls, essentially limiting, or even banning, investment in other countries to help them to implement independent domestic monetary policies while maintaining fixed exchange rates. Not until the end of the Bretton Woods fixed exchange-rate era in the early 1970s would capital flow freely across international borders once again. As a result, capital flows as a percentage of US GDP dropped to just 0.4%, well below the pre-Depression level of 1.7%.[96]

Instead of investing in American industry, for example, France invested in gold, increasing its share of world gold reserves from 7% pre-Crash to 27% in 1932. Instead of benefitting from corporate profits, the French paid high interest rates to attract and retain their stash of the yellow stuff, thus dragging their own economy through a longer and harder downturn than even that suffered by the United States.[97]

Despite financing, taxation, and regulatory obstacles, many businesses continued operating throughout the Depression and some even expanded or improved productivity. Although Hopkins thought that cotton tenant incomes, whether working on shares or on cash-rent, were far too low, he had to acknowledge that mechanization had "been proceeding very rapidly" since 1934. That reduced labor costs by 16% per acre and 20% per cotton bale even as the boll weevil infestation and declining soil fertility in the east drove cotton production westward. The large number of families "tractored off" their land by the 66% increase in the number of farm tractors and the 100% increase in the number of farm trucks between 1930 and 1938 decreased agricultural employment, Hopkins admitted, but he realized that it stimulated employment in industrial farm equipment production.[98]

Despite those few bright spots, two in three Americans in a 1939 Gallup poll said that they believed that FDR's anti-business policies and rhetoric were thwarting recovery.[99] That should have led him to bow out of his unprecedented third attempt at the presidency in 1940 but FDR had two powerful allies on his side, propaganda and corruption.

Gaslighting Like a Statist

New Dealers defended FDR and his radical policies with various forms of propaganda, including cancellation, gaslighting, use of the memory hole, and language manipulation much like the techniques described in the dystopian novel *1984*. Or, less anachronistically given that *1984* did not appear until 1949 and focused on Britain, the techniques described in Garet Garrett's 1938 essay "The Revolution Was." It described how brilliantly FDR had kept Americans "fixed in the delusion that they were talking about the same things because they were using the same words. Opposite and violently hostile ideas were represented by the same word signs. This was the American people's first experience with dialectic according to Marx and Lenin."[100]

The biggest lie of all, perhaps, was framing the economic "emergency" in militaristic terms. The U.S. government, FDR claimed, needed to "wage a war against" the economy.[101] He hoped that, as in the Civil and Great Wars, the American people would suffer diminution of their civil and economic liberties for a greater, collectivist cause, though this time against an invisible foe. By early 1934, regular Americans already perceived that it was "almost dangerous to question any" of FDR's "theories or statements."[102] That was partly because many of FDR's views were clothed in scientistic garb by the 370 socioeconomic studies produced by the Natural Resources Planning Board, one of the bureaucracies established by the NIRA.[103]

With help from the friendly or cowed parts of the mass media,[104] old words like liberal, freedom, and individualism were redefined, and their old connotations denigrated. Freedom in the sense of the ability to ignore government decrees became a bad thing. "Rugged" individualism transmogrified into greed.[105] Many Americans rightly sensed that the New Deal was not "The American Way," no matter how "ill-defined" New Dealers found that term.[106] What they meant by the American Way was the unwritten economic constitution and classical liberalism, not FDR's gaslighting. "I am fighting Communism," FDR once began a word salad that included the word "capitalistic" (not capitalism, but something like capitalism), and that ended "I want to equalize the distribution of wealth."[107]

One of FDR's speechwriters admitted that FDR lied like all politicians do. The brazenness of his falsehoods, though, were perhaps unmatched until the series of strange events that began in 2020. FDR claimed, for example, that he authored the constitution of Haiti even after being called out on it. Why he would want to take credit for that is another story completely but at least it was a relatively innocuous falsehood. More serious was reneging on a promise to consider the Clark Amendment, which would have allowed businesses to opt out of Social Security by providing workers with company pensions. Tellingly, nobody in the administration trusted any of the president's promises.[108] Members of the public who noticed FDR's broken policy promises, meanwhile, were fed a line about how changing circumstances necessitated the implementation of a very different set of policies.[109]

FDR's 1932 campaign promises were almost all broken, badly. Three weeks before his election, in a campaign speech in Pittsburgh, the future president promised "to reduce the cost of the current federal government operations by 25 per cent" by completely realigning "the unprecedented bureaucracy that has assembled in Washington in the last 4 years."[110] Also shoved down the memory hole was the 1932 Democratic platform promise to enforce the antitrust laws strictly and impartially, the very laws nullified by the Blue Eagle, the FCC, the Civil Aeronautics Board, the Robinson-Patman Act of 1936, and other New Deal deals.[111] Turns out that government-controlled monopolies were good but presumed private ones were not; the administration in 1938 staved off recovery yet again by filing 150 antitrust lawsuits, few of which did anything economically beneficial for consumers.[112] One key component of the New Deal's propaganda strategy was to never admit to being wrong, especially in an election year.[113]

Other campaign promises also entered the memory hole. As Garrett later explained, Americans in 1932 "thought they were voting: for less government, not more; for an end of deficit spending by government, not deficit spending raised to the plane of a social principle, and, for sound money, not as the New Deal afterward defined it, but as everybody then understood it."[114]

The administration also took credit for putative successes in which it played little role. In 1938, for example, Hopkins claimed that "when millions of people needed to be fed, the Federal Government fed them."[115] The problem is that the federal government didn't feed Americans, farmers, nonprofits, and local governments did. The U.S. government ordered the destruction of cotton and foodstuffs while Americans shivered and starved.[116]

To cover their disinformation campaigns, New Dealers sought to criminalize "false news." Senator Sherman Minton took the lead in 1938 but his bill, which targeted anti-New Deal papers like the *Philadelphia Inquirer* and *Chicago Daily Tribune* by imposing a $10,000 fine or 2 years in prison upon publishers who knowingly printed anything "known to be false," spurred the creation of a pro-free speech coalition with members from both sides of the political aisle unwilling to give any government agency the power to determine truth. The bipartisan backlash thankfully squelched the bill. When Minton again stirred up the issue, the *San Francisco Chronicle* boldly and effectively retorted, "This is fascism" and noted that the federal government could and did pay to produce and mail its own propaganda.

New Dealers also used the media to push out messages that aided their causes. Many were innocuous but helped to get people into seats in auditoriums where they could be induced to sign up for electrical grids that they did not really want or need.[117] Gordon Persons, the head of Alabama's REA, for example, asked Bill Pape of Mobile's WALA radio station to run a free advertisement for a meeting in Baldwin County six times each day under the free access or "right of way" understanding that FDR had forged with a frightened radio industry early in his first administration. "It is necessary," Persons explained, "that the meeting mentioned be given the widest publicity."[118] He also hit up several local newspaper editors for good press. "We want to thank you in anticipation of your usual cooperation," he reminded one of them.[119] Anything for the righteous cause of collectivism.

Turns out, for example, that FDR knew that rumors of Stalin-induced famine in Ukraine were true. He urged the *New York Times* to suppress the story so that his plan to recognize the U.S.S.R. diplomatically would not get waylaid. The number of additional Ukrainians who would have been available to fight Russia's 2022 invasion had FDR tied humanitarian aid to Ukraine to diplomatic recognition can only be guessed, but undoubtedly is substantial. Instead of destroying American-produced food, FDR could have purchased it and gifted it to the 3 to 8 million victims of the Holodomor. But that would have crashed the positive image of communism that he wanted to cultivate so he suppressed stories of horrific famine by independent journalists like Gareth Jones.[120]

To ensure that a cult of personality enveloped New Dealers, especially FDR, the regime cozied up to entertainers. Starting in 1934, many stars appeared annually at FDR's Birthday Ball, ostensibly thrown to raise money for FDR's charity, the Warm Springs Foundation for Infantile Paralysis. Mickey Rooney, Janet Gaynor, Lucille Ball, and others attended over the years. Most surprisingly of all, even staunch Republicans like Robert Taylor appeared because they were contractually obligated to do so. The iconography of the events depicted FDR as a father not just to "crippled children" (FDR's words, not mine) but to the nation, a saintly savior of the American way of life. The propaganda became so blatant that the theme of the 1941 Inaugural Gala was, in Orwellian style, proclaimed to be "Anti-propaganda."[121] Also Orwellian was FDR's claim that "the freedom of the press is in jeopardy, not from the Government but from certain types of newspaper owners," i.e., those who questioned his policies.[122]

FDR also turned the annual state of the union address into a campaign opportunity. Instead of informing Congress of conditions in the country in writing like most of his predecessors had, FDR began to deliver the message in person and "over a national hookup" to the radio networks, the dominance of which he encouraged in order to exert his control over the airwaves more efficiently than he ever could in a decentralized, segmented market.[123] When he turned his 1936 address into a campaign stump speech, Republicans in Congress booed him. The budget he delivered the next day basically asked for a blank check but promised no new taxes, another promise broken.[124]

New Dealers also engaged in hypocrisy on a grand scale. FDR admitted that he could not do his own taxes while at the same time shaming rich men who engaged in legal tax avoidance and trying to get the Treasury to assume that taxpayers who failed to file correctly were guilty of tax evasion.[125] He claimed that the papers falsified news to protect their rich owners and so bypassed them whenever he had to by taking to the airwaves, much as President Donald J. Trump would later communicate largely via Twitter and other forms of social media. That was ironic in FDR's case, though, as he had much of the print media in his pocket. The publisher of the *Seattle Post-Intelligencer*, for example, married FDR's daughter Anna, and loyal newspaper reporters throughout the country forewarned him of potentially damaging articles, some of which he was able to suppress before they appeared. Even the opposition press refrained from reminding the American people that their leader was sickly and dependent on a wheelchair and yet also a serial philanderer.[126]

New Dealers understood that certain "litanies," or rhetorical lines that could not be crossed, existed. They would not attack private enterprise, capitalism, or the Constitution directly, as that would lead to electoral defeat. But they could ask questions like "shall the Constitution be construed to hold property rights above human rights?" as if property rights were not one of the core human rights. They could create symbols meant to get people asking their own questions, about wealthy financiers for example. The stigmatized could then be targeted, creating precedents for later attacks on yet other groups.[127] And New Dealers could extol the Bill of Rights while undermining it at every turn, in part by renaming concentration camps as internment camps and calling those who asserted their right to free speech "un-Americans."[128]

Moreover, some claims about New Dealers that threatened the litanies had to be censored or rebutted at any cost.[129] Their response to criticism was therefore often overwhelming, even when the transformational nature of its policies was not directly assailed with accusations of collectivism, fascism, or communism. When Republicans attacked Social Security by stressing its costs in broadsides, for example, the Social Security Board retorted with movies that many theaters showed due to the cozy relationship that developed between the New Deal and Hollywood.[130] The latter got money and political favors and the former got eyeballs and expert persuasion techniques. Some people were outraged but nobody was surprised when FDR's son Jimmy took a job with Samuel Goldwyn, the Academy Award winning producer. Ditto the Department of Justice backing off on its antitrust suit against the film industry, which responded by launching a "Hollywood for Roosevelt" campaign in support of his third term.[131]

Other "dirty tricks" played by New Deal operatives have also come to light in recent years. To remove roadblocks to a massive executive branch "reorganization" bill, FDR's minions sent lobbyist Charles G. Dunwoody implied threats, a detective tail, a $1500 check from the "American Nazi Party," and, eventually, a prostitute.[132] The 1938 reorganization bill failed to pass, in large measure because Americans feared that it would consolidate FDR's power too much.[133]

More urban, more affluent Americans were easily swayed by photographic "evidence" of poverty, the pictures and movies of grinding poverty and soup lines that have become iconic. That's because they did not understand the dire conditions in places like the mill towns in the sand hills of North Carolina prior to the downturn, where even economic improvements could be easily portrayed as setbacks.[134]

To distract from the radical nature of their policies, New Dealers also regularly disparaged critics and their views. New Dealer Harold O. Hunter told a youth audience in 1939, for example, that he hoped they were "not too much confused ... by partisan political debate or distorted and inaccurate comments in some of our leading newspapers."[135] That reiterated talking points from the Minton Committee that tried to force nonprofits to reveal the sources of their funding so that their presumably evil motives would face public scrutiny. The ploy failed and the committee fell into disfavor, but the aspersions had been cast.[136] Indian New Deal creator John Collier was also noted for the vitriol he sprayed at his critics, who were legion.[137]

New Dealers were also adept spin artists. When critics accused the WPA of being excessively bureaucratic, its leader, F.C. Harrington, responded with a non sequitur: the WPA could not possibly be too bureaucratic because "WPA workers are selected locally." In the same document, in the same paragraph, Harrington explained that the WPA paid a monthly wage equivalent to the WPA's best estimate of a "subsistence standard of living in the locality in which the worker resides" but that it also had four wage scales, for unskilled, skilled, professional, and technical workers.[138] Left unstated was how "subsistence" standards changed with occupation.

Instead of a nuanced discussion about WPA workers and the incentives they faced, Harrington tried to refute the widespread notion that WPA projects were "little better than leaf raking"[139] and that WPA workers were "lazy, good-for-nothing bums" who turn down private-sector jobs. He did so, lamely, by noting that 4.5 million workers left the WPA's rolls between 1935 and 1939. But some of those were involuntary separations and there was no evidence that WPA workers "take jobs in private industry the minute they can get them." The WPA's own investigations revealed that only one-half of 1% of public complaints about WPA workers refusing jobs had any merit. The rest "were the most amazing collection of rumors, wish-fulfillments, axe-grindings and idle dreams you ever saw."[140] Contrary to Harrington's claims, though, it isn't clear that the WPA had the incentive to uncover anything that would make it look bad and, more importantly, whistleblowers had good reasons rooted in community norms not to identify specific people as public employment-free riders. Moreover, most people receiving private-sector job offers had applied for work, implying that wage or condition of work negotiations had broken down when they decided to remain with the WPA.

In other words, instead of gaslighting critics, Harrington could have explained that WPA workers did not have homogenous goals or values, so some workers may have chafed and left as soon as possible while others clung to what to them was a good thing. As rational people, though, most workers would have weighed the cost and benefits of private-sector offers. They would be more likely to leave a steady WPA job for fifty cents more an hour than a nickel—an-hour raise in a riskier private position. They would also be more likely to leave to the extent that they disliked some aspect of their WPA job (type of work, other workers, relationship with boss, commuting costs, etc.) relative to their expectation of the private-sector job. Most probably were risk-adverse, so the private job needed to have a clear margin of superiority before they could be induced to give up the status quo.

Even if the lazy bum stereotype was inaccurate, there is some indication that WPA workers were not as productive as other workers. In 1939, when industrial activity was increasing rapidly, 87% of WPA workers terminated under a new 18-month rule could not find employment, and half those who did were employed at lower wages than paid by the WPA.[141]

Administration discussions around the need for Social Security were also odd, to say the least. While it was true that the population was aging and that economic activity was shifting out of agriculture and toward manufacturing and services, all three sectors were becoming increasingly automated or mechanized, effectively extending the usefulness of older workers, and not putting a premium on youth as some claimed. Other New Dealers engaged in ageism, arguing, without evidence, that older workers were slower to learn new skills.[142]

FDR also engaged in ageism in his assault on SCOTUS. In doing so, he employed the infamous false metaphor technique in the first fireside chat of his second term on 9 March 1937 in which he likened the federal government to a three-horse team, with voters as the driver. In his metaphor, FDR himself was just a horse, the executive branch, while Congress represented another steed. Those two horses were pulling in the same direction but the tired old third horse, a veiled reference to the Four Horsemen of the Supreme Court, was preventing the field from being plowed, or economic progress in other words. A return to the darkest depths of depression would occur unless that third horse started to pull its weight. While rhetorically brilliant, FDR's metaphor was false because he was in the de facto driver's seat, steering both Congress and the executive horse. More importantly, it was the third horse's job under the Constitution's system of checks and balances to stop the tractor if it perceived trouble ahead, as it clearly and rightly did even though its classical liberal view of the world was largely hidden behind blinkers.[143]

New Dealers also fancied false dichotomies. In his 1925 textbook, *American Economic Life*, Tugwell noted that "no individual ever built a skyscraper" so society should encourage "more collective effort." That was true in a sense, but Tugwell conveniently left off the fact that successful "collective" endeavors were also voluntary, not forced by politicians from above.[144] Top-down command economies were unsustainable and, more importantly, only as democratic as the governance system itself. America under the New Deal was Democratic, not democratic, because

Democrats controlled all the major purse strings, and converted them into votes.

Sometimes when New Dealers could not lie, spin, or otherwise talk their way out of trouble, they told critics to just grin and bear it until they got used to the imposition on their liberty. One New Dealer told critics that issues that had "created hot controversy" all eventually came to be accepted as "necessary and that its effect was not to topple the country into ruin as, in the heat of argument, they had prophesied it would."[145] The nation, though, was indeed *ruined* by the New Deal, which of course is not the same condition as being destroyed.

To help push all those messages, FDR invested heavily in government public relations. Inhouse organs spouted the administration line, putting out pamphlets printed *en masse* by the Government Printing Office and distributed by the U.S. Postal Service, increasing its already embarrassing deficits.[146]

Heavy-handed techniques like censorship also regularly occurred, especially in radio. As historian David Beito recently explained, "Roosevelt had few, if any, scruples about hatching schemes to covertly sideline, or even quash, dissenting radio voices." The Federal Radio Commission requested stations to supply the text of addresses on public affairs so that they could ward off critical commentary before it reached any ears.[147] When decorated war veteran Eddie Rickenbacker, for example, went on NBC Radio in 1934 to expose a new policy that aimed to use the military, instead of commercial airlines, to deliver the U.S. mail by air, somebody from the administration so frightened NBC executive William B. Miller that he threatened to take Rickenbacker off the air if he "said anything controversial."[148] Famed aviator Charles Lindbergh also denounced the use of relatively untrained and untested military pilots to deliver the mails and after several crashes FDR had to reverse course. The president still held a grudge about it 5 years later when the two butted heads over America's involvement in the brewing global war.[149]

A year later, NBC refused to air the radio sitcom *The American Family Robinson* because its message, though veiled in comedy and drama, seemed too anti-New Deal because it stressed traditional American values like thrift, property rights, and limited government.[150] It became widely popular on independent stations but after new regulations came into effect in 1939, its plots became anodyne, indistinguishable from any soap opera. It ceased in September 1941, a pathetic shell of its former self.[151]

New Dealers also had no qualms about engaging in creative budget accounting. They realized that "a program that entails a continuing series of budgetary deficits will encounter strong popular resistance and is politically vulnerable. The solution," Lauchlin Currie later revealed, "is to develop wholly or partially self-liquidating projects financed outside the budget." The goal was to preserve "a technically balanced budget" while achieving New Deal aims.[152] The most creative budget accounting propaganda of all was the effort to equate FDR with Santa Claus, the great gift giver, not the one who took all the credit for the toys his elves made.[153]

During the war phase of the Long New Deal, propaganda kicked into high gear. The radio industry was not just effectively muzzled, it was turned into a potent tool for spreading the administration's messages. Socialist presidential candidate Norman Thomas complained that "we are dealing with a situation on the radio in which practically all commentators are one side," that of intervention in the European war.[154]

In Executive Order 8922 promulgated in October 1941, FDR established an Office of Facts and Figures tasked with formulating "programs designed to facilitate a widespread and accurate understanding of the status and progress of the national defense effort."[155] The fact that it was involved in the massive investigation of the black press exposes its real intent as a sort of mini-Ministry of Truth.[156] Hollywood was happy to aid both the administration and the war effort, partly to wash itself of accusations of communist sympathies that would resurface again in the 1950s. Starlet Bette Davis, for example, combined war bond rallies with pitches for FDR during his 1944 campaign, while Orson Welles went on air to warn of dire consequences for the war effort should a Republican administration come to power.[157]

It Pays to Be Purple or Organized

In March 1934, on the first anniversary of FDR's inauguration, Ohio Republican Benjamin Roth conceded that despite his abject policy failures FDR remained popular. "It seems he and the Democrats will be in power for some time," a prediction that proved prescient. But why did FDR's following among the working class remain "tremendous?" How did he win re-election in 1936, when polling indicated that three in five Americans opposed the New Deal?[158] In short, some pollsters predicted a Landon victory because they had not factored in the fact that FDR's programs paid off many voters.[159] As Roth noted on the eve of the

1938 Congressional elections, Americans were "slowly turning back to the Republican Party—but New Deal money with millions on W.P.A. and relief still give the Democrats the edge."[160] It was no coincidence that WPA employment always peaked in the third quarter of even-numbered years.[161] Republicans gained 81 seats in the House of Representatives and 8 in the Senate in 1938, a blow to FDR for sure, but Democrats still maintained control of the federal government.[162]

FDR was a master politician who employed the patronage power of his office to great effect.[163] "His appointments," biographer Jean Edward Smith noted, "were calculated not only to reward, but to co-opt." He made Tennessee Senator Cordell Hull his secretary of state, for example, "to protect the administration from carping redneck legislators," while largely ignoring Hull and working through Undersecretary of State and fellow New York patrician Benjamin Sumner Welles. Similarly, John Nance Garner of Texas became his VP to solidify southern support.[164]

Some policies, like the Indian New Deal, directly moved voters from the Republican to the Democratic column. While hardly a good deal, the Indian New Deal was a big enough improvement to induce members of the Five Civilized Tribes of Oklahoma to forget their hatred of Andrew Jackson and the Trail of Tears and vote Democrat for the first time.[165]

Money, though, played the biggest role in getting FDR and his New Deal allies re-elected to political office. "Nearly all studies find," economist historian Price Fishback and two coauthors noted in a 2005 survey, "that the administration distributed more funds to areas that tended to be more volatile in their support for Democrats."[166] And that holds even when accounting for regional cost of living differences, which were not so large as New Deal apologists claimed. Solidly Democratic Tennessee, for example, had to fund a third of its own relief funding, while richer but purple Pennsylvania pitched in only a dime of every relief dollar spent in the Keystone State. That was why Georgia congressman Richard Russell in 1939, who had voted for every New Deal poor relief bill, reluctantly conceded that he had been wrong to do so. "The poorer States," he finally figured out, "would have been better off if they had gone along with their own poverty-stricken people and endeavored to take care of them."[167]

Not all New Deal spending went to swing voters, of course. Many Southerners felt like they were getting their fair share and a Georgian felt pleased to be "in on the big money. It makes us feel for the first time as if we have really been taken into the Union!" suggesting that an expectations effect was at play psychologically. In other words, they expected a paltry pittance, so they felt great when they received a little.[168]

Political considerations, however, influenced spending, with purple areas getting more FERA and CWA dollars than solidly red or blue places, all else constant.[169] (Economist historian John Wallis, however, claimed that such findings rely largely on Nevada, which had a very small population in the 1930s.[170]) Given that every two government relief jobs crowded out at least one private-sector job, the effect was to buy allegiance to the Democratic Party by making the recipient purple counties yet more dependent on federal aid.[171]

Contemporaries also noted the spending skew and something much worse, direct corruption. Frank Hague, the mayor of Jersey City, pushed FDR over the line in 1932, in part by denying meeting halls to opponents through fire codes and other regulations.[172] So Hague got to control all the WPA jobs in purple New Jersey, which ended up with the highest WPA wages in the nation. Hague screened the men politically and insisted on a 3% kickback to the Democratic Party. Meanwhile, FDR made sure that rival Huey Long could not use federal dollars to bolster his popularity in Louisiana.[173]

New Jersey was perhaps the worst case, but Hopkins received letters from throughout the country crying foul, and some written solicitations survived. One from Indiana informed a woman that unless she quickly came to appreciate her position enough to donate $28.08 to the Indiana Democratic Party, her name was to be placed "on the list of those who will not be given consideration for any other appointment."[174]

Despite such evidence, however, Hopkins adamantly argued that "all WPA workers" enjoyed "absolute political freedom … to vote as they please." He "proved" that in 1938 by posting 7000 copies of a letter stating it at WPA work sites throughout the country. Interestingly, the letter did not explain how employees were supposed to report violations of the policy, nor did it provide even paper protections for whistleblowers.[175]

Tellingly, the following year Hopkins' replacement, Colonel F.C. Harrington, praised Congress for finally passing a law making it a felony for anyone to promise a job in the WPA in exchange for a vote or campaign contribution and termination for any WPA supervisor or administrator to use "his official authority or influence to interfere in an election." Harrington then admitted that Hopkins had fought "for years to keep politics out of this program" and did "everything in his power," which wasn't much given the lack of legal penalties.[176]

Implementation of the law, though, resembled something that in the 2020s would be described as a "clown world" and in the 1930s was called "inane buffoonery."[177] As Harrington explained in March 1939, "all cases involving possible felonies" had to be forwarded to the "WPA Division of Investigation." Only then could the Department of Justice get involved, based on the "findings" of the WPA's investigation of itself.[178] "Now you might think that nothing will come of investigations made by WPA about itself," Harrington admitted in another context. "But think for a minute," he wrote. "If we don't investigate these charges," he asked, "who else is going to bother?"[179] State election officials and prosecutors seem like the obvious answer.

New Dealers also used their stash of cash to collect data. If that sounds innocuous, read James C. Scott's *Seeing Like a State*, which shows that data collection often served as the first step in the government expansion process.[180] Once a bureaucrat credibly quantifies something, it can be turned into a "problem," the mere continuance of which begs for a government program to "fix." In 1939, for example, Harrington released a report on Urban Housing, 1934–1936, begun under the CWA and FERA and completed by the WPA. The tell was in how the data was presented: not that 84% of homes remained habitable after a decade of depression, but that 16% were uninhabitable; not that 80% had a private bath or shower, but that 20% did not; not that half the structures were less than a quarter century old, but that half were built before 1915.[181]

In addition, some New Deal programs initially run through independent agencies were shifted into executive branch departments as part of FDR's 1939 Reorganization Plan Number I. Although ostensibly implemented to streamline government, many people feared it was simply a way to augment governmental power even though it was much less potent a bill than the one that a dictatorship-fearing Congress had rejected in 1938.[182] Moving the Farm Credit Administration into the Department of Agriculture, for example, started a 14-year-long controversy because "the cooperative Farm Credit System did not want to risk its usefulness to farmers by getting involved in such [politicized] issues."[183]

Government employees became an important voting bloc for the first time in the 1930s, as the number of federal employees soared and state and local officials learned how to become supplicants, looking to receive federal grant money in exchange for their political obedience.[184] And due to the growth of New Deal programs, "federal agencies are all around us," monitoring state and even county governments. "The whole warp and woof of local government," the governor of Kansas Andrew F. Schoeppel complained in 1943, "is enmeshed in the coils of bureaucratic control and regulation."[185]

New Deal money also gravitated toward better-organized special interest groups, like farmers and retirees, on the supposition that they could, and would, get the vote out in favor of FDR. And within hard-core Democratic states in the South, New Dealers concentrated on the primaries to ensure that more radical candidates defeated traditional Southern conservative Democrats.[186]

In short, FDR and most New Dealers were "HELL BENT FOR ELECTION" and did whatever they could to ensure they won again, and again, and yet again.[187] By 1936, FDR controlled a political machine and millions of voters depended on his ability to subsidize them.[188] He could push the envelope of the New Deal without risking his power base and did just that.

Notes

1. Harry Hopkins, Public Works Administration, "Resurgent Democracy," 8 Oct. 1938, FRASER.
2. James Ledbetter and Daniel B. Roth, eds., *The Great Depression: A Diary by Benjamin Roth* (New York: Public Affairs, 2009), 208.
3. Marion Turner Sheehan, ed. *The World at Home: Selections from the Writings of Anne O'Hare McCormick* (New York: Alfred A. Knopf, 1956), 173–227, 248, 278.
4. Betty Houchin Winfield, *FDR and the News Media* (New York: Columbia University Press, 1994), 103.
5. Harry Hopkins, Public Works Administration, "Resurgent Democracy," 8 Oct. 1938, FRASER.
6. John Gunther, *Inside U.S.A.* (New York: Harper & Brothers, 1947), 811.
7. Garet Garrett, *A Bubble That Broke the World* (Boston: Little, Brown, and Company, 1932), 5.
8. Anothony J. Bolton, "'The Best Form of Assistance Always Is the Kind That Enables Folks to Help Themselves': Public Reaction to the New Deal in Hancock, Seneca, and Wood Counties of Ohio," (MA Thesis: Bowling Green State University, 2021), 99.

9. Bolton, "'Best Form of Assistance'," 82–83.
10. Bolton, "'Best Form of Assistance'," 105.
11. Ledbetter and Roth, *Great Depression*, 139–40.
12. Harry L. Hopkins, "The Essence of Democracy," The Works Program, Works Progress Administration, (30 Aug. 1938), 7–9.
13. Ledbetter and Roth, *Great Depression*, 23.
14. Sylvester J. Schieber and John B. Shoven, *The Real Deal: The History and Future of Social Security* (New Haven: Yale University Press, 1999), 25.
15. As quoted in John F. Cogan, *The High Cost of Good Intentions: A History of U.S. Federal Entitlement Programs* (Stanford: Stanford University Press, 2017), 68–69.
16. Alan de Bromhead, Barry Eichengreen, and Kevin H. O'Rourke, "Right-Wing Political Extremism in the Great Depression," NBER Working Paper No. 17871 (Feb. 2012).
17. Bolton, "'Best Form of Assistance'," 90–91.
18. David T. Beito, *The New Deal's War on the Bill of Rights: The Untold Story of FDR's Concentration Camps, Censorship, and Mass Surveillance* (Oakland: Independent Institute, 2023), 124–28.
19. SEC Memorandum, 30 April, 1937, Accession Number 57A153, Box 321, Records of the Securities and Exchange Commission, RG 266, National Archives and Records Administration, College Park, Maryland.
20. Bolton, "'Best Form of Assistance'," 96–8.
21. Winfield, *FDR and the News*, 231–39.
22. Jim Powell, *FDR's Folly: How Roosevelt and His New Deal Prolonged the Great Depression* (New York: Crown Forum, 2003), 76.
23. David Beito, *From Mutual Aid to the Welfare State: Fraternal Societies and Social Services, 1890–1967* (Chapel Hill: University of North Carolina Press, 2000), 230.
24. Justin Raimondo, *Reclaiming the American Right: The Lost Legacy of the Conservative Movement* (Wilmington, DE: ISI Books, 2008), 149–54.
25. Amity Shlaes, "Introduction," in Amity Shlaes, ed. *New Deal Rebels* (Great Barrington, Mass.: American Institute for Economic Research, 2023), ix–lv.
26. Gregory L. Schneider, ed., *Conservatism in America Since 1930: A Reader* (New York: New York University Press, 2003), 5.

27. Schneider, ed., *Conservatism*, 9–28.
28. Schneider, ed., *Conservatism*, 7; Raimondo, *Reclaiming the American Right*, 130–31.
29. Lawrence W. Reed, *Great Myths of the Great Depression* (Mackinac Center for Public Policy and the Foundation for Economic Education, 2011), 14.
30. Guy J. Forgue, ed., *Letters of H.L. Mencken* (New York: Alfred A. Knopf, 1961), 403.
31. Schneider, ed., *Conservatism*, 29–44, 53–67.
32. Albert Jay Nock, *Our Enemy, the State* (New York: William Morrow & Co., 1935), 3.
33. Raimondo, *Reclaiming the American Right*, 131–33.
34. Raimondo, *Reclaiming the American Right*, 51–108.
35. Bruce Ramsey, *Unsanctioned Voice: Garet Garrett, Journalist of the Old Right* (New York: Caxton Press, 2009).
36. Forgue, ed., *Mencken*, 438.
37. Beito, *New Deal's War on the Bill of Rights*, 102–3.
38. Kari Frederickson, "Cathrine Curtis and Conservative Isolationist Women, 1939–1941," *The Historian* 58, 4 (1996): 825–39.
39. E.C. Harwood, *The Counterrevolution* (Great Barrington, Mass.: AIER, 1951), 28.
40. E.C. Harwood, "The Hopeless Folly of Inflating Commodity Prices," (March 1932), Box 1, E.C. Harwood Archives, AIER, Great Barrington, Mass.
41. See, for example, E.C. Harwood, "The First Step Toward Reform of the Money-credit System," "Alterations to the Federal Reserve Act in the Interest of Money-Credit Reform," "Inflation Again! What Are We Going to Do About It?," "Inflation Is Here! What Does This Mean to Labor?" (May 1928), "Co-ordination of National and State Banks with Money-credit Reform," "What's Wrong with the Money-Credit System?" (June 1928), Box 1, E.C. Harwood Archives, AIER, Great Barrington, Mass.
42. E.C. Harwood, "A Better Monetary Unit for Use with a Reformed Money-credit System," (June 1928) Box 1, E.C. Harwood Archives, AIER, Great Barrington, Mass.
43. E.C. Harwood, "Calculations on the Credit Expansion Limit to Present Prosperity," *The Annalist* (25 Jan. 1929), 227–28; E.C. Harwood, "Speculation in Securities vs. Commodity Speculation," *The Annalist* (15 Feb. 1929), 347, 380.

44. E.C. Harwood, "The Hoover-Foster and Catchings Plan an Economic Absurdity," (December 1928) Box 1, E.C. Harwood Archives, AIER, Great Barrington, Mass.
45. E.C. Harwood, "What Does Mr. Hoover Think of the Debenture Plan Now?" (April 1929) Box 1, E.C. Harwood Archives, AIER, Great Barrington, Mass.
46. Benjamin Baker to E.C. Harwood, 29 Nov. 1929, in re: E.C. Harwood, "The Aftermath of Getting Something for Nothing; Causes, Effects, Remedies," *The Annalist* (29 Nov. 1929), 1,052, 1,095.
47. E.C. Harwood, "A Criticism of Stimulated Construction As a Cure for Business Depression," *The Annalist* (30 May 1930), 1,155, 1,170.
48. Lawrence W. Reed, "Henry Flipper Rose from Slavery to Become West Point's First Black Graduate—and a Staunch Anti-New Dealer," *FEE* (17 July 2022).
49. Josiah Bailey, "The Conservative Manifesto," in Shlaes, *New Deal Rebels*, 199–204.
50. Kathryn Cramer Brownell, *Showbiz Politics: Hollywood in American Political Life* (Chapel Hill: University of North Carolina Press, 2014), 38.
51. John P. Davis, "A Black Inventory of the New Deal," in Shlaes, *New Deal Rebels*, 91–97.
52. Lauchlin Currie, "Lauchlin Currie's Memoirs," *Journal of Economic Studies* 31, 3/4 (2004), 227.
53. Hugh Rockoff, "By Way of Analogy: The Expansion of the Federal Government in the 1930s," in Michael D. Bordo, Claudia Goldin, and Eugene N. White, eds., *The Defining Moment: The Great Depression and the American Economy in the Twentieth Century* (Chicago: University of Chicago Press, 1998): 134.
54. Robert E. Wright and George D. Smith, *Mutually Beneficial: The Guardian and Life Insurance in America* (New York: New York University Press, 2004), 137–39.
55. Lewis W. Douglas, *The Liberal Tradition: A Free People and a Free Economy* (New York: D. Van Nostrand, 1935).
56. James P. Warburg, *Hell Bent for Election* (New York: Doubleday, Doran & Company, 1935), vii–ix.
57. Ranjit S. Dighe, "Al Smith, Economic Conservative?" Economic and Business History Society Conference (April 2012).

58. Alfred E. Smith, "Democrat or Socialist?" in Shlaes, *New Deal Rebels*, 123.
59. Davis, "Not Democratic," in Shlaes, *New Deal Rebels*, 171–78.
60. Louis Adamic, *Dynamite: The Story of Class Violence in America*, rev. ed. (1934) (Oakland: AK Press 2008), 296–97, 315–16.
61. Gary Dean Best, *Pride, Prejudice, and Politics: Roosevelt Versus Recovery, 1933–1938* (New York: Praeger, 1991), xi-xii.
62. As quoted in Raimondo, *Reclaiming the American Right*, 112.
63. Alan Brinkley, *Culture and Politics in the Great Depression* (Waco: Baylor University Press, 1998), 6–7, 25, 31–32.
64. Michael Schearer, "Batteryman versus the New Deal: The Life of Fred C. Perkins," Working Paper (9 May 2021), 16.
65. Powell, *FDR's Folly*, 49–51.
66. David M. Kennedy, "What the New Deal Did," *Political Science Quarterly* 124, 2 (Summer 2009), 252; Burton Folsom, Jr. *New Deal or Raw Deal? How FDR's Economic Legacy Has Damaged America* (New York: Simon & Schuster, 2008), 164.
67. Harry L. Hopkins, *The Realities of Unemployment* (WPA, 1937), 19.
68. Reed, *Great Myths*, 15. As quoted in Warburg, *Hell Bent*, 56.
69. Kristin S. Williams and Albert J. Mills, "Frances Perkins: Gender, Context, and History in the Neglect of a Management Theorist," *Journal of Management History* 23, 1 (2017), 37.
70. Quoted in Kennedy, "What the New Deal Did," 264.
71. As quoted in Amity Shlaes, *The Forgotten Man: A New History of the Great Depression* (New York: HarperCollins, 2007), 226.
72. Jim F. Couch and William F. Shughart, *The Political Economy of the New Deal* (Northampton, MA: Edward Elgar, 1998), 30.
73. Reed, *Great Myths*, 16.
74. Lawrence J. Christiano, Roberto Motton, Massimo Rostagno, "The Great Depression and the Friedman-Schwartz Hypothesis," NBER Working Paper 10255 (2004), 5–7.
75. Edward C. Prescott, "Some Observations on the Great Depression," *Federal Reserve Bank of Minneapolis Quarterly Review* 23. 1 (Winter 1999): 25–31.
76. Ledbetter and Roth, *Great Depression*, 50.
77. William Shughart, "The New Deal and Modern Memory," *Southern Economic Journal* 77, 3 (2011), 530.

78. J. Peter Ferderer and David A. Zalewski, "Uncertainty as a Propagating Force in the Great Depression," *Journal of Economic History* 54, 4 (Dec. 1994): 825–49.
79. Charles W. Calomiris, "Financial Facts in the Great Depression," *Journal of Economic Perspectives* 7, 2 (Spring 1993): 67.
80. Ledbetter and Roth, *Great Depression*, 71.
81. Charles W. Calomiris, "Financial Facts in the Great Depression," *Journal of Economic Perspectives* 7, 2 (Spring 1993): 68–69.
82. Shlaes, *Forgotten Man*, 347–48; Ledbetter and Roth, *Great Depression*, 72.
83. Ledbetter and Roth, *Great Depression*.
84. Shlaes, *Forgotten Man*, 8–9, 338–39.
85. Ledbetter and Roth, *Great Depression*, 23; Leonard P. Ayres, *Turning Points in Business Cycles* (New York: Macmillan Company, 1939), 129–30.
86. Powell, *FDR's Folly*, 90, 107, 109.
87. Ledbetter and Roth, *Great Depression*, 103.
88. Powell, *FDR's Folly*, 80–82.
89. Shlaes, *Forgotten Man*, 269.
90. Charles W. Calomiris and R. Glenn Hubbard, "Internal Finance and Investment: Evidence from the Undistributed Profits Tax of 1936–1937," NBER Working Paper #4288 (March 1993).
91. Benjamin Graham, "The Undistributed Profits Tax and the Investor," *Yale Law Journal* 46, 1 (Nov. 1936): 1–18.
92. Harry G. Guthmann, "The Effect of the Undistributed Profits Tax Upon the Distribution of Corporate Earnings: A Note," *Econometrica* 8, 4 (Oct. 1940): 354–56.
93. Powell, *FDR's Folly*, 81.
94. John R. Graham and Krishnamoorthy Narasimhan, "Corporate Survival and Managerial Experiences During the Great Depression," SSRN Working Paper (15 Jan. 2004); John R. Graham, Sonali Hazarika, and Krishnamoorthy Narasimhan, "Financial Distress in the Great Depression," NBER Working Paper 17388 (September 2011).
95. Ramana Nanda and Tom Nicholas, "Did Bank Distress Stifle Innovation During the Great Depression?" NBER Working Paper 20392 (August 2014).

96. Maurice Obstfeld and Alan M. Taylor, "The Great Depression as a Watershed: International Capital Mobility Over the Long Run," NBER Working Paper 5960 (1997), 7.
97. Douglas A. Irwin, "Did France Cause the Great Depression?" NBER Working Paper 16350 (September 2010).
98. "For Release to Newspapers," Works Progress Administration, No. 4-1805, (15–16 October 1938); "Mechanization Reduces Farm Labor Requirements, WPA Study Shows," WPA, 4-1884, (12 Feb. 1939), FRASER.
99. Folsom, *New Deal?*, 140.
100. Garet Garrett, *The People's Pottage* (Caldwell, ID: Caxton Printers, 1953), 17.
101. Folsom, *New Deal?*, 42.
102. Ledbetter and Roth, *Great Depression*, 149.
103. John M. Jordan, *Machine-Age Ideology: Social Engineering and American Liberalism, 1911–1939* (Chapel Hill: University of North Carolina, 1994), 236–43.
104. Winfield, *FDR and the News.*
105. Garrett, *People's Pottage*, 10, 56.
106. Works Progress Administration, The Works Program, Press Release, 16 Jul. 1938, FRASER.
107. As quoted in Schieber and Shoven, *Real Deal*, 25.
108. Folsom, *New Deal?*, 27–28, 40, 118, 220.
109. Best, *Pride*, 23.
110. Warburg, *Hell Bent*, 8.
111. Warburg, *Hell Bent*, 16–17; Powell, *FDR's Folly*, 233–35.
112. Powell, *FDR's Folly*, 235–40.
113. Ledbetter and Roth, *Great Depression*, 209.
114. Garrett, *People's Pottage*, 26.
115. Harry Hopkins, Public Works Administration, "Resurgent Democracy," 8 Oct. 1938, FRASER.
116. Gary Libecap, "The Great Depression and the Regulating State: Federal Government of Agriculture, 1884–1970," in Bordo, Gold, and White, eds. *Defining Moment*, 181–224; Naomi R. Lamoreaux and Jean-Laurent Rosenthal, "Corporate Governance and the Plight of Minority Shareholders in the United States Before the Great Depression," in Edward L. Glaeser and Claudia Goldin, eds. *Corruption and Reform: Lessons from America's*

Economic History (Chicago: University of Chicago Press, 2006), 125–52.
117. Beito, *New Deal's War on the Bill of Rights*, 59–60, 67–68, 112.
118. Gordon Persons to Bill Pape, 18 Jan. 1937, Folder 2, Baldwin County Electric Membership Corporation, Rural Electrification, SG51084, Alabama Department of Archives and History, Montgomery, Alabama.
119. Gordon Persons to Jimmy Faulkner of the Baldwin County Times, 26 Apr. 1937, Gordon Persons to Editor, Fairhope Courier, 26 Apr. 1937, Folder 2, Baldwin County Electric Membership Corporation, Rural Electrification, SG51084, Alabama Department of Archives and History, Montgomery, Alabama.
120. Ray Gamache, "Contextualizing FDR's Campaign to Recognize the Soviet Union, 1932–1933," *Harvard Ukrainian Studies* 37, 3/4 (2020): 287–322.
121. Brownell, *Showbiz*, 29, 31, 38.
122. As quoted in Winfield, *FDR and the News*, 127.
123. Beito, *New Deal's War on the Bill of Rights*, 111.
124. Ledbetter and Roth, *Great Depression*, 163.
125. Shlaes, *Forgotten Man*, 312–14.
126. Folsom, *New Deal?*, 134, 225–28.
127. Garrett, *People's Pottage*, 43–44.
128. Beito, *New Deal's War on the Bill of Rights*, 155–56, 198, 204.
129. Nock, *Our Enemy*, 25–26.
130. Schieber and Shoven, *Real Deal*, 25.
131. Brownell, *Showbiz*, 30, 33–36.
132. Beito, *New Deal's War on the Bill of Rights*, 45–48.
133. Richard Polenberg, *Reorganizing Roosevelt's Government: The Controversy Over Executive Reorganization* (Cambridge, Mass.: Harvard University Press, 1966), vii, 191–95.
134. John Doe, "A True Story from the Sand Hills" (May 1929), Box 1, E.C. Harwood Archives, AIER, Great Barrington, Mass.
135. "Howard O. Hunter Discusses Relief Needs on 'Youth Meets Government' Program Over NBC Network," WPA, 4–1904 (26 Feb. 1939).
136. Beito, *New Deal's War on the Bill of Rights*, 50.
137. W. Roger Buffalohead, "The Indian New Deal: A Review Essay," *Minnesota History* 48, 8 (Winter 1983), 339–41.

138. F. C. Harrington, "Misconceptions Concerning the WPA Program," WPA, 4-1901, (26 Feb. 1939), 5, FRASER.
139. Currie, "Memoirs," 205.
140. F.C. Harrington, "Do WPA Workers Refuse Jobs in Private Industry?" WPA, 4-1973, (3 June 1939), 1–3, FRASER.
141. "Survey of WPA Workers Dismissed Under 18-Months Rule Shows 87 Percent Without Jobs," WPA 4–2082, (26 Jan. 1940), FRASER.
142. Glenn W. Miller, *Problems of Labor* (New York: Macmillan Co., 1951), 260–61, 269–70.
143. Shlaes, *Forgotten Man*, 305.
144. As quoted in Amity Shlaes, *Great Society: A New History* (New York: HarperCollins, 2019), 67.
145. Malcolm Ross, *All Manner of Men* (New York: Harcourt, Brace, & World, 1948), 287.
146. Winfield, *FDR and the News*, 92.
147. Beito, *New Deal's War on the Bill of Rights*, 112–13.
148. Folsom, *New Deal?*, 96.
149. Lynne Olson, *Those Angry Days: Roosevelt, Lindbergh, and America's Fight Over World War II, 1939–1941* (New York: Random House, 2014), xiv.
150. Naomi Oreskes and Erik M. Conway, *The Big Myth: How American Business Taught Us to Loathe Government and Love the Free Market* (New York: Bloomsbury Publishing, 2023), 101; Beito, *New Deal's War on the Bill of Rights*, 116.
151. Beito, *New Deal's War on the Bill of Rights*, 128–29.
152. Currie, "Memoirs," 220, 224.
153. Folsom, *New Deal?*, 181, 186, 256–57.
154. Beito, *New Deal's War on the Bill of Rights*, 129–30.
155. https://www.presidency.ucsb.edu/documents/executive-order-8922-establishing-the-office-facts-and-figures
156. Patrick S. Washburn, *A Question of Sedition: The Federal Government's Investigation of the Black Press During World War II* (New York: Oxford University Press, 1986), 8.
157. Brownell, *Showbiz*, 42–74, 80, 87.
158. Ledbetter and Roth, *Great Depression*, 154, 161.
159. D. Lusinchi, "'President Landon' and the 1936 *Literary Digest* Poll: Were Automobile and Telephone Owners to Blame?" *Social Sciences History* 36, 1 (2012): 23–54.

160. Ledbetter and Roth, *Great Depression*, 214.
161. Shughart, "New Deal," 535; Neumann, Fishback, and Kantor, "Dynamics of Relief Spending," 197–98, 200.
162. Best, *Pride*, 202.
163. Folsom, *New Deal?*, 168–91.
164. Jean Edward Smith, *FDR* (New York: Random House, 2007), xi.
165. Gunther, *Inside U.S.A.*, 875.
166. Price V. Fishback, William C. Horrace, and Shawn Kantor, "Did New Deal Grant Programs Stimulate Local Economies? A Study of Federal Grants and Retail Sales During the Great Depression," *Journal of Economic History* 65, 1 (March 2005), 54–55.
167. Couch and Shughart, *Political Economy*, 139–40, 205, 217.
168. Sheehan, ed., *World at Home*, 263.
169. Price Fishback, "The Newest on the New Deal," *Essays in Economic and Business History* 36, 1 (2018): 7–9.
170. John J. Wallis, "The Political Economy of New Deal Spending Revisited, Again: With and Without Nevada," *Explorations in Economic History* 35, 2 (April 1998): 140–70.
171. John J. Wallis and Daniel K. Benjamin, "Public Relief and Private Employment in the Great Depression," *Journal of Economic History* 41, 1 (1981): 97–102; Robert A. Margo, "Employment and Unemployment in the 1930s," *Journal of Economic Perspectives* 7, 2 (Spring 1993): 56.
172. Beito, *New Deal's War on the Bill of Rights*, 7.
173. Folsom, *New Deal?*, 87–88, 147–49, 153–55.
174. Quoted in Folsom, *New Deal?*, 182.
175. "Hopkins Reaffirms Absolute Political Freedom of WPA Workers," WPA, 4-1814 (25 October 1938), FRASER.
176. F.C. Harrington, "The Outlook for the WPA," WPA, 4-1883 (5 Feb. 1939), 2–3, FRASER.
177. Nock, *Our Enemy*, 24.
178. F.C. Harrington, "WPA Issues Regulations to Prevent Illegal Political Activities," WPA 4-1913, (9 March 1939), FRASER.
179. F.C. Harrington, "Do WPA Workers Refuse Jobs in Private Industry?" WPA, 4-1973, (3 June 1939), 2, FRASER.
180. James C. Scott, *Seeing Like a State: How Certain Schemes to Improve the Human Condition Have Failed* (New York: Yale University Press, 1998).

181. "WPA Report Finds That Only 40 Percent of Urban Homes in 'Good Condition'," WPA, 4-1869, (9 Jan. 1939), FRASER.
182. Polenberg, *Reorganizing*, 184–88.
183. W. Gifford Hoag, *The Farm Credit System: A History of Financial Self-Help* (Danville, Ill.: Interstate Printers & Publishers, Inc., 1976), 249–50.
184. Nock, *Our Enemy*, 13–14.
185. Garrett, *People's Pottage*, 65.
186. Couch and Shughart, *Political Economy*, 37–38, 119–21, 190–94.
187. Warburg, *Hell Bent*, 78.
188. Shlaes, *Forgotten Man*, 375.

CHAPTER 8

Emasculating SCOTUS

With New Dealers in charge of the executive and legislative branches of the federal government from 1933 until 1947, only two parts of government could slow the massive transformation that was occurring, state governments and the U.S. Supreme Court (SCOTUS). The former could be won over with federal money but the latter, by Constitutional design, enjoyed some fiscal and political independence from the other two branches of government. Although somewhat constrained by previous precedent (*stare decisis)* and without the physical means of enforcing its rulings, SCOTUS, by a majority vote of its justices, could declare whole or parts of federal and state laws, policies, and practices unconstitutional, essentially rendering them illegal. Even early in the Depression, it did not uniformly support classical liberal views of some important laws, but it did at least tacitly support economic freedom and the unwritten constitution on many important issues. When SCOTUS finally gave itself over to the New Deal, the customary way of thinking about the Constitution and law disappeared, perhaps forever, opening the floodgates to almost a century of federal administrative bloat.[1]

Some of the justices in the U.S. Supreme Court that FDR inherited still clung to traditional views regarding the unwritten economic constitution, unenumerated rights, and federal power more generally. It therefore looked at much of the New Deal with disdain, and the feeling was mutual. New Dealers like Harry Hopkins did not believe that "the written words

R. E. Wright, *FDR's Long New Deal*,
https://doi.org/10.1007/978-3-031-74141-8_8

of the constitution" were that important because they were "merely the mechanics through which the American way finds expression."[2] Words, in other words, should not stand in the way of progress, i.e., those in power, like Hopkins, "helping" Americans.

The high court's 1934 ruling in *Nebbia*, which upheld a New York law regulating milk prices,[3] was instructive. The court made clear that its decision rested solely on the facts of the case and that in this specific instance, the statute in question was, like hoary state inspection laws, a reasonable response to a perceived "evil." The court was duped as the law, like so many other presumably Progressive measures, was purely an exercise in rent-seeking, in increasing the profits of one group at the expense of another,[4] but the precedent remained limited and of course, what a state might do under traditional police powers was not the same as what the federal government might do.

On 18 February 1935, the court, following contradictory and injudicious post-Civil War precedents, decided the Gold Clause Cases 5–4 in favor of the Federal government despite calling its confiscation of gold and its abrogation of the gold clauses in public contracts unconstitutional and in private contracts immoral.[5] Gold clauses were designed to thwart market-induced inflation, not a government-proclaimed devaluation, by forcing borrowers to repay creditors in gold should the dollar lose purchasing power. The government argued that it had sole discretion to regulate the nature and value of lawful money and because gold was no longer legal money, gold contract clauses were senseless. Moreover, gold confiscation, dollar devaluation, and abrogation had been necessary emergency measures, and they could not be reversed without severely disrupting a still shaky economy.

Claimants retorted that creditors should be repaid in paper dollars sufficient to buy the quantity of gold implicit in their contracts, i.e., the nominal debt due times 1.69, to make up for the dollar devaluation. In other words, they wanted $59.15 in the new less valuable paper dollars to satisfy an old $35.00 debt denominated in gold.[6]

The so-called Four Horsemen, conservative justices Pierce Butler, James McReynolds, George Sutherland, and Willis Van Devanter, argued that upholding abrogation would destroy the Constitution by violating Fifth Amendment protections of due process and property rights. In his minority opinion, McReynolds exclaimed that "The Constitution as many of us understood it, the instrument that has meant so much to us is gone. … Shame and humiliation are upon us now."[7]

The majority on the Court sidestepped the issue, though, by arguing that abrogation of public contracts was indeed unconstitutional but caused bondholders no loss in real terms, in terms of purchasing power, so they had no claim to extra compensation. That position also had implications for a technical sovereign debt default, as did the fact that the Treasury had already managed to retire about half of its old bonds with gold clauses, most issued during the Great War, between the abrogation and the SCOTUS decision.

To understand how the High Court could conclude that bondholders suffered no loss, it is important to understand that most justices believed that devaluation and inflation were inherently different, though they both reduced the nominal value of the dollar. Devaluation was a sovereign act that occurred all at once, and to all equally, without changing market interest rates. It did not directly raise the domestic price level, which was still well below its 1929 level. Inflation was a market phenomenon that came in fits and starts and that raised market interest rates and hence reduced asset prices. Gold clauses were meant to protect investors from inflation, not devaluation, which essentially simply changed the numeraire or unit of account, much like adding or subtracting one or more zeroes from all prices and contract values. In short, the Court saw no reason to disrupt global commercial activities, or bankrupt debtors, including potentially the U.S. government, by disavowing abrogation, a minor and rare exception to the Fifth Amendment implied by the explicit constitutional right of the federal government to regulate the value of the nation's money.[8]

Although the Four Horsemen's spirited dissent failed, they remained hopeful that in other cases they could win over one or both swing justices, Owen Roberts and Chief Justice Charles Evans Hughes. They did but rued the day, 27 May 1935, otherwise known in New Deal circles as Black Monday.

Black Monday

That day, SCOTUS unanimously struck down three pillars of the New Deal, the NIRA in *Schechter Poultry Company v. United States*, the Frazier-Lemke Farm Bankruptcy Act in *Louisville Joint Stock Land Bank v. Radford*, and presidential overreach in *Humphrey's Executor v. United States*. The court ruled in the third case that FDR had illegally fired a commissioner in the FTC.[9] In the second, it ruled that the bankruptcy law stripped mortgage lenders of property without compensation, contra the Fifth Amendment.[10] And in *Schechter*, it held that the entire NIRA was an unconstitutional delegation of legislative power to the executive.

Even though the NIRA and its Blue Eagle were already fading by 1935, the Schechter decision constituted a major blow to FDR, who responded by pushing for laws, like the Bituminous Coal Conservation Act of 1935, that implemented NIRA-like codes for specific industries.[11] He also reinstated the gist of the NIRA's labor codes in the National Labor Relations Act, or Wagner Act, of 1935 and the minimum wage in the Fair Labor Standards Act of 1938.[12]

Also in May 1935, SCOTUS nixed the Railroad Retirement Act (RRA) for violating the interstate commerce clause and the Fifth Amendment's stricture against taking property without due process. That posed a major threat to FDR's plan for implementing a sweeping social insurance act. Later, a revised RRA passed constitutional muster.[13]

In January 1936 in *U.S. v. Butler*, SCOTUS also invalidated parts of the original AAA, including a tax on food processors designed to fund payments to farmers for reducing their output.[14] FDR responded by reinstating production restrictions but tied them to so-called "soil conservation" practices. Tellingly, all the crops it claimed depleted the soil were cash crops, while so-called soil-conserving crops all happened to be forage cover crops that generally traded only in local markets. In 1938, a revamped AAA reinstated many earlier policies under a SCOTUS with a radically new view of the Constitution.[15]

FDR's Court Pack Panic Attack

After SCOTUS killed additional New Deal policies in *Carter v. Carter Coal Co.* (1936), which brought down the Bituminous Coal Conservation Act,[16] *Morehead v. New York ex rel Tipaldo* (1936), which nixed a New York minimum wage law for women and children, and some other cases, FDR's empire decided that it had to strike back. Over 330 newspaper editorials attacked the Morehead decision and FDR argued that it created a "no man's land" where no government could regulate, a bad thing from the perspective of a politician eager to augment his power. Two paid hitmen, journalists Drew Pearson and Robert Allen, slapped together a book called *The Nine Old Men* that castigated the court, especially the Four Horsemen. They called McReynolds "Scrooge" and claimed that court insiders finally settled their longstanding debate about him by concluding that he was equally stupid and lazy.[17]

Bad jurisprudence must be due to the justices being overworked, FDR claimed. He could not just fire the older justices, however, or enlarge the court through executive order. In 1937, therefore, he sent to Congress the Judicial Procedures Reform Bill, which would have allowed him to appoint a new justice whenever a sitting justice reached 75 years of age and did not retire. With six justices already aged 70 plus, the law would have allowed FDR to transform the court by "packing" it with his own appointments favorable to the New Deal.

FDR botched his own ploy, though, by arguing that more members would make the court more efficient when obviously it would simply lengthen the period of deliberation. Within days of the public announcement of his bill, publisher Frank Gannett, civil libertarian Amos Pinchot, farm equipment manufacturer Edward A. Rumely, and others formed the National Committee to Uphold Constitutional Government (NCUCG) to combat court packing. Soon hundreds of thousands of Americans had joined its mailing list and began to deluge Senators with telegrams and phone calls urging them to resist legislation granting the president sufficient power to become a dictator, like Mussolini or that guy in Germany.[18] To NCUCG, FDR, like those dictators, was a smooth-talking egotist who believed he knew more about economics and business than businessmen and economists did.[19] In July, Congress rightly rejected FDR's bill as a threat to the delicate Constitutional balance between the three main branches of government and as a dangerous precedent that could one day, sooner or later, send America straight into the jaws of totalitarianism.[20]

FDR's attempt to pack the court, combined with a relentless campaign against the free speech of critical newspaper editors, nevertheless frightened the justices into submission.[21] The high court soon reversed *Carter* and *Tipaldo*. The political pressure also hastened the retirement of Van Devanter, one of the conservative Four Horsemen. His departure made room for FDR's first SCOTUS appointee, Hugo Black. FDR would appoint eight more justices during his long tenure in office, transforming the court for decades.[22] Two of his appointees, Robert H. Jackson and Stanley Reed, served into the 1950s, Felix Frankfurter continued into the 1960s, and Black and William O. Douglas continued in active service until the 1970s, with Douglas, who was confirmed in April 1939, continuing in retired service until 1980.

Arguably the worst of the batch, Black served on the bench until 1971, retiring just 8 days before his death, a New Dealer with a shaky record on civil rights to the end.[23] A member of the second Ku Klux Klan (KKK), Black was, ironically, a major problem for people with dark skin, especially if formerly enslaved or the descendant of a former slave, or if from or descended from someone from a certain rapidly growing East Asian empire.[24] After the press dug up undeniable evidence of Black's dark past,[25] FDR denied knowledge of Black's KKK membership, but surely the president knew that almost all Alabama Democratic leaders active in the early 1920s were Klan members.[26] Black also "owned and studied Hitler's *Mein Kampf*," though presumably just to be able to study the mind of the evil dictator.[27] Yet he still supported the internment of Americans in concentration camps during World War II, as did FDR himself.[28]

FDR had to repay Black for supporting him in the 1932 election. To racists like Black and FDR, membership in the 1920s Klan was little different from membership in the Odd Fellows, Knights of Pythias, Masons, or other fraternal lodges.[29] Were that not enough, Black was hardly qualified for the job.[30] In fact, according to one of his biographers, "probably no other Justice's jurisprudence … has been subjected to such systematic and extensive criticism." His decisions were uneven at best and frequently he squabbled with Frankfurter and Jackson, the former because he was a Jew, and the latter due to jealousy.[31] Black and Frankfurter both agreed, however, that "due process clauses had to go"[32] and Jackson as attorney general had shown little interest in black civil rights and even squelched the investigation of one of FDR's urban political bosses credibly accused of intimidating black Republican voters in the 1940 election.[33] Black was also decidedly hostile to the Ninth Amendment because it could be interpreted to mean that much of the expansion of the federal government since the rise of Progressivism disparaged unenumerated rights and hence was unconstitutional.[34]

Black and most other FDR appointments were faithful followers of the New Deal, though none of them knew entirely what it entailed. But they were "modern liberals," a.k.a. Progressives, and hence willing to talk about the importance of the Constitution while decimating traditional interpretations of it in their decisions.[35] Unlike classical liberals, Black believed that the Constitution granted the federal government broad powers restricted mainly by the Bill of Rights.[36] Yet in addition to allowing FDR to do as he pleased, Black trashed parts of the Bill of Rights related to due process and other limits on federal power on numerous occasions too.[37] He remained solid only on the First Amendment. Throughout his long tenure, he decided cases based on how he felt about their impacts on real people, the law, and the Constitution, countervailing views of what constitutes a good and just society be damned. *Stare decisis*, he argued, *obiter dictum*, "has only a limited application in the field of constitutional law!".[38]

Douglas has been called the most lefty liberal in the high court's history and was also its longest serving, over 36 years. Like FDR's other appointees, he had proven himself down with the New Deal by serving as the third chairman of the SEC, an organization that pestered for-profit corporations enough to stymie any natural economic rebound from the pit of the Depression. Handpicked by the justice he replaced, another corporation basher named Louis Brandeis, author of the infamous Progressive tract, *Other People's Money*, Douglas would not disappoint. Like Black but unlike Frankfurter, Douglas did not value *stare decisis* or even judicial consistency. Allegedly a genius, Douglas behaved in an overbearing manner, particularly toward his clerks and other staff members.

Like FDR, Douglas seems to have believed that if you did not agree with him, it was because he was smarter and/or better informed than you, the sort of hubris that lent itself to the slipshod opinions, often written within 20 min, for which he became infamous. Frequently divorced, he made extra cash by writing travel books and serving as president of the Parvin Foundation. The latter connection led to an impeachment investigation in 1970 that brought about the resignation of his protégé, justice Abe Fortas. An aging vestige of the New Deal, Douglas tried to cling to his seat until a Democrat sat in the Oval Office, but a stroke forced his retirement in 1975.[39]

FDR's other appointments were not quite as jurisprudentially disruptive as Black or Douglas, but all supported the New Deal's radical agenda. Although he did not have a law degree, Jackson evolved into a much better jurist than Black. He remained most solid on civil liberties, dissenting on Japanese internment camps and serving as America's Chief Prosecutor at Nuremberg. Before joining the high court, Jackson had served FDR's tax and antitrust law enforcers. FDR groomed him as his potential successor in 1940 until FDR convinced himself that only FDR could save America. Looking to eliminate a potential rival in 1944, FDR in 1941 nominated Jackson to SCOTUS. To his great credit,

Jackson immediately began to feud with Black, who tended to settle cases based on his biases rather than *stare decisis*. Like all of FDR's appointments, however, Jackson's jurisprudence was far from above reproach. For example, he initially wanted to uphold the separate but equal doctrine of *Plessy v. Ferguson* by voting against the majority in *Brown v. Board of Education*.[40]

Reed was another New Dealer, the general counsel of the RFC and later FDR's Solicitor General. He greatly aided the government's case in the Gold Clause Cases, the AAA, the Securities Act of 1933, and other legislative pillars of the New Deal. Although he lost some of those battles, we won numerous others upholding minimum wage laws, the National Labor Relations Act, and Social Security. FDR rewarded him with a seat on the high court and he dutifully voted along with Jackson and Frankfurter on most matters, especially decisions that upheld or increased the power of the federal government. He was the final holdout on *Brown* and reportedly cried when the opinion was read.

Perhaps the most important FDR appointee, however, was Felix Frankfurter, leader of the staunchly pro-New Deal "Happy Hot Dogs," which included key policymakers like Dean Acheson, Tom Corcoran, James Landis, Jerome Frank, and Alger Hiss. From January 1939 until August 1962, Frankfurter served on the high court and authored 247 opinions, 132 concurring opinions, and 251 dissents. An advocate of judicial restraint, Frankfurter thought that the other two branches of government should have broad discretion to impose the policies that they saw fit without worrying about what the constitution or SCOTUS may have to say about the matter. In 1940, he wrote in *Minersville School District* that a local school board could expel students who refused to salute the American flag and recite the Pledge of Allegiance because the board's authority was more important than freedom of expression or religion. Forgetting about the First Amendment and other pesky parts of the Constitution was necessary to forge the brave new world envisaged by FDR and his New Dealers.[41]

"The Great Forgetting"

After FDR's victory in the 1936 election, the Court shifted in favor of the New Deal. The remaining conservative Horsemen stayed firmly opposed while Brandeis, Harlan F. Stone, Benjamin Cardozo, and soon Black, stood staunchly in favor. Hughes and Roberts, both unsurprisingly the appointees of progressive Republican Herbert Hoover, switched from generally opposed to generally in favor of the new order, which eschewed *Lochner* and other cases defending freedom of contract.[42] Some claim that they switched sides before the court-packing plan but certainly the threat implicit in FDR's attack reinforced their politically, rather than juridically, grounded flip-flop.[43] After their "switch in time," SCOTUS assaulted the commerce and general welfare clauses, turning them into tools of federal power.[44] In what has been called the "Great Forgetting," jurisprudence eschewed common law economic regulation and the unwritten constitution in favor of allowing a political movement to run roughshod over economic freedom.[45] As Arthur Krock put it, SCOTUS reprinted the Constitution on rubber so that it could be stretched to support FDR's policies.[46] Given that the New Deal did not improve the economic situation, the court's flip-flop helped to prolong the Depression as well as to empower the continued expansion of the federal government into the next century.[47]

In other words, the high court's general demeanor switched from "if in doubt, knock it out" to if in doubt, let New Dealers have their way with the Constitution. The privacy protections inherent in the Fourth Amendment, for example, were weakened by Black's uneven jurisprudence because he thought it quite reasonable for law enforcement to infringe the rights of criminals,[48] i.e., in Black's race-addled brain, black people.

Within a few years, the remnants of the unwritten constitution also lost any remaining power to check government overreach into Americans' economic freedom, though it was occasionally later invoked to support liberal causes like abortion.[49] The New Deal finally subsumed SCOTUS in 1937–38, ending the long ascendance of what has been termed legal classicism. As in all revolutions, the collapse of the old order came shockingly suddenly as Constitutional protections for economic freedom were entombed, in some cases likely forever.[50]

In March 1937, in *West Coast Hotel v. Parrish*, the court 5–4 overturned its 1923 decision in *Adkins v. Children's Hospital* by upholding the constitutionality of a state minimum wage law. In the majority opinion, Chief Justice Hughes seemed to go out of his way to kill the notion of unenumerated rights, arguing point blank that "the Constitution does not speak of freedom of contract." It safeguards liberty, "but the liberty safeguarded is liberty in a social organization which requires the protection of law against the evils which menace the health, safety, morals, and welfare of the people." Americans, in other words, were free, but only to be protected by government decree. Such a shaky decision could have been overturned but then Black arrived on the court, sealing sure victory for the New Deal in any future challenges.[51]

Another 1937 case, decided in April, *NLRB v. Jones and Laughlin Steel Corp.*, reversed the court's earlier strict interpretation of the commerce clause by upholding the National Labor Relations Act of 1935 and the Board that it created. According to jurist Richard Epstein, the 5–4 ruling was "wrong on historical, structural, and textual grounds"[52] because it overturned the commerce as trade doctrine established by John Marshall's opinion in *Gibbons v. Odgen*.[53] In the process, it upheld the ability of Congress to establish new federal agencies with the power to do just about anything given the country's integrated national economy and the Court's broad construction of "commerce" and "interstate."[54]

The following month in *Helvering v. Davis*, SCOTUS upheld the Social Security Act as coming within the "general welfare" clause. While it conceded that America's great statesmen had long debated the extent of that clause, it claimed that the issue had been settled in favor of a presumption that whatever Congress wanted was constitutional, "unless the choice is clearly wrong, a display of arbitrary power, not an exercise of judgment." Thereafter, America devolved into a majoritarian democracy from its origins as a republic with a limited government.[55] In 1938, SCOTUS in *United States v. Carolene Products Co.* upheld a state law that banned "filled milk," an inexpensive substitute product, thus opening the floodgates to yet more anticompetitive rent-seeking legislation.[56] Again in its 1939 decision in *Currin v Wallace*, the high court ruled that the federal government could do anything, including regulating local tobacco auctions, under the general welfare clause.

In 1941, SCOTUS decreed, in *United States v. Hutcheson*, that the Sherman Antitrust Act didn't apply to labor unions. Businesses that tried to consort, without the administration's consent, were subject to stringent enforcement and fines but violent labor unions became sacrosanct, even if they deliberately interfered with interstate commerce. In a 1945 decision, it decided that unions and union leaders did not have to answer for violence they instigated workers into committing.[57]

In case any doubt of the federal government's overarching powers lingered, the 1942 decision in *Wickard v. Filburn* settled the matter firmly. In 1936, an editorialist in a small paper in Ohio stated what was then obvious: America was not Soviet Russia, so "what a farmer plants in his own fields should be his own business." Moreover, government bureaucrats in neither place knew what producers and consumers wanted more than the producers and consumers themselves did.[58] By 1942, though, the by then thoroughly New-Deal-friendly Supreme Court upheld the right of the Secretary of Agriculture to prevent a farmer from growing wheat on his own land for his family's own consumption on the grounds that the farmer's actions would affect the interstate price for wheat.[59] Were not the country focused on fighting fascism abroad at that moment, some may have taken up arms against the fascists in Washington over the *Wickard* decision, which collectivists praised and then sent down the memory hole as a clear judicial error that removed almost any limit to the national government's reach under the federal commerce power.[60]

Good thing Agriculture Secretary Henry A. Wallace didn't think he should force Americans to eat more bread, eggs, or arsenic to increase the demand, and hence their prices, because Black and the rest of the pro-government Supreme Court would have allowed it. If it was something that could be sold, it was interstate commerce, and if Congress proclaimed it for the general welfare, it was constitutional, case closed. As Garet Garrett complained, Black especially undertook "extreme and fantastic extensions of the interstate commerce clause."[61]

When President Hoover had wanted to restrict credit to farmers so they would not produce so much, however, Black attacked the plan in no uncertain terms. "Mr. Jefferson in one of his letters states," Black recalled, "that when the time came that he could be directed from Washington when to sow and when to reap and how much to plant and how much to reap, the days of the independence of the farmer would be at an end."[62] What Jefferson actually wrote in his 1821 autobiography was much more concrete and ominous: "were we directed from Washington when to sow and when to reap, we should soon want bread."[63]

With the capitulation and then transformation of SCOTUS, only an electoral revolution could have stopped the New Deal's complete triumph and the nationalization of the American economy. Geopolitical, and then military, competition from Germany and Japan, though, forced FDR to head down the somewhat different path of wartime central planning. His death and the return of prosperity following the war brought with it the return of competitive two-party politics. Moreover, the existential threat shifted away from big business and capitalism and toward the Soviet Union. So instead of ending in fascistic socialism, the Long New Deal resulted in the formation of a permanent surveillance state that slowly merged big business with big government. The balance of this book describes the beginnings of that transformation before moving on to two critiques of New Deal policies, one from the perspective of vulnerable populations and the other from the standpoint of their long-term economic consequences.

Notes

1. William M. Wiecek, *The Lost World of Classical Legal Thought: Law and Ideology in America, 1886–1937* (New York: Oxford University Press, 1998).
2. Works Progress Administration, The Works Program, Press Release, 16 Jul. 1938, FRASER.
3. Colin Gordon, "Rethinking the New Deal," *Columbia Law Review* 98, 8 (Dec. 1998): 2050.
4. William F. Shughart, "Bending Before the Storm: The U.S. Supreme Court in Economic Crisis, 1935–1937," *The Independent Review* 9, 1 (Summer 2004), 61–62.
5. Richard Timberlake, *Constitutional Money: A Review of the Supreme Court's Monetary Decisions* (New York: Cambridge University Press, 2013), 221–28.
6. Sebastian Edwards, *American Default: The Untold Story of FDR, the Supreme Court, and the Battle Over Gold* (Princeton: Princeton University Press, 2018), 148–54.
7. As quoted in Edwards, *American Default*, 178.
8. Edwards, *American Default*, 158, 171–3.
9. James P. Warburg, *Hell Bent for Election* (New York: Doubleday, Doran & Company, 1935), 77.
10. Warburg, *Hell Bent*, 5.
11. Daniel J. Gifford, "The New Deal Regulatory Model: A History of Criticism and Refinements," *Minnesota Law Review* 68 (1983), 308.
12. David E. Bernstein, *Only One Place of Redress: African Americans, Labor Regulations, and the Courts from Reconstruction to the New Deal* (Durham: Duke University Press, 2001), 94–101.
13. Sylvester J. Schieber and John B. Shoven, *The Real Deal: The History and Future of Social Security* (New Haven: Yale University Press, 1999), 47.

14. Shane Hamilton, "Crop Insurance and the New Deal Roots of Agricultural Financialization in the united States," *Enterprise & Society* 21, 3 (Sept. 2020), 648–80; Bill White, *America's Fiscal Constitution: Its Triumph and Collapse* (New York: PublicAffairs, 2014), 193.
15. Gary Libecap, "The Great Depression and the Regulating State: Federal Government of Agriculture, 1884–1970," in Michael D. Bordo, Claudia Goldin, and Eugene N. White, eds. *The Defining Moment: The Great Depression and the American Economy in the Twentieth Century* (Chicago: University of Chicago Press, 1998), 195.
16. James Ledbetter and Daniel B. Roth, eds., *The Great Depression: A Diary by Benjamin Roth* (New York: Public Affairs, 2009), 172.
17. Amity Shlaes, *The Forgotten Man: A New History of the Great Depression* (New York: HarperCollins, 2007), 272–73.
18. David T. Beito, *The New Deal's War on the Bill of Rights: The Untold Story of FDR's Concentration Camps, Censorship, and Mass Surveillance* (Oakland: Independent Institute, 2023), 40–41.
19. Gary Dean Best, *Pride, Prejudice, and Politics: Roosevelt Versus Recovery, 1933–1938* (New York: Praeger, 1991), 3–4.
20. Jim Powell, *FDR's Folly: How Roosevelt and His New Deal Prolonged the Great Depression* (New York: Crown Forum, 2003), 209–11.
21. Beito, *New Deal's War on the Bill of Rights*, 41–42.
22. Shughart, "Bending," 55–83.
23. Tinsley E. Yarbrough, *Mr. Justice Black and His Critics* (Durham: Duke University Press, 1988), 256–62; John O. McGinnis, "Revisiting the Logic of Court Packing," *Law and Liberty* (29 November 2022); Beito, *New Deal's War on the Bill of Rights*, 13–14.
24. Tony A. Freyer, *Hugo L. Black and the Dilemma of American Liberalism* (New York: Pearson, 2008), 42–51, 72–74, 172–73.
25. Betty Houchin Winfield, *FDR and the News Media* (New York: Columbia University Press, 1994), 136–37.
26. Shawn Lay, ed., *The Invisible Empire in the West: Toward a New Historical Appraisal of the Ku Klux Klan* (Champaign: University of Illinois Press, 1992).
27. Freyer, *Hugo L. Black*, 104.
28. Yarbrough, *Mr. Justice Black*, 1; Beito, *New Deal's War on the Bill of Rights*, 165–200.

29. Freyer, *Hugo L. Black*, 16, 59.
30. Freyer, *Hugo L. Black*, 83; Yarbrough, *Mr. Justice Black*, 1.
31. Yarbrough, Mr. *Justice Black*, xi, 2–3.
32. As quoted in Thomas C. Grey, "The Uses of an Unwritten Constitution," *Chicago-Kent Law Review* 64, 1 (April 1988): 219.
33. Beito, *New Deal's War on the Bill of Rights*, 154–55.
34. John Hart Ely, "The Ninth Amendment," in Randy E. Barnett, ed. *The Rights Retained by the People: The History and Meaning of the Ninth Amendment* (Fairfax, Va.: George Mason University Press, 1989), 185.
35. Yarbrough, *Mr. Justice Black*, 20.
36. Freyer, *Hugo L. Black*, xvii.
37. Shughart, "Bending," 59–60.
38. Yarbrough, *Mr. Justice Black*, 22, 28, 46–63.
39. Henry J. Abraham, *Justices and Presidents: A Political History of Appointments to the Supreme Court* 3d ed. (New York: Oxford University Press, 1992).
40. Abraham, *Justices and Presidents*; Mark Tushnet and Katya Lezin, "What Really Happened in *Brown v. Board of Education*," *Columbia Law Review* 91, 8 (1991): 1867–1930.
41. Abraham, *Justices and Presidents*.
42. Shughart, "Bending," 58 n5, 67; Bernstein, *Only One Place of Redress*, 2, 7.
43. Freyer, *Hugo L. Black*, 79.
44. Gordon, "Rethinking," 2031.
45. Jeremy K. Kessler, "The Political Economy of 'Constitutional Political Economy'," *Texas Law Review* 94 (2016), 1528–29.
46. Best, *Pride*, 5.
47. Shughart, "Bending," 57.
48. Yarbrough, *Mr. Justice Black*, 198–99.
49. Grey, "Uses," 219–20.
50. Wiecek, *Lost World*, 218.
51. Freyer, *Hugo L. Black*, 79.
52. Richard A. Epstein, *Forbidden Grounds: The Case Against Employment Discrimination Laws* (Cambridge: Harvard University Press, 1992), 138.
53. Shughart, "Bending," 74.
54. Freyer, *Hugo L. Black*, 81.

55. John F. Cogan, *The High Cost of Good Intentions: A History of U.S. Federal Entitlement Programs* (Stanford: Stanford University Press, 2017), 110–12.
56. Shughart, "Bending," 74.
57. Powell, *FDR's Folly*, 216–17, 220.
58. "This Is Not Russia," *Fostoria Daily Review* (30 Oct. 1936), 4.
59. Freyer, *Hugo L. Black*, 101.
60. Epstein, *Forbidden Grounds*, 139.
61. Garet Garrett, *The People's Pottage* (Caldwell, ID: Caxton Printers, 1953), 64.
62. As quoted in Freyer, *Hugo L. Black*, 55.
63. https://avalon.law.yale.edu/19th_century/jeffauto.asp.

CHAPTER 9

In Bed with the Fed and the Red

Some of the New Deal's critics on the Right referred not to Russians but "Roosian Reds" to stress the similarities between the policies of Roosevelt and communists.[1] Such claims were not as hyperbolic as they might at first seem as the economic poverty of communism was not yet widely understood and some even argued, plausibly in the early 1930s, that it provided superior economic outcomes.[2] Moreover, one of FDR's first acts as president was to recognize the Soviet Union, though it remained godless and was in the process of starving millions in Ukraine.[3] The move surprised most American voters as it was not a plank in the 1932 Democratic Party platform.[4] Ostensibly, the move was made to aid America's foreign trade but no big uptick occurred.[5]

Several New Dealers were not just Progressives, but members of the radical collectivist left. Frances Perkins, for example, was widely known as a communist sympathizer[6] and South Dakota's Ellis Yarnel Berry considered Indian New Deal leader John Collier "a socialist ... a pure unadultered socialist."[7] Lauchlin Currie and Harry Dexter White at Treasury were communists.[8] Decisions like *Wickard* indicated that New Dealers saw nothing unconstitutional about central planning, especially when the economy wallowed in a putative crisis. By mid-1933 many on the right, like Ohio attorney Benjamin Roth, had already noticed "that the U.S. has traveled a long way toward some form of socialism or managed economy."[9] Whether card-carrying communists or not, many

R. E. Wright, *FDR's Long New Deal*,
https://doi.org/10.1007/978-3-031-74141-8_9

New Dealers advocated for government ownership of the Federal Reserve and the nation's railroads in addition to the TVA.[10]

In 1935, former New Dealer James Warburg laid out in detail how the New Deal did not fulfill promises FDR made during the 1932 campaign but rather closely matched the planks of the Socialist party platform. America rejected the Socialist candidate, Eugene Debs' successor Norman Thomas, in that election but ended up with his policy agenda anyway.[11] Al Smith made the same point a year later.[12]

The notion that the New Deal aimed to establish a command economy should not be confused with FDR's hesitation to adopt the fiscal theories of John Maynard Keynes, who argued that governments could manage their macroeconomies by borrowing and spending during downturns. In fact, Currie claimed that "Keynes was for years regarded as the archpriest of economic unsoundness."[13] FDR himself tried to minimize federal government budget deficits, especially in his first years in office, even forcing through Congress an "Economy Act" that made such drastic cuts in civilian and military pay and veterans benefits that Congress reversed most of it the next year over his veto.[14] Slowly, however, New Dealers came around to the Keynesian notion that the government could, and should, smooth output fluctuations by increasing borrowing and spending during recessions. Currie admitted that it was difficult for the government to micromanage the macroeconomy, but nevertheless concluded that it should try by slowing its "rate of expenditures during the inventory buying upswings ... and then a greatly accelerated rate of expenditure when such buying decreases."

Currie admitted "we had very little current idea of the movement of inventories" and in fact they "had no idea of the magnitude," i.e., whether the correct figure was in the 10s or the 100s.[15] But the allure of being able to spend money on pet projects and purple election districts without the tight traditional constraint of taxes waxed so strong that Hopkins tried to convince people that American governments had engaged in anti-cyclical macroeconomic policies for 150 years prior to the New Deal. "Pump priming," he claimed, "is as American as corn-on-the-cob." That included "pump priming away our national domain."[16]

After 1934, the Fed lost power relative to Treasury, which allowed the latter to force the former to monetize the debts it began to run up.[17] It ran involuntary deficits during the early part of the Depression and New Deal but later in the New Deal it started to make a virtue of necessity and began to trumpet the potential benefits of government borrowing, a habit that only grew worse in the decades to follow.[18]

Signs of economic recovery began to appear again in 1936, when even permabears like Ohio attorney Benjamin Roth believed "the depression is about over." The stock market showed the initial signs of bubble formation as investors dumped low-yield bonds for rebounding common stocks.[19] New Deal pump primers attributed the revival not to increases in the money supply, or the restoration of some business confidence, but to their own policies. Currie claimed the "general upswing" was due largely to "the excess of federal expenditures over tax revenues," i.e., deficit financing, forced upon the administration by the passage of a $2 billion veterans bonus bill.[20]

Roosevelt Depression of 1937–38

While New Dealers like Currie sought "to make the upswing as steady and as orderly as possible," the Federal Reserve, with help from Treasury, managed to botch up the money supply situation again.[21] The undistributed profits tax of 1936–37 certainly did not help matters as it reduced investment in physical capital and employment, which remained low due to continued regulatory hostility.[22] The government nixed the tax but too late to stop a drop in output largely caused by a dramatic slowdown in money growth. As gold poured into the United States again, FDR began to worry about inflation even though domestic consumer prices were still twenty percent below their 1926 level. Treasury, which retained much control over the money supply, therefore slowed money growth by sterilizing the gold inflows and signaling the administration's resolve to not allow inflation.[23]

Another major blunder occurred in 1936 when the Fed, which had been under the leadership of Marriner Eccles since November 1934, interpreted the excess reserves of commercial banks to mean that banks wanted to make loans when in fact they were simply trying to protect themselves in the event of more bank runs. The Fed feared that the excess reserves could serve as inflationary bubble tinder and that it owned too few securities to soak up enough dollars to stop such an episode. Under new powers granted to it in the Banking Act of 1935, the Fed could raise the reserve requirement, essentially reclassifying excess reserves as required and thereby making them unavailable to lend. Banks responded to the doubling of reserve requirements by selling securities and increasing loans but took the increases as a signal that the government wanted to tighten monetary policy again.[24]

After the required reserve increases and continued gold inflow sterilization, the money supply indeed tightened and eventually the price level dropped a bit.[25] It did not help that the Federal government's deficit was at the same time shrinking as the stimulus provided by the bonus bill petered out. Output dropped from May 1937 until June 1938.[26] Industrial output fell by a third in that period,[27] with steel mills in places like Youngstown dropping from 80 to just 20 percent capacity at the nadir. As conditions worsened, the stock market plummeted and many people who had bought automobiles and consumer appliances in 1935 and 1936 found themselves struggling to keep up with their bills.[28]

"The President clearly did not understand what had happened to the recovery," Currie later explained, "and was uncertain what to do."[29] So rumors that he would take "some drastic step to break" the depression his policies created went unfulfilled.[30]

Instead of trying to fix its mistake, the Fed at first remained as passive as ever, content to take orders from Morgenthau, who used the Exchange Stabilization Fund, the windfall from the 1934 dollar devaluation, to engage in open market operations, essentially desterilizing $300 million.[31] In August 1937, the Fed also cut interest rates, lowered the reserve requirement, and bought some securities in the open market, thereby increasing the money supply and finishing the reflation. The economy rebounded, even as the 1938 federal budget deficit declined yet further, to 1.2 percent of GDP, from its 1936 high of 4.4 percent.[32]

Some of the more self-aware New Dealers realized that the "Roosevelt Recession" of 1937–38, really a depression-within-a-depression, threatened the New Deal's legitimacy, especially its emerging pump priming or deficit financing approach. That forced advisers like Currie to urge that FDR double down on deficit financing. As Currie put it, "there is grave danger that the principle of conducting fiscal policy to compensate for excessive variations in private spending will be discredited unless the new spending program is immediately effective. This principle is the most important contribution of the New Deal," he claimed, so it would be a shame if it faltered due to execution errors.[33] Currie got the sign correct—fiscal belt-tightening did contribute to the 1937–38 recession—but was way off on the magnitude.[34] Monetary policy, albeit aided and abetted by labor, tax, and trade policies, constituted the leading cause of the output decline in 1929 and the big bounce out of the bottom of 1933.

That bounce would have been bigger and permanent had the government not interfered ham-handedly in almost every aspect of the economy. As investor Benjamin Roth put it in March 1938, "real prosperity cannot return until Roosevelt stops trying to reform and lets business alone under fair restrictions but with a reasonable chance to earn a profit—and also no more currency manipulation."[35] Even with such meddling, economic growth would have continued had not the Fed and Treasury mismanaged monetary policy again in 1936–37.[36] A pause in the New Deal in 1939 eventually helped too, as did the war in Europe, especially in the industrial heartland.[37]

Treasury's Wartime Capture of Monetary Policy

After the 1937 debacle, the U.S. money supply grew at a quick clip, at first due to an unprecedented inflow of gold from abroad and then because the Fed agreed to monetize increasingly large U.S. government deficits. It did so by pegging the market interest rate on Treasuries at a low level. That meant that when Treasury prices dipped (their yields went up), the Fed bought, driving bond prices up (and yields back down to their pegs). Buying bonds required putting money into circulation so, due to the peg, the money supply grew by more than 20 percent in the first two years of America's involvement in the war, and about 15 percent during the last two. The Fed continued to peg until the Treasury Accord of 1951 restored some semblance of its policy independence.[38]

Interestingly, in the early postwar years declining market interest rates meant that the peg worked in reverse, forcing the Fed to sell Treasuries and hence to reduce the money supply. Money supply growth, therefore, slowed to 6.5 percent in 1946 and declined more each year until it went slightly negative in 1949. The big postwar inflation proved transitory because a one-time postwar price-level readjustment, not easy monetary policy, caused it. Its effect was to reduce real interest rates below zero. Recall the Fisher equation, where the real interest rate is equal to the nominal interest rate minus inflation. A nominal rate of 6 percent with 10 percent inflation is therefore a − 4 percent real rate. Such a strong inducement to borrow, combined with President Truman's more business-friendly policies and postures, made business investment soar, and ensured that the U.S. economy did not suffer a postwar depression, as many feared it would.[39] Thankfully, Truman's fears of a looming "speculative financial boom" proved unfounded.[40]

Ending America's Universal Basic Asset Program

In 1934, FDR's Taylor Grazing Act ended America's longstanding universal basic asset program. Under various nineteenth-century laws, the U.S. government sold vast amounts of land, in small parcels, to anyone willing and able to work the land and pay a small fee. Beginning with FDR, the federal government began to hoard its remaining land. One might think that Progressives would have supported America's land redistribution policies but alas not when it meant that New Dealers had fewer assets to appropriate for their cause, especially as their deficits began to attract unwanted attention in the late 1930s.[41]

Moreover, America's nineteenth-century land redistribution policies ran in the "wrong" direction, from public to private. The "right" way was to make private land public again so that the government could put it to its best use, which presumably only it knew. As a result of the New Deal, government land constitutes 40 percent of the entire landmass of the continental United States. The National Park System comprises a small percentage of the total, most of which falls under the management of the Department of Defense, U.S. Fish and Wildlife (USFW), the U.S. Forest Service (USFS), or the Bureau of Land Management (BLM), which lease land for private uses like timber, grazing, or energy extraction. Despite controlling lands worth an estimated $1.8 trillion, the USFW, USFS, and BLM manage each year to expend more than they bring in, by an order of magnitude.[42]

The Natural Gas Act of 1938 gave the Federal Power Commission, which had been established in 1920 under Wilson to regulate hydroelectric dams, power over interstate natural gas pipelines and rates. A 1942 law further augmented its power. FDR's SCOTUS of course upheld its constitutionality and gave it broad scope, including the regulation of gas production itself, even by independent producers that sold their gas to pipelines, another unprecedented extension of the power of the federal government.[43] The unnecessary regulation worsened the energy crisis in the 1970s.[44]

In 1944, New Deal critic and army officer Colonel E.C. Harwood argued that the government should open up government lands, or at least natural resource rights, to returning service personnel. "Those who fight for the Nation," he argued, "have earned the right to share in its natural resources," resources that may otherwise remain under or completely unutilized. As Harwood himself noted, though, America's future prosperity lay not in the physical frontier, which had closed a generation before, but in metaphorical technological "frontiers," the number and speed of development of which "staggers the imagination." The key to those frontiers, like the physical frontier, was to allow "employers or producers [to] be influenced by the demands of buyers in free markets rather than by politically granted subsidies of any kind."[45] Unfortunately, during its war phase, the Long New Deal began a long tradition of government meddling in most technological fields, in fact all with even the remotest connection to national defense.

Creating a Communitarian Folk Mythology

As another part of the Long New Deal agenda, Roosevelt and his followers took every opportunity to move the nation down the road to serfdom. Some of the "piddling around" conducted by the WPA, for example, entailed a concerted effort to create a "folk" mythology that could stimulate class consciousness. While Joseph Stalin forced the production of art that celebrated workers and Hitler grounded Nazism in the unifying concept of *der Volk*, FDR forced the production of legends of an American people united in their opposition to Big Business. The Mayflower Compact and Constitutional Convention, for example, New Dealers set forth as examples of America's long history of central planning.[46]

Interest in American folk culture existed before the Depression, but the New Deal fueled it with cash. Numerous productions were either directly funded by the federal government or indirectly encouraged by its support of artists who showed a predilection to mock concepts underpinning classical liberalism like the notion of the "self-made man" and "rugged individualism." Documentary films like Pare Lorentz's *The Plow That Broke the Plains* (1936) and *The River* (1937) utilized a new "voice-of-God" style of narration designed to add an air of authority to very unfolksy interpretations of the devastation wrought by the Depression.[47]

The WPA's Federal Theater Project (FTP) also supported the administration with a new kind of theater called the "Living Newspaper." Actors portrayed the news of the day, often in ways skewed toward the New Deal.

In one play, "Power," an Insull character bilked an investor while electricity consumers complained of high prices. Some 60,000 people bought tickets before its New York opening. Hopkins admitted the propaganda aspect of the play but insisted that it educated consumers about the evils of private electricity companies.[48]

In another FTP play, "Triple A Plowed Under," New Dealers used public funds to strike back at the Supreme Court for rejecting large parts of the AAA. The pretext was that actors deserved to eat too but the context was to rally the radical base of the New Deal, militant workers and farmers and members of CPUSA. The FTP's head, Hallie Flanagan, had studied the Soviet theater in Russia and wrote a book about it, so she knew how to turn even marionettes into the agents of "modern social and economic ideas." No matter whether free or subsidized tickets drove commercial theaters out of business and actors into the arms of the propagandists.[49]

The WPA also ran its own radio program, aired free by many stations that realized that if they did not comply their broadcast licenses could be revoked. The Federal Housing Authority/Federal Housing Administration also ran radio shows for free, some 8000 hours worth over 375 stations in 1938 alone.[50]

To ensure that his view of the New Deal prevailed, FDR worked closely with Postmaster Frank Walker to make his papers available to scholars soon after his death. By 1970, the number of books and dissertations "resting upon the material at Hyde Park" was "already extensive." With additional records available at the National Archives, few scholars touch local documents, let alone private records that produce very different views of FDR and his policies. Unsurprisingly, the historiography of FDR's presidency, with a few notable exceptions, began to sound much like Stephen Colbert during the George W. Bush administration: was FDR just a great president or was he the greatest president? The point was to leave no room for those who find him the worst president ever to join the conversation.[51]

In fact, criticizing FDR or the New Deal long had to be done lightly or obliquely or only after paying due homage to the greatness of the great one and his great policies. A 1983 *Minnesota Law Review* article that critiqued the New Deal regulatory model, for example, began by explaining that the Depression was so bad that no matter what, scholars must praise the Roosevelt administration for having "the courage to act despite incomplete and uncertain information and theory."[52] In fact, the "staggering complexity" of the economic problem was the reason that FDR, had he been interested in the American people, should have not done anything other than increase the money supply and improve banking regulation by discouraging unit banking.

New Dealers argued that big government became increasingly necessary "as the industrial system grew complex" and small businesses could no longer compete with bigger farmers, stores, or manufacturers.[53] The biggest reason why small businesses could not compete, though, was because government regulations hit them hardest. Most were Republican stalwarts, though, so their calls for fairer treatment went unheeded. World War II and the eventual end of the Long New Deal, though, gave America's small business sector a reprieve that lasted until 2020.

Notes

1. Robin O.G. Kelley, *Hammer and Hoe: Alabama Communists During the Great Depression* (Chapel Hill: University of North Carolina Press, 2015), 78.
2. Sylvester J. Schieber and John B. Shoven, *The Real Deal: The History and Future of Social Security* (New Haven: Yale University Press, 1999), 23.
3. Ray Gamache, "Contextualizing FDR's Campaign to Recognize the Soviet Union, 1932–1933," *Harvard Ukrainian Studies* 37, 3/4 (2020): 287–322.
4. James P. Warburg, *Hell Bent for Election* (New York: Doubleday, Doran & Company, 1935), 25; Amity Shlaes, *The Forgotten Man: A New History of the Great Depression* (New York: HarperCollins, 2007), 171.
5. James Ledbetter and Daniel B. Roth, eds., *The Great Depression: A Diary by Benjamin Roth* (New York: Public Affairs, 2009), 134.
6. Kristin S. Williams and Albert J. Mills, "Frances Perkins: Gender, Context, and History in the Neglect of a Management Theorist," *Journal of Management History* 23, 1 (2017), 41–42.
7. Steven C. Schulte, "Removing the Yoke of Government: E.Y. Berry and the Origins of Indian Termination Policy," *South Dakota History* 14, 1 (1984), 52.
8. Shlaes, *Forgotten Man*, 6.
9. Ledbetter and Roth, eds., *Great Depression*, xxiii, 115, 160.
10. Warburg, *Hell Bent*, 26–27.

11. Warburg, *Hell Bent*, 3–6; Naomi Oreskes and Erik M. Conway, *The Big Myth: How American Business Taught Us to Loathe Government and Love the Free Market* (New York: Bloomsbury Publishing, 2023), 131.
12. Alfred E. Smtih, "Democrat or Socialist?" in Amity Shlaes, ed. *New Deal Rebels* (Great Barrington, Mass.: American Institute for Economic Research, 2023), 117–26.
13. Lauchlin Currie, "Lauchlin Currie's Memoirs," *Journal of Economic Studies* 31, 3/4 (2004), 227.
14. Bill White, *America's Fiscal Constitution: Its Triumph and Collapse* (New York: PublicAffairs, 2014), 190–91.
15. Currie, "Memoirs," 211.
16. Harry Hopkins, Works Progress Administration, The Works Program, Press Release, 16 July 1938.
17. Charles W. Calomoris and David C. Wheelock, "Was the Great Depression a Watershed for American Monetary Policy?" in Michael D. Bordon, Claudia Goldin, and Eugene N. White, eds. *The Defining Moment: The Great Depression and the American Economy in the Twentieth Century* (Chicago: University of Chicago Press, 1998), 23–65.
18. J. Bradford De Long, "Fiscal Policy in the Shadow of the Great Depression," in Bordo, Goldin, and White, *Defining Moment*, 67–85.
19. Ledbetter and Roth, eds., *Great Depression*, 13, 167–69, 175–77, 189, 192.
20. Currie, "Memoirs," 209; Ledbetter and Roth, eds., *Great Depression*, 172.
21. Currie, "Memoirs," 210.
22. Shlaes, *Forgotten Man*, 334–35; Jim Powell, *FDR's Folly: How Roosevelt and His New Deal Prolonged the Great Depression* (New York: Crown Forum, 2003), 231–43.
23. George Selgin, *False Dawn: The New Deal and the Promise of Recovery, 1933–1947* (Chicago: University of Chicago Press, 2025).
24. Selgin, *False Dawn*; Robert Hetzel, *The Great Recession: Market Failure or Policy Failure?* (New York: Cambridge University Press, 2012), 71–72.
25. Powell, *FDR's Folly*, 221–30.

26. Roger W. Garrison, "The Great Depression Revisited," *Independent Review* 3, 4 (Spring 1999): 600.
27. Selgin, *False Dawn*.
28. Ledbetter and Roth, eds., *Great Depression*, 209, 213.
29. Currie, "Memoirs," 212.
30. Ledbetter and Roth, eds., *Great Depression*, 210.
31. Allan Meltzer, *A History of the Federal Reserve: Volume I: 1913–1951* (Chicago: University of Chicago Press, 2003), 574–75; Hetzel, *Great Recession*, 73.
32. Thomas E. Hall and J. David Ferguson, *The Great Depression: An International Disaster of Perverse Economic Policies* (Ann Arbor: University of Michigan Press, 1998), 153–54.
33. Currie, "Memoirs," 216.
34. Selgin, *False Dawn*.
35. Ledbetter and Roth, eds., *Great Depression*, 209.
36. Selgin, *False Dawn*.
37. Ledbetter and Roth, eds., *Great Depression*, 215–35.
38. Meltzer, *History of the Federal Reserve*, 707–12.
39. Selgin, *False Dawn*; Johan Norberg, *Financial Fiasco: How America's Infatuation with Homeownership and Easy Money Created the Economic Crisis* (Washington, DC: Cato Institute, 2009), 109; Burton Folsom, Jr. *New Deal or Raw Deal? How FDR's Economic Legacy Has Damaged America* (New York: Simon & Schuster, 2008), 248.
40. Harry Truman to Ganson Purcell, Chairman of the SEC, 17 May 1945, Ganson Purcell to Harry Truman, 3 July 1945, Files of Chairmen Ganson Purcell and James J. Caffrey, and Commissioners Robert H. O'Brien and Robert K. McConnaughey, 1939–1948, Box 50, Records of the Securities and Exchange Commission, RG 266, National Archives and Records Administration, College Park, Maryland.
41. Currie, "Memoirs," 208.
42. Steve Hanke, "Public Lands: America's Great Anomaly," *Independent Institute Blog* (6 Oct. 2022).
43. Clair Wilcox, *Public Policies Toward Business* rev. ed. (Homewood, Ill., Richard D. Irwin, Inc., 1960), 623–29.
44. Oreskes and Conway, *Big Myth*, 314–15.

45. E.C. Harwood, "Stimulating Postwar Employment in the United States," (1944), Box 2, E.C. Harwood Archives, AIER, Great Barrington, Mass.
46. John M. Jordan, *Machine-Age Ideology: Social Engineering and American Liberalism, 1911–1939* (Chapel Hill: University of North Carolina, 1994), 232, 238.
47. Sonnet Retman, *Real Folks: Race and Genre in the Great Depression* (Durham, N.C.: Duke University Press, 2011), 3–7.
48. Shlaes, *Forgotten Man*, 305.
49. Garet Garrett, "Federal Theater for the Masses," in Shlaes, ed. *New Deal Rebels*, 133–41.
50. David T. Beito, *The New Deal's War on the Bill of Rights: The Untold Story of FDR's Concentration Camps, Censorship, and Mass Surveillance* (Oakland: Independent Institute, 2023), 115.
51. G.Q. Flynn, "The New Deal and Local Archives: The Pacific Northwest," *The American Archivist* 33, 1 (Jan. 1970), 44; Folsom, *New Deal?*, 14.
52. Daniel J. Gifford, "The New Deal Regulatory Model: A History of Criticism and Refinements," *Minnesota Law Review* 68 (1983), 300.
53. Works Progress Administration, The Works Program, Press Release, 16 July 1938, FRASER.

CHAPTER 10

Wartime Blues

New Dealers judged markets by their apparent effects but government officials by their announced intentions. It is little wonder, then, that when global war erupted they instinctively increased the power of those officials, in the name of peace and/or victory, of course.[1] "Dr. New Deal," FDR, morphed into "Dr. Win-the-War" with the same general policies augmented by new and more invasive ones. Americans were not allowed to question whether America's involvement in the war was more about saving the British Empire, aiding communists, and/or helping to extend the New Deal than about democracy.[2] Those who did over radio lost their broadcast licenses and those who did in print lost their second-class mail franking privileges on FDR's insistence.[3] FDR even chastised his bureaucrats when they publicly criticized "other agencies of the Government." All should just fall into line because only FDR knew everything; others should not make "public statements based either on inadequate information or on failure to appreciate all the aspects of a complex subject which is only partially in their jurisdiction."

To ensure compliance with his demands, FDR not only countenanced but encouraged men in his administration like assistant secretary of war John J. McCloy, who considered the U.S. Constitution "just a scrap of paper."[4] More independent men he simply threatened. He told the head of the SEC, for example, that the next time he felt like going to the press

R. E. Wright, *FDR's Long New Deal*,
https://doi.org/10.1007/978-3-031-74141-8_10

instead of going through him, "I ask that when you release the statement for publication, you send to me a letter of resignation."[5]

As the war geared up, the administration set out to crush any remaining opposition to the Long New Deal, including having Garet Garrett and his editor at the *Saturday Evening Post*, Wesley Stout, sacked and blacklisted. The government even cut Garrett's paper rations when he tried to self-publish using an old printing press out of his home in Tuckahoe, New Jersey. It also went after the livelihood of John T. Flynn, who had had the temerity to suggest that FDR should be impeached for secretly swapping U.S. warships for British base leases. FDR wanted America to go to war, Flynn explained, to mask the New Deal's many failures. "That Man in the White House" personally admonished the *Yale Review* and all other "respectable" outlets to bar Flynn's submissions. Old Right noninterventionist Frank Chodorov also found himself unceremoniously relieved of his duties at *The Freeman* soon after Pearl Harbor. Although FDR was not likely personally responsible for that one, he certainly created the atmosphere that encouraged such rash actions. FDR sycophants went so far as to call for Robert McCormick, the publisher of the anti-administration *Chicago Tribune*, to be hanged, shot, or locked up "in a concentration camp."[6]

If FDR had paid more attention to foreign policy, he would have earlier understood the threat posed by foreign totalitarian states and done more to nip them in the bud before they grew too powerful to thwart short of war. Focusing on policies that stood a chance of spurring economic recovery, instead of on policies that augmented his power and helped him get re-elected, would have made America look more formidable to European and Asian fascists.[7]

In fact, FDR openly admired Mussolini, who deftly positioned himself as the only viable alternative between communism and the even more extreme form of fascism that controlled Germany. FDR might have even been able to deter America's enemies had he allowed America's economy to regain its 1920s vigor by decreasing tariffs, increasing the money supply, and allowing supply and demand to determine the number and wages of workers.[8] As it turned out, an economically weak and autarkic America proved no barrier to imperial expansionism in Africa, Europe, western Asia, or east Asia.

Global war, though, helped FDR to further his domestic policy agenda. As the U.S. economy began to recover from the depression-within-a-depression that bears his name, FDR began to focus increasingly on the international scene. The domestic New Deal by 1938 was as complete as it was likely to become without another crisis, and what better crisis than a two-front war?[9]

Regardless of its causes, World War II's effect on America's mass unemployment problem was clear and salutary. By early 1942, the WPA had morphed into a job training and skills matching administration that cajoled employers to hire everyone regardless of age, race, or sex, not because it was the right policy, but to defeat foreign fascism.[10] The war also staved off several more rounds of the Long New Deal, including the Temporary National Economic Committee (TNEC), a joint Congressional and executive committee created in 1939 "to inquire into the working of our economic systems," New Dealer code for identifying new targets for regulation and taxation in faux concern over "monopoly."[11] After 18 months of testimony and the production of 3300 exhibits and 43 studies, TNEC proved unable to show that private monopolies dominated the economy or even that significant concentration occurred. All it managed to do was worry business executives enough to further mute recovery.[12]

The global conflict, however, allowed New Dealers to implement several policies that haunt Americans to this day, including job-based health insurance and the permanent surveillance state. It also allowed them to impose a regime of price controls and rationing that, along with the failure of the New Deal to end high unemployment and the postwar economic prosperity, put economic planning and other forms of technocracy back on their heels and wrecked any hopes of implementing postwar socialism.[13] Instead of socialism, America devolved into what political economist Sam Gregg calls "state capitalism"[14] and what was known in the postwar period as a "mixed economy," an economy where the government directly controlled, or controlled access to, the commanding heights of economic power, especially credit.[15]

Worst of all, perhaps, war justified more FDR power grabs. Critics like James Warburg had already warned that to affect his economic goals, FDR would have to be omnipotent as well as omniscient. Moving toward those ends forced him into "being a dictator."[16] FDR died before the war's end but left America with a form of "administrative absolutism" that has plagued its citizens and economy ever since.[17]

Birth of the "Snoopnocracy"

FDR used all the tools at his disposal, including those of the deep surveillance state, to aid allies and crush opponents.[18] As poet Berton Braley put it, "You may have thoughts but you must not speak or you'll be summoned by a New Deal Sneak!"[19] The federal government's politicized weaponization of state power was not, however, a laughing matter for many, including even Democrats like New York's Emanuel Celler, who likened Hugo Black to Benito Mussolini in his use of espionage.

FDR even weaponized the post office, instructing postmaster general James Farley to monitor Father Coughlin's mail after Coughlin began to call his one-time ally Franklin Double-Crossing Roosevelt. The administration also went after the many independent radio stations that carried Coughlin's popular jeremiads.[20] When FDR political ally Frank Hague of Jersey City got caught going through his opponents' mail, FDR instructed Farley not to prosecute because he needed Hague's support to carry purple New Jersey.[21]

Those existing tools were not always enough to ensure success, though, so FDR augmented his portfolio of surveillance. His KKK-affiliated buddy and future SCOTUS justice Senator Hugo Black, for example, used his subpoena power to force corporations to turn over records, including millions of private telegrams, to aid the investigation of the utilities industry.[22]

The FCC reduced broadcast licensing from 3 years to 6 months so that it could better control dissenting voices. Critics were known to run into mounds of red tape that did not seem to get in the way of friendlies, and a few even had their license renewals denied.[23] This was just one of many examples of administrative overreach aided and abetted by the New Deal administrative state.[24] Even minor infractions, like not airing a fireside chat, would induce punishment, like a reduction in campaign ad purchases for the offending stations.[25]

While using the power of the state to bash his enemies, FDR also employed it to boost his friends, like radio megastar Boake Carter, until they turned against him, as Carter did in 1937. FDR retaliated by pressuring Carter's main sponsor, General Foods, to muzzle him. When that tactic backfired, Carter's 1936 tax returns, and apparently other aspects of his life, suddenly became interesting to federal investigators. Not long after, Carter stopped criticizing the administration on air. His ratings plummeted and his contract was discontinued. During his final broadcast, Carter read from John Stuart Mill's *On Liberty*.

The FBI apparently played no role in the dirt digging on Carter, who had always gushed about the FBI (technically the Bureau of Investigation until 1935) and even called for the enlargement of its budget.[26] Most other administration targets, however, did not escape its wrath. The FBI was formed during the presidency of Theodore Roosevelt, ER's uncle. It attracted little attention until its involvement in the kidnapping of the infant son of famed aviator Charles Lindbergh in 1932. Passage of the anti-kidnapping Lindbergh Law in 1933 made the FBI lead investigator in any interstate kidnapping case. Led by the ambitious Anthony Fauci of his day, J. Edgar Hoover, for almost half a century (from 1924 until 1972), the FBI soon developed a reputation for being an elite law enforcement unit, aided in part by two 1935 movies, *"G" Men* and *Show Them No Mercy!*, perhaps properly considered propaganda films, and the 1935 launch of *Gang Busters*, a real crime radio show that aired until 1957.

Comic strips and pulp magazines puffing the FBI also found success. High profile arrests and shootouts with the likes of John Dillinger and Baby Face Nelson further fueled a publicity machine geared toward aggrandizing the Bureau and its leader, who became the most respected crime fighter in the nation although he mostly sat behind a desk engaging in crimes himself, including surveilling former treasury secretary Andrew Mellon.[27] The FBI above all protected the apparatus of state and naturally the sitting president. So, it is not surprising to learn that individual agents often held reactionary views. One, for example, thought a newspaper "biased" because it used "such well-known Communistic phrases as 'Civil Liberties,' 'Inalienable Rights,' and 'Freedom of Speech and of the Press'."[28]

During the run-up to World War II, the FBI investigated 180,000 Americans, including Ben Botkin, a folklorist who ran several WPA projects like the famous slave narrative compilation. The FBI officially opened his file in 1941 fearful that Botkin might be a communist and hence a critic of the president, or the war. Because of his association with the WPA, though, anti-New Dealers within the FBI were also interested in pinning something on Botkin to discredit the president. Such is the nature of a surveillance state.[29]

FDR also turned the FBI against the black press, the many newspapers written for, and by, African-Americans that had sprouted up, and grown to a significant size, after the Great War. As the war drums beat louder beginning in 1938, some black newspaper editors had the audacity to not bash Japanese incursions into China, which was the equivalent of not criticizing Putin after the 2022 invasion of Ukraine. While FDR did not prosecute any for sedition, his administration used intimidation tactics and paper rationing to ensure that they kept their criticisms of him, and the war effort, in check. For the most part, they did toe the line by, for instance, condemning black draft dodgers and "Black Hitler" Robert O. Jordan, who argued that a victorious Japanese would "liberate" people of color throughout the world.[30]

Tellingly, the first African-American White House Secretary was not appointed until February 1944. That same man, Harry McAlpin, was denied a congressional press pass. He later related that there had been plans in place to demoralize the black press by charging the editors of the leading papers with sedition, but he would not reveal his sources. Archival documents later proved that McAlpin had underestimated the size and scope of the massive investigation, which included executive departments like the Department of Justice, the Post Office, the U.S. Army, the War Productions Board, the Office of Facts and Figures, and, of course, the FBI.

The administration feared that the black press's complaints about Jim Crow, voter suppression, lynchings, and other aspects of black life in America would aid America's enemies and perhaps induce black men to avoid the draft. Attempts to gain freedom and equal rights were unpatriotic, FDR and his followers told themselves. FDR, it turns out, did not so much like the press as he liked to use reporters for his personal political gain. He would have persecuted the press mercilessly had not Attorney General Francis Biddle, a staunch defender of civil liberties, refused to go along.[31]

The FBI also investigated other critics of FDR under the 1940 Smith Act, which made it unlawful to be a member of any organization advocating for the violent overthrow of the United States, and other laws designed to augment the government's power and reach. Apologists claimed that governments possess the right to protect themselves, thus conflating the protection of politicians with the protection of the state itself. Hoover and his agents certainly used illegal surveillance techniques, including warrantless wiretaps and break-ins. They also concentrated their efforts on political, rather than national security, threats and kept their notes in secret files. Ironically, aviator Charles Lindbergh, spokesman for the noninterventionist America First Committee, which counted over 800,000 members at its height, found himself targeted. Gerald Nye, a U.S. Senator from North Dakota with the audacity to argue against FDR's cash-and-carry proposal, and Senator David I. Walsh of Massachusetts were other targets. In FDR's mind, the so-called Great Debate over American involvement in the war was simply a propaganda campaign to garner support for America's entry into the conflict.[32] Many Americans, however, still felt betrayed by Woodrow Wilson, France, and Britain regarding the nation's expensive entry into the Great War in 1917.

Most astonishingly of all, FDR also turned for aid to a covert British intelligence operation, called the British Security Coordination (BSC), in his "dirty fight" against the isolationist anti-interventionists. Led by Canadian business mogul William Stephenson, one of the real-life models for the fictional James Bond, the BSC waged information war "on all of Britain's enemies in the United States—whether German, Italian, Vichy French, or American isolationists," including sitting members of Congress. The BSC, which conducted spying missions as well as creating and disseminating propaganda, coordinated with both FDR and the FBI. BSC agents taught FBI agents how to open a target's mail surreptitiously and the latter developed a habit of doing so.[33]

After Pearl Harbor, most anti-interventionists sought to aid the American war effort, either through genuine patriotism or fear that FDR would treat dissident voices even more harshly than Wilson had done during the Great War, or FDR himself had done before the outbreak of hostilities.[34] FDR would suffer no "Quislings" (a reference to a pro-Nazi Norwegian traitor) in his war party, so he "canceled" high profile political opponents, including Lindbergh, a highly skilled pilot denied jobs in both the military and private aircraft design. Winning the next election, apparently, sat higher on FDR's agenda than winning the war.

Even the *New York Times* believed that Lindbergh would provide material support in the fight against the fascists, but FDR remained steadfast, using his influence to induce Pan American and other companies to reject Lindbergh's employment overtures. At first, only Henry Ford had the chops to defy the president and put Lindbergh to work on B-24 bomber and P-47 fighter designs and dangerous high altitude test flights. Later, the aviator helped United Aircraft to develop the Corsair for the naval and marine air forces. Were that not enough, without FDR's knowledge, Lindbergh flew combat missions in the Pacific theater as a civilian, splashed a Japanese Zero, and improved the P-38 fighter's range by some 500 miles by suggesting modifications. By no means did he single-handedly win the war in the Pacific, but few individuals matched his contribution.

FDR also kept America First chairman Robert Wood out of military uniform but allowed Hap Arnold to use him as a civilian advisor working on logistics for the Army Air Force. Wood, who was also chairman of Sears, Roebuck, won the Legion of Merit for his exceptional services. Younger America First leaders FDR allowed into low-level officer positions where they might be killed in combat, as Sargent Shriver almost was in the battle for Guadalcanal, and as Neal Anderson Scott, who proclaimed in a 1940 commencement speech that the "Yanks are *not* coming," was in the Battle of Santa Cruz.[35]

FDR also weaponized the IRS against his political opponents, including House Representative Hamilton Fish, a supporter of African-American rights and a federal antilynching bill and a critic of FDR and the New Deal, which he said was leading America "down the road to socialism and dictatorship." Payments from a German caviar retailer triggered the IRS review, which was accompanied by an FBI investigation into a sketch of a British flag flying above Roosevelt's library that Fish possessed. Investigators found nothing untoward, and Fish did not even learn of the probes until 1951.[36]

The IRS also went after Huey Long at FDR's behest. Morgenthau made sure the 250 agents on the case reported weekly on the progress of the investigation, which included planting an agent in Long's organization and using RFC funds to finance informants. They continued to prosecute members of the Long organization even after Huey's assassination in 1935 until the executors of his estate promised to back FDR in 1936. They did so, and FDR garnered 9 out of every 10 votes cast in Louisiana.

FDR also used the IRS to attack other opponents, including Mellon when the FBI could not turn up sufficient dirt on him. The audit also proved meritless, though Mellon did pay almost half a million simply to get the decade of torment to end.[37] Before joining SCOTUS, FDR hitman and Alabama Senator Hugo Black used IRS records to investigate journalist and New Deal critic David Lawrence.[38]

The IRS also went after Moses Annenberg at FDR's behest. An immigrant and a Republican, Annenberg used his *Philadelphia Inquirer* to lambaste the New Deal and to take readership away from the FDR-friendly *Philadelphia Record*. After stunning defeats in Pennsylvania in the

1938 Congressional election, FDR directed the RFC to lend money to *The Record* and released his Treasury hounds. Less fastidious than Mellon, Annenberg was found to owe some $8 million. He promised to pay it all immediately, plus penalties, but FDR wanted him in jail, so there he went in time for the 1940 presidential contest. Pennsylvania, unsurprisingly, went for FDR.

And as in the case of the post office, FDR also used the IRS to support friends, including future President Lyndon B. Johnson (LBJ). A loyal New Dealer, LBJ supported FDR even during the court packing scheme and helped put down the presidential run of fellow Texan John Nance Garner in 1940. When LBJ and his main benefactor, the huge construction company Brown & Root, got into trouble with the IRS in 1944, FDR interceded, letting the company off with a minimal payment and no publicity. LBJ himself got off Scot free, keeping his political career intact. He repaid FDR posthumously by extending the New Deal with his Great Society programs in the 1960s.[39]

In 1934, Morgenthau floated "the possibility of a house-to-house canvass throughout the United States by Treasury representatives to make certain that income tax returns are filed by all who should file them and to promote better collection of taxes." The goal was "a considerable gain in revenue to the Government."[40] The canvas did not happen, but the IRS gained even more tremendous surveillance capabilities during World War II. To prosecute the war, Congress in 1942 increased income taxes significantly, definitively turning the Progressive levy from a class to a mass tax. The following year, to ensure a steady stream of green and to reduce collection costs, it introduced mandatory payroll withholding, basically the system in place to this day. Instead of canvassing door-to-door to induce people to file, the IRS took money right out of their paychecks, forcing taxpayers to lend money to the government and to have to fill out intrusive and arcane documents to claw back misnamed tax "refunds."

FDR also weaponized the SEC. In addition to refusing a registration exemption to Dr. Townsend, the SEC scrutinized the disclosures of prominent New Deal critics, like Hearst Magazines. Finding nothing explicitly wrong with its 1937 registration filing, staffers nevertheless chastised the corporation for failing to make "prominent disclosure of certain important facts."[41]

Wartime Controls and the End of the Socialist Dream

In April 1941, months before America became an active combatant in the global war, FDR created by executive order the Office of Price Administration and Civilian Supply to combat rising prices. The Emergency Price Control Act passed in late January 1942 created a successor agency, the Office of Price Administration (OPA). From then until late 1946, the OPA administered a price control and rationing system encompassing most civilian goods and services and even rents.[42] Ironically, given the New Deal's penchant for high real wages, it tried to limit wage increases while still allowing employers to compete for employees based on fringe benefits, like health insurance.[43] In addition to setting price ceilings, the OPA also issued ration cards designed to limit the quantity of goods that Americans could buy. One could lawfully buy a desired item cheaply only if one also possessed a ration card or stamp, creating a nightmare for shoppers.[44]

Industrial inputs were subject to quantity rationing as well, through a top-down allocation system designed to ensure that war industries were fully supplied with strategic materials like aluminum, copper, and steel before any were released for consumer use. Certain classes of skilled workers were also rationed but left free to decide which employer to join when they lost their jobs at companies producing nonessential goods.

The usual story is that price controls and ration cards "worked" to limit inflation—and available price level indices suggest it did—because Americans were willing to sacrifice for the war effort. What goes unexplained, though, is why the OPA system was superior to simply allowing market prices to emerge, even if that meant a higher price level.[45] What difference did it make to Americans if they sacrificed by putting up with ration cards or if they had to pay a higher nominal price for the stuff they wanted? Indeed, until Progressives and New Dealers oversaw the federal government, wartime inflation was as American as apple pie. But, of course, allowing supply and demand free reign would have meant reducing the power of FDR and his army of federal bureaucrats. Instead of producers deciding how to adulterate goods to "stretch" their supply, government bureaucrats got to decide instead.[46]

Moreover, many Americans resisted the price and rationing regime by exchanging for goods in underground markets. Beef and gasoline were frequently traded illegally, and housewives routinely but illicitly sold or bartered unwanted ration stamps. While more efficient than waiting in long lines for desired goods, such activities constituted deadweight losses and thus hurt the war effort. Other workarounds and costs also dragged down the war effort, arguably much more than inflation would have. Thieves stole and sold ration coupons from OPA offices, while counterfeiters simply made their own, and cattle rustling became common for the first time in generations. The costs imposed by the system were so high that one in every 15 businesses got caught breaking the rules, while one in every five received warnings. Due to the wartime shortage of workers, though, OPA employed only about 5000 investigators at its height, suggesting that evasion rates were much, much higher.[47]

Americans truly suffered under wartime price controls and rationing and supported them to the minimal extent they did only to aid the war effort. They also recalled a decade earlier when the Blue Eagle had flummoxed economic recovery with price and wage floors.[48] When shortly after the war Hayek, Harwood, and Henry Hazlitt articulated the many problems with government price controls and planning, many Americans understood their message clearly. Because the postwar economy proved prosperous and robust, they would not countenance further centrally planned incursions on their economic liberty. Already by 1944, Harwood had laid out the argument that all that the American economy needed to re-achieve full employment was a return to high levels of economic freedom, i.e., low taxes, labor mobility, and effective regulation designed to ensure competition and voluntary choice.[49]

Americans could not, or would not, roll back most aspects of the New Deal, but they were happy to allow Joseph McCarthy to do his thing, and to fight a Cold War against the Soviet Union, so long as store shelves remained stocked with good goods at affordable prices.

Resetting Healthcare Policy

Like Adolf Hitler, FDR suffered from numerous maladies. Along with the complications from polio, FDR suffered from gallstones, high blood pressure, and heart disease. He smoked tobacco anyway, cutting consumption to six cigarettes per day only as his conditions worsened.[50] Doctors prescribed dietary restrictions, laxatives, barbiturates, and "a minimum of 10 hours of sleep" per night. FDR was also to avoid, to the extent possible, the "tension and irritations" of being president but that did not stop him from serving in that office from 1933 until his death in 1945, the longest stint in U.S. history by far.[51] Yet the man who did not even know what was good for himself decided that he knew what was best for everyone else by tightly linking health insurance to employment.

Critics of big government like Milton Friedman have long understood that America's healthcare system remains fundamentally flawed because of its reliance on employment-based insurance.[52] The details, though, deserve close attention because they reveal how, as with retirement savings, the Long New Deal destroyed a flexible system of private security and replaced it with a monstrosity that augmented FDR's power, at the expense of Americans' wallets and health. Tellingly, FDR purposely left health insurance out of Social Security for fear that its inclusion would have defeated the entire measure. Americans had solidly rejected government health insurance in the Progressive era and matters had not changed much due to the Depression.[53]

Interestingly, the Great Depression did not foment a healthcare crisis so New Dealers had little reason to reform health insurance or healthcare.[54] Mortality rates dropped due to fewer automobile fatalities and improvements in treating respiratory ailments like tuberculosis, pneumonia, and influenza. Death from suicide and suspicious accidents,[55] heart disease, cancer, and diabetes increased, the first two likely due to economic distress and the last likely from deteriorating diets, especially of the poor.[56] As Benjamin Roth told his diary in 1932, soup kitchens in Youngstown filled the buckets of 500 poor mendicants with soup "and a loaf of stale bread."[57] And poor tenant farmers working rich soil in Iowa often could afford only "plain lard on bread with nothing at all to help it out."[58] Roth noted that "insanity and suicide among prominent business men is on the increase."[59] The "lotta people" who committed suicide "couldn't face the disgrace" of losing their livelihoods and were part of the collateral damage of the New Deal.[60] The uptick in death from cancer, by contrast, was part of a long-term trend.[61]

Lacking sufficient reason and with other priorities, New Dealers did not directly assault America's evolving healthcare and insurance ecosystem at first, though they did, ironically, give regulatory preference to commercial insurers over nonprofit ones, especially fraternals and employee benefit organizations, like industrial sickness funds. Industrial sickness funds thrived during the Depression, in part because more sickly workers were the ones most likely to be laid off. They covered the lost wages of a large percentage of Americans at a time when medical care was still affordable out-of-pocket. Instead of using actuarial tables, though, the sickness funds and fraternals limited adverse selection and moral hazard in old-fashioned but effective ways, like initiation periods and personal visitation. New Deal technocrats wanted numbers, not stories, so they preferred the salaried actuaries of commercial insurers over volunteer administrators even though the latter typically enjoyed superior information about individual cases.[62] New Dealers did not effectively counter the increasingly powerful American Medical Association (AMA), which favored policies that maintained the power of doctors over bureaucrats and, unfortunately, patients. "We can't go up against the State Medical Societies," Roosevelt lamented, "we just can't do it."[63]

Americans seeking to cover the cost of medicine, seeing a doctor, or visiting a hospital could join a fraternal society, many of which directly employed doctors to attend to sick members. Some fraternals even had their own hospitals. When Ruth Papon of Olathe, Kansas fell ill in February 1934, the Security Benefit Association paid for her major surgery and to heal the pneumonia she contracted after the procedure. The doctors and nurses, she later reported, took a "personal interest" in her health and well-being. Millions of other Americans received similar care, with a "homey air," before FDR broke a system that had remained unbroken.

Doctors responded to the competition from the so-called contract or "lodge practice" model with uncompetitive practices like penalizing lodge doctors and unfairly disparaging their education and skill level.[64] They also allowed Americans to bypass fraternal membership by contributing directly to pre-payment plans. For a monthly or quarterly payment, subscribers to such plans were treated when they fell ill and did not have to make payments when they were laid low, thus incentivizing healthcare providers to restore them to health as quickly and efficiently as then technologically possible. Pre-paid plans especially flourished in the 1930s because they helped both patients and healthcare providers to smooth their expenditures and revenues, respectively.[65]

During World War II, less productive, more sickly workers flooded into fraternal sickness funds as most healthy prime age males found themselves in a military uniform. The influx stressed the funds and provided FDR's technocrats the opportunity to reset the industry indirectly, in a way that kept workers, employers, and doctors happy, at least at first.[66] As described above, during World War II the U.S. federal government imposed strict price controls, including on wages. In their competition for workers, companies began to offer so-called "fringe" benefits not considered wages. One of those benefits was health insurance, which the administration further encouraged by not taxing. In 1949, the NLRB further tightened the tie by asserting that unions could bargain on behalf of workers for pension and insurance benefits in addition to straight up wages, a claim that SCOTUS upheld in its *Inland Steel* and *W.R. Cross* decisions.[67]

Between 1945 and 1950, commercial health insurers came to dominate the market for actuarially based group insurance sold to employers.[68] Fraternal sickness funds soon vanished and the market for individual healthcare insurance atrophied.[69] Nonprofit and hence tax-exempt Blue Cross hospitalization and Blue Shield medical plans also thrived, gobbling up existing independent pre-paid doctor and hospital insurance programs.[70]

Like many of his other policies, FDR's great health insurance reset did not cause too much economic damage at first. Healthcare was still affordable without insurance and many adults enjoyed stable employment and the health insurance that came with it. By the time the true costs of the employer-based system became apparent, though, entrenched interests made reform politically impossible. The AMA, for example, used its deep coffers to buy advertisements in almost every newspaper in the country, thus not-so-subtly influencing their editorial policies regarding healthcare reforms. "The voluntary way," their ads stated, "is the American Way." After almost two decades of failed New Deal promises, Americans were happy to keep the federal government out of the doctor's office. Little did they know the steep price they would pay for the tragic employment-based insurance system in the ensuing decades.[71]

The Long New Deal failed to bring about socialized medicine, let alone socialism or some other form of forced collectivism, but it did move America a long way from its classical liberal roots and in so doing damaged the overall economy and the lives of many of its most vulnerable people, a tragic story is taken up in Chapter 11.

Notes

1. Jim Powell, *FDR's Folly: How Roosevelt and His New Deal Prolonged the Great Depression* (New York: Crown Forum, 2003), 26.
2. Betty Houchin Winfield, *FDR and the News Media* (New York: Columbia University Press, 1994), 191–208.

3. David T. Beito, *The New Deal's War on the Bill of Rights: The Untold Story of FDR's Concentration Camps, Censorship, and Mass Surveillance* (Oakland: Independent Institute, 2023), 214–16.
4. As quoted in Beito, *New Deal's War on the Bill of Rights*, 172.
5. Franklin D. Roosevelt to Ganson Purcell, Chairman of the SEC, 20 August 1942, 15 July 1943, Files of Chairmen Ganson Purcell and James J. Caffrey, and Commissioners Robert H. O'Brien and Robert K. McConnaughey, 1939–1948, Box 50, Records of the Securities and Exchange Commission, RG 266, National Archives and Records Administration, College Park, Maryland.
6. Justin Raimondo, *Reclaiming the American Right: The Lost Legacy of the Conservative Movement* (Wilmington, DE: ISI Books, 2008), 87–88, 92–93, 113–16, 137, 149.
7. Gary Dean Best, *Pride, Prejudice, and Politics: Roosevelt Versus Recovery, 1933–1938* (New York: Praeger, 1991), x.
8. David F. Schmitz, *The United States and Fascist Italy, 1922–1940* (Chapel Hill: University of North Carolina Press, 1988).
9. Douglas M. Charles, *J. Edgar Hoover and the Anti-Interventionists: FBI Political Surveillance and the Rise of the Domestic Security State, 1939–1945* (Columbus: Ohio State University Press, 2007), 30, 37.
10. "Dryden Calls for Intensified Effort to Train and Employ Older Workers," WPA, 4–2313, (3 May 1942), FRASER.
11. Lauchlin Currie, "Lauchlin Currie's Memoirs," *Journal of Economic Studies* 31, 3/4 (2004), 224–25.
12. Powell, *FDR's Folly*, 236–37.
13. John M. Jordan, *Machine-Age Ideology: Social Engineering and American Liberalism, 1911–1939* (Chapel Hill: University of North Carolina, 1994), 255, 261–79.
14. Samuel Gregg, *The Next American Economy: Nation, State, and Markets in an Uncertain World* (New York: Encounter Books, 2022).
15. Garet Garrett, *The People's Pottage* (Caldwell, ID: Caxton Printers, 1953), 72.
16. James P. Warburg, *Hell Bent for Election* (New York: Doubleday, Doran & Company, 1935), 36.
17. Garrett, *People's Pottage*, 17.
18. Arthur Krock called it "Snoopnocracy." Beito, *New Deal's War on the Bill of Rights*, 26.

19. As quoted in Beito, *New Deal's War on the Bill of Rights*, 28–29.
20. Beito, *New Deal's War on the Bill of Rights*, 30, 117.
21. Burton Folsom, Jr. *New Deal or Raw Deal? How FDR's Economic Legacy Has Damaged America* (New York: Simon & Schuster, 2008), 155.
22. Alice Roosevelt Longworth, "What Alice Thinks," in Amity Shlaes, ed. *New Deal Rebels* (Great Barrington, Mass.: American Institute for Economic Research, 2023), 127; Beito, *New Deal's War on the Bill of Rights*, 12–18.
23. Folsom, *New Deal?*, 234.
24. Philip Hamburger, *Is Administrative Law Unlawful?* (Chicago: University of Chicago Press, 2014), 120.
25. Winfield, *FDR and the News Media*, 109–10.
26. Beito, *New Deal's War on the Bill of Rights*, 117–21.
27. William H. Young and Nancy K. Young, "Federal Bureau of Investigation," *The Great Depression in America: A Cultural Encyclopedia, Volume 1: A—M* (Westport, Conn.: Greenwood Press, 2007), 161–64.
28. As quoted in Patrick S. Washburn, *A Question of Sedition: The Federal Government's Investigation of the Black Press During World War II* (New York: Oxford University Press, 1986), 170.
29. Susan G. Davis, "Ben Botkin's FBI File," *Journal of American Folklore* 123, 487 (Winter 2010): 3–30.
30. Washburn, *Question*, 172–73.
31. Washburn, *Question*, 3–10, 32–40, 50–52, 166–67; Beito, *New Deal's War on the Bill of Rights*, 7.
32. Charles, *J. Edgar Hoover*, 1–13, 42–52.
33. Lynne Olson, *Those Angry Days: Roosevelt, Lindbergh, and America's Fight Over World War II, 1939–1941* (New York: Random House, 2014), xvii, xix, 115–21.
34. Beito, *New Deal's War on the Bill of Rights*, 201–2.
35. Olson, *Angry Days*, 439–46.
36. Charles, *J. Edgar Hoover*, 107–13.
37. Folsom, *New Deal?*, 149–53, 160–61, 208.
38. Beito, *New Deal's War on the Bill of Rights*, 6.
39. Folsom, *New Deal?*, 156–57, 162–64, 265.
40. "For Immediate Release," 17 Jan. 1934, U.S. Treasury Press Releases, Vol. 11, 1933–34. FRASER.

41. Emphasis in original. Memorandum to Mr. Bane, 29 April 1937, Accession Number 57A153, Box 321, Records of the Securities and Exchange Commission, RG 266, National Archives and Records Administration, College Park, Maryland.
42. Clair Wilcox, *Public Policies Toward Business* rev. ed. (Homewood, Ill., Richard D. Irwin, Inc., 1960), 724–25.
43. Melissa Thomasson, "Health Insurance in the United States," *EH.Net Encyclopedia*, ed. Robert Whaples (17 April 2003); Wilcox, *Public Policies*, 726–27.
44. Robert Higgs, "The Two-Price System: U.S. Rationing During World War II," *Foundation for Economic Education* (24 April 2009): https://fee.org/articles/the-two-price-system-us-rationing-during-world-war-ii/.
45. Wilcox, *Public Policies*, 723, 727–30.
46. Higgs, "Two-Price System."
47. Hugh Rockoff, *Drastic Measures: A History of wage and Price Controls in the United States* (New York: Cambridge University Press, 1984).
48. Amity Shlaes, *The Forgotten Man: A New History of the Great Depression* (New York: HarperCollins, 2007), 203.
49. E.C. Harwood, "Stimulating Postwar Employment in the United States," (1944), Box 2, E.C. Harwood Archives, AIER, Great Barrington, Mass.
50. H. W. Brands, *A Traitor to His Class: The Privileged Life and Radical Presidency of Franklin Delano Roosevelt* (New York: Anchor Books, 2008), 778–83.
51. As quoted in Liran Einav, Amy Finkelstein, and Ray Fisman, *Risky Business: Why Insurance Markets Fail and What to Do About It* (New Haven: Yale University Press, 2022), 215.
52. Milton Friedman, "Why Government Is the Problem," *Essays in Public Policy* No. 39 (Stanford: Hoover Institution, 1993), 9–10.
53. John F. Cogan, *The High Cost of Good Intentions: A History of U.S. Federal Entitlement Programs* (Stanford: Stanford University Press, 2017), 146.
54. Colin Gordon, *Dead on Arrival: The Politics of Health Care in Twentieth-Century America* (Princeton: Princeton University Press, 2003), 190.
55. Best, *Pride*, xv.

56. Burton A. Abrams, *The Terrible Ten: A Century of Economic Folly* (Oakland: Independent Institute, 2013), 23; Shlaes, *Forgotten Man*, 1, 352; Folsom, *New Deal?*, 5.
57. James Ledbetter and Daniel B. Roth, eds., *The Great Depression: A Diary by Benjamin Roth* (New York: Public Affairs, 2009), 48.
58. Richard Willis, *Long Gone* (New York: Greenpoint Press, 2007), 37.
59. Ledbetter and Roth, *Great Depression*, 49.
60. Alan Brinkley, *Culture and Politics in the Great Depression* (Waco: Baylor University Press, 1998), 8.
61. David Stuckler, Christopher Meissner, Price Fishback, Sanjay Basu, and Martin McKee, "Banking Crises and Mortality During the Great Depression: Evidence from US Urban Populations, 1929–1937," *Journal of Epidemiology and Community Health* (March 2011).
62. John E. Murray, *Origins of American Health Insurance: A History of Industrial Sickness Funds* (New Haven: Yale University Press, 2007), 203–17.
63. Gordon, *Dead on Arrival*, 215–18.
64. David Beito, *From Mutual Aid to the Welfare State: Fraternal Societies and Social Services, 1890–1967* (Chapel Hill: University of North Carolina Press, 2000), 1, 109–28, 164–80.
65. Thomasson, "Health Insurance."
66. Gordon, *Dead on Arrival*, 219–21.
67. Thomasson, "Health Insurance"; Gordon, *Dead on Arrival*, 57–67.
68. Gordon, *Dead on Arrival*, 67–76.
69. Murray, *Origins*, 218–36.
70. Thomasson, "Health Insurance."
71. Gordon, *Dead on Arrival*, 222–24.

CHAPTER 11

Structural Discrimination and the New Deal

Most aspects of the New Deal directly hurt members of numerous vulnerable populations, including American Indians, immigrants, minors, people of color, and women. James Warburg noted in 1935 that "we are living in a time when it is fashionable to be 'social-minded'." He thought that a good thing but then noted that people too often "make the mistake of taking for granted that anything that is proposed for the good of the less fortunate elements in our social structure will actually redound to their benefit."[1] Consider, for example, that in 1930 the unemployment rate among blacks was lower than that of whites but by 1940 it was considerably higher and continued to trend higher until plateauing for decades at double the white rate starting in 1954. Minimum wage laws, pro-union policies, and occupational licensing, not a doubling of racial discrimination, explain the flip-flop and trend.[2]

Moreover, New Deal spending was lowest in the poorest states and in states with a higher percentage of black residents and tenant farmers.[3] Yet the New Deal's effects on the most vulnerable Americans remain shrouded in a mist of scholarly disinformation, like that of economist Benjamin M. Friedman, who in 2005 argued against one of the main themes of his own book to claim that "the depression experience, on balance, fostered a broader commitment to opportunity and mobility for all citizens" and that the New Deal sought "more equal economic opportunity."[4]

R. E. Wright, *FDR's Long New Deal*,
https://doi.org/10.1007/978-3-031-74141-8_11

Warburg and Friedman both missed the fact that government programs could be steered to help the better off. While New Deal housing policies did little to help the poor, for example, they greatly aided homeownership for the wealthy and middle class. America emerged from the New Deal with a dual housing policy, one part of which generously subsidized the better off through income tax deductions and the other part of which produced poor housing for the poor.[5]

The New Deal concentrated control of social welfare in the nation's capital. While that made outcomes more equal across the country, centralization came at the cost of compounding mistakes. By crowding out local charities and governments, the federal government increased its power and budget. When its policies failed, as they often did, however, the costs fell on everyone.[6]

Incomes apparently did become more equal between 1929 and 1950 because the New Deal was more supportive of low-skilled workers than professionals like attorneys and doctors,[7] who tended to be Republican. Increased income equality was a goal of socialists, after all, but the overall trend does not mean that the New Deal helped all lower income people. The most marginalized were most likely to have gotten relatively better off but worse off in absolute terms. To their stories we now turn.

American Indians

The so-called Indian New Deal began with the Wheeler-Howard or Indian Reorganization Act of 1934.[8] It allowed tribal governments to form and ended the allotment system created by the 1887 General Allotment or Dawes Act, which FDR's Indian Commissioner John Collier understood stole natives' souls as well as their lands, and tried to stop forced assimilation policies and practices.[9] Those were improvements,[10] but Collier and his legal guru Felix Solomon Cohen failed to end fractionation, one of the biggest problems facing Indians who wished to own land in large enough plots to regain economic independence.[11] They also misunderstood the root economic problem in Indian Country, which was a Federal bureaucracy that stifled Indian entrepreneurship and hence Reservation economic development.[12] As John Gunther put it shortly after World War II, "those Indians who still remain on reservations are ... still hedged in and perplexed with some bothersome restrictions" that rendered them wards of the state.[13]

Moreover, the Indian New Deal treated American Indians as homogenous tribal communities instead of individual members of their respective—and culturally, economically, and politically highly variegated—tribes.[14] That led to the misallocation of the little credit available in Indian Country and to the top-down imposition of culturally and historically inappropriate tribal governance structures. Numerous historians have noted that Collier's rhetoric and the reality of life under the Bureau of Indian Affairs (BIA) often dramatically diverged.[15] The Navajo completely rejected Collier and his Indian New Deal, in part because the BIA tried to reduce the number of sheep that they could graze, as if they could not manage natural resources themselves. Over 70 other tribes, almost a third of the total, also rejected the top-down plan.[16]

Meanwhile, Collier's daughter Nina convinced Congress to fund the Indian Arts and Crafts Board. Its leader, Rene d'Harnoncourt, has been credited with revivifying American Indian arts and crafts traditions by stimulating demand among non-Indians. To the extent that increased demand for Indian goods was genuine, and not mere virtue signaling, however, it was a profit opportunity missed by the private sector due largely to the federal government's own harshly restrictive Indian policies.[17] Overall, federal Indian policies remained abysmal, forcing most Indians who chose to remain on Reservations to live in rural squalor.[18]

Immigrants

Immigrants were less likely to receive federal work relief than the native born, all else equal.[19] That might have been because their political allegiances were changing, unformed, or heterogeneous. As noted previously, many immigrants from Mexico were ejected from the country to reduce relief rolls and competitors for jobs. Others returned home voluntarily.[20]

The politicization of government giveaways may not seem important until one realizes that during the Depression it was often a life and death matter. Areas that received more funding suffered lower suicide and infant mortality rates and higher birthrates. In the 1930s, for example, 30 infants per 1000 died in lily-white Newton, Massachusetts, while a staggering 104.5 died in heavily Latino El Paso, Texas.[21]

Although the oldest and most justifiable occupational licensing laws, like for doctors, did not discriminate overtly based on race or ethnicity, the batch that passed during the Great Depression were certainly designed to protect incumbents, mostly white native-born Americans, from competition from immigrants, especially Mexican, Chinese, and Japanese ones. In Arizona, New Mexico, California, and several other states, for example, accountants had to be full citizens. Public works project workers in Arizona, California, and Illinois also had to be citizens, as did highway workers in Texas. Private investigators in California also needed citizenship, as did mine owners in Nevada and poison sellers in South Dakota. Many other ridiculous examples could be adduced. Other citizenship-only restrictions on dog ownership, fishing, hunting, and receipt of relief were designed to make life more difficult for immigrants, especially brown-skinned ones. If nothing else, such regulations signaled that the foreign-born were not welcomed in America anymore.[22]

Minors

The Depression caused many children "acute suffering, both physical and mental."[23] Hundreds of thousands of boys, for example, ran away from home to "get by" as transients rather than burden their families further.[24] Instead of directly aiding minors, who then as now could not vote,[25] FDR in the Economy Act of 1933 slashed pension benefits paid to their widowed mothers for the wartime services of their deceased fathers. When Congress later tried to reverse the move, FDR fought it hard enough to retain 90% of his cuts.[26]

Were that not enough, various New Deal labor policies forced children out of the labor force and into government schools, which had rapidly crowded out private academies in the two decades before the Depression began.[27] Outlawing child labor had been a Progressive goal, but the Constitutional amendment they brought in 1924 was not ratified.[28] New Dealers eagerly took up the cause. The policy was clearly dubious as it involuntarily reduced family income during the most severe depression in the nation's history without palpably improving the unemployment crisis. Despite the downturn, over 2 million minors remained formally employed in 1930, but as employment opportunities decreased, many voluntarily returned to school.[29] The unemployment rate for teens still willing and able to work was 36.5% in 1937, twice the national average.[30]

Instead of allowing unemployed grandmothers or mothers to make some money by watching neighborhood children who were too young for school, or afterschool, as they traditionally had, the WPA set up subsidized childcare facilities.[31] The federal government also gave block grants to states to fund new daycare licensing programs. Both policies gave governments more control over who could provide childcare services and made working parents yet more beholden to FDR and state-level bureaucrats.[32]

Forced schooling seemed salutary for the children themselves but only to the extent that they received an education of sufficient quality to make up for their lost income and work experience. We know that despite the decisions in *Plessy v. Ferguson* (1896) and *Brown v. Board of Education* (1954) the quality of government schooling remained uneven across the United States, with poorer districts more likely to produce poorer outcomes.[33] During the Depression itself, in many districts public high school attendance rates increased as funding decreased, leading to overcrowded classrooms and relatively low-quality outcomes.[34] The big jump in high school graduation rates applauded by some scholars, in other words, came at the cost of increasing the education gap between whites and non-whites and the rich and the poor.[35]

A longitudinal study that tracked the social mobility of thousands of fathers and their sons over the 1930s shows that what New Dealers saw as preventing "child labor" and saving jobs for adult men was a bane to poor adolescent men who lost valuable job experience. Specifically, sons living in the cities where the Depression struck hardest were less socially mobile than the sons living in cities that fared better. They were also less socially mobile than they expected to be given the degree of intergenerational mobility in their cities between 1900 and 1920. New Deal spending, the study showed, did nothing to improve the social mobility of any group of sons. It did not aid the American Dream, but rather allowed the Depression to calcify the mobility ladder, especially for sons born in the cities that suffered the biggest downturns.[36]

A similar study tracked children residing within a HOLC mortgage map redline in the 1930s with children from similar backgrounds and neighborhoods living outside of the redlined area. It found that through the 1970s and up to at least the 2000 Census, the children who had lived in the New Deal mortgage credit desert were more likely in later life to have lower levels of educational achievement and income and to live in high poverty neighborhoods.[37]

Social Security also hurt minors by reducing their inheritance to an annuity that ceased when they turned 18 (at times 21). While that annuity has saved many a minor from penury, it is not free but rather paid through the Social Security payroll tax. Without it, parents would purchase inexpensive industrial or term-life insurance instead. Such policies are much more flexible than the one-size-fits-all Social Security survivorship annuity and could be structured to fund college or to seed a business in addition to meeting consumption needs. While FDR boasted that Social Security protected Americans from "poverty-ridden old age," he neglected to note that it came at the cost of poverty for youths whose parents were unable to accumulate and bequeath assets due to the payroll tax.[38]

While ER's pet NYA doubtless helped youngsters under 21, almost three in five were male and almost nine in ten were white.[39] Although remembered for aiding blacks and other minorities, ER always kept an eye on the political consequences of her causes.[40] Her husband, after all, was an inveterate racist who once proclaimed that everyone knew that "the mingling of Asiatic blood with European or American blood produces, in nine cases out of ten, the most unfortunate results." After all, aggression "was in the blood" of the Japanese.[41]

People of Color

Despite continuing racism and repressive state laws, mostly the product of the Democratic Party,[42] African-Americans made tremendous economic gains in the half century after Emancipation. They would have made even more rapid strides without Jim Crow laws and with greater access to the financial system but by the eve of the Great War blacks in the United States owned almost a million farms, about 40,000 nonfarm businesses, over half a million homes, and an estimated $700 million in wealth. In 1924, African-American George Schuyler noted that most blacks had not joined radical movements, like those of Marcus Garvey, because they knew that they "were so much better fixed financially than anywhere else."[43] Most, however, remained vulnerable to the economic and policy shocks awaiting them.[44]

Although the federal government sometimes helped African-Americans, as during Reconstruction and the Civil Rights Movement, it often hurt them too. "The centralization of power," two scholars of the subject recently noted, "can often mean the uniform imposition of an unjust system instead of a merely balkanized one."[45] The New Deal was one such episode. The Depression decimated blacks, with almost nine out of ten families living below the federal poverty threshold. Life expectancy dropped overall, but much more for Blacks than for whites.[46]

Yet FDR did little to help. Several New Deal programs, including Social Security, excluded farm and domestic workers in part of a compromise with Southern paternalists who feared loss of control over workers, especially black workers, due to the expansion of federal power.[47] Half of black Americans were farmers in 1932 and a large percentage of the other half worked as domestics.[48] The sums lost were so large that at least one historian has called for reparations for the losses incurred by black families denied Social Security payments when they were a windfall early in the program's history.[49] Similarly, states with a higher percentage of black farmers received less federal agricultural aid per farmer.[50]

The federal minimum wage in effect from 1933 until 1935 under the Blue Eagle, and then from 1938 onward, along with state minimum wages when they were higher than the federal, also decreased employment. Indeed African-Americans, then routinely referred to as "Negroes," called the NRA the "Negro Removal Act," "Negro Robbed Again," or "Negro Rarely Allowed," because of its negative effects on their employment. According to one contemporary estimate, the NRA cost African-Americans half a million jobs during its two-year existence.[51]

The NRA's minimum wage requirements hurt blacks because they were traditionally the first fired.[52] Urban blacks were the last hired and first fired.[53] In January 1931 in Buffalo, New York, for example, 35.5% of white males were jobless while black male unemployment was over 50%. In only one of the 19 cities where surveys were conducted that month, Boston, did the white unemployment rate (28.2%) exceed that of blacks (26.2%). The disparity between white and black female workers was even bigger. In Detroit, for example, exactly 3 in 4 black women in the labor force were out of work, while "only" 17.4% of white women could not find work.[54]

The federal minimum wage constrained employment mostly in the South. By some accounts, though, it was routinely evaded.[55] In Greensboro, North Carolina, for example, the blacks who kept their jobs did so only by working long hours for wages well below those mandated by government.[56] Where it was binding, though, blacks (and immigrants) typically lost their jobs first.[57] And that outcome was exactly what many economists and New Dealers wanted.[58] Denied union and non-union private-sector jobs due to the minimum wage, blacks also faced direct discrimination from New Deal policies. The 1934 revisions to the Railway

Labor Act worked to exclude blacks from high wage railroad employment, as did the NRA, the codes of which could officially prefer whites over blacks who, if hired at all, received lower pay for the same work.[59]

Members of other disadvantaged groups also found the NRA and other labor laws restricted their employment opportunities.[60] Enforcement of state and federal minimum wages, plus whatever else caused real wages to increase during the Depression, especially hurt the prospects of the so-called "hardcore" unemployed, which included minorities, older workers, and those who, for whatever reasons, had long been out of the formal private labor force.[61]

Because FDR lacked the fortitude to stand up to the Southern bigots he needed to win re-election, the NLRB also excluded agricultural and domestic workers, or in other words the poorest workers of all. Recall that the Progressive movement from which FDR and the New Deal sprang was highly racist, pro-KKK, and pro-eugenics. There was a reason why the Nazis cited American eugenic thinkers to justify their infamous 1933 Law for the Prevention of Progeny with Hereditary Disease.[62]

In Alabama, actual card-carrying communists tried to drum up support by attacking overt acts of racism, like the Scottsboro Frame-up of nine black teenagers riding the rails near Paint Rock. The tactic backfired at first because the KKK and other racists successfully framed Alabama's communist party as part of a global communist conspiracy to "nationalize" the mothers, sisters, wives, and daughters of broke and broken American workers. To side with the communists, they argued, was to accept miscegenation and, if that was not bad enough for the less bigoted, public promiscuity. Nevertheless, the ranks of the communist party in Alabama swelled, in large part due to an influx of blacks fed up with lynchings and their second-class treatment by the courts.[63] But FDR would not support a federal antilynching law because he remained in league with white Southern leaders determined to control blacks.[64]

New Dealers steered clear of socializing healthcare in part because they did not want to provide African-Americans with quality healthcare. Their destruction of fraternal greatly hurt blacks, many of whom looked to their fraternals for health insurance and other forms of community-based self-help.[65]

Social Security's means-tested welfare program, Aid to Families with Dependent Children (AFDC), crowded out industrial life insurance. More importantly, it ravaged some families composed of people of color, particularly African-Americans, in part by preventing children from adding much to family income even though that usually meant they were left unsupervised at home when not forced to spend time in a compulsory government school. Many working mothers had to work through periods of illness and yet in 1945 two in five still did not meet government minimum budget guidelines.[66]

Benefit formula changes made in the 1960s worsened AFDC's effects by denying benefits to women who worked or had any live-in male companionship. AFDC provided disincentives to work and to form stable nuclear family units that arguably destroyed the black family and community.[67] In 1996, the failed program was scrapped in favor of a new and somewhat improved approach, Temporary Assistance for Needy Families but governments today implement new welfare programs under the guise of "universal basic income" policies paid only to black women.

Social Security's old-age annuity program has also hampered wealth acquisition by African-Americans, Hispanics, and other people of color. Initially, Social Security excluded the self-employed and those in domestic service and agriculture, the majority of whom were people of color.[68] That was when the program was a boon to participants, many of whom received much more in benefits than they had paid out in taxes.[69] (The first recipient, Ida Fuller, received almost $23,000 for total taxes paid of just $24.75.[70]) As returns dropped, additional occupational groups were added, including many dominated by African-Americans. That was not, however, a boon for them as the program was structured so that it redistributes wealth from black and Hispanic males to old white women. That is because many people of color receive little if they die before retirement age, but after their children remain eligible for survivorship benefits, a common occurrence for African-American males.[71]

As noted previously, after emancipation, and especially after their Great Migration to northern cities, African-Americans made progress in wealth holdings relative to whites. Convergence between the wealth holdings of whites and blacks stalled again after 1950, however, as the effects of World War II and the Great Migration wore off.[72] Convergence began to reverse in the 1980s, arguably due to Social Security making it more difficult for black households to purchase business equity or financial securities that could be bequeathed to heirs.

During the New Deal, blacks received fewer public construction dollars per capita and some major public works programs disproportionately displaced them. "Across the country," one scholar recently argued, "Black workers were employed on projects so long as they did not threaten the status quo."[73] Federal support for labor unions in the Davis-Bacon Act (1931) and state-level equivalents, the Wagner Act, and the Fair Labor Standards Act (1938) also hurt people of color because they tended to be less educated and lower skilled than whites and could no longer lawfully compete for jobs by accepting a lower wage.[74] Some unions banned people of color from membership while others steered them into the lowest-paid job categories.[75] The Davis-Bacon act effectively kept blacks out of the construction trades for decades.[76] Little wonder that Frederick Douglass, Booker T. Washington, and even, at times, the socialist W.E.B. DuBois thought unions harmful to people of color.[77]

Urban blacks faced disproportional loss of their homes. The Wagner-Steagall Act of 1937 created a U.S. Housing Authority (USHA) charged with constructing housing for low-income Americans. The USHA "did not work," in the frank assessment of one historian, "to increase the supply of affordable housing nor did it promote low-income homeownership."[78] Another historian explained that because the law left decision-making in the hands of local governments, instead of USHA bureaucrats, little could be accomplished. Public housing was generally received, in the words of one contemporary commentator, with "the same enthusiasm as they might have greeted the introduction of bubonic plague."[79] Low rent housing under government ownership usually quickly deteriorated physically and were soon seen as "ghettos" for minority groups.[80]

Another barrier to the USHA's success was the stipulation that federal construction projects be tied to "slum" clearance. In other words, instead of building in attractive locations on new land, USHA had to tear down existing low-income housing and rebuild on the same site. An earlier program created to clear slums in the nation's capital, the D.C. Alley Dwelling Authority, had experienced some success but worked more closely with tenants and builders than the USHA did.[81] Moreover, unlike some PWA projects that people enjoyed living in due to architectural features and amenities like swimming pools, the USHA projects created cheap high-density units that quickly deteriorated into ramshackle, crime-ridden hellholes.[82]

Rural blacks were also hurt by the New Deal, which did nothing to stop the continuous transfer of farmland owned by African-Americans to whites. The farmland loss trend reversed slightly during World War II, only to accelerate after 1950.[83] The crop destruction program of the AAA displaced over 100,000 African-American tenant farmers.[84] Subsequent efforts to help farmers also primarily aided whites rather than farmers of color,[85] although because the AAA was "built around commodities instead of people" it did not help many farmers of any skin hue.[86]

The TVA displaced many tenant farmers, too, some white but many black. In 1932, after all, four in five black farmers were tenants.[87] Unlike landowners, tenants received no compensation when the TVA flooded the land they worked to create hydroelectric dams of dubious necessity.[88] Still, Agriculture Secretary Henry Wallace feared that the New Deal might be helping blacks too much, thus risking white backlash at the all-important polls.[89]

In the South, blacks stayed away from programs administered by state and local officials and remained distrustful of federal officials as well. So, they received less relief than they should have in some rural areas. In some urban areas, blacks received more than they should have,[90] suggesting attempts to win them over to the Democrats politically and/or to immiserate them.

FDR's administration put a few African-Americans in positions of influence, honor, and some power to try to convince them that the Democrats were now their friends. It was only virtue signaling, though, as two National Conferences on the Problems of the Negro and Negro Youth concluded that FDR's administration had failed "to include adequate Negro personnel in administrative and supervisory positions throughout the government."[91] Moreover, lynchings and the persecution of young black men, like the Scottsboro Boys, continued without federal intrusion.[92] And while FDR allegedly had a "black cabinet," he rarely met with them, and when he did he talked at them rather than listening to them.[93] FDR even allowed his weaponized IRS to harry African-American athletes, outspoken Republican ones like Jesse Owens and Joe Louis anyway.[94]

Overall, it made little sense to try to win the votes of African-Americans in the South, many of whom were happy with whatever aid they could get. Democrats suppressed or even directly purchased their votes. The secret ballot had not de facto reached the South by the New Deal, so voters who turned in their ballots marked the right way could be identified and rewarded. Those who refused to sell their votes, or who voted in districts with minimum secrecy precautions, still could be identified later and punished in various ways, including job loss and stringent application of building codes and real estate tax laws.[95] In the North, blacks left the Republican party more than they flocked to the Democratic one.[96]

Only when the economy began to transition back toward full employment due to the global war did the New Deal start to push for some semblance of civil rights for African-Americans with the 1941 creation, by executive order, of the Fair Employment Practice Committee (FEPC).[97] One early assessment by an FEPC insider concluded that any progress that "Negroes and Mexican-American mass workers" made was due to wartime conditions, not the FEPC. The FEPC, he noted, remained so singularly focused on the workplace that it was nowhere to be found when it came to Japanese-American internment camps because the "Nisei" did "not generally seek industrial jobs, or go in for government service."[98] FDR supported internment because he didn't care much about the civil liberties of anyone, much less people of color.[99] He was known in private to mock Japanese speech patterns and far from simply allowing internment he sought reasons to put Japanese-Americans in "concentration" camps.[100] As his first SCOTUS appointee Justice Hugo Black noted, "Japs" had to be watched in camps because all Japanese-Americans "look alike to a person not a Jap."[101] Even after it was clearly not militarily necessary to inter Japanese-Americans, FDR left them to rot in their camps for fear of losing votes in the 1944 election.[102]

Despite high-quality and highly committed staff, the FEPC remained ineffective, especially in the South where it was most needed, because of political wrangling, a tiny budget, and the inability of government to force a man "to alter his feelings."[103] According to one scholar's assessment, "at its worst, the FEPC was completely ineffective. At its best, it froze an unfavorable status quo."[104] In short, it largely constituted a form of virtue signaling but extended tentative precedents that would bear more copious fruit in the 1960s.[105]

Meanwhile, the Mexicans and other Hispanics not booted out of the country early in the Great Depression struggled to earn adequate wages, even during World War II. Non-citizens were denied WPA jobs and many communities would not provide relief even to American-born itinerants.[106]

Women

Although not implemented until the Eisenhower administration, America's woefully inadequate "any occ" disability system can also be blamed on the New Deal because it would not have been implemented were Social Security not in place.[107] Social Security's Disability Insurance (SSDI) crowded out the low end of private disability insurance, forcing tens of millions of Americans to accept the judgments of government workers when filing disability claims, which, unlike retirement and survivorship claims, are subject to considerable discretion and ambiguity. Sometimes, claims analysts were too lax, accepting people who were not really disabled to win their political allegiance. Other times, claims analysts were too stringent, rejecting truly disabled applicants in order to meet budgetary or political goals.[108] All of the time, applicants risked rejection solely on the basis of their skin color, marital status, or gender, or other forms of bias that commercial providers find more costly to get away with in competitive markets or in heavily regulated industries, like insurance.[109] Eligibility requirements also stymie people of color and women because they tend to possess less stable employment histories. At least one study has found that SSDI fails to serve older women, in particular.[110]

Women were also not well served by the Blue Eagle as many of the codes included lower pay scales for females. That may have increased their employability but to the extent that employers substituted women for men it cut into the administration's stated goal of bolstering wages.[111]

The New Deal's effects on employment hurt women, especially poorer ones. But it also affected wealthy women too. NYA grants to elite women-only private colleges, for example, proved highly problematic. Less than 4% of the adult female population, and 5.5% of the adult male population, had a college degree in 1940, and most degrees were conferred by state universities or teacher training colleges. Elite colleges were where the wealthiest of the wealthy, the elites of the elite class, went to find a spouse and learn how to become productive members of the ruling class. Many elite female colleges resented the strings attached to FDR's aid and some of Massachusetts' Seven Sisters, fearful of losing their recently acquired and hard-won autonomy, joined 130-plus other private institutions to reject the federal monies, much of which was slated for work-study programs so students could cover their tuition and fees. The over 1400 public and private institutions that accepted the aid soon rued the decision due to the onerous nature of the accompanying regulations, which included regulation of the political beliefs of students and faculty.[112] The New Deal, in other words, taught the federal government that it could use money to control institutions of higher education, giving it almost total control over most of them today, to disastrous ends.

Finally, FDR's friends at the FBI secretly investigated lesbians as well as gays. It remains unclear whether ER's proclivities played a part or not, but it certainly reflected the homophobia of the age. The FBI, for example, tracked Senator Walsh to a "house of degradation," a male-only brothel frequented by homosexual members of the armed services allegedly used by Nazi spies to discover deep, dark military secrets. The FBI's interest in homosexuals, however, began in 1937, years before the war.[113]

In short, although a few women like ER and female cabinet members like Frances Perkins personally gained from the New Deal, most became worse off materially.[114]

Notes

1. James P. Warburg, *Hell Bent for Election* (New York: Doubleday, Doran & Company, 1935), 28–29.
2. David E. Bernstein, *Only One Place of Redress: African Americans, Labor Regulations, and the Courts from Reconstruction to the New Deal* (Durham: Duke University Press, 2001), 103.
3. Jim Powell, *FDR's Folly: How Roosevelt and His New Deal Prolonged the Great Depression* (New York: Crown Forum, 2003), 100–4.
4. Benjamin M. Friedman, *The Moral Consequences of Economic Growth* (New York: Alfred A. Knopf, 2005), 158–59, 173.
5. Gail Radford, "The Federal Government and Housing During the Great Depression," in John F. Bauman, Roger Biles, and Kristin M. Szylvian, eds. *From Tenements to the Taylor Homes: In Search of an Urban Housing Policy in Twentieth Century America* (University Park: Pennsylvania State University Press, 2000), 102–20.
6. John J. Wallis, "Lessons from the Political Economy of the New Deal," *Oxford Review of Economic Policy* 26, 3 (Autumn 2010): 442–62.
7. Jeffrey G. Williamson and Peter H. Lindert, *American Inequality: A Macroeconomic History* (New York: Academic Press, 1980), 82–88.
8. David M. Kennedy, "What the New Deal Did," *Political Science Quarterly* 124, 2 (Summer 2009), 266.
9. Dalia Tsuk, "Pluralisms: The Indian New Deal As a Model," *University of Maryland Law Journal of Race, Religion, Gender and Class* 1, 2 (2001): 393–449.

10. T.H. Watkins, *The Great Depression: America in the 1930s* (New York: Little, Brown & Co., 1993), 131.
11. Kenneth H. Bobroff, "Retelling Allotment: Indian Property Rights and the Myth of Common Ownership," *Vanderbilt Law Review* 54, 4 (May 2001): 1559–623.
12. Steven C. Schulte, "Removing the Yoke of Government: E.Y. Berry and the Origins of Indian Termination Policy," *South Dakota History* 14, 1 (1984), 48–67; Robert E. Wright, *Little Business on the Prairie: Entrepreneurship, Prosperity, and Challenge in South Dakota* (Sioux Falls: Center for Western Studies, 2015).
13. John Gunther, *Inside U.S.A.* (New York: Harper & Brothers, 1947), 871–73.
14. Watkins, *Great Depression*, 134.
15. W. Roger Buffalohead, "The Indian New Deal: A Review Essay," *Minnesota History* 48, 8 (Winter 1983), 339–41.
16. Watkins, *Great Depression*, 135–36.
17. Buffalohead, "Indian New Deal," 341.
18. Naomi Schaefer Riley, *The New Trail of Tears: How Washington Is Destroying American Indians* (New York: Encounter Books, 2016).
19. Price Fishback, Jessamyn Schaller, Evan Taylor, "Racial Differences in Access to New Deal Work Relief in 1940," Working Paper (December 2020), 7.
20. James Ledbetter and Daniel B. Roth, eds., *The Great Depression: A Diary by Benjamin Roth* (New York: Public Affairs, 2009), 63.
21. Price V. Fishback, Michael R. Haines, Shawn Kantor, "Births, Deaths and New Relief During the Great Depression," NBER Working Paper No. 11246 (March 2005).
22. Abraham Hoffman, *Unwanted Mexican Americans in the Great Depression* (Tucson: University of Arizona Press, 1974), 18.
23. Grace Abbott, *From Relief to Social Security: The Development of the New Public Welfare Service* (Chicago: University of Chicago Press, 1941), 162.
24. St. Louis Bureau for Men, *Missourians on the Move: A Study of Intra-State Transient Men and Boys Applying at St. Louis April 1934–August 1935* (St. Louis: St. Louis Bureau for Men, 1938), 30; Abbott, *Relief*, 168.
25. Abbott, *Relief*, 229.

26. John F. Cogan, *The High Cost of Good Intentions: A History of U.S. Federal Entitlement Programs* (Stanford: Stanford University Press, 2017), 71–4.
27. David M. Kennedy, "What the New Deal Did," *Political Science Quarterly* 124, 2 (Summer 2009), 259.
28. James M. Strickland and Ken Kollman, "Constitutional Change and Interest Mobilization: Insight from the Progressive Era," Working Paper (7 April 2023), 14.
29. Abbott, *Relief*, 170–71.
30. Richard K. Vedder and Lowell E. Gallaway, *Out of Work: Unemployment and Government in Twentieth-Century America*, updated ed. (New York: New York University Press, 1997), 75.
31. Geraldine Youcha, *Minding the Children: Child Care in America from Colonial Times to the Present* (New York: Scribner, 1995), 13–14.
32. Erica B. Grubb, "Day-Care Regulation: Legal and Policy Issues," *Santa Clara Law Review* 25, 2 (1985), 311–12.
33. John Gunther, *Inside U.S.A.* (New York: Harper & Brothers, 1947), 781; Glenn W. Miller, *Problems of Labor* (New York: Macmillan Co., 1951), 425; Rachel S. Ferguson and Marcus M. Witcher, *Black Liberation Through the Marketplace: Hope, Heartbreak, and the Promise of America* (New York: Post Hill Press, 2002), 290–91.
34. Claudia Goldin and Lawrence F. Katz, *The Race Between Education and Technology* (Cambridge, Mass.: Belknap Press, 2008), 7–8, 223–27, 245; Ledbetter and Roth, eds., *Great Depression*, 60.
35. John Steele Gordon, *An Empire of Wealth: The Epic History of American Economic Power* (New York: HarperCollins, 2004), 336.
36. James J. Feigenbaum, "Intergenerational Mobility During the Great Depression," Working Paper, 1 Dec. 2015.
37. Daniel Aaronson, Daniel Hartley, Bhashkar Mazumder, and Martha Stinson, "The Long-run Effects of the 1930s Redlining Maps on Children," Center for Economic Studies Working Paper (December 2022); Mario L. Small and Devah Pager, "Sociological Perspectives on Racial Discrimination," *Journal of Economic Perspectives* 34, 2 (Spring 2020), 58.
38. As quoted in Cogan, *High Cost*, 79.

39. Jim F. Couch and William F. Shughart, *The Political Economy of the New Deal* (Northampton, MA: Edward Elgar, 1998), 117.
40. David T. Beito, *The New Deal's War on the Bill of Rights: The Untold Story of FDR's Concentration Camps, Censorship, and Mass Surveillance* (Oakland: Independent Institute, 2023), 158–59.
41. As quoted in Beito, *New Deal's War on the Bill of Rights*, 166.
42. Nancy J. Weiss, "The Negro and the New Freedom: Fighting Wilsonian Segregation," *Political Science Quarterly* 84, 1 (March 1969): 61–79.
43. George Schuyler, "A Tribute to Caesar," *The Messenger* (Jul. 1924), 225–226, 231.
44. Juliet E.K. Walker, *The History of Black Business in America: Capitalism, Race, Entrepreneurship*, 2nd ed., (Chapel Hill: University of North Carolina Press, 2009), 1:272–73; Richard Sterner, *The Negro's Share: A Study of Income, Consumption, Housing and Public Assistance* (Westport, CN: Negro Universities Press, 1943), 26–27, 195–96.
45. Ferguson and Witcher, *Black Liberation*, 195.
46. Burton Folsom, Jr. *New Deal or Raw Deal? How FDR's Economic Legacy Has Damaged America* (New York: Simon & Schuster, 2008), 6.
47. Lee J. Alston and Joseph P. Ferrie, *Southern Paternalism and the American Welfare State: Economics, Politics, and Institutions in the South, 1865–1965* (New York: Cambridge University Press, 1999), 61–72.
48. Paul Moreno, "An Ambivalent Legacy: Black Americans and the Political Economy of the New Deal," *Independent Review* 6, 4 (Spring 2002): 515.
49. David Stoesz, "Reparations from Social Security," SSRN Working Paper (3 Mar. 2023).
50. Couch and Shughart, *Political Economy*, 192.
51. Bernstein, *One Place*, 89.
52. Powell, *FDR's Folly*, 118.
53. William A. Sundstrom, "Last Hired, First Fired? Unemployment and Urban Black Workers During the Great Depression," *Journal of Economic History* 52, 2 (June 1992): 415–29; Malcolm Ross, *All Manner of Men* (New York: Harcourt, Brace, & World, 1948), 20.
54. Sterno, *Negro's Share*, 362.

55. Price Fishback, "The Newest on the New Deal," *Essays in Economic and Business History* 36, 1 (2018): 14–15.
56. Jill Watts, "New Deal or Raw Deal? Black Americans in the Roosevelt Years," *Financial History* (Summer 2020), 21.
57. Ralph J. Bunche, *The Political Status of the Negro in the Age of FDR* (Chicago: University of Chicago Press, 1973), 608.
58. Ferguson and Witcher, *Black Liberation*, 207–9, 222.
59. David E. Bernstein, "Racism, Railroad Unions, and Labor Regulations," *Independent Review* 5, 2 (Fall 2000): 237–47.
60. Colin Gordon, "Rethinking the New Deal," *Columbia Law Review* 98, 8 (Dec. 1998): 2,039.
61. Harry L. Hopkins, *The Realities of Unemployment* (WPA, 1937), 10; Vedder and Gallaway, *Out of Work*, 75.
62. Ferguson and Witcher, *Black Liberation*, 183–84, 197–98, 201–2.
63. Robin O.G. Kelley, *Hammer and Hoe: Alabama Communists During the Great Depression* (Chapel Hill: University of North Carolina Press, 2015), 79–89.
64. Ferguson and Witcher, *Black Liberation*, 222–24; Alston and Ferrie, *Southern Paternalism*, 45.
65. Colin Gordon, *Dead on Arrival: The Politics of Health Care in Twentieth-Century America* (Princeton: Princeton University Press, 2003), 51, 190–91.
66. Ruth A. Kasman, "Employed Mothers of Children in the A.D.C. Program," in Gwendolyn Mink and Rickie Solinger, eds., *Welfare: A Documentary History of U.S. Policy and Politics* (New York: New York University Press, 2003), 120–24.
67. Charles Murray, *Losing Ground: American Social Policy, 1950–1980* (New York: Basic Books, 1984), 162–66.
68. Fishback, "Newest," 9 n.1.
69. John B. Shoven, "Social Security Reform: Two Tiers Are Better Than One," in Benjamin M. Friedman, ed., *Should the United States Privatize Social Security?* (Cambridge, Mass.: MIT Press, 1999), 23; Robert J. Barro, "Comments," in Friedman, ed., *Privatize Social Security?*, 123.
70. Sylvester J. Schieber and John B. Shoven, *The Real Deal: The History and Future of Social Security* (New Haven: Yale University Press, 1999), 8; Folsom, *New Deal?*, 117.

71. Schieber and Shoven, *Real Deal*, 224–27; Folsom, *New Deal?*, 264.
72. Eliora Derenoncourt, Chi Hyun Kim, Moritz Kuhn, and Moritz Schularick, "Wealth of Two Nations: The US Racial Wealth Gap, 1860–2020," CRC TR 225 Discussion Paper Series (September 2022).
73. Darryle Ulama, "Black Public Works: The Political Economy of Race and New Deal Infrastructure," (MA Thesis: Massachusetts Institute of Technology, 2021), 75–81, 97–98.
74. Ferguson and Witcher, *Black Liberation*, 286–88; Bernstein, *One Place*, 6.
75. Miller, *Problems*, 425–26.
76. Bernstein, *One Place*, 66, 78.
77. Ferguson and Witcher, *Black Liberation*, 211–15; Amity Shlaes, *Great Society: A New History* (New York: HarperCollins, 2019), 59–60.
78. Theresa A. Glanz, "Federal Land-Use Policy and Resettlement in the Great Plains: An Experiment in Community Development During the New Deal Years, 1933–1941," (Ph.D. Diss., University of Nebraska, 2020), 2–3.
79. As quoted in Radford, "Federal Government," in Bauman, Biles, and Szylvian, eds. *Tenements*, 111.
80. Davis McEntire, *Residence and Race: Final and Comprehensive Report to the Commission on Race and Housing* (Los Angeles: University of California Press, 1960), 316.
81. Bell Clement, "Wagner-Steagall and the D.C. Alley Dwelling Authority," *Journal of the American Planning Association* 78, 4 (Autumn 2012): 434–48.
82. Radford, "Federal Government," in Bauman, Biles, and Szylvian, eds. *Tenements*, 111–15.
83. Dania V. Francis, Darrick Hamilton, Thomas W. Mitchell, Nathan A. Rosenberg, and Bryce Wilson Stucki, "Black Land Loss: 1920–1997," *AEA Papers and Proceedings* 112 (2022): 38–42.
84. Ferguson and Witcher, *Black Liberation*, 222.
85. Bunche, *Political Status*, 610.
86. Amity Shlaes, *The Forgotten Man: A New History of the Great Depression* (New York: HarperCollins, 2007), 168.
87. Moreno, "Ambivalent Legacy," 515.
88. Powell, *FDR's Folly*, 151–52.

89. Moreno, "Ambivalent Legacy," 516.
90. Fishback, "Newest," 10.
91. Bunche, *Political Status*, 630.
92. Watts, "New Deal?," 22–25.
93. Folsom, *New Deal?*, 211.
94. Folsom, *New Deal?*, 210.
95. Dewey W. Grantham, "Editor's Introduction," in Bunche, *Political Status*, xvii-xviii; Bunche, *Political Status*, 106, 134–42; Beito, *New Deal's War on the Bill of Rights*, 142–43.
96. Moreno, "Ambivalent Legacy," 531–34.
97. Jean Edward Smith, *FDR* (New York: Random House, 2007), xiii.
98. Ross, *All Manner*, 19, 27–28, 31.
99. Ferguson and Witcher, *Black Liberation*, 221.
100. Beito, *New Deal's War on the Bill of Rights*, 169–70.
101. Tinsley E. Yarbrough, *Mr. Justice Black and His Critics* (Durham: Duke University Press, 1988), 1.
102. Beito, *New Deal's War on the Bill of Rights*, 193–94.
103. Ross, *All Manner*, 31–33.
104. Bernstein, *One Place*, 82.
105. Miller, *Problems*, 428; Merl E. Reed, *Seed Time for the Modern Civil Rights Movement: The President's Committee on Fair Employment Practice, 1941–1946* (Baton Rouge: Louisiana State University Press, 1991).
106. Amber Arthun Warburton, Helen Wood, and Marian M. Crane, "The Work and Welfare of Children of Agricultural Laborers in Hidalgo Conty, Texas," in Mink and Solinger, eds., *Welfare*, 110–14.
107. Dominick Pratico, *Eisenhower and Social Security: The Origins of the Disability Program* (New York Writers Club Press, 2001).
108. Linda G. Mills, "A Calculus for Bias: How Malingering Females and Dependent Housewives Fare in the Social Security Disability System," *Harvard Women's Law Journal* 16 (1993): 211; Jason D. Vendel, "General Bias and Administrative Law Judges: Is There a Remedy for Social Security Disability Claimants?" *Cornell Law Review* 90 (2004–5): 769–807; Frank Griffin, "Implicit Disability Bias Disinterred by Zombie Factors in Social Security Disability Determinations," *Nevada Law Journal* 21 (2020–21): 161ff; John Gettens, Pei-Pei Lei, and Alexis D. Henry,

"Accounting for Geographic Variation in Social Security Disability Program Participation," *Social Security Bulletin* 78 (2018): 29ff; Richard V. Burkhauser, J.S. Butler, and Robert R. Weathers, II, "How Policy Variables Influence the Timing of Applications for Social Security Disability Insurance," *Social Security Bulletin* 64 (2001–2): 52ff.; David H. Autor and Mark G. Duggan, "The Growth in the Social Security Disability Rolls: A Fiscal Crisis Unfolding," *Journal of Economic Perspectives* 20, 3 (Summer 2006): 71–96.

109. Robert E. Wright, *Financial Exclusion: How Competition Can Fix a Broken System* (Great Barrington, Mass.: AIER 2019), 10–11.
110. Olivia S. Mitchell and John W. R. Phillips, "Eligibility for Social Security Disability," Michigan Retirement Research Center Paper No. WP 2001–011 (17 Jan. 2008).
111. Folsom, *New Deal?*, 57.
112. Jon Gorgosz, "'No Formal Cooperation Needed': Federal New Deal Policy at Elite Massachusetts' Women's Colleges, 1933–1942," *Historical Journal of Massachusetts* 49 (Summer 2021): 100–27.
113. Douglas M. Charles, *J. Edgar Hoover and the Anti-Interventionists: FBI Political Surveillance and the Rise of the Domestic Security State, 1939–1945* (Columbus: Ohio State University Press, 2007), 106.
114. Betty Houchin Winfield, *FDR and the News Media* (New York: Columbia University Press, 1994), 81.

CHAPTER 12

The Miseries Continue

FDR's New Deal not only failed to make America socialist or even collectivist, it failed on its own terms. The U.S. economy not only failed to return to anything close to full employment, but it also became one of the worst performers in the world in the 1930s after being one of the top performers in the 1920s.[1]

Alone among FDR's policies, reflation of the money supply stimulated output, in part because it helped to reduce real wages and reduce bankruptcies. Other New Deal policies, like the NIRA and the NLRB, muted its salutary effects on employment and output, however. Relief and work agencies helped individuals to survive but they, too, may have slowed recovery. As explained above, too much monetary and fiscal policy fiddling also helped to return the economy to depression in 1937–38.

The Great Depression undoubtedly had a silver lining.[2] As Friedrich Nietzsche said, that which does not kill us makes us stronger. Some scholars, for example, have found that the children of people living in the areas worst hit by the Depression were thriftier and more entrepreneurial than their peers in more fortunate areas of the country.[3] Others noted that library circulation went up "and people are once again turning to home pleasures, etc. and to simple living."[4] A few people, like public relations whiz Wilma Soss, and Charles Darrow, inventor of the board game Monopoly,[5] even managed to thrive economically during the Depression.[6] As the old joke goes, the Depression was not so bad if you had

R. E. Wright, *FDR's Long New Deal*,
https://doi.org/10.1007/978-3-031-74141-8_12

a job.[7] Nevertheless, nobody could seriously argue that the Depression increased well-being on net. Most tellingly, perhaps, the body mass index (BMI) of the poor declined during the Depression.[8]

Even if the Federal Reserve was not completely culpable for the initial downturn, its policies exacerbated the recession and caused the deflation that turned it into a depression. Its policies, along with most New Deal policies, did nothing to reverse the prolonged period of unemployment that followed the 1933 and 1937 output bottoms. Restoring full private employment was paramount for macroeconomic but also socioeconomic reasons, like a reduction in the number and boldness of beggars and crime reduction.[9] For every 10% increase in New Deal spending, crime decreased only 1%. For every 10% increase in private employment, by contrast, crime decreased 10%.[10] It was another great global war, not the New Deal, that finally returned the macroeconomy to full private employment, where it stayed in the postwar period due to a lucky confluence of factors, including FDR's death and a transitory bout of postwar inflation that supercharged business investment after a decade and a half of malaise and wartime planning.

The macroeconomic outcome alone, in other words, should indict FDR and his New Deal. The point of this chapter is to show that to this day the costs of FDR's New Deal continue to outweigh its putative benefits. At best, a few policies, like federal deposit insurance, remain a wash on net. Most, though, impose significant net costs on overall economic efficiency, yet they remain politically untouchable. Social Security and employment-based healthcare constitute two important examples.[11]

Progressives retort that the New Deal helped society's most vulnerable groups, including children, people of color, and women.[12] Chapter 11 showed that it did no such thing, in part due to policy incompetence and in part due to political chicanery. As Walter Lippmann once wrote of FDR, "his mind is not very clear, his purposes are not simple, and his methods are not direct."[13] So with all due respect for FDR biographer Jean Edward Smith, it is not a riddle "to explain how this Hudson River aristocrat ... became the champion of the common man."[14] The only things that FDR truly championed were himself and a paternalist federal government that jousted with, and eventually vanquished, older, more personal forms of paternal control of blacks and poor whites.[15]

FDR's New Deal sometimes hurt vulnerable groups indirectly by reducing productivity and output, but sometimes it did so directly, and even purposefully. Harry Hopkins argued in 1938 that "in this administration there must be no discrimination and no coercion."[16] FDR's electoral success, however, required the support of the South, which accepted New Deal nostrums only so long as they did not threaten racial segregation.[17]

Consider, for example, the allocation of federal highway funds in Georgia, which went to political cronies instead of the most economically pressing projects. With the racist Eugene Talmadge in Georgia's governor's office from 1933 to 1937 and 1941 to 1943, few road resources aided predominantly black districts.[18] Talmadge went so far as to declare martial law in Georgia over control of the state's Highway Commission, but up until then he had supported Roosevelt, so Washington did not respond.[19] After he consolidated his power, though, he became a "relentless New Deal hater" who called FDR "that cripple in the White House."[20]

Tellingly, African-Americans received more federal relief outside of the South. They had little political power in the South but in the North they were still swing voters as late as 1940. The New Deal, therefore, used relief to lure them out of the party of Lincoln.[21]

New Deal Policy Defects

Many New Deal policies remain politically ensconced despite their palpably negative effects on overall economic efficiency.[22] That is an esoteric point only to those who do not understand that lost efficiency reduces overall output, so it hurts everyone, especially the poorest and least powerful members of society. Inefficiencies also contribute to crises, which also hurt the most vulnerable the most. True champions of the underclasses would not countenance New Deal policies another minute and would never have allowed them in the first place.

Agricultural, Energy, and Environmental Policies

FDR's acolytes also proudly proclaim that his New Deal presaged today's Green New Deal. They come to such conclusions easily, by downplaying the negative environmental impacts of rural electrification, forest, soil, and water "conservation" (i.e., nonprice rationing), the TVA and other dam projects, and by pointing approvingly to the growth of an inflexible, top-down regulatory model[23] that continues to crowd out more effective, sustainable, nuanced, and flexible bottom-up, private initiatives.[24] They also ignore the negative impacts of federal agricultural policies on the stewards of much of the nation's private land, farmers and ranchers.

New Deal programs did little to help agriculturalists overall. Although a few managed to reduce debt and grow assets during the 1930s, most increased debt while the value of their assets shrank, increasing average leverage (debt as a percentage of assets) for the worst-off farms from 33% in the 1920s to 50% by 1940.[25] Already by 1935, FDR had made the Secretary of Agriculture, in the words of erstwhile New Dealer James Warburg, "an absolute czar over the farmers of the United States."[26] If anyone doubted that claim, SCOTUS affirmed its constitutionality 6 years later in *Wickard*. By the early postwar period, authors like pro-FDR journalist John Gunther[27] could write, matter-of-factly, that "the whole national crop is (since the New Deal) controlled by Washington, D.C." Despite, or more likely because of, federal agricultural subsidies and other forms of top-down control, many farmers' earnings remained "too low to afford an acceptable way of living," at least according to New Dealers like Claude R. Wickard, the former secretary of agriculture and head of the REA.[28]

As noted previously, the REA subsidized grid electricity for farmers who did not really need their power to be electric, or to be delivered over lines from a central generation facility. One major long-term cost of FDR's meddling was greatly reduced demand for, and supply of, better batteries and green energy technologies. Due to rural electrification, battery manufacturers like Fred Perkins were less motivated to improve battery technology, putting the world decades behind when it later came to believe that battery storage constituted the key to slowing anthropogenic global climate change.[29]

Moreover, many farm windmills fell into disrepair due to the availability of subsidized grid electricity. Many windmills were also abandoned because the small family farm disintegrated during the 1930s and 1940s. As Richard Willis, who was a boy on a traditional Iowa mixed-produce farm (butter and eggs, milk, corn, forage, beans) in the 1930s, later recalled, "government policies seemed to say 'get big or get out'." He wasn't wrong. Small farmers, like other small proprietors, proved a bane to FDR's agenda because they were too economically, and hence politically, independent. They could grow their own food and barter for the rest without any help from DC bureaucrats. Willis's own parents, for example, "stayed Republican until the day they died" more than 30 years after FDR's reign ended.[30]

Health Insurance and Healthcare Regulation

As historian Christy Ford Chapin documents, America's health insurance system continued to evolve in the postwar period, specifically away from the nonprofit Blue Cross and Blue Shield system and toward commercial group insurance. Many more policy mistakes were made along the way, but nobody rectified the core problem, the close tie between health insurance and employment, a uniquely bad system found nowhere else in the world that created a large number of uninsured, and largely uninsurable, Americans.[31]

By the 2000s, major reforms were clearly necessary, but inertia won until the Great Recession threw many Americans out of work. In my 2010 book *Fubarnomics*, I entitled a chapter on America's healthcare system "House Scrubs" to highlight its bimodal nature. *House* referred to a popular television show about a skilled doctor who saved many patients suffering from unusual, but usually deadly, maladies. "House" also harkened back to the good old days, when doctors made house calls. *Scrubs* referred to a popular television comedy about clownish doctors. "Scrubs" also referenced scrubs as in healthcare worker attire and an ineffectual person. In the chapter, I made several serious proposals for the integration of life insurers, health insurers, and healthcare providers that, alas, policymakers did not take seriously. They implemented the Affordable Care Act (ACA, a.k.a. "Obamacare") instead and even maintained the inexcusable tie between employment and health insurance.[32]

Despite its hopeful sounding official name, ACA did not stop runaway healthcare spending increases, nor did it improve the bimodal nature of the American healthcare system, which remains the most expensive in the world by far yet barely middling by three key, and difficult to fudge, health metrics. Granted, the system is weighed down by the Indian Health Service and, more importantly, the Medicaid and Medicare programs implemented during the Great Society, LBJ's New Deal lite.[33]

The best, or one of the best, healthcare systems in the world, by contrast, is also by far the cheapest because it maintained market competition and its attendant discipline on both costs and quality and did so without abandoning the poor. That country is Singapore, and its system was largely copied from the system the United States had in place before the New Deal, with other American ideas not implemented in the United States due to its idiosyncratic FDR-era linkage of employment and insurance.[34]

Securities Regulation

As James Warburg noted in 1935, FDR "brought about a certain amount of hasty reform of our banking and investment system" that failed to fix much, if anything. "He has carried out his promises where it mattered least," Warburg concluded, "and failed to do so where it mattered most."[35]

Blue-Sky Laws and the SEC could only do so much to prevent the sale of fraudulent securities. Financial literacy could have ameliorated the problem, but it received almost no public support.[36] Nonprofit organizations, like AIER and Wilma Soss's Federation of Women Shareholders in American Business, and commercial financial intermediaries, which could hardly be counted on to give unbiased advice, helped but faced the constraints imposed by the country's often substandard primary and secondary educational institutions.[37]

Soon after its formation, the SEC attacked regional exchanges in Buffalo, Pittsburgh, and Denver.[38] For decades after, it pushed for the regionals to give up listing local stocks in favor of channeling order flow to the New York Stock Exchange,[39] ignoring the anticompetitive implications of its centralization policies, which made staffers' jobs easier and helped powerful friends in New York.[40]

The SEC nevertheless continued to act as if it was helping small investors when it hurt them by regulating brokerage fees, essentially enforcing a brokerage cartel arrangement.[41] It finally gave up that charade in 1975 when it deregulated commissions and allowed the growth of discount brokerages. At the same time, though, it allowed bond rating agencies to morph from being companies that competed to provide investors with accurate assessments of issuers into a government-protected cartel beholden to issuer interests. That change degraded the quality of bond ratings and thus created one of the conditions necessary for the subprime mortgage crisis that led to the Global Financial Crisis of 2008 (GFC) and the Great Recession of 2008–9.[42]

Banking Regulation

"In the early days of the administration," James Warburg admitted in 1935, "I was shocked by the slapdash slipshod methods by which the administration sought to solve problems that had baffled the wisest minds for years."[43] New Deal banking regulations were among the most slipshod. Breaking investment and commercial banks apart served no economic purpose and, numerous claims to the contrary notwithstanding, had nothing to do with the half century of relative banking stability that followed. No major banking crises hit until the Savings and Loan Crisis in the 1980s because of America's victory in World War II and financial repression. The former meant that the U.S. economy would boom for a quarter century after the war as economic rivals like Japan and Germany rebuilt and caught up. The latter meant that banking became cartelized, with the rates that banks could charge depositors capped and competition minimized by branching restrictions. A far better reform than Glass-Steagall, which no other country willingly adopted and enforced (the U.S. forced it upon postwar Japan), would have been to increase competition by allowing interstate branching. That reform would come only in the final decades of the twentieth century although its importance in mitigating the effects of the Depression in Canada and California was well understood before then.[44]

Federal deposit insurance proved successful, except when it didn't. While physical bank run scenes like that depicted in the movie *It's a Wonderful Life* rarely occurred after 1933, so-called quiet bank runs still took place behind the scenes.[45] One federal deposit insurance corporation, the Federal Savings and Loan Insurance Corporation (FSLIC), botched things so badly that Congress shut it down.[46] FSLIC greatly exacerbated the 1980s Savings and Loan Crisis by engaging in the same regulatory forbearance that Herbert Hoover had forced on federal regulators in the early 1930s.

Another, the Federal Deposit Insurance Corporation (FDIC), handled itself with more aplomb, though technically many of the bank bailouts following the GFC were as much bailouts of the FDIC, which failed to see the crisis coming or to do anything about it, as they were bailouts of the failed banks that it oversaw.[47] Moreover, while everyone sees the benefit that deposit insurance provides depositors by allowing them not to worry about the safety of their cash balances, few perceive its costs, including its tendency to increase bank risk-taking by reducing the incentives of private monitoring by depositors when deposit insurance is too inexpensive, and its added operating costs when it is too dear. Because the FDIC never seriously attempted to price the risks posed by individual banks, most banks, perhaps all, impose one or the other of those costs on taxpayers or customers.[48]

Housing Regulation

According to Davis McEntire, the director of the Commission on Race and Housing, it remained "a cardinal policy" of the U.S. federal government in 1960 "not to replace but to support private enterprise." Since the New Deal, however, "the amount of housing produced, the types and locations of new dwelling units, the terms of their sale or rental, and the volume of consumer demand for housing depend in large measure upon decisions taken by the federal government."[49] Its power, based largely on its regulation of the mortgage market and the construction of public housing, only waxed thereafter.[50]

It would be unfair to lay the entire blame for the subprime mortgage crisis and subsequent global financial crisis on the New Deal. FDR's policies, though, started the long chain of events that led to disaster in 2008. It was FDR who decided that the federal government had to meddle in the market to induce more Americans to buy houses.[51] The original sin was to base federal tax deductions on mortgage interest payments instead of homeowner equity, thus inducing Americans to stay as heavily mortgaged as possible instead of encouraging them to own their land outright, their traditional goal. The deduction was as old as the income tax itself but only became important when the percentage of Americans who had to pay income taxes increased during the 1930s and 40s.[52]

Were that not bad enough, the HOLC embraced redlining, the practice of excluding people of color, especially African-Americans, from buying houses in all-white neighborhoods by denying them mortgages. Mixed-race neighborhoods, lenders and New Deal bureaucrats believed, posed credit risks because many of them witnessed rapid price collapses associated with "white flight." So, government appraisers marked them on the so-called Residential Security Maps that HOLC's parent, the FHLB board, ordered created between 1935 and 1940. The maps and attendant descriptive documents were ordered destroyed in 1942 in part because of the "harsh, racist, and negative language" they contained. The forms utilized used terms like "infiltration by" next to blanks designed to be filled in with "negro" or "foreign-born." Examples of "detrimental influences" included "heavy concentration of negro" even if they were considered a "Better class negro."[53]

Also, HOLC may have been relatively stingy with mortgages within redlined low-income housing neighborhoods. Denied easy HOLC renewals, many African-Americans, other people of color, and recent immigrants may have faced foreclosure, and its attendant hardships, while similarly situated whites with homes in higher-graded neighborhoods obtained refinancing. Such claims must remain tentative, however, because even in more recent times it has proven difficult to parse location from racial or nationality effects in lending decisions due to lack of individual data on mortgage rates, fees, and delinquencies. Nevertheless, even scholars sympathetic to HOLC writing in the journal of a New Deal-era institution (the government-sponsored wholesale mortgage buyer Fannie Mae) concluded that it "incorporated racial labeling into its appraisals and assessment of neighborhood risk," while stressing that it was not the sole cause of such outcomes because the FHA (Federal Housing Administration) and private lenders were also involved in the creation and widespread use of redlining.[54]

Later, blacks and white developers trying to create low-income housing also found it difficult to secure subsidized FHA-insured loans.[55] In addition to refusing to guarantee any mortgages in certain neighborhoods, the FHA encouraged the use of racist deed covenants that blocked the sale of homes to people of color until public pressure in 1947 induced it to obscure its racist policies with *1984*-like doublespeak.[56] Soon after, SCOTUS deemed the clauses unconstitutional in *Shelley v. Kraemer* and the FHA finally adopted race-neutral language and policies.[57]

Since about 1910, however, local zoning laws had been used to keep blacks and whites, or at least the poor and the well-heeled, apart. Zoning that allowed only large lots and single-family homes was for the (white) rich, while zoning that favored multifamily units attracted the less desirable (displaced, immigrant, black) poor. The New Deal did nothing to challenge those practices. Moreover, many local, state, and federal public housing projects were also racially segregated by force of law and later by custom.[58] The ones destined for blacks remained subpar, often intentionally so, because controlled by powerful Democrat political bosses like Edward H. Crump in Memphis, Tennessee.[59]

Labor Regulation

Several New Deal programs supported Big Labor even though unions were known to reduce employment.[60] FDR's pro-union stance tripled the number of union workers over the 1930s. The policy followed logically from FDR's high wage hypothesis, which few believed at the time and no serious economist supports today. Nevertheless, the federal government still generally supports unions, except when they threaten other priorities, as they did during a threatened freight rail strike in the Fall of 2022, and in 1938 when Aubrey Williams advised truck operators threatening to strike Ohio WPA projects "that no strike against the government will be tolerated." Specifically, Williams threatened to shut down WPA projects in the state rather than "recognize such a strike." The truckers wanted an established hourly rate for their work rather than to competitively bid for routes. Williams cited "arbitration and settlement … facilities" as the reason for the strict policy.[61]

Many Depression-era employers allowed positions to go unfilled rather than fill them with laborers who had signaled, through long-term unemployment, that their labors were worth less than the minimum or prevailing wage. As previously noted, the law, and the policy stance of both Hoover's and FDR's administrations, urged employers to pay efficiency wages, i.e., top dollar for top workers. As a consequence, firms laid off the least productive workers first.[62] That helped overall productivity but hurt workers, especially those who needed any sort of training.[63] Unsurprisingly, analysis of the 1940 Census shows that the young, the old, and the less educated and skilled were much more likely to be unemployed. Those who signaled their weakness by accepting a relief job in the CCC or WPA also found themselves stigmatized until the global war restored full employment, and then necessitated "scraping the bottom of the barrel" for workers.[64] Labor economists have found that employers will frequently pay known quality workers more, or pay high wages to lure workers away from competitors, rather than hire unemployed workers who may well have become unemployed because they had proven themselves relatively unproductive.[65]

Hopkins' dubious claim that the Wagner Act and unions looked out for all workers because they could no longer look out for themselves[66] was belied by the rise of the right to work, or open shop movement late in the war. Florida and Arkansas voters approved right-to-work referenda in 1944. South Dakota followed in 1945. South Dakota's law, emulated by Arizona and Nebraska in 1946 and half a dozen more states in 1947, declared that "the right of persons to work shall not be denied or abridged on account of membership or non-membership in any labor organization." Soon after, at the federal level, the Taft-Hartley Act of 1947, over President Truman's veto, also took a few of the sharper edges off Wagner by explicitly allowing state right-to-work laws and outlawing closed shops. It, however, still countenanced union shops where workers vote for or against unionization and hence was a far cry from federal right-to-work legislation. Moreover, unions continued to control non-union workers due to the unwillingness or inability of federal regulators to enforce Taft-Hartley's few protections. Political battles over unionism, therefore, continued for decades.[67]

The Long New Deal and Globalism

Despite FDR's Long New Deal, America remained a rich country, and an economically free one, at least relative to most other countries. What it could have achieved with better economic policies we can never know with precision, but undoubtedly everyone, including its poorest members, would have enjoyed even higher incomes and fewer restrictions on how they made their respective livelihoods.[68]

FDR's New Deal and wartime policies inspired major expansions of state power later in the century, including Eisenhower's extension of Social Security into disability "insurance" and the Medicare and Medicaid programs of LBJ's "Great Society."[69] Like FDR's New Deal, the globalist movement that pushed for lockdowns and other extreme government power in 2020 had ample radical progressive precursors, like the 2001 book *Empire*, which launched two decades of misanthropic thought and social subversion culminating with the rise of Antifa and Black Lives Matter.[70] But the roots run even deeper, back to the New Deal, which initiated major policy trends that have waxed ominous since March 2020.

Specifically, like many current policy developments, FDR's New Deal:

- began the vilification of successful people regardless of the sources of their income.[71]
- turned social emphasis away from individual responsibility and toward paternalism, especially that of the federal government.[72]
- began the process of inuring American voters to politician dissembling and the weaponization of parts of the government for partisan purposes.[73]
- started the process of almost completely ending the distinction between the public and private spheres.[74]
- empowered the peacetime growth of the administrative state and the powerful presidency.[75]
- rendered the notion of large-scale "experimentation" in public policy acceptable, even laudatory.

- extended and cemented the notion that "military necessary" justified suspending parts of the U.S. Constitution and that only the executive branch knew what constituted a military emergency.[76]
- showed that civil liberties groups could be co-opted or cowed into following blatantly unconstitutional decrees, like Japanese internment.[77]
- forced publishers to advocate war over peace or face accusations of sedition, and treason, and equated loyalty to the administration with loyalty to the nation.[78]
- introduced the notion that the Federal government had to backstop and bail out every group that experienced trouble, even from localized natural disasters.[79]
- began the process of privileging vague "environmental" goals over the needs of human beings while deprecating their right to own property.[80]
- started the construction of "racist roads," like I-84 through Hartford, Connecticut, announced in 1940, and of "urban renewal" projects really aimed at "Negro removal."[81]
- introduced many of the policy falsehoods and half-truths heard today, including ones that attempt to justify running up the national debt in the name of "capital investments" or "human capital" accumulation.[82]
- began to normalize the notion that politicians worked for their parties instead of their constituents.[83]

Worst of all, perhaps, FDR's New Deal turned the proverbial power of the purse over to the federal government, thus nationalizing policies traditionally the purview of state or local governments or the once mighty voluntary Third Sector.[84] As colonists, Americans long struggled to maintain their right to pay colonial governors, a right that British policymakers wished to wrest away from them. Both sides understood that governors would be beholden to those who paid them. The power of the purse, they knew, would prove paramount.[85]

During the depths of the Depression, though, many state and local politicians and even nonprofit presidents gladly accepted the help of FDR, who happily helped them back to their financial feet for the low price of their autonomy.[86] The New Deal government literally swamped religious charity, crowding out some 30% of it.[87] (New Deal propagandists spread the myth that private charity collapsed in the first years of the Depression.

That collapse, though, was exaggerated and to the extent it occurred was likely the administration's fault.[88])

State and local governments had already taken over transportation infrastructure from the private sector but during the New Deal the federal government moved in with its billions. The states jauntily moved aside.[89] Thenceforth, whenever Washington wanted something, like a reduction in speed limits or an increase in the legal drinking age, it simply threatened to withhold highway or other funds from the states or nonprofits opposing it. Compliance typically resulted. American democracy found root in coercion, instead of consent.[90]

The fact that Americans' liberty could not be reconciled with the dominion of the federal government constituted the core conundrum. With states' rights, local autonomy, and voluntarism reduced in power, other checks and balances within the federal government became vulnerable to erosion. And erode they did, to the point that both purse and sword came to rest in the hands of the executive branch, if not the presidency itself.[91] Resistance continued,[92] led by business interests, conservative politicians like Ronald Reagan, and a revivified, some say radicalized, classical liberal movement called libertarianism.[93] In the face of the Great Inflation of the 1970s and the need to win the Cold War against the communist Soviet Union, those forces managed to slow the advance of the state in the final quarter of the twentieth century, much to the chagrin of Progressives, some of whom saw a nefarious conspiracy theory where existed only a revitalization of ideas, like economic freedom and limited government, that dated, in America, from the eighteenth century.[94]

By the end of the second decade of the Third Millennium AD, however, the policies of the New Deal had regained ascendancy as America devolved into the sort of mobocracy that the Founders and Framers had feared. Instead of prioritizing "prudence and gradualism over fanaticism and ideology," the new "woke" Progressives favored fear and faction over tried-and-true constitutional principles.[95] In the name of amorphous concepts like "social justice," the Woke Ones burned and pulled down symbolic buildings and statues, destroyed faith in public health and national election results, ran up the national debt to a level unprecedented in peacetime, and eroded the domestic value of the dollar. The level of state surveillance is at an all-time high, as are propaganda efforts and the fusing of private corporations with government goals.

Where the recent changes will end, no one can know for certain. How they could end, however, remains clear.

Beyond the New Deal

Harry Hopkins argued that government and business could never be in conflict because if public officials ever lost their concern for business or workers, "they will be replaced by officials who do."[96] That has not happened because FDR's New Deal cemented the foundations of the administrative state and corrupted federalism with cash. As New Deal critic Albert Jay Nock warned, the government "conditioned" its citizens to believe the New Deal was all well and good through its long-held near monopoly on K-12 education and its increasing influence on post-secondary formal education as well. Much as everyday people in 1500 accepted the word of The Church as final, most Americans have come, as Nock put it, to "an unreasoned acceptance of the State on its own terms and at its own valuation."[97] As Garet Garrett added, much of the New Deal "is irreversible … because habits of dependence are much easier to form than to break."[98]

In his 2021 book *Public Citizens*, Paul Sabin argues that a new breed of "public interest" liberals, led by outspoken critics of government policies like Rachel Carson, Jane Jacobs, and Ralph Nader, destroyed the New Deal coalition of big government, big labor, and big business by showing how feckless the government had become by the 1960s. Much truth suffuses that analysis, but Sabin goes too far when he claims that "New Deal big-government liberalism contained within it the seeds of its own decline." While it is true that after the Great Society, until 2020 anyway, the federal government attempted few major Progressive policy initiatives, it did not roll back the New Deal in any significant way.[99] America remains shackled by Social Security, the least efficient healthcare system in the developed world, and politicized court precedents that allow the federal government to be much more active in the everyday affairs of everyday Americans than the Framers and Founders intended.[100]

Many nonprofit policy organizations call for incremental reforms like health savings accounts, less occupational licensure, Social Security formula adjustments, and the like. Tweaks are all well and good, insofar as they go, but what the American people, and the people of most nations, need to do is to scale back significantly the power of their governments.

In the American case, that would entail keeping the written U.S. Constitution, as amended. Even FDR in his fourth inaugural address said that "it provided a firm base upon which all manner of men ... could build our solid structure of democracy."[101] Keep core military defense capabilities, too, lest some other country try to invade. But boot all incumbent politicians and bureaucrats, subject all past SCOTUS decisions to rigorous analysis, and repeal most laws, or at least have them sunset if not renewed.[102] Finally, the unwritten constitution should also be revivified.

Precedent for such a fundamental reformation exists. "The Whigs," Albert Nock reminded readers, "proceeded by the negative method of repealing existing laws, not by the positive method of making new ones. They combed the Statute-book, and when they found a statute which bore against 'the liberty of the subject' they simply repealed it and left the page blank. This purgation ran up into the thousands."[103] Such a purge might be most easily affected by allowing 5% of laws each year to expire unless explicitly renewed. Time was, all laws contained sunset clauses so that they automatically expired after a decade or so unless renewed. The useless or pernicious ones passed away automatically, and no legislature ever forgot to reinstate laws against murder or rape.

Other checks against government power should be reinstated, too. The custom of reading a bill aloud, in its entirety, on the floor of the legislature at least three times before it could be put to a vote helped to keep laws from growing too prolix. Another, to limit bills to one subject except in rare instances when putting two or three changes into one law was needed to affect great compromises, allowed legislators to express the will of their constituents on all matters and not have to compromise on A to get B.

State governments need to wrest back some of the power of the purse, perhaps by insisting that all federal monies go to each state on an equal per capita basis, and sequestering federal taxes paid by their residents and corporations until their federal allotment is paid. More generally, America needs to reinstate its fiscal constitution, the set of institutions that ensured that the federal government increased its debt burden only when necessary, like during a declared war, and paid them down, at least as a percentage of overall economic output, in peacetime.[104]

Something needs to be done about political parties, too, as they were not countenanced in the original frame of government. They should be banned by Constitutional amendment or, if that cannot be done, then by application of RICO statutes or antitrust law, if those laws remain in place. Political parties have become protection rackets and a duopoly in restraint of trade in policy ideas.

If political parties cannot be outlawed directly, then maybe the country should move to a sortition model whereby representatives are randomly selected from a pool, like jurors. In addition to negating the need for parties, sortition would eliminate campaign contributions as a source of corruption, defang strategic redistricting, and make term limits unnecessary. Moreover, odds are that the median legislator would improve in quality, especially if, unlike trial jurors, they are paid twice or thrice their pre-selection daily income if they serve faithfully.

Most importantly, Americans and their institutions need to again recognize the presumption of liberty. That includes recognizing the existence and power of the unwritten constitution, and all their customary, natural economic, and personal rights to be left alone so long as their behaviors do not palpably physically or economically harm others. That means making cases like *Wickard's* examples of federal power gone wrong and declaring paternalism inherently unconstitutional at the national, state, and local levels. Some "police powers" will remain, but not the power to legislate against victimless crimes or to move resources from one person or group to another under their guise.

Progressives will bemoan such reforms, but their policies failed to achieve their stated goals during and after the Great Depression and the Covid pandemic. Classical liberal America remained imperfect, but over time it emancipated immigrants, slaves, and women to live their lives on their own terms, and it could emancipate us all again today. As James Wilson wrote, "man does not exist for the sake of government, but government is instituted for the sake of man."[105]

Notes

1. Burton Folsom, Jr. *New Deal or Raw Deal? How FDR's Economic Legacy Has Damaged America* (New York: Simon & Schuster, 2008), 6, 243.
2. Alexander J. Field, *A Great Leap Forward: 1930s Depression and U.S. Economic Growth* (New Haven: Yale University Press, 2011), 294–311.
3. Christos A. Makridis and Erin McGuire, "Refined by Fire: The Great Depression and Entrepreneurship," SSRN Working Paper, (2 Apr. 2020).

4. James Ledbetter and Daniel B. Roth, eds., *The Great Depression: A Diary by Benjamin Roth* (New York: Public Affairs, 2009), 63.
5. Amity Shlaes, *The Forgotten Man: A New History of the Great Depression* (New York: HarperCollins, 2007), 227.
6. Janice Traflet and Robert E. Wright, *Fearless: Wilma Soss and America's Forgotten Investment Movement* (New York: All Seasons Press, 2022).
7. Shlaes, *Forgotten Man*, 9.
8. John Komlos and Scott Carson, "The BMI Values of the Lower Classes Likely Declined During the Great Depression," *Economics & Human Biology* 26 (Aug. 2017): 137–43.
9. Ledbetter and Roth, *Great Depression*, 17, 65; Folsom, *New Deal?*, 6.
10. Price Fishback, "The Newest on the New Deal," *Essays in Economic and Business History* 36, 1 (2018): 5.
11. Sylvester J. Schieber and John B. Shoven, *The Real Deal: The History and Future of Social Security* (New Haven: Yale University Press, 1999), 14.
12. Schieber and Shoven, *Real Deal*, 22; Malcolm Ross, *All Manner of Men* (New York: Harcourt, Brace, & World, 1948), 21.
13. As quoted in James P. Warburg, *Hell Bent for Election* (New York: Doubleday, Doran & Company, 1935), 33.
14. Jean Edward Smith, *FDR* (New York: Random House, 2007), x.
15. H. W. Brands, *A Traitor to His Class: The Privileged Life and Radical Presidency of Franklin Delano Roosevelt* (New York: Anchor Books, 2008), 306, 563–64; Lee J. Alston and Joseph P. Ferrie, *Southern Paternalism and the American Welfare State: Economics, Politics, and Institutions in the South, 1865–1965* (New York: Cambridge University Press, 1999), 8–10, 13–23, 34–44.
16. Harry L. Hopkins, "The Essence of Democracy," The Works Program, Works Progress Administration, (30 Aug. 1938), 2, FRASER.
17. Colin Gordon, "Rethinking the New Deal," *Columbia Law Review* 98, 8 (Dec. 1998): 2046; Lee J. Alston and Joseph P. Ferrie, *Southern Paternalism and the American Welfare State: Economics, Politics, and Institutions in the South, 1865–1965* (New York: Cambridge University Press, 1999), 44.

18. William Anderson, *The Wild Man from Sugar Creek: The Political Career of Eugene Talmadge* (Baton Rouge: Louisiana State University Press, 1975).
19. "National Affairs: Martial Law," *Time* (3 July 1933).
20. John Gunther, *Inside U.S.A.* (New York: Harper & Brothers, 1947), 778.
21. Price Fishback, Jessamyn Schaller, Evan Taylor, "Racial Differences in Access to New Deal Work Relief in 1940," (December 2020), 12; Ralph J. Bunche, *The Political Status of the Negro in the Age of FDR* (Chicago: University of Chicago Press, 1973), 610–11.
22. Robert E. Wright, *Fubarnomics: A Lighthearted, Serious Look at America's Economic Ills* (Amherst, N.Y.: Prometheus Books, 2010).
23. Richard N.L. Andrews, "Recovering FDR's Environmental Legacy," in Henry L. Henderson and David B. Woolner, eds., *FDR and the Environment* (New York: Palgrave, 2005), 221–43.
24. Robert E. Wright, "Improving Sustainability by Privatizing Wildlife Conservation," *Natural Resources* 14, 4 (2023).
25. Donald C. Horton, *Patterns of Farm Financial Structure: A Cross-Section View of Economic and Physical Determinants* (Princeton: Princeton University Press, 1957), 38.
26. Warburg, *Hell Bent*, 13.
27. Jean Edward Smith, *FDR* (New York: Random House, 2007), 336n.
28. Gunther, *Inside U.S.A.*, 791–92.
29. Michael Schearer, "Batteryman vs. the New Deal: The Life of Fred C. Perkins," Working Paper (9 May 2021), 1, 8.
30. Richard Willis, *Long Gone* (New York: Greenpoint Press, 2007), 150, 174, 185–86.
31. Christy Ford Chapin, *Ensuring America's Health: The Public Creation of the Corporate Health Care System* (New York: Cambridge University Press, 2015).
32. Wright, *Fubarnomics*, 177–97; Burton A. Abrams, *The Terrible Ten: A Century of Economic Folly* (Oakland: Independent Institute, 2013), 77.
33. Abrams, *Terrible Ten*, 85–100.

34. Sean Masaki Flynn, *The Cure that Works: How to Have the World's Best Healthcare—At a Quarter of the Price* (New York: Regnery Publishing, 2019).
35. Warburg, *Hell Bent*, 30.
36. Thomas Nixon Carver, *The Present Economic Revolution in the United States* (Boston: Little, Brown, and Co., 1925), 196.
37. Edward P. Stringham, ed., *How to Invest Wisely* (Great Barrington, Mass.: AIER, 2019/1947); Traflet and Wright, *Fearless*.
38. SEC Memorandum, 15, 18, 21 March, 28 April 1937, Accession Number 57A153, Box 321, Records of the Securities and Exchange Commission, RG 266, National Archives and Records Administration, College Park, Maryland.
39. Tom Arnold, Philip Hersch, J. Harold Muhlerin, and Jeffrey Netter, "Merging Markets," *Journal of Finance* 54, 3 (June 1999): 1083–107.
40. Norman S. Poser, "Restructuring the Stock Markets: A Critical Look at the SEC's National Market System," *New York University Law Review* 56 (1988): 883–922.
41. Jim Powell, *FDR's Folly: How Roosevelt and His New Deal Prolonged the Great Depression* (New York: Crown Forum, 2003), 111.
42. Andrew Smith and Robert E. Wright, "Sowing the Seeds of a Future Crisis: The SEC and the Emergence of the Nationally Recognized Statistical Rating Organization (NRSRO) Category, 1971–75," *Business History Review* (Winter 2021): 739–64; Robert L. Hetzel, *The Great Recession: Market Failure or Policy Failure?* (New York: Cambridge University Press, 2012).
43. Warburg, *Hell Bent*, 61.
44. Robert E. Wright and Richard E. Sylla, *Genealogy of American Finance* (New York: Columbia University Press, 2015), 1–7.
45. Robert E. Wright, "What George Bailey's Building and Loan Company Can Still Teach Us About Banking," *Zocalo Public Square* (6 Dec. 2018).
46. Robert E. Wright, "FSLICing America's Public Health Bureaucracies," *AIER Daily Economy* (10 Feb. 2022).
47. Robert E. Wright, ed. *Bailouts: Public Money, Private Profit* (New York: Columbia University Press, 2010), 21.

48. Thomas L. Hogan and William J. Luther, "The Implicit Costs of Government Deposit Insurance," SSRN Working Paper (19 Feb. 2015).
49. Davis McEntire, *Residence and Race: Final and Comprehensive Report to the Commission on Race and Housing* (Los Angeles: University of California Press, 1960), 291.
50. Kristen B. Crossney and David W. Bartelt, "The Legacy of the Home Owners' Loan Corporation," *Housing Policy Debate* 16, 3/4 (2005), 548.
51. Mechele Dickerson, *Homeownership and America's Financial Underclass: Flawed Premises, Broken Promises, New Prescriptions* (New York: Cambridge University Press, 2014), 1; McEntire, *Residence*, 291–92.
52. Dickerson, *Homeownership*, 51.
53. Crossney and Bartelt, "Legacy," 553–55.
54. Crossney and Bartelt, "Legacy," 568.
55. Rachel S. Ferguson and Marcus M. Witcher, *Black Liberation Through the Marketplace: Hope, Heartbreak, and the Promise of America* (New York: Post Hill Press, 2002), 233, 239.
56. McEntire, *Residence*, 301–2.
57. Dickerson, *Homeownership*, 146–49.
58. Ferguson and Witcher, *Black Liberation*, 230–31.
59. David T. Beito, *The New Deal's War on the Bill of Rights: The Untold Story of FDR's Concentration Camps, Censorship, and Mass Surveillance* (Oakland: Independent Institute, 2023), 140–41.
60. Ledbetter and Roth, *Great Depression*, 111.
61. "Williams Warns That No Strike Against Government Will Be Tolerated," WPA No. 4-1803 (8 Oct. 1938).
62. John E. Murray, *Origins of American Health Insurance: A History of Industrial Sickness Funds* (New Haven: Yale University Press, 2007), 203.
63. Richard J. Jensen, "The Causes and Cures of Unemployment in the Great Depression," *Journal of Interdisciplinary History* 19, 4 (Spring 1989): 553–83.
64. Robert A. Margo, "Employment and Unemployment in the 1930s," *Journal of Economic Perspectives* 7, 2 (Spring 1993): 53–54.

65. Liran Einav, Amy Finkelstein, and Ray Fisman, *Risky Business: Why Insurance Markets Fail and What to Do About It* (New Haven: Yale University Press, 2023), 236.
66. Works Progress Administration, The Works Program, Press Release, 16 Jul. 1938, FRASER.
67. Matt Pehl, "The Frustrations of Organized Labor in South Dakota and the Making of a Conservative Coalition in the Mid-Century United States," in Jon Lauck, John Miller, and Don Simmons, eds. *The Plains Political Tradition*, Volume 2 (Pierre: South Dakota State Historical Society Press, 2014), 103–25; George Leef, *Free Choice for Workers: A History of the Right to Work Movement* (Ottawa, Illinois: Jameson Books, 2005), 28–32, 35–37; Glenn W. Miller, *Problems of Labor* (New York: Macmillan Co., 1951), 451–54.
68. Abrams, *Terrible Ten*, xiii-xv; Michael J. Graetz and Jerry L. Mashaw, *True Security: Rethinking American Social Insurance* (New Haven: Yale University Press, 1999), 10.
69. Dominick Pratico, *Eisenhower and Social Security: The Origins of the Disability Program* (New York Writers Club Press, 2001); Amity Shlaes, *Great Society: A New History* (New York: Harper-Collins, 2019), 2–3, 14, 52, 63, 78, 99–103, 141; Abrams, *Terrible Ten*, 85–100; Folsom, *New Deal?*, 263–64.
70. Brian C. Anderson, *Democratic Capitalism and Its Discontents* (Wilmington, Del.: ISI Books, 2007), 23–34.
71. Dalia Tsuk, "Pluralisms: The Indian New Deal As a Model," *University of Maryland Law Journal of Race, Religion, Gender and Class* 1, 2 (2001): 446.
72. Garet Garrett, *The People's Pottage* (Caldwell, ID: Caxton Printers, 1953), 6–7.
73. Folsom, *New Deal?*, 235–36.
74. Gary Libecap, "The Great Depression and the Regulating State: Federal Government of Agriculture, 1884–1970," in Michael D. Bordon, Claudia Goldin, and Eugene N. White, eds. *The Defining Moment: The Great Depression and the American Economy in the Twentieth Century* (Chicago: University of Chicago Press, 1998), 181–82.
75. Daniel J. Gifford, "The New Deal Regulatory Model: A History of Criticism and Refinements," *Minnesota Law Review* 68 (1983), 306–8; Mariano-Florentino Cuellar, "James Landis and the

Dilemmas of Administrative Government," 83, 4/5 *George Washington Law Review* (September 2015): 1330–57.

76. Beito, *New Deal's War on the Bill of Rights*, 184.
77. Beito, *New Deal's War on the Bill of Rights*, 189–90, 218, 239.
78. Beito, *New Deal's War on the Bill of Rights*, 212–13.
79. One can almost see FEMA rising from Harry Hopkins's description of the devastation wrought by the hurricane that slammed New England in September 1938. "How awful the carnage; how decisive and imperative to response of the gallant government! People who did not seek aid at the nadir of the depression pleaded for it in the aftermath and the New Deal was there to help!" Harry Hopkins, "Meeting the Challenge of Disaster," Works Progress Administration, NBC Radio Announcement, 26 Sept. 1938, FRASER.
80. Roger G. Kennedy, "A New Deal for Nature—And Nature's People," in Henderson and Woolner, eds., *FDR and the Environment.*
81. Completed in the 1960s, I-84 raised the value of homes in predominantly upper and middle class white neighborhoods a half mile to a mile away from the road, while crushing home values in the black, immigrant, and poor white neighborhoods that the interstate bisected. Jeffrey P. Cohen, Nicholas Lownes, and Bo Zhang, "1960s Interstate Highways and Homeowner Wealth Distribution," *St. Louis Federal Reserve Review* 104, 4 (21 Oct. 2022). For the destruction wrought by the system, see Ferguson and Witcher, *Black Liberation*, 244–57.
82. Harry Hopkins, Works Progress Administration, The Works Program, Press Release, 16 Jul. 1938, FRASER; Garrett, *People's Pottage*, 69.
83. "National Affairs: Martial Law," *Time* (3 July 1933).
84. Robert E. Wright, *Liberty Lost: Rise and Demise of Voluntary Association in America Since 1700* (Great Barrington, Mass.: American Institute for Economic Research, 2023); Brian C. Anderson, *Democratic Capitalism and Its Discontents* (Wilmington, Del.: ISI Books, 2007), 37–49.
85. John Phillip Reid, *Constitutional History of the American Revolution*, abridged ed. (Madison: University of Wisconsin Press, 1995), 70.
86. Folsom, *New Deal?*, 81.

87. Jonathan Gruber and Daniel M. Hungerman, "Faith-Based Charity and Crowd Out During the Great Depression," NBER Working Paper 11332 (May 2005).
88. "Howard O. Hunter Discusses Relief Needs on 'Youth Meets Government' Program Over NBC Network," WPA, 4-1904 (26 Feb. 1939), 3, FRASER; Naomi Oreskes and Erik M. Conway, *The Big Myth: How American Business Taught Us to Loathe Government and Love the Free Market* (New York: Bloomsbury Publishing, 2023), 190.
89. Folsom, *New Deal?*, 110.
90. Thomas R. Dye, *Understanding Public Policy* 14th ed. (New York: Pearson, 2013), 91–95.
91. Garrett, *People's Pottage*, 9.
92. Reid, *Constitutional History*, 99.
93. Matt Zwolinski and John Tomasi, *The Individualists: Radicals, Reactionaries, and the Struggle for the Soul of Libertarianism* (Princeton: Princeton University Press, 2023).
94. Philip Magness, "Free Enterprise as Conspiracy," *Law and Liberty* (23 Dec. 2019).
95. Allen Mendenhall, "The Lineaments of the Ancient Constitution," *Law and Liberty* (22 June 2022).
96. Works Progress Administration, The Works Program, Press Release, 16 Jul. 1938.
97. Albert Jay Nock, *Our Enemy, the State* (New York: William Morrow & Co., 1935), 10, 33.
98. Garrett, *People's Pottage*, 73.
99. Paul Sabin, *Public Citizens: The Attack on Big Government and the Remaking of American Liberalism* (New York: W.W. Norton & Co., 2021), 1–9.
100. Randy E. Barnett, *Restoring the Lost Constitution: The Presumption of Liberty* (Princeton: Princeton University Press, 2004), 354–58.
101. As quoted in Ross, *All Manner*, 21.
102. On the costs and benefits of incrementalism and other policy models, see Dye, *Understanding Public Policy*, 14–31.
103. Albert Nock, "Liberalism, Properly So Called," Working Paper (1943).
104. Bill White, *America's Fiscal Constitution: Its Triumph and Collapse* (New York: PublicAffairs, 2014).

105. Kermit L. Hall, ed. *Collected Works of James Wilson* (Indianapolis: Liberty Fund, 2007), 1083.

Bibliography

Archives

American Presidency Project, University of California, Santa Barbara, Santa Barbara, California: https://www.presidency.ucsb.edu/documents.
E.C. Harwood Archives, American Institute for Economic Research, Great Barrington, Massachusetts.
Franklin D. Roosevelt Presidential Library and Museum, Hyde Park, New York: https://www.fdrlibrary.org/digital-collections.
FRASER, St. Louis Federal Reserve, St. Louis, Missouri: https://fraser.stlouisfed.org/.
Treasury Records
Works Progress Administration Records
Gareth Jones Publications: https://www.garethjones.org/index.htm.
Records of the Securities and Exchange Commission, RG 266, National Archives and Records Administration, College Park, Maryland.
Rural Electrification Administration Records, Alabama Department of Archives and History, Montgomery, Alabama.

Printed Sources

Aaronson, Daniel, Daniel Hartley, Bhashkar Mazumder, and Martha Stinson. "The Long-run Effects of the 1930s Redlining Maps on Children," Center for Economic Studies Working Paper (Dec. 2022).
Abbott, Grace. *From Relief to Social Security: The Development of the New Public Welfare Service* (Chicago: University of Chicago Press, 1941).

R. E. Wright, *FDR's Long New Deal*,
https://doi.org/10.1007/978-3-031-74141-8

Abraham, Henry J. *Justices and Presidents: A Political History of Appointments to the Supreme Court*, 3d ed. (New York: Oxford University Press, 1992).

Abrams, Burton A. *The Terrible Ten: A Century of Economic Folly* (Oakland: Independent Institute, 2013).

Abramowitz, Mildred W. "Eleanor Roosevelt and the National Youth Administration 1935–1943—An Extension of the Presidency," *Presidential Studies Quarterly* 14, 4 (Fall 1984): 569–80.

Adamic, Louis. *Dynamite: The Story of Class Violence in America*, rev. ed. (1934) (Oakland: AK Press 2008).

Alston, Lee J. and Joseph P. Ferrie. *Southern Paternalism and the American Welfare State: Economics, Politics, and Institutions in the South, 1865–1965* (New York: Cambridge University Press, 1999).

Amenta, Edwin. *When Movements Matter: The Townsend Plan and the Rise of Social Security* (Princeton: Princeton University Press, 2006).

Anderson, Richard G., Michael Bordo, and John V. Duca, "Money and Velocity During Financial Crises: From the Great Depression to the Great Recession," NBER Working Paper No. 22100 (Mar. 2016).

Anderson, William. *The Wild Man from Sugar Creek: The Political Career of Eugene Talmadge* (Baton Rouge: Louisiana State University Press, 1975).

Antonucci, Ryan J. "Building a New (Deal) Identity: The Evolution of Italian-American Political Culture and Ideology, 1910–1940," (Ph.D. diss.: University of South Carolina, 2021).

Ardelt, Monika. "Social Credit and Individual Growth: The Long-Term Effects of the Great Depression," *Journal of Aging Studies* 12, 3 (Sept. 1998): 291–314.

Arnold, Tom, Philip Hersch, J. Harold Muhlerin, and Jeffrey Netter. "Merging Markets," *Journal of Finance* 54, 3 (Jun. 1999): 1083–107.

Arrupe, Javier San Julian. "When Lawmakers Met Progressives: Debating the American Federal Income Tax of 1894," University of Barcelona School of Economics Working Paper No. 418 (Mar. 2022).

Asp, David. "Espionage Act of 1917," *The First Amendment Encyclopedia* (Murfreesboro, TN: Free Speech Center, 2024): https://firstamendment.mtsu.edu/article/espionage-act-of-1917/#.

Asquith, Benjamin Sherman. "Some Substitutes for the General Property Tax," (MA Thesis: University of Iowa, 1912).

Autor, David H. and Mark G. Duggan. "The Growth in the Social Security Disability Rolls: A Fiscal Crisis Unfolding," *Journal of Economic Perspectives* 20, 3 (Summer 2006): 71–96.

Ayres, Leonard P. *Turning Points in Business Cycles* (New York: Macmillan Company, 1939).

Ballinger, Kenneth. *Miami Millions: The Dance of the Dollars in the Great Florida Land Boom of 1925* (Miami: Franklin Press, 1936).

Banfield, Edward C. "Ten Years of the Farm Tenant Purchase Program," *Journal of Farm Economics* 31, 3 (Aug. 1949): 469–86.

Barnett, Randy E. *Restoring the Lost Constitution: The Presumption of Liberty* (Princeton: Princeton University Press, 2004).

Barnett, Randy E. ed. *The Rights Retained by the People: The History and Meaning of the Ninth Amendment* (Fairfax, Va.: George Mason University Press, 1989).

Bauman, John F., Roger Biles, and Kristin M. Szylvian, eds. *From Tenements to the Taylor Homes: In Search of an Urban Housing Policy in Twentieth Century America* (University Park: Pennsylvania State University Press, 2000).

Beito, David T. *From Mutual Aid to the Welfare State: Fraternal Societies and Social Services, 1890–1967* (Chapel Hill: University of North Carolina Press, 2000).

Beito, David T. *The New Deal's War on the Bill of Rights: The Untold Story of FDR's Concentration Camps, Censorship, and Mass Surveillance* (Oakland: Independent Institute, 2023).

Benmelech, Efraim, Carola Frydman, and Dimitris Papanikolaou, "Financial Frictions and Employment during the Great Depression," NBER Working Paper No. 23216 (Mar. 2017).

Bernanke, Ben S. "Non-Monetary Effects of the Financial Crisis in the Propagation of the Great Depression," NBER Working Paper Series No. 1054 (Jan. 1983).

Bernanke, Ben S. "The Macroeconomics of the Great Depression: A Comparative Approach," NBER Working Paper No. 4814 (Aug. 1994).

Bernanke, Ben S. *Essays on the Great Depression* (Princeton: Princeton University Press, 2000).

Bernanke, Ben S. and Kevin Carey. "Nominal Wage Stickiness and Aggregate Supply in the Great Depression," NBER Working Paper No. 5439 (Jan. 1996).

Bernanke, Ben S. and Harold James. "The Gold Standard, Deflation, and Financial in the Great Depression: An International Comparison," NBER Working Paper No. 3488 (Oct. 1990).

Bernstein, David E. "Racism, Railroad Unions, and Labor Regulations," *Independent Review* 5, 2 (Fall 2000): 237–47.

Bernstein, David E. *Only One Place of Redress: African Americans, Labor Regulations, and the Courts from Reconstruction to the New Deal* (Durham: Duke University Press, 2001).

Best, Gary Dean. *Pride, Prejudice, and Politics: Roosevelt Versus Recovery, 1933–1938* (New York: Praeger, 1991).

Betten, Neil and Raymond A. Mohl. "From Discrimination to Repatriation: Mexican Life in Gary, Indiana, During the Great Depression," *Pacific Historical Review* 42, 3 (Aug. 1973): 370–88.

Betti, Daniel. "G.K. Chesterton on the Fundamentals of Liberalism," *AIER Daily Economy* (27 Sep. 2022): https://www.aier.org/article/g-k-chesterton-on-the-fundamentals-of-liberalism/.

Blum, John Morton, ed. *Public Philosopher: Selected Letters of Walter Lippmann* (New York: Ticknor & Fields, 1985).

Bobroff, Kenneth H. "Retelling Allotment: Indian Property Rights and the Myth of Common Ownership," *Vanderbilt Law Review* 54, 4 (May 2001): 1559–623.

Bolton, Anthony J. "'The Best Form of Assistance Always Is the Kind That Enables Folks to Help Themselves': Public Reaction to the New Deal in Hancock, Seneca, and Wood Counties of Ohio," (MA Thesis: Bowling Green State University, 2021).

Bonham, Mark S. ed., *Becoming 150: 150 Years of Canadian Business History* (Toronto: Canadian Business History Association, 2018).

Bordo, Michael D., Christopher J. Erceg, and Charles L. Evans. "Money, Sticky Wages, and the Great Depression," NBER Working Paper 6071 (Jun. 1997).

Bordo, Michael D., Claudia Goldin, and Eugene N. White, eds. *The Defining Moment: The Great Depression and the American Economy in the Twentieth Century* (Chicago: University of Chicago Press, 1998).

Bordo, Michael D. and Arunima Sinha. "A Lesson from the Great Depression that the Fed Might Have Learned: A Comparison of the 1932 Open Market Purchases with Quantitative Easing," Working Paper (Sep. 2015).

Boyd, Christina L. "Sedition Act of 1918," *The First Amendment Encyclopedia* (Washington, DC: CQ Press, 2009): https://sk.sagepub.com/cqpress/encyclopedia-of-the-first-amendment.

Brady, David, Richard Brody, and David Epstein. "Heterogeneous Parties and Political Organization: The U.S. Senate, 1880–1920," *Legislative Studies Quarterly* 14, 2 (May 1989): 205–23.

Brandeis, Louis. *Other People's Money and How the Bankers Use It* (New York: Harper Torchbooks, 1974).

Brands, H. W. *A Traitor to His Class: The Privileged Life and Radical Presidency of Franklin Delano Roosevelt* (New York: Anchor Books, 2008).

Brinkley, Alan. *Culture and Politics in the Great Depression* (Waco: Baylor University Press, 1998).

Bromhead, Alan de, Barry Eichengreen, and Kevin H. O'Rourke, "Right-Wing Political Extremism in the Great Depression," NBER Working Paper No. 17871 (Feb. 2012).

Brownell, Kathryn Cramer. *Showbiz Politics: Hollywood in American Political Life* (Chapel Hill: University of North Carolina Press, 2014).

Bruner, Robert F. *The Panic of 1907: Lesson Learned from the Market's Perfect Storm* (Hoboken, N.J.: Johne Wiley & Sons, 2007).

Bruner, Robert F. and Scott C. Miller. "The Great Crash of 1929: A Look Back After 90 Years," *Journal of Applied Corporate Finance* 31, 3 (Fall 2019): 43–58.

Buffalohead, W. Roger. "The Indian New Deal: A Review Essay," *Minnesota History* 48, 8 (Winter 1983): 339–41.

Bunche, Ralph. *The Political Status of the Negro in the Age of FDR* (Chicago: University of Chicago Press, 1973).

Burke, Edmund, and David Bromwich, ed. *On Empire, Liberty, and Reform: Speeches and Letters* (New Haven: Yale University Press, 2000).

Burkhauser, Richard V., J.S. Butler, and Robert R. Weathers. "How Policy Variables Influence the Timing of Applications for Social Security Disability Insurance," 64 *Social Security Bulletin* (2001–2): 52–83.

Cagigas, Leonardo de las and Andre Straus, eds. *Role of Reinsurance in the World* (Cham, Switz.: Palgrave, 2021).

Calomiris, Charles W. "Financial Factors in the Great Depression," *Journal of Economic Perspectives* 7, 2 (Spring 1993): 61–85.

Calomiris, Charles W. and R. Glenn Hubbard, "Internal Finance and Investment: Evidence from the Undistributed Profits Tax of 1936–1937," NBER Working Paper No. 4288 (Mar. 1993).

Calomiris, Charles W. and Joseph R. Mason. "Contagion and Bank Failures During the Great Depression The June 1932 Chicago Banking Panic," NBER Working Paper No. 4934 (Nov. 1994).

Carver, Thomas Nixon. *The Present Economic Revolution in the United States* (Boston: Little, Brown, and Co., 1925).

Cecchetti, Stephen G. "Prices During the Great Depression: Was the Deflation of 1930–32 Really Unanticipated?" NBER Working Paper No. 3174 (Nov. 1989).

Cecchetti, Stephen G. "Understanding the Great Depression: Lessons for Current Policy," NBER Working Paper No. 6015 (Apr. 1997).

Cecchetti, Stephen and Georgios Karras. "Sources of Output Fluctuations During the Interwar Period: Further Evidence on the Causes of the Great Depression," NBER Working Paper 4049 (Apr. 1992).

Chandler, William U. *The Myth of TVA: Conservation and Development in the Tennessee Valley, 1933–1983* (Cambridge, Mass.: Ballinger Publishing Co., 1984).

Chapin, Christy Ford. *Ensuring America's Health: The Public Creation of the Corporate Health Care System* (New York: Cambridge University Press, 2015).

Charles, Anthony P. *The Great Reset Explained: Corporate Plot, Economic Pipe Dream, or Global Panacea?* (New York: Kindle, 2022).

Charles, Douglas M. *J. Edgar Hoover and the Anti-Interventionists: FBI Political Surveillance and the Rise of the Domestic Security State, 1939–1945* (Columbus: Ohio State University Press, 2007).

Christiano, Lawrence J., Roberto Motton, and Massimo Rostagno. "The Great Depression and the Friedman-Schwartz Hypothesis," NBER Working Paper 10255 (2004).

Clement, Bell. "Wagner-Steagall and the D.C. Alley Dwelling Authority," *Journal of the American Planning Association* 78, 4 (Autumn 2012): 434–48.

Cogan, John F. *The High Cost of Good Intentions: A History of U.S. Federal Entitlement Programs* (Stanford: Stanford University Press, 2017).

Cogley, Timothy and Thomas J. Sargent. "The Market Price of Risk and the Equity Premium: A Legacy of the Great Depression?" UC Davis Department of Economics Working Paper Series No. 05–22 (Mar. 2005).

Cohen, Jeffrey P., Nicholas Lownes, and Bo Zhang. "1960s Interstate Highways and Homeowner Wealth Distribution," *St. Louis Federal Reserve Review* 104, 4 (21 Oct. 2022): 317–36.

Cole, Harold L. and Lee E. Ohanian. "The Great Depression in the United States from a Neoclassical Perspective," *Federal Reserve Bank of Minneapolis Quarterly Review* (Winter 1999): 2–24.

Cole, Harold L. and Lee E. Ohanian. "Re-examining the Contributions of Money and Banking Shocks to the U.S. Great Depression," *NBER Macroeconomics Annual* 15 (2000): 183–227.

Cole, Harold L. and Lee E. Ohanian. "New Deal Policies and the Persistence of the Great Depression: A General Equilibrium Analysis," *Journal of Political Economy* 112, 4 (Aug. 2004): 779–816.

Conti-Brown, Peter and Sean H. Vanatta. "The Logic and Legitimacy of Bank Supervision: The Case of the Bank Holiday of 1933," *Business History Review* 95, 1 (Spring 2021): 87–120.

Cooper, John Milton, Jr. *Woodrow Wilson: A Biography* (New York: Random House, 2009).

Costa, Dora L. *The Evolution of Retirement: An American Economic History, 1880–1990* (Chicago: University of Chicago Press, 1998).

Cotter, Christopher and Peter L. Rousseau. "Correspondent Banking, Systematic Risk, and the Panic of 1893," MPRA Paper No. 113340 (May 2022).

Cowle, Jefferson and Nick Salvatore. "The Long Exception: Rethinking the Place of the New Deal in American History," *International Labor and Working-Class History* 74, 1 (Fall 2008): 3–32.

Couch, Jim F. and William F. Shughart. *The Political Economy of the New Deal* (Northampton, MA: Edward Elgar, 1998).

Crossney, Kristen B. and David W. Bartelt. "The Legacy of the Home Owners' Loan Corporation," *Housing Policy Debate* 16, 3/4 (2005): 547–74.

Crucini, Mario J. and James Kahn. "Tariffs and the Great Depression Revisited," Federal Reserve Bank of New York Staff Report No. 172 (Sep. 2003).

Cuellar, Mariano-Florentino. "James Landis and the Dilemmas of Administrative Government," 83, 4/5 *George Washington Law Review* (Sep. 2015): 1330–57.

Cunfer, Geoff. "The Southern Great Plains Wind Erosion Maps of 1936–1937," *Agricultural History* 85, 4 (Fall 2011): 540–59.

Currie, Lauchlin. "Lauchlin Currie's Memoirs: The New Deal," *Journal of Economic Studies* 31, 3/4 (2004): 201–34.

Davis, Susan G. "Ben Botkin's FBI File," *Journal of American Folklore* 123, 487 (Winter 2010): 3–30.

DeFalco, Ralph L., III. "Was There Ever a Neoliberal Order?" *Law and Liberty* (18 Oct. 2022): https://lawliberty.org/book-review/was-there-ever-a-neoliberal-order/.

DeLong, J. Bradford. "'Liquidation' Cycles: Old-Fashioned Real Business Cycle Theory and the Great Depression," NBER Working Paper 3546 (Dec. 1990).

Derenoncourt, Eliora, Chi Hyun Kim, Moritz Kuhn, and Moritz Schularick. "Wealth of Two Nations: The US Racial Wealth Gap, 1860–2020," CRC TR 225 Discussion Paper Series (Sept. 2022).

DeTocqueville, Alexis. *Democracy in America*, Henry Reeve, trans. (New York: Pratt, Woodford & Co., 1848).

Dickerson, Mechele. *Homeownership and America's Financial Underclass: Flawed Premises, Broken Promises, New Prescriptions* (New York: Cambridge University Press, 2014).

Diggins, John P. "Flirtation with Fascism: American Pragmatic Liberals and Mussolini's Italy," *American History Review* 71, 2 (Jan. 1966): 487–506.

Dighe, Ranjit S. "America's High Wage Economy in the 1930s," (Ph.D. diss., Yale University, 1997).

Dighe, Ranjit S. "Al Smith, Economic Conservative?" Economic and Business History Society Conference (Apr. 2012).

Dighe, Ranjit S., ed. *The Historian's Wizard of Oz: Reading L. Frank Baum's Classic as a Political and Monetary Allegory* (Westport, CT: Praeger Publishers, 2002).

Douglas, Lewis W. *The Liberal Tradition: A Free People and a Free Economy* (New York: D. Van Nostrand, 1935).

Dugger, William M. "The Reform Method of John R. Commons," *Journal of Economic Issues* 13, 1 (Jun. 1979): 369–81.

Duke, Rebecca K. "From Dewey to Skyline Farms: Progressive Education in New Deal Resettlement Communities," (Ph.D. Diss., Middle Tennessee State University, 2020).

Dye, Thomas R. *Understanding Public Policy* 14th ed. (New York: Pearson, 2013).

Ealy, Lenore. "Philanthropy and Civil Society: An Ethic of Beneficence for the Modern Age," Acton University Working Paper, (2015).

Ealy, Lenore and Steven D. Ealy. "Progressivism and Philanthropy," *The Good Society* 15, 1 (2006): 35–42.

Edwards, Sebastian. *American Default: The Untold Story of FDR, the Supreme Court, and the Battle Over Gold* (Princeton: Princeton University Press, 2018).

Eggertsson, Gauti B. "Was the New Deal Contractionary," *American Economic Review* 102, 1 (Feb. 2012): 524–55.

Eichengreen, Barry. "The Gold-Exchange Standards and the Great Depression," NBER Working Paper No. 2198 (Mar. 1987).

Eichengreen, Barry and Douglas A. Irwin. "The Slide to Protectionism in the Great Depression: Who Succumbed and Why?" NBER Working Paper No. 15142 (Jul. 2009/Feb. 2010).

Eichengreen, Barry and Kris Mitchener. "The Great Depression as a Credit Boom Gone Wrong," BIS Working Papers No. 137, (Sep. 2003).

Eichengreen, Barry and Peter Temin. "The Gold Standard and the Great Depression," NBER Working Paper 6060 (Jun. 1997).

Einav, Liran, Amy Finkelstein, and Ray Fisman. *Risky Business: Why Insurance Markets Fail and What to Do About It* (New Haven: Yale University Press, 2022).

Epstein, Richard A. *Forbidden Grounds: The Case Against Employment Discrimination Laws* (Cambridge: Harvard University Press, 1992).

Eslake, Saul. "The Difference Between a Recession and a Depression," *Economic Papers* 28, 2 (Jun. 2009): 75–81.

Escarraz, Donald Ray and Thomas Yirak. "The Evolution of Georgia's Tax Structure," *Georgia Government Review* 1, 2 (Summer 1968): 1–6.

Feigenbaum, James J. "Intergenerational Mobility During the Great Depression," Working Paper (1 Dec. 2015).

Ferderer, J. Peter and David A. Zalewski. "Uncertainty as a Propagating Force in the Great Depression," *Journal of Economic History* 54, 4 (Dec. 1994): 825–49.

Ferguson, Rachel S. and Marcus M. Witcher. *Black Liberation Through the Marketplace: Hope, Heartbreak, and the Promise of America* (New York: Post Hill Press, 2022).

Field, Alexander J. *A Great Leap Forward: 1930s Depression and U.S. Economic Growth* (New Haven: Yale University Press, 2011).

Fishback, Price V. "How Successful Was the New Deal? The Microeconomic Impact of New Deal Spending and Lending Policies in the 1930s," NBER Working Paper 21925 (Jan. 2016).

Fishback, Price V. "The Newest on the New Deal," *Essays in Economic and Business History* 36, 1 (2018): 1–22.

Fishback, Price V., Michael R. Haines, Shawn Kantor, "Births, Deaths and New Relief During the Great Depression," NBER Working Paper No. 11246 (Mar. 2005).

Fishback, Price V., William C. Horrace, and Shawn Kantor. "Did New Deal Grant Programs Stimulate Local Economies? A Study of Federal Grants and Retail Sales During the Great Depression," *Journal of Economic History* 65, 1 (Mar. 2005): 36–71.

Fishback, Price V., Alfonso Lagunes, William Horrace, Shawn Kantor and Jaret Treber, "The Influence of the Home Owners' Loan Corporation on Housing Markets During the 1930s," NBER Working Paper Series 15824 (Mar. 2010).

Fishback, Price V., Jonathan Rose, and Kenneth Snowden, *Well Worth Saving: How the New Deal Safeguarded Home Ownership* (Chicago: University of Chicago Press, 2013).

Fishback, Price V., Jessamyn Schaller, Evan Taylor, "Racial Differences in Access to New Deal Work Relief in 1940," Working Paper (Dec. 2020)

Florida, Richard. *The Great Reset: How the Post-Crash Economy Will Change the Way We Live and Work* (New York: HarperCollins, 2010).

Flynn, G.Q. "The New Deal and Local Archives: The Pacific Northwest," *The American Archivist* 33, 1 (Jan. 1970): 41–52.

Flynn, John T. *Country Squire in the White House* (New York: Doubleday, 1940).

Flynn, Sean Masaki. *The Cure that Works: How to Have the World's Best Healthcare—At a Quarter of the Price* (New York: Regnery Publishing, 2019).

Folsom, Burton, Jr. *New Deal or Raw Deal? How FDR's Economic Legacy Has Damaged America* (New York: Simon & Schuster, 2008).

Francis, Dania V., Darrick Hamilton, Thomas W. Mitchell, Nathan A. Rosenberg, and Bryce Wilson Stucki, "Black Land Loss: 1920–1997," *AEA Papers and Proceedings* 112 (2022): 38–42.

Fraser, Steve and Gary Gerstle, eds. *The Rise and Fall of the New Deal Order, 1930–1980* (Princeton: Princeton University Press, 1989).

Frazer, William and John J. Guthrie, Jr., *The Florida Land Boom: Speculation, Money, and the Banks* (Westport, Conn.: Quorum Books, 1995).

Frederickson, Kari. "Cathrine Curtis and Conservative Isolationist Women, 1939–1941," *The Historian* 58, 4 (1996): 825–39.

Freyer, Tony A. *Hugo L. Black and the Dilemma of American Liberalism* (New York: Pearson, 2008).

Friedman, Benjamin M. ed., *Should the United States Privatize Social Security?* (Cambridge, Mass.: MIT Press, 1999).

Friedman, Benjamin M. ed., *The Moral Consequences of Economic Growth* (New York: Alfred A. Knopf, 2005).

Friedman, Milton. "Why Government Is the Problem," *Essays in Public Policy* No. 39 (Stanford: Hoover Institution, 1993).

Forgue, Guy J., ed. *Letters of H.L. Mencken* (New York: Alfred A. Knopf, 1961).

Fulmer, Sean. "United States: Aldrich-Vreeland Emergency Currency During the Crisis of 1914," *Journal of Financial Crises* 4, 2 (2022): 1156–79.

Gamache, Ray. "Contextualizing FDR's Campaign to Recognize the Soviet Union, 1932–1933," *Harvard Ukrainian Studies* 37, 3/4 (2020): 287–322.

Gamm, Gerald H. *The Making of New Deal Democrats: Voting Behavior and Realignment in Boston, 1920–1940* (Chicago: University of Chicago Press, 1989).

Gan, Jie, Paul Mahoney, and Jianping Mei, "IPO Underpricing: A Tale of a Different 1920s," SSRN Working Paper (20 Apr. 2022).

Garrett, Garet. *A Bubble That Broke the World* (Boston: Little, Brown, and Company, 1932).

Garrett, Garet. *The People's Pottage* (Caldwell, ID: Caxton Printers, 1953).

Garrison, Roger W. "The Great Depression Revisited," *Independent Review* 3, 4 (Spring 1999): 595–603.

Gatch, Loren. "Local Money in the United States During the Great Depression," *Essays in Economic & Business History* 26 (2008): 47–61.

Gerstle, Gary. *The Rise and Fall of the Neoliberal Order: America and the World in the Free Market Era* (New York: Oxford University Press, 2022).

Gettens, John, Pei-Pei Lei, and Alexis D. Henry. "Accounting for Geographic Variation in Social Security Disability Program Participation," *Social Security Bulletin* 78, 2 (2018): https://www.ssa.gov/policy/docs/ssb/v78n2/v78n2p29.html.

Gifford, Daniel J. "The New Deal Regulatory Model: A History of Criticism and Refinements," *Minnesota Law Review* 68 (1983): 299–332.

Glaeser, Edward L. and Claudia Goldin, eds. *Corruption and Reform: Lessons from America's Economic History* (Chicago: University of Chicago Press, 2006).

Glanz, Theresa A. "Federal Land-Use Policy and Resettlement in the Great Plains: An Experiment in Community Development During the New Deal Years, 1933–1941," (Ph.D. Diss., University of Nebraska, 2020).

Goldin, Claudia and Lawrence F. Katz. *The Race Between Education and Technology* (Cambridge, Mass.: Belknap Press, 2008).

Gordon, Colin. "Rethinking the New Deal," *Columbia Law Review* 98, 8 (Dec. 1998): 2029–54.

Gordon, Colin. *Dead on Arrival: The Politics of Health Care in Twentieth-Century America* (Princeton: Princeton University Press, 2003).

Gordon, John Steele. *An Empire of Wealth: The Epic History of American Economic Power* (New York: HarperCollins, 2004).

Gorgosz, Jon. "'No Formal Cooperation Needed': Federal New Deal Policy at Elite Massachusetts' Women's Colleges, 1933–1942," *Historical Journal of Massachusetts* 49, 2 (Summer 2021): 100–27.

Grabar, Mary. *Debunking FDR: The Man and the Myths* (New York: Regnery, 2024).
Graetz, Michael J. and Jerry L. Mashaw, *True Security: Rethinking American Social Insurance* (New Haven: Yale University Press, 1999).
Graham, Benjamin. "The Undistributed Profits Tax and the Investor," *Yale Law Journal* 46, 1 (Nov. 1936): 1–18.
Graham, John R., Sonali Hazarika, and Krishnamoorthy Narasimhan, "Financial Distress in the Great Depression," NBER Working Paper 17388 (Sept. 2011).
Graham, John R. and Krishnamoorthy Narasimhan, "Corporate Survival and Managerial Experiences During the Great Depression," SSRN Working Paper (15 Jan. 2004).
Gregg, Samuel. *The Next American Economy: Nation, State, and Markets in an Uncertain World* (New York: Encounter Books, 2022).
Grey, Thomas C. "Origins of the Unwritten Constitution: Fundamental Law in American Revolution Thought," *Stanford Law Review* 30, 5 (May 1978): 843–93.
Grey, Thomas C. "The Uses of an Unwritten Constitution," *Chicago-Kent Law Review* 64, 1 (Apr. 1988): 211–38.
Griffin, Frank. "Implicit Disability Bias Disinterred by Zombie Factors in Social Security Disability Determinations," *Nevada Law Journal* 21 (2020–21): 161–207.
Grubb, Erica B. "Day-Care Regulation: Legal and Policy Issues," *Santa Clara Law Review* 25, 2 (1985): 303–74.
Gruber, Jonathan and Daniel M. Hungerman. "Faith-Based Charity and Crowd Out During the Great Depression," NBER Working Paper 11332 (May 2005).
Gunther, John. *Inside U.S.A.* (New York: Harper & Brothers, 1947).
Guthmann, Harry G. "The Effect of the Undistributed Profits Tax Upon the Distribution of Corporate Earnings: A Note," *Econometrica* 8, 4 (Oct. 1940): 354–56.
Hall, Kermit L., ed. *Collected Works of James Wilson* (Indianapolis: Liberty Fund, 2007).
Hall, Thomas E. and J. David Ferguson. *The Great Depression: An International Disaster of Perverse Economic Policies* (Ann Arbor: University of Michigan Press, 1998).
Hamburger, Philip. *Is Administrative Law Unlawful?* (Chicago: University of Chicago Press, 2014).
Hamilton, James D. "Was the Deflation During the Great Depression Anticipated? Evidence from the Commodity Futures Market," *American Economic Review* 82, 1 (1992): 157–78.

Hamilton, Shane. "Crop Insurance and the New Deal Roots of Agricultural Financialization in the United States," *Enterprise & Society* 21, 3 (Sept. 2020): 648–80.

Hanke, Steve. "Public Lands: America's Great Anomaly," *Independent Institute Blog* (6 Oct. 2022): https://www.independent.org/news/article.asp?id=14299&omhide=true&trk=title.

Harwood, E.C. "The Underlying Causes of Our Recent Prosperity: Why the End Is Near," *The Annalist* (13 Apr. 1928): 3–13.

Harwood, E.C. "How the Army Officer Builds His Future Income," *Magazine of Wall Street* (29 Aug. 1928): 1116–51.

Harwood, E.C. "Calculations on the Credit Expansion Limit to Present Prosperity," *The Annalist* (25 Jan. 1929).

Harwood, E.C. "Speculation in Securities vs. Commodity Speculation," *The Annalist* (15 Feb. 1929).

Harwood, E.C. "The Aftermath of Getting Something for Nothing; Causes, Effects, Remedies," *The Annalist* (29 Nov. 1929).

Harwood, E.C. "Effects of Currency Hoarding," *Barron's* (15 Feb. 1932).

Harwood, E.C. "The Full Significance of Freedom," *American Journal of Economics and Sociology* 4, 2 (Jan. 1945): 185–92.

Harwood, E.C. *The Counterrevolution* (Great Barrington, Mass.: AIER, 1951).

Hausman, Joshua K., Paul W. Rhode, and Johannes F. Wieland. "Recovery from the Great Depression: The Farm Channel in Spring 1933," *American Economic Review* 109, 2 (2019): 427–72.

Hautcoeur, Pierre-Cyrille. "Financial Crisis and Depression: Are There Lessons to Draw from the Great Depression?" *Realities Industrielles* 2018, 3 (Aug. 2018): 7–13.

Henderson, Henry L. and David B. Woolner, eds. *FDR and the Environment* (New York: Palgrave, 2005).

Hess, Karl. *Visions Upon the Land: Man and Nature on the Western Range* (Washington, DC: Island Press, 1992).

Hetzel, Robert. *The Great Recession: Market Failure or Policy Failure?* (New York: Cambridge University Press, 2012).

Higgs, Robert. "Regime Uncertainty: Why the Great Depression Lasted So Long and Why Prosperity Resumed After the War," *Independent Review* 1, 4 (1977): 561–90.

Higgs, Robert. *Crisis and Leviathan: Critical Episodes in the Growth of American Government* (New York: Oxford University Press, 1987).

Higgs, Robert. "Wartime Prosperity? A Reassessment of the U.S. Economy in the 1940s, *Journal of Economic History* 52, 1 (Mar. 1992): 41–60.

Higgs, Robert. "The Two-Price System: U.S. Rationing During World War II," *Foundation for Economic Education* (24 Apr. 2009): https://fee.org/articles/the-two-price-system-us-rationing-during-world-war-ii/.

Hoag, W. Gifford. *The Farm Credit System: A History of Financial Self-Help* (Danville, Ill.: Interstate Printers & Publishers, Inc., 1976).
Hoffman, Abraham. *Unwanted Mexican Americans in the Great Depression* (Tucson: University of Arizona Press, 1974).
Hoffner, Benjamin. "United States: New York Clearing House Association, the Panic of 1884," *Journal of Financial Crises* 4, 2 (2022): 1278–99.
Hoffner, Benjamin. "United States: New York Clearing House Association, the Panic of 1890," *Journal of Financial Crises* 4, 2 (2022): 1300–21.
Hogan, Thomas L. and William J. Luther. "The Implicit Costs of Government Deposit Insurance," SSRN Working Paper (19 Feb. 2015).
Hopkins, Harry L. *The Realities of Unemployment* (Washington, DC: WPA, 1937).
Hormats, Robert. *The Price of Liberty: Paying for America's Wars* (New York: Henry Holt, 2007).
Horpedahl, Jeremy, Phillip Magness, and Marcus Witcher. "Teaching the Causes of Great Depression to College Students: Evidence from History, Economic, and Economic History Textbooks," *Journal of Economics and Finance Education* 21, 2 (Fall 2023): 22–37.
Horton, Donald C. *Patterns of Farm Financial Structure: A Cross-Section View of Economic and Physical Determinants* (Princeton: Princeton University Press, 1957)
Hoyt, Homer. *One Hundred Years of Land Values in Chicago: The Relationship of the Growth of Chicago to the Rise of Its Land Values, 1830–1933* (Chicago: University of Chicago Press, 1933).
Hsieh, Chang-Tai and Christina D. Romer. "Was the Federal Reserve Constrained by the Gold Standard During the Great Depression? Evidence from the 1932 Open Market Purchase Program," *Journal of Economic History* 66, 1 (Mar. 2006): 140–76.
Irwin, Douglas A. "The Smoot-Hawley Tariff: A Quantitative Assessment," *Review of Economics and Statistics* 80, 2 (May 1998): 326–44.
Irwin, Douglas A. "Did France Cause the Great Depression?" NBER Working Paper 16350 (Sept. 2010).
Jalil, Andrew J. "Monetary Intervention Really Did Mitigate Banking Panics During the Great Depression: Evidence Along the Atlanta Federal Reserve District Border," *Journal of Economic History* 74, 1 (Mar. 2014): 259–73.
Jensen, Richard J. "The Causes and Cures of Unemployment in the Great Depression," *Journal of Interdisciplinary History* 19, 4 (Spring 1989): 553–83.
Ji, Yangyang. "The Effect of New Deal Policies Revisited," *CESifo Economic Studies* (2021): 238–49.
Johnson, C. Donald. *The Wealth of a Nation: A History of Trade Politics in America* (New York: Oxford University Press, 2018).

Johnson, H. Clark. *Gold, France, and the Great Depression, 1919–1932* (New Haven: Yale University Press, 1997).

Johnson, Marianne. "Taxation in the Early Progressive Era: From Revenue to Social Policy," SSRN Working Paper, (14 Jun. 2022).

Jordan, John M. *Machine-Age Ideology: Social Engineering and American Liberalism, 1911–1939* (Chapel Hill: University of North Carolina, 1994).

Kabiri, Ali, Harold James, John Landon-Lane, David Tuckett, and Rickard Nyman, "The Role of Sentiment in the US Economy: 1920 to 1934," *Economic History Review* 76, 3 (2022): 1–28.

Keck, Richard P. "Reevaluating the Rural Electrification Administration: A New Deal for the Taxpayer," *Environmental Law* 16, 1 (Fall 1985): 39–89.

Kelley, Robin O.G. *Hammer and Hoe: Alabama Communists During the Great Depression* (Chapel Hill: University of North Carolina Press, 2015).

Kennedy, David M. "What the New Deal Did," *Political Science Quarterly* 124, 2 (Summer 2009): 251–68.

Kessler, Jeremy K. "The Political Economy of 'Constitutional Political Economy'," *Texas Law Review* 94, 7 (2016): https://texaslawreview.org/the-political-economy-of-constitutional-political-economy/.

Kitchens, Carl and Price Fishback. "Flip the Switch: The Impact of the Rural Electrification Administration, 1935–1940," *Journal of Economic History* 75, 4 (Dec. 2015): 1161–95.

Kleck, Gary. *Targeting Guns: Firearms and Their Control* (New York: Aldine DeGruyter, 1997).

Klehr, Harvey. *The Heyday of American Communism: The Depression Decade* (New York: Basic Books, Inc., 1984).

Knowles, Anne Kelly, ed. *Placing History: How Maps, Spatial Data, and GIS are Changing Historical Scholarship* (Redlands, CA: ESRI Press, 2008).

Komlos, John and Scott Carson. "The BMI Values of the Lower Classes Likely Declined During the Great Depression," *Economics & Human Biology* 26 (Aug. 2017): 137–43.

Lauck, Jon, John Miller, and Don Simmons, eds. *The Plains Political Tradition*, Vol. 2 (Pierre: South Dakota State Historical Society Press, 2014).

Lay, Shawn, ed., *The Invisible Empire in the West: Toward a New Historical Appraisal of the Ku Klux Klan* (Champaign: University of Illinois Press, 1992).

Lambert, Jeremiah D. *The Power Brokers: The Struggle to Shape and Control the Electric Power Industry* (Cambridge: The MIT Press, 2015).

Leab, Daniel J. "'United We Eat': The Creation and Organization of the Unemployed Councils in 1930," *Labor History* 8, 3 (1967): 300–15.

Ledbetter, James and Daniel B. Roth, eds. *The Great Depression: A Diary by Benjamin Roth* (New York: Public Affairs, 2009).

Leef, George. *Free Choice for Workers: A History of the Right to Work Movement* (Ottawa, Illinois: Jameson Books, 2005).
Leonard, Natalie. "United States: Federal Home Loan Bank Advances, 1932–1941," *Journal of Financial Crises* 4, 2 (2022): 1180–1200.
Leonard, Natalie. "United States: New York Clearing House Association, the Crisis of 1893," *Journal of Financial Crises* 4, 2 (2022): 1222–40.
Lusinchi, D. "'President Landon' and the 1936 *Literary Digest* Poll: Were Automobile and Telephone Owners to Blame?" *Social Sciences History* 36, 1 (2012): 23–54.
Magness, Philip. "Free Enterprise as Conspiracy," *Law and Liberty* (23 Dec. 2019): https://lawliberty.org/book-review/free-enterprise-as-conspiracy/.
Mahoney, Paul G. "The Political Economy of the Securities Act of 1933," *Journal of Legal Studies* 30 (Jan. 2001): 1–31.
Mahoney, Paul G. "The Common Law and Economic Growth: Hayek Might Be Right," *Journal of Legal Studies* 30 (Jun. 2001): 503–25.
Mahoney, Paul G. "The Origins of the Blue-Sky Laws: A Test of Competing Hypotheses," *Journal of Law and Economics* 46 (Apr. 2003): 229–51.
Makridis, Christos A. and Erin McGuire, "Refined by Fire: The Great Depression and Entrepreneurship," SSRN Working Paper, (2 Apr. 2020).
Margo, Robert A. "Employment and Unemployment in the 1930s," *Journal of Economic Perspectives* 7, 2 (Spring 1993): 41–59.
Marquis, Ralph W. and Frank P. Smith, "Double Liability for Bank Stock," *American Economic Review* 27, 3 (Sep. 1937): 490–502.
Martin, Joe. "The 1929 Stock Market Crash, A Tale of Two Cities," *Prospectus* (18 Oct. 2022).
Mason, Robert. *The Republican Party and American Politics from Hoover to Reagan* (New York: Cambridge University Press, 2011).
McCallum, Bennett. "Could a Monetary Base Rule Have Prevented the Great Depression?" NBER Working Paper No. 3162 (Nov. 1989).
McElvaine, Robert S. *The Great Depression: America, 1929–1941* (New York: Random House, 1984).
McEntire, Davis. *Residence and Race: Final and Comprehensive Report to the Commission on Race and Housing* (Los Angeles: University of California Press, 1960).
McGinnis, John O. "Revisiting the Logic of Court Packing," *Law and Liberty* (29 Nov. 2022): https://lawliberty.org/book-review/revisiting-the-logic-of-court-packing/.
Mendenhall, Allen. "The Lineaments of the Ancient Constitution," *Law and Liberty* (22 Jun. 2022). https://lawliberty.org/classic/the-lineaments-of-the-ancient-constitution/.
Mink, Gwendolyn and Rickie Solinger, eds. *Welfare: A Documentary History of U.S. Policy and Politics* (New York: New York University Press, 2003).

Meltzer, Allan. "Monetary and Other Explanations of the Start of the Great Depression," *Journal of Monetary Economics* 2 (1976): 455–71.

Meltzer, Allan. *A History of the Federal Reserve: Volume I: 1913–1951* (Chicago: University of Chicago Press, 2003).

Michener, Ron. "Money in the American Colonies," *EH.Net Encyclopedia*, ed. Robert Whaples (8 Jun. 2003, rev. 13 Jan. 2011): http://eh.net/encyclopedia/money-in-the-american-colonies.

Miller, Glenn W. *Problems of Labor* (New York: Macmillan Co., 1951).

Mills, Linda G. "A Calculus for Bias: How Malingering Females and Dependent Housewives Fare in the Social Security Disability System," *Harvard Women's Law Journal* 16 (1993): 211–32.

Mitchell, Olivia S. and John W. R. Phillips. "Eligibility for Social Security Disability," Michigan Retirement Research Center Paper No. WP 2001–011 (17 Jan. 2008).

Mitchener, Kris James. "Bank Supervision, Regulation, and Instability During the Great Depression," NBER Working Paper 10475 (May 2004).

Moore, Lydon and Gertjan Verdickt. "Railroad Bailouts in the Great Depression," Working Paper, n.d.: https://cepr.org/system/files/2022-11/Railroad%20Bailouts.pdf.

Moreno, Paul. "An Ambivalent Legacy: Black Americans and the Political Economy of the New Deal," *Independent Review* 6, 4 (Spring 2002): 513–39.

Moskowitz, Seymour. "Adult Children and Indigent Parents: Intergenerational Responsibilities in International Perspectives," *Marquette Law Review* 86, 3 (Winter 2002): https://scholarship.law.marquette.edu/mulr/vol86/iss3/1/.

Murray, Charles. *Losing Ground: American Social Policy, 1950–1980* (New York: BasicBooks, 1984).

Murray, John E. *Origins of American Health Insurance: A History of Industrial Sickness Funds* (New Haven: Yale University Press, 2007).

Nanda, Ramana and Tom Nicholas. "Did Bank Distress Stifle Innovation During the Great Depression?" NBER Working Paper 20392 (Aug. 2014).

Nelson, Aaron G. and Gerald E. Korzan, *Profits and Losses in Ranching, Western South Dakota, 1931–1940 Bulletin 352* (Brookings, S.D.: South Dakota State College, 1941).

Neumann, Todd C., Price V. Fishback, and Shawn Kantor, "The Dynamics of Relief Spending and the Private Urban Labor Market During the New Deal," *Journal of Economic History* 70, 1 (Mar. 2010): 195–220.

Nicholas, Tom and Anna Scherbina. "Real Estate Prices During the Roaring Twenties and the Great Depression," *Real Estate Economics* 41, 2 (2013): 278–309.

Nock, Albert Jay. *On Doing the Right Thing, And Other Essays* (New York: Harper and Brothers, 1928).

Nock, Albert Jay. *Our Enemy, the State* (New York: William Morrow & Co., 1935).

Nock, Albert Jay. "Liberalism, Properly So Called," Working Paper, (1943): https://www.panarchy.org/nock/liberalism.html.

Norberg, Johan. *Financial Fiasco: How America's Infatuation with Homeownership and Easy Money Created the Economic Crisis* (Washington, DC: Cato Institute, 2009).

Ohanian, Lee E. "What—or Who—Started the Great Depression?" *Journal of Economic Theory* 144, 6 (2009): 2310–35.

Obstfeld, Maurice, Jay C. Shambaugh, and Alan M. Taylor. "The Trilemma in History: Tradeoffs Among Exchange Rates, Monetary Policies, and Capital Mobility," NBER Working Paper 10396 (Mar. 2004).

Obstfeld, Maurice and Alan M. Taylor. "The Great Depression as a Watershed: International Capital Mobility Over the Long Run," NBER Working Paper 5960 (1997).

Olson, Lynne. *Those Angry Days: Roosevelt, Lindbergh, and America's Fight Over World War II, 1939–1941* (New York: Random House, 2014).

Oreskes, Naomi and Erik M. Conway. *The Big Myth: How American Business Taught Us to Loathe Government and Love the Free Market* (New York: Bloomsbury Publishing, 2023).

Ostrom, Vincent. *The Intellectual Crisis in American Public Administration*, 3rd ed. (Tuscaloosa: University of Alabama Press, 2008).

Paige, John C. *The Civilian Conservation Corps and the National Park Service, 1933–1942: An Administrative History* (Washington, DC: U.S. Department of the Interior, 1985).

Panne, Jean-Louis, et al. *The Black Book of Communism: Crimes, Terror, Repression* (Cambridge: Harvard University Press, 1999).

Patel, Kiran Klaus. *Soldiers of Labor: Labor Service in Nazi Germany and New Deal America, 1933–1945* (New York: Cambridge University Press, 2005).

Patel, Kiran Klaus. *The New Deal: A Global History* (Princeton: Princeton University Press, 2016).

Paul, Jeffrey. *Winning America's Second Civil War: Progressivism's Authoritarian Threat, Where It Came From, and How to Defeat It* (New York: Encounter, 2024).

Person, H.S. "The Rural Electrification Administration in Perspective," *Agricultural History* 24, 2 (Apr. 1950): 70–89.

Poelmans, Eline, Jason E. Taylor, Samuel Raisanen, and Andrew C. Holt. "Estimates of Employment Gains Attributable to Beer Legalization in Spring 1933," *Explorations in Economic History* 84 (Apr. 2022): https://doi.org/10.1016/j.eeh.2021.101427.

Polenberg, Richard. *Reorganizing Roosevelt's Government: The Controversy Over Executive Reorganization* (Cambridge, Mass.: Harvard University Press, 1966).

Poser, Norman S. "Restructuring the Stock Markets: A Critical Look at the SEC's National Market System," *New York University Law Review* 56 (1988): 883–922.

Powell, Jim. *FDR's Folly: How Roosevelt and His New Deal Prolonged the Great Depression* (New York: Crown Forum, 2003).

Pratico, Dominick. *Eisenhower and Social Security: The Origins of the Disability Program* (New York Writers Club Press, 2001).

Prescott, Edward C. "Some Observations on the Great Depression," *Federal Reserve Bank of Minneapolis Quarterly Review* 23, 1 (Winter 1999): 25–31.

Quincy, Sarah. "Loans for the 'Little Fellow': Credit, Crisis, and Recovery in the Great Depression," NBER Working Papers, 31779 (Oct. 2023).

Rabushka, Alvin. *Taxation in Colonial America* (Princeton: Princeton University Press, 2008).

Raimondo, Justin. *Reclaiming the American Right: The Lost Legacy of the Conservative Movement* (Wilmington, DE: ISI Books, 2008).

Rakove, Jack N. *Original Meanings: Politics and Ideas in the Making of the Constitution* (New York: Vintage 1996).

Ramsey, Bruce. *Unsanctioned Voice: Garet Garrett, Journalist of the Old Right* (New York: Caxton Press, 2009).

Rauchway, Eric. "The New Deal Was on the Ballot in 1932," *Modern American History* (2019): 1–13.

Rauchway, Eric. *Why the New Deal Matters* (New Haven: Yale University Press, 2021).

Reed, Lawrence W. *Great Myths of the Great Depression* (Michigan: Mackinac Center for Public Policy and the Foundation for Economic Education, 2011).

Reed, Lawrence W. "Henry Flipper Rose from Slavery to Become West Point's First Black Graduate—and a Staunch Anti-New Dealer," *FEE Stories* (17 July 2022): https://fee.org/articles/henry-flipper-rose-from-slavery-to-become-west-point-s-first-black-graduate-and-a-staunch-anti-new-dealer/

Reed, Lawrence W. "What Calvin Coolidge's 'Common Sense' Vetoes of Two Farm Bills Can Teach about Price Controls," *FEE* (23 Sept. 2022): https://fee.org/articles/what-calvin-coolidge-s-common-sense-vetoes-of-two-farm-bills-can-teach-about-price-controls/.

Reed, Merl E. *Seed Time for the Modern Civil Rights Movement: The President's Committee on Fair Employment Practice, 1941–1946* (Baton Rouge: Louisiana State University Press, 1991).

Reid, John Phillip. *Constitutional History of the American Revolution*, abridged ed. (Madison: University of Wisconsin Press, 1995).

Reinhart, Carmen M. and Kenneth S. Rogoff. *This Time Is Different: Eight Centuries of Financial Folly* (Princeton: Princeton University Press, 2009).

Retman, Sonnet. *Real Folks: Race and Genre in the Great Depression* (Durham, N.C.: Duke University Press, 2011).

Reynolds, Alan. "The Economic Impact of Tax Changes, 1920–1939," *CATO Journal* (Winter 2021): https://www.cato.org/cato-journal/winter-2021/economic-impact-tax-changes-1920-1939.

Richardson, Gary and William Troost. "Monetary Intervention Mitigated Banking Panics During the Great Depression: Quasi-Experimental Evidence from the Federal Reserve District Border in Mississippi, 1929 to 1933," NBER Working Paper No. 12591 (Oct. 2006).

Riley, Naomi Schaefer. *The New Trail of Tears: How Washington Is Destroying American Indians* (New York: Encounter Books, 2016).

Ripley, William Z. *Main Street and Wall Street* (Boston: Little, Brown and Co., 1929).

Robertson, Ross. *The Comptroller and Bank Supervision: A Historical Appraisal* (Washington, D.C.: Officer of Comptroller of the Currency, 1968).

Rockoff, Hugh. *Drastic Measures: A History of Wage and Price Controls in the United States* (New York: Cambridge University Press, 1984).

Romer, Christina D. and David H. Romer, "The Missing Transmission Mechanism in the Monetary Explanation of the Great Depression," NBER Working Paper 18746 (Jan. 2013).

Rosenbloom, Joshua L. and William A. Sundstrom, "The Sources of Regional Variation in the Severity of the Great Depression: Evidence from U.S. Manufacturing, 1919–1937," NBER Working Paper No. 6288 (Nov. 1997).

Rosenzweig, Roy. "'Socialism in Our Time': The Socialist Party and the Unemployed, 1929–1936," *Labor History* 20, 4 (1979): 485–509.

Ross, Malcolm. *All Manner of Men* (New York: Harcourt, Brace, & World, 1948).

Rothbard, Murray N. *America's Great Depression* 5th ed. (Auburn, Ala.: Ludwig von Mises Institute, 1963, 2000).

Rothbard, Murray N. "World War I as Fulfillment: Power and the Intellectuals," *Mises Daily* (9 Nov. 2018): https://mises.org/library/world-war-i-fulfillment-power-and-intellectuals.

Sabin, Paul. *Public Citizens: The Attack on Big Government and the Remaking of American Liberalism* (New York: W.W. Norton & Co., 2021).

Saloutos, Theodore. "New Deal Agricultural Policy: An Evaluation," *Journal of American History* 61, 2 (Sept. 1974): 394–416.

Salter, Alexander W., Vipin Veetil, and Lawrence H. White. "Extended Shareholder Liability as a Means to Constrain Moral Hazard in Insured Banks," *Quarterly Review of Economics and Finance* 63, 1 (Feb. 2017): 153–60.

Sanborn, F.B., ed. *The Single Tax Discussion* (Concord, Mass.: American Social Science Association, 1890).
Sanders, Anthony B. *Baby Ninth Amendments: How Americans Embraced Unenumerated Rights and Why It Matters* (Ann Arbor: University of Michigan Press, 2023).
Schearer, Michael. "Batteryman vs. the New Deal: The Life of Fred C. Perkins," Working Paper (9 May 2021).
Schieber, Sylvester J. and John B. Shoven. *The Real Deal: The History and Future of Social Security* (New Haven: Yale University Press, 1999).
Schmitz, David F. *The United States and Fascist Italy, 1922–1940* (Chapel Hill: University of North Carolina Press, 1988).
Schneider, Gregory L. ed. *Conservatism in America Since 1930: A Reader* (New York: New York University Press, 2003).
Schulte, Steven C. "Removing the Yoke of Government: E.Y. Berry and the Origins of Indian Termination Policy," *South Dakota History* 14, 1 (1984): 48–67.
Schwab, Klaus and Thierry Malleret. *Covid-19: The Great Rese*t (Geneva, Switzerland: World Economic Forum, 2020).
Scott, James C. *Seeing Like a State: How Certain Schemes to Improve the Human Condition Have Failed* (New York: Yale University Press, 1998).
Selgin, George. *False Dawn: The New Deal and the Promise of Recovery, 1933–1947* (Chicago: University of Chicago Press, 2025).
Sherraden, Michael. "The Local Impact of the Civilian Conservation Corps, 1933–1942," *Journal of Sociology & Social Welfare* 10, 3 (Dec. 2014): 514–29.
Sheehan, Marion Turner, ed. *The World at Home: Selections from the Writings of Anne O'Hare McCormick* (New York: Alfred A. Knopf, 1956).
Sherry, Suzanna. "The Founders' Unwritten Constitution," *University of Chicago Law Review* 54, 4 (Fall 1987): 1127–77.
Shlaes, Amity. *The Forgotten Man: A New History of the Great Depression* (New York: HarperCollins, 2007).
Shlaes, Amity. *Great Society: A New History* (New York: HarperCollins, 2019).
Shlaes, Amity, ed. *New Deal Rebels* (Great Barrington, Mass.: American Institute for Economic Research, 2023).
Shughart, William F. "Bending Before the Storm: The U.S. Supreme Court in Economic Crisis, 1935–1937," *The Independent Review* 9, 1 (Summer 2004): 55–83.
Shughart, William F. "The New Deal and Modern Memory," *Southern Economic Journal* 77, 3 (2011): 515–42.
Slaboch, Matthew W. *A Road to Nowhere: The Idea of Progress and Its Critics* (Philadelphia: University of Pennsylvania Press, 2017).

Small, Albion. "The Social Gradations of Capital," *American Journal of Sociology* 9, 6 (May 1914): 721–52.

Small, Mario L. and Devah Pager. "Sociological Perspectives on Racial Discrimination," *Journal of Economic Perspectives* 34, 2 (Spring 2020): 49–67.

Smith, Adam and Bruce Yandle. *Bootleggers & Baptists: How Economic Forces and Moral Persuasion Interact to Shape Regulatory Policies* (Washington, DC: Cato Institute, 2014).

Smith, Andrew and Robert E. Wright, "Sowing the Seeds of a Future Crisis: The SEC and the Emergence of the Nationally Recognized Statistical Rating Organization (NRSRO) Category, 1971–75," *Business History Review* 95, 4 (Winter 2021): 739–64.

Smith, Jean Edward. *FDR* (New York: Random House, 2007).

Sowell, Thomas. *A Conflict of Visions* (New York: William Morrow & Co., 1987).

Sowell, Thomas. *The Vision of the Anointed: Self-Congratulation as a Basis for Social Policy* (New York: Basic Books, 1995).

Sowell, Thomas. *Social Justice Fallacies* (New York: Basic Books, 2023).

Sprague, O.M.W. *History of Crises Under the National Banking System* (Washington: General Printing Office, 1910).

Steig, Olga M. "What Can the Regulatory Securities Act Accomplish?," *Michigan Law Review* 31, 6 (1933): 775–84.

Sterner, Richard. *The Negro's Share: A Study of Income, Consumption, Housing and Public Assistance* (Westport, CN: Negro Universities Press, 1943).

Stoesz, David. "Reparations from Social Security," SSRN Working Paper (3 Mar. 2023).

Stokes, W.N. Jr. *Credit to Farmers: The Story of Federal Intermediate Credit Banks and Production Credit Associations* (Washington, DC: Farm Credit Administration, 1973).

Strickland, James M. and Ken Kollman. "Constitutional Change and Interest Mobilization: Insight from the Progressive Era," Working Paper (7 Apr. 2023).

Stringham, Edward P. ed., *How to Invest Wisely* (Great Barrington, Mass.: AIER, 2019/1947).

Stuckler, David, Christopher Meissner, Price Fishback, Sanjay Basu, and Martin McKee. "Banking Crises and Mortality During the Great Depression: Evidence from US Urban Populations, 1929–1937," *Journal of Epidemiology and Community Health* 66, 5 (Mar. 2011): https://jech.bmj.com/content/66/5/410 .

Sumner, Scott. "Roosevelt, Warren, and the Gold-Buying Program of 1933," *Research in Economic History* 20 (2001): 135–72.

Sundstrom, William A. "Last Hired, First Fired? Unemployment and Urban Black Workers During the Great Depression," *Journal of Economic History* 52, 2 (Jun. 1992): 415–29.

Sylla, Richard E. and David J. Cowen. *Alexander Hamilton on Finance, Credit, and Debt* (New York: Columbia University Press, 2018).

Taylor, Jason E. "Work-sharing During the Great Depression: Did the 'President's Reemployment Agreement' Promote Reemployment?" *Economica* 78, 309 (Jan. 2011): 133–58.

Taylor, Jason E. *Deconstructing the Monolith: The Microeconomics of the National Industrial Recovery Act* (Chicago: University of Chicago Press, 2019).

Taylor, Jason E. and Todd C. Neumann. "The Effect of Institutional Regime Change Within the New Deal on Industrial Output and Labor Markets," *Explorations in Economic History* 50 (2013): 582–98.

Taylor, Jason E. and Todd C. Neumann. "Recovery Spring, Faltering Fall: March to November 1933," *Explorations in Economic History* 61 (Jul. 2016): 54–67.

Thomasson, Melissa. "Health Insurance in the United States," *EH.Net Encyclopedia*, ed. Robert Whaples (17 Apr. 2003): https://eh.net/encyclopedia/health-insurance-in-the-united-states/.

Timberlake, Richard. *Constitutional Money: A Review of the Supreme Court's Monetary Decisions* (New York: Cambridge University Press, 2013).

Tocci, Charles and Ann Marie Ryan. "Conserving the American Man: Gender, Eugenics and Education in the Civilian Conservation Corps," *History of Education* 51, 2 (2022): 224–43.

Traflet, Janice M. *A Nation of Small Shareholders: Marketing Wall Street After World War II* (Baltimore: Johns Hopkins University Press, 2013).

Traflet, Janice M. and Robert E. Wright. *Fearless: Wilma Soss and America's Forgotten Investor Movement* (New York: All Seasons Press, 2022).

Triebel, Ethel H. "The Department of Commerce Under Herbert Hoover, 1921–1928," (MA Thesis: Loyola University, 1939).

Tsuk, Dalia. "Pluralisms: The Indian New Deal as a Model," *University of Maryland Law Journal of Race, Religion, Gender and Class* 1, 2 (2001): 393–449.

Tugwell, Rexford G. and Michael Namorato, ed. *The Diary of Rexford G. Tugwell: The New Deal, 1932–1935* (New York: Greenwood Press, 1992).

Tushnet, Mark and Katya Lezin. "What Really Happened in *Brown v. Board of Education*," *Columbia Law Review* 91, 8 (1991): 1867–930.

Ulama, Darryle. "Black Public Works: The Political Economy of Race and New Deal Infrastructure," (MA Thesis: Massachusetts Institute of Technology, 2021).

VanGiezen, Robert and Albert E. Schwenk. "Compensation From Before World War I Through the Great Depression," *Monthly Labor Review*

(Sept. 2001): https://www.bls.gov/opub/mlr/2001/article/compensation-from-before-world-war-i-through-the-great-depression.htm.

Vendel, Jason D. "General Bias and Administrative Law Judges: Is There a Remedy for Social Security Disability Claimants?" *Cornell Law Review* 90 (2004–5): 769–807.

Vedder, Richard K. and Lowell E. Gallaway. *Out of Work: Unemployment and Government in Twentieth-Century America*, updated ed. (New York: New York University Press, 1997).

Walker, Juliet E.K. *The History of Black Business in America: Capitalism, Race, Entrepreneurship*, 2nd ed. (Chapel Hill: University of North Carolina Press, 2009).

Wallis, John J. "The Political Economy of New Deal Spending Revisited, Again: With and Without Nevada," *Explorations in Economic History* 35, 2 (Apr. 1998): 140–70.

Wallis, John J. "Lessons from the Political Economy of the New Deal," *Oxford Review of Economic Policy* 26, 3 (Autumn 2010): 442–62.

Wallis, John J. and Daniel K. Benjamin. "Public Relief and Private Employment in the Great Depression," *Journal of Economic History* 41, 1 (1981): 97–102.

Warburg, James P. *Hell Bent for Election* (New York: Doubleday, Doran & Company, 1935).

Warburg, Paul M. *The Federal Reserve System: Its Origin and Growth, Reflections and Recollections* Vol. 1 (New York: Macmillan Co., 1930).

Washburn, Patrick S. *A Question of Sedition: The Federal Government's Investigation of the Black Press During World War II* (New York: Oxford University Press, 1986).

Washburn, Watson "Anti-Fraud Legislation," *Michigan Law Review* 31 (1933): 768–75.

Watkins, T.H. *The Great Depression: America in the 1930s* (New York: Little, Brown & Co., 1993).

Watson, Bradley C.S. *Progressivism: The Strange History of a Radical Idea* (Notre Dame: University of Notre Dame Press, 2020).

Watts, Jill. "New Deal or Raw Deal? Black Americans in the Roosevelt Years," *Financial History* 134 (Summer 2020): 20–25.

Weiss, Nancy J. "The Negro and the New Freedom: Fighting Wilsonian Segregation," *Political Science Quarterly* 84, 1 (Mar. 1969): 61–79.

West, Robert Craig. *Banking Reform and the Federal Reserve, 1863–1923* (Ithaca: Cornell University Press, 1974).

Wheelock, David C. "Monetary Policy in the Great Depression: What the Fed Did, and Why," *St. Louis Federal Reserve Review* (Mar./Apr. 1992): 3–28.

Whaples, Robert. "Where Is There Consensus Among American Economic Historians? The Results of a Survey on Forty Propositions," *Journal of Economic History* 55, 1 (Mar. 1995): 139–54.

Whaples, Robert and Randall Parker, eds., *Handbook of Major Events in Economic History* (New York: Routledge, 2013).

White, Bill. *America's Fiscal Constitution: Its Triumph and Collapse* (New York: PublicAffairs, 2014).

White, Larry. *Better Money: Gold, Fiat, or Bitcoin?* (New York: Cambridge University Press, 2022).

Wiebe, Robert H. *The Search for Order, 1877–1920* (New York: Hill and Wang, 1967).

Wiecek, William M. *The Lost World of Classical Legal Thought: Law and Ideology in America, 1886–1937* (New York: Oxford University Press, 1998).

Wilcox, Clair. *Public Policies Toward Business* rev. ed. (Homewood, Ill., Richard D. Irwin, Inc., 1960).

Williams, Kristin S. and Albert J. Mills. "Frances Perkins: Gender, Context, and History in the Neglect of a Management Theorist," *Journal of Management History* 23, 1 (2017): 32–50.

Williamson, Harold F. *Edward Atkinson: The Biography of an American Liberal, 1827–1905* (Boston: Old Corner Book Store, Inc., 1934).

Williamson, Jeffrey G. and Peter H. Lindert. *American Inequality: A Macroeconomic History* (New York: Academic Press, 1980).

Willis, Richard. *Long Gone* (New York: Greenpoint Press, 2007).

Wilson, Woodrow. *The New Freedom: A Call for the Emancipation of the Generous Energies of a People* (New York: Doubleday, Page & Co., 1913).

Winfield, Betty Houchin. *FDR and the News Media* (New York: Columbia University Press, 1994).

Wormser, I. Maurice. *Frankenstein, Incorporated* (New York: McGraw Hill Book Co., 1931).

Wright, Robert E. *One Nation Under Debt: Hamilton, Jefferson, and the History of What We Owe* (New York: McGraw-Hill, 2008).

Wright, Robert E. *Fubarnomics: A Lighthearted, Serious Look at America's Economic Ills* (Amherst, N.Y.: Prometheus Books, 2010).

Wright, Robert E. *Corporation Nation* (Philadelphia: University of Pennsylvania Press, 2014).

Wright, Robert E. *Little Business on the Prairie: Entrepreneurship, Prosperity, and Challenge in South Dakota* (Sioux Falls: Center for Western Studies, 2015).

Wright, Robert E. *The Poverty of Slavery: How Unfree Labor Pollutes the Economy* (Cham, Switzerland: Palgrave, 2017).

Wright, Robert E. "What George Bailey's Building and Loan Company Can Still Teach Us About Banking," *Zocalo Public Square* (6 Dec. 2018): https://www.zocalopublicsquare.org/2018/12/06/george-baileys-building-loan-company-can-still-teach-us-banking/ideas/essay/.

Wright, Robert E. *Financial Exclusion: How Competition Can Fix a Broken System* (Great Barrington, Mass.: AIER 2019).

Wright, Robert E. "Elites Gone Wild," *AIER Daily Economy Blog* (19 Feb. 2021). https://www.aier.org/article/elites-gone-wild/.

Wright, Robert E. "FSLICing America's Public Health Bureaucracies," *AIER Daily Economy* (10 Feb. 2022): https://www.aier.org/article/fslicing-americas-public-health-bureaucracies/.

Wright, Robert E. "Improving Sustainability by Privatizing Wildlife Conservation," *Natural Resources* 14, 4 (2023): https://doi.org/10.4236/nr.2023.144004.

Wright, Robert E. *Liberty Lost: Rise and Demise of Voluntary Association in America Since 1700* (Great Barrington, Mass.: American Institute for Economic Research, 2023).

Wright, Robert E., ed. *Bailouts: Public Money, Private Profit* (New York: Columbia University Press, 2010).

Wright, Robert E. and Aleksandra Przegalinska. *Debating Universal Basic Income: Pros, Cons, and Alternatives* (Cham, Switzerland: Palgrave, 2022).

Wright, Robert E. and George D. Smith. *Mutually Beneficial: The Guardian and Life Insurance in America* (New York: New York University Press, 2004).

Yarbrough, Tinsley E. *Mr. Justice Black and His Critics* (Durham: Duke University Press, 1988).

Youcha, Geraldine. *Minding the Children: Child Care in America from Colonial Times to the Present* (New York: Scribner, 1995).

Young, William H. and Nancy K. Young. "Federal Bureau of Investigation," *The Great Depression in America: A Cultural Encyclopedia, Volume 1: A—M* (Westport, Conn.: Greenwood Press, 2007).

Zalewski, David A. "A Reconsideration of the Revenue Act of 1932," *Essays in Economic and Business History* 24 (2006): 56–68.

Zwolinski, Matt and John Tomasi. *The Individualists: Radicals, Reactionaries, and the Struggle for the Soul of Libertarianism* (Princeton: Princeton University Press, 2023).

Index

R. E. Wright, *FDR's Long New Deal*,
https://doi.org/10.1007/978-3-031-74141-8

G

The manufacturer's authorised representative in the EU is Springer Nature Customer Service Centre GmbH, Europaplatz 3, 69115 Heidelberg, Germany. If you have any concerns regarding our products, please contact ProductSafety@springernature.com

Printed and bound by CPI Group (UK) Ltd, Croydon, CR0 4YY
30/09/2026
02225583-0013